ART IS ELEMENTARY
Teaching Visual Thinking Through Art Concepts

Ivan E. Cornia
Charles B. Stubbs, 1930-
Nathan B. Winters

GIBBS·SMITH
→P
PUBLISHER

D1089422

Original Contributors

John Anderson
Louise Beck
Rhoda Bierstadt
Dorothy S. Borovatz
Steve N. Borovatz
Barbara Brown
Carolyn Carson
David C. Chaplin
Darryl L. Colton
Wayne A. Graybill

Dale F. Gibbs
Jerry R. Hancock
G. Norleen Harding
Marian Hyde
Barbara N. Jeppsen
Max Johns
Lorna C. Kennedy
Ruth K. Lyon
Dick L. Powell
David R. Roberts

William R. Shaw
Norman R. Skanchy
Ronald L. Snow
Mary Stirland
Julie Todd
Calvin Toone
The Utah State Board of Education
The Teachers of the Davis School District
University of Utah Art Education Students

Art prints for use as visual aids with the lessons in **ART IS ELEMENTARY** may be purchased from:
Shorewood Fine Art Reproductions, Inc.
27 Glen Road
Sandy Hook, CT 06482
Telephone (203) 426-8100

The following prints are no longer in print:
El Greco, *Virgin with Saint Ines and Saint Tecla*
Kollwitz, *Mother and Child*
Morreau, *Knockout*
Picasso, *Les Miserables*

The following prints are substitutions for those out of print:
El Greco, *St. Martin and the Beggar*
Picasso, *Mother and Child*
Morisot, *Jeanne Pontillon*
Picasso, *The Tragedy*

Art prints to accompany lessons are available from the publisher. Call 1-800-421-8714 for information.

Revised edition © 1994
1st edition 1983

This is a Peregrine Smith Book, published by Gibbs Smith, Publisher, PO Box 667, Layton, UT 84041 — 1-800-421-8714.

Manufactured in the United States of America

Library of Congress Cataloging in Publication Data

Stubbs, Charles B., 1930-
    Art is elementary.

    Rev. ed. of: Art is elementary / Ivan E. Cornia, Charles B. Stubbs, Nathan B. Winters. c1976.
    Includes bibliographical references.
    1. Art--Study and teaching (Elementary)--United States. I. Cornia, Ivan, E., 1920-   Art is elementary. II. Winters, Nathan B., 1937-
III. Title.
N353.S87   1983   372.5'044   83-3929
ISBN 0-87905-138-8

TABLE OF CONTENTS

PRONUNCIATION GUIDE
FOR ARTISTS' NAMES
AND ART TERMS

Baroque	Ba ROKE
Bas relief	BAH relief
Batik	Ba TEEK'
Bauhaus	BOUGH house
Bonnard, Pierre	Bo nar', Pyair
Botticeili, Sandro	Bot tee CHEL' lee, San dro
Braque, Georges	Brock, Zhorzh
Brouwer, Adriaen	BROW' er, Ad ree ON
Brueghel, Pieter	BROO' gul, Peter
Canaletto	Kan a LET' toe
Caravaggio	Car a VOD' jo
Cezanne	Say zan'
Chagall	Shah GAHL'
Chardin	Shar dan'
Chartres	SHAR' t'r
Chiaroscuro	Key AH ro SKOO' ro
Corot, Camille	Kaw roe', Ca meel
Courbet, Gustave	Coor bay', Gew Stahv
Cuyp, Aelbert	Kipe, Ay I burt
Dali, Salvador	DAH' lee, Salvador
Daumier, Honore	Dome yay, On o ray
David, Jacques Louis	Dah veed', Zhock Loo eee
Degas, Edgar	D'gah', Edgar
De La Tour, Georges	Day la tour', Zhorzh
Delvaux, Paul	Del voh', Pole
Demuth, Charles	D'mooth', Charles
Duchamp, Marcel	Dew shahm', Mar sell
Dufy, Raoul	Dew fee', Rah ool
Durer, Albrecht	DURE' er, AL brekt
Eakins, Thomas	EEK' ins, Thomas
Encaustic	En COST' ick
Fauvism	Fove' ism
Feininger, Lyonel	FINE' inger, Lionel
Fragonard, Jean Honore	Frag' o nar, Zhon On o ray
Gainsborough, Thomas	GAINES' burrough, Thomas
Genre	Zhon r (or) ZHON' ruh
Gericault, Jean Louis	Zhay' ree co, Zhon Loo ee
Gogh, Vincent Van	GO, Vincent van
Gouache	Gwahsh
Goya, Francesco de	GOY' a, Frahn thees co day
Grande Jatte	Grahnd Zhot
Greco, El	GRECK' o, El
Gruenwald, Mathias	GREW' en vahlt, Ma TEE us
Gurenica	GWARE' nee ca
Hals, Frans	Hahls, Fronz
Hassam, Childe	Ha Sawm', Child
Horatii	Ho RAY' she eye
Icarus	IK' a rus
Ingres, Jean Auguste Dominique	Ang're', Zhahn O gewst Doh me neek
Intaglio	In TALL' yo
Klee, Paul	Clay, Paul
Kollwitz, Kathe	CALL' vits, Katy
Koryusai	Koh roo sigh
Koson	Koh sone
Leger, Fernand	Lay zhay', Fair non

Leonardo da Vinci	Lay o NAR' doe da VIN' chee
Magritte, Rene	Mah greet', Ra nay
Manet, Edouard	Mah nay', Aid wahr
Matisse, Henri	Ma teess', On ree
Medici	MAY' dee chee
Metsys, Quentin	Met' sees, Quentin
Michelangelo Buonarotti	Michael AN jel o Bwoe na ROT tee
Millet	Mee lay'
Miro, Joan	Mee ROE', Wahn
Modigliani, Amedeo	Mo dill YAH' nee, Am a Day o
Monet	Mo nay'
Montmartre	Mawn mart'
Morreau, Luc-Albert	Mo ROW, Look Albert
Morisot, Berthe	Maw' ree zo, Bairt
Patina	Pa TEEN' a
Picasso, Pablo	Pea CASS' o, Pablo
Pieta	Pea ay TAH'
Redon, Odilon	Ray doh', Ah di lawn
Rembrandt, Van Rijn	Rem'brandt, Van Rine
Renoir, Pierre Auguste	R'n wahr, Peer Ah goost'
Rococo	Ro co co (or) Ro CO co
Rouault	Roo oh
Rousseau	Roo so
Salon des Refuses	Sa lawn day R' few zay
Seurat	Sir ah
Shahn, Ben	Shawn, Ben
Toulouse-Lautrec, Henri	Too looze Lo trek, On ree
Triptych	Trip tick
Velasquez	Ve LASS kess (or) Ve LATH keth
Vasarely, Victor	Vazar ELL ee, Victor
Vermeer	Ver MARE
Vlaminck, Maurice de	Vlahm ink, Mawr ees de
Vuillard, Edouard	Wee LAR, Aid wahr
Watteau, Jean Antoine	Wah toe, Jean An twan
Wyeth, Andrew	Wy uth, Andrew

Stress the syllable that is printed in capital letters. No stress has been provided for the French names, which are properly pronounced with equal stress on each syllable.

GLOSSARY

Abstract and abstraction—any deviation from a standard photographic representation of something; such abstraction may be found in any degree, variety, or form.

Accent—specific areas within a composition that are given greater emphasis by the use of more intense tone, by size change, or by other means that exaggerate these specific parts.

Aesthetic—anything relating to or dealing with the beautiful.

Aesthetic quality—infers beauty based on some set of criteria.

After image—a visual sensation occurring after the external stimulus that is causing it has ceased to operate.

Analogous colors—colors that are closely related to each other and in which a common hue can be found, such as blue, blue-violet, and violet.

Applique—a cutout design fastened (sewn, stitched, or glued) to a larger piece of material.

Armature—a frame or shape made of wire, wood, paper, or some similar material, and that is used as a skeleton to hold clay, plaster, or some other sculpture material. The sculpture is built on top of the armature.

Asymmetrical balance (informal balance)—unequal distribution of art elements, resulting in a visually pleasing balance.

Balance—A visual impression of equilibrium between all interactive parts in any art work.

Brayer—a rubber or gelatin roller that is used in printing to spread ink evenly over a surface.

Calligraphy—the use of lines in varying widths and rhythms, such as those commonly used in brush lettering.

Cartoon—a preliminary drawing for a painting or mural.

Ceramics—a term representing objects made from clay and then fired in an oven.

Collage—an arrangement of various materials such as cloth, wood, paper, and various scraps into a visually pleasing art form. The materials are affixed to a backing by pasting.

Complement and complementary color—in color, the hue directly opposite on the color wheel.

Composite shadows—when the cast shadows of two or more things overlap, they are seen as one, or as *composite* shadows.

Composition—the arrangement and organization of parts into a unified whole; all parts unite to form a new total relationship. (Sometimes the terms *composition* and *design* are used interchangeably.)

Contour—the outer surface of an object or figure, usually bounded by a line, by a change of color, or by a change of texture.

Convex—a shape that curves out from the center (where it is thickest) to thinner tapered edges.

Concave—a shape that curves inward and appears to be hollow.

Decorative texture—a textural pattern that serves as decoration on a form.

Design—infers some way of organizing space. (See *composition*.)

Diffused light—light that has been broken up, extended, or scattered by the material it passes through.

Draping—a process of hanging or arranging a pliable material over a stationary form so that it will take on a new shape.

Embossed—a design that is raised slightly from the surface.

Emotive—deals with the expression and interpretation of emotions.

Etching—a method of engraving a design on a copper or zinc plate by means of acid; from this plate, a print is made.

Form—shapes that have length, width, and depth of volume.

Fresco—a painting done on moist plaster in which the pigments become incorporated with the plaster.

Geometric/organic forms—forms that are based on or derived from those in nature are said to be organic; forms that are invented by man are geometric.

Gouache—refers to opaque water colors.

Grog—fired clay that has been broken up and mixed with fresh unfired clay for texture.

Harmony—a result that occurs when all of the art elements have been organized into a visually pleasing relationship.

Illusion of line—a misleading image of line; an impression.

Illusion of movement—a psychological movement or an impression of movement.

Illusion of texture—being visually deceived by an impression of texture when none can be felt other than the natural surface it is seen on.

In-relief—sculpture in which the subject is raised from the surface it is placed on or carved from.

Illustration—refers to an art product in which the story content is clearly evident.

In-the-round—sculpture that stands apart from any background.

Intensity—refers to the amount of pigment in a color; bright colors contain considerable amounts of pigment.

Linear—something that is line-like or that has an emphasis on a line.

Linear shape—a shape that has the appearance of a line, such as string, tree branches, or cables on a bridge.

Lithography—refers to the printing of an image on a surface material executed by using a stone plate and a grease pencil.

Lost wax process—a method of casting objects that have been made from clay or other plastic materials in metal.

Mendala—in children's art, a doubly crossed circle that is the basis for the images drawn by all normal children at about the ages of three or four. Mendala grows out of the child's scribbling when he was an earlier age.

Mat—a heavy border of paper or cardboard used to frame a drawing or painting.

Matte—a surface deprived of luster or gloss, and free from shine or highlights.

Media—the art materials to be used in a project.

Mobile—a hanging three-dimensional design that has moving parts.

Mount—to place, paste, or attach something on a suitable support of backing. Mounting enriches the visual appearance of an art work.

Natural form—a form taken from nature or akin to nature.

Naturalistic—lifelike, or like the "real thing."

Oil paint—paint made from the pigment in linseed, poppy, or nut oil.

Opaque—a surface that cannot be penetrated by rays of light. Opaque color or paint, such as tempera, completely covers any drawing or color that is underneath it.

Open and closed forms—forms that reflect the original shape they are carved or chiseled from are closed forms; those that have openings, projections, and/or protuberances are called open forms.

Optical vibration—the illusion of vibration or movements created by an artist.

Optical weight—the weight that one judges an object has by looking at it, but without lifting it or weighing it.

Pastel—ground pigment that is combined with gum arabic and that is used in solid form. Pastel colors are often tinted in appearance.

Patina—the greenish incrustation of old bronze that results from weathering. Sculptors now create a wide variety of patinas by inducing them with various chemicals.

Perspective—the art of creating an illusion of depth on a two-dimensional surface; a visual method of drawing objects as they appear to the eye.

Picture plane—refers to the surface on which the artist makes his drawing, painting, or design.

Plane—an existing surface with no elevations or depressions.

Point of emphasis—an accent or center of interest.

Positive/Negative space—in its simplest terms, positive space is the foreground and negative space is the background; either may change, depending upon the viewer focus.

Primary colors—the basic colors of red, yellow, and blue.

Proportion—may refer to size relationships within an art work, or may refer to quantities of tone or color in an art work.

Raffia—a material that is used in the making of baskets, mats, and other objects of that type.

Relief—in sculpture, the exposure of certain parts away from a base or foundation.

Representational—made to look like the real thing or to create an illusion of the actual object or scene.

Rigid/pliable—rigid forms retain their shape until their composition is altered by heating or by other means; pliable forms, when moved, punched, pinched, or otherwise altered, retain the new shape that is imposed on them (soft clay is a pliable object).

Rhythm—a regulated flow of colors, lines, textures, or other art elements that achieve a pleasing effect.

Shade—a color to which one has added black in order to darken it.

Shape—defined areas that are two-dimensional, such as a ball drawn on paper.

Spatial—related to the occupying or nature of space.

Spectrum—a band of colors derived from wave lengths of light when seen through a prism or other reflective material.

Still life—any combination of inanimate objects, such as fruits, books, or vases, that the artist arranges for use as subject matter.

Style—the manner in which an individual artist approaches his work and his particular method of working, such as applying pigment to a surface, carving, modeling, and so on.

Stylized—slight distortions of a naturalistic subject that are created to dramatize a mood, feeling, or idea; the first step in abstraction.

Symbol—something that stands for or represents the actual image or idea.

Tactile—refers to the sense of touch.

Texture—the way an object looks or feels to our touch or vision.

Three-dimensional and two-dimensional—an object with height, width, and depth is three-dimensional; if an object has only height and width, it is two-dimensional, but the illusion of the third dimension can be created on a two-dimensional space.

Tint—a color to which one has added white in order to lighten it.

Value—in art, *value* refers to all different degrees of darkness or lightness.

View finder—a small opening cut out of paper or cardboard through which the artist can frame possibilities for a picture or design of the subject he is looking at.

Visual balance—an arrangement that visually or psychologically appears to be balanced.

Visual field—all that can be seen without turning one's head.

Visual order—all arrangement that visually appears to have absense of order.

Visual perception—what one perceives visually or the concepts one develops as a result of what he sees determine the extent of his *visual perception*.

Visual rhythm—an arrangement that seems to lead the eye from one part to another in a rhythmical or orderly manner.

Volume/mass—*volume* refers to the space an object or form occupies (or has within it), and *mass* refers to its weight or appearance of weight.

Warp—the threads from which a loom is strung, warp threads run lengthwise.

Wash—a watered-down pigment that causes a transparent effect when used over other lines or colors.

Wedge—to cut and pound clay in order to prepare it for work in ceramics; wedging removes the air bubbles.

Weft (woof)—the thread used in weaving.

INTRODUCTION

Why teach art?

The intrinsic values of art education are fundamental to the development of a productive, creative human being; therefore, a sound, successful teaching program in this field is the birthright of every child in school.

Some people ask "Why *teach* art?" — assuming that art is a gift to a few and that "either you have it or you don't."

But the truth is, art can be learned like any other subject. Further, it not only *can* but *must* be learned, for it is the foundation for effective visual perception, and the development of visual perception is fundamental to learning in any field.

Art, for the most part, deals with sight, and to be visually literate requires the same processes of learning as those found in any other form of study. To begin with, it is revealing to know that at birth we do not have sight. A newborn infant has only the feeling or sensation of light — purely a kinetic experience. Dark and light images produce different sensations, but no particular image is "mother" or "father" until these concepts exist in the child's mind. The newborn baby cannot perceive specific shapes. If mother holds him tightly and caresses him, he has the feeling of being loved; but the concept of love will be far into his future. So it is with sight. The images are even recorded upside down. The eye is like the lens of a camera, and the retina is like the film, recording everything in an inverted position. It is the brain that turns it right side up, and this only when it has enough information or experience to compare one thing with another.

This whole process is referred to as visual perception. It starts the day we are born, and it should continue throughout our lives to be a part of our thinking process.

Visual perception is, after all, the ability to use imagery; to perceive objects in space; to use and to comprehend graphic language such as maps, blueprints, drawings, and diagrams; to see visual order; to recognize beauty, symbols, excellence, and expression.

Before he comes to a carefully worded explanation of his thoughts, man begins to perceive. Anciently, the respected philosopher, Aristotle, observed, "The soul never thinks without an image." More recently, the great creative physicist, Albert Einstein, who gave us the revolutionary theory of relativity, declared, "The words or the language, as they are written and spoken, do not seem to play any role in my mechanism of thought."* Both Aristotle and Einstein seem to be saying that symbols and images first clothed their creative thinking, not written words. We believe that something valuable is being overlooked in our education — the perceptual development of the learner.

We know that art concepts can now be identified and taught in a systematic method that will give students a highly developed skill in visual perception, and we believe that such skill will enhance their potential to provide the world with creative, innovative thinking in all fields of study.

The fact that art concepts can be identified and learned is exciting, for it offers every student a new pathway to continued growth and development. This new understanding offers to each of us who have eyes — and see not — an opportunity to begin to see and appreciate.

*Einstein, A. Quoted by Ha'damard, J., in *The Psychology of Invention in the Mathematical Field*, Princeton University Press

This is not to say that some are not more gifted than others, but this comparative capability factor is true in reading, math, science, or any other subject. The fact that some have more ability is no reason to take all understanding away from the least talented.

Furthermore, it is our belief that the use of visual thinking skills and evaluative processes will lead students to responsible value judgments that will carry over to all areas of life.

By teaching a basic set of art concepts, a teacher gives each student the tools by which art can be judged. This in turn becomes an exercise in value judging. Value selection by nature is abstract, but when taught in an art education context, it becomes more concrete; it becomes something which can be stopped, run in slow motion, taken out, observed, and analyzed.

Through aesthetics students can be given experience with the concepts of goodness and badness, rightness, beauty and ugliness, and other abstractions. Experience with these ideas will be effective value training, and value training is necessary to develop responsible citizenry.

In nineteenth-century England, well-bred ladies and gentlemen were extremely accomplished in all of the arts. Indeed, it was the "fashion" to be able to draw. But in the fearful age of Sputnik, the arts were almost completely neglected in favor of science and "progress." Now the pendulum seems to be swinging back toward the arts. We do not desire to produce a society of professional "artists" but to make students at large more visually literate. We believe with Rudolf Arnheim that "visual thinking is not the exclusive reserve of the artist — it is used by every truly productive person." And we agree with Sir Herbert Read, the great British educator, that "when a civilization begins to neglect the arts, it soon loses its balance and topples into chaos."

Why this art program?

This art program successfully combines the knowledge, imagination, and evaluative factors of creativity for a productive pattern of growth in perception, thinking, valuing, and art skills.

We have identified 206 basic concepts and have arranged them in a logical, developmental order that we believe will give the student a body of valuable knowledge. Instruction must focus on the concept, and the teacher must do everything possible to make each concept a useful bit of information that has application in numerous aspects of the student's life.

It is our conviction that learning these basic concepts will provide the student with the necessary knowledge and skill base for greater visual perception, which will in turn lead him into greater creative thinking and higher value judgments in all fields, thus enriching his life.

The need for awareness and skills is apparent. So-called "natural" creativity is not enough. Fifty years ago, "progressive educators" told us to give children the supplies and some encouragement, like "a pat on the head," but not to inhibit their "natural creativity" by giving them something to do. Practical application of this idea has proved that this perception of creativity was incomplete. The results were not satisfactory, and investigation into the field continued. Through persistent research we now have greater insight into this aspect of the human personality.

We recognize that creativity is not unique to art. Only recently have we begun to realize that conceptual knowledge is an indispensable ingredient of creativity.

Dr. Sidney J. Parnes, Director of Creative Education, University of New York at Buffalo, describes creativity as a function of knowledge, imagination, and evaluation. Written as a formula, it may be expressed in this manner:

$$C = f(K I E)$$

Creativity = a function of:
knowledge — imagination — evaluation

As the formula indicates, teachers who foster the development of imagination without knowledge and evaluation will do little to enhance the creative talents of their students; indeed, they will likely stifle them. All the materials and pats on the head you can give a student will not encourage creativity without the conceptual base.

The K (Knowledge) factor is the conceptual base. According to Dr. Asahel Woodruff, educational researcher, a concept is a relatively complete and meaningful idea in the mind of a person. It is an understanding of something. At its most abstract and complex level, it is a synthesis of a number of conclusions drawn from particular experiences.

Percepts are the sensory beginnings of concepts. As meanings from past perceptions become associated with one another, they form concepts. As concepts are formed, choices or evaluations are made based on those accumulated ideas or concepts. And these evaluations or decisions determine behavior. When a child has his first experience with a dog, his concept of a dog may consist of just two or three percepts, e.g., the noise it makes, its size compared to him, and how it feels when he touches it. As the child has additional experiences with dogs, he will have an increase in the number of percepts received, and his concept will change. Each change will influence the child's behavior.

Understanding these things, we have chosen for this program those concepts that, when linked together, will provide the significant base of knowledge each individual needs in art education. The concepts are categorized as "awareness" concepts and "skill" concepts, and each of these areas has both two- and three-dimensional ideas. The concepts are geared to eight different levels of understanding and competency — or student "readiness" — and are in a sequence for systematic growth and progression.

It is important to know that all children go through a sequence of visual and graphic development. The child's symbols are indicators of his "visual level." This program will help the parent or teacher to develop an awareness and recognition of the developmental stages. It will also prescribe the experiences that are needed for their further growth and development. As a baby begins life virtually sightless and grows in perception, so he also begins his artistic efforts with scribbling. It is an important link in his growth pattern and comes at a time when his ability to speak is somewhat limited. These experiences satisfy both the need to communicate ideas and feelings and the need to express one's uniqueness. The child's art activity becomes a foundation for understanding himself and his environment.

When instruction is given on a cognitive or memory plane, sequence is unimportant. For example, teaching a student "about" bicycles requires no sequence. What difference would it make if you started with the spokes, sprocket, or fender? If, however, you wanted to teach someone to *ride* a bike, instruction must come in sequence and at a time or level appropriate for the learner.

Therefore our program is not designed to teach "about" art — though it does that. It is designed to teach students how to increase their skills in both understanding and doing. This means that the teacher must present the concepts in sequence and at a time or level appropriate for the learner.

The teacher can tell if his or her instruction is effective because learning will not take place if the instruction is out of sequence or if the instruction is given before the child is mentally or physically ready for the experience. The teacher can tell, as can a parent, because *no learning has taken place unless the behavior of the student has changed.* In teaching a student to ride a bicycle, an instructor can tell if a student has learned by observing whether or not the student can ride. In teaching art concepts, an instructor can tell if a student has learned by observing what he or she does with the new information.

The I (Imagination) factor we shall refer to as *productive thinking.* Productive thinking has four elements:
- *Convergent thinking* is learning to find the one correct or best answer to a problem.
- *Divergent thinking* is the process of searching for all the possibilities — expanding the number of ideas (fluency) and the kinds of ideas (flexibility). (Brainstorming is a form of divergent thinking.)
- *Evaluative thinking* is used in value selections and in evaluating applications of the concepts relative to the goals.
- *Visual thinking,* or perception, is the ability to think in imagery. Concepts cannot be formed without first having concrete *images.* Divergent thinking and visual thinking are typically left out of most educational programs but are an integral part of this one. Since we mentioned visual thinking earlier in this chapter, we shall dwell here primarily with divergent thought processes as related to the I factor.

Divergent thinking exercises are built into almost every suggested lesson activity. Most classroom activity is geared to the cognitive-memory thought processes, but it is through divergent thinking that one feels his mind shift gears and go searching. Such "games" as, "List everything you can which has an orange hue," "Now categorize these according to bright or dull," hunting for analogies, comparisons, writing similes — all these expand one's imagination. These divergent exercises are usable in any teaching situation and help students learn to think productively.

The E (evaluation) factor was discussed earlier, but we believe that evaluation should be an essential part of learning and should occur at all stages of the child's development. Concept application, teacher effectiveness, and changes in awareness are the focus of evaluation rather than whether or not the student does "good" art. Open discussion and verbal analysis at all levels of instruction are helpful in learning. To fail to acquaint students with the insights of visually literate people is to deny them an opportunity for development.

The affective (aesthetic-feeling) and cognitive (understanding) elements of a concept are formed at the same time. If we ignore the basic art concepts, we may not have an aesthetic standard with which to evaluate quality. With no judicial standard, there are too many trails, mostly leading up blind alleys.

Since the focus of the program's conceptual approach rests on increasing the students' awareness (perception), the needs of each student can be met — whether the student be a potential Frank Lloyd Wright, Albert Einstein, or Wordsworth, a future mayor, brick mason, teacher, executive, or parent.

With a "product approach" many teachers are relieved that they must spend an equivalent of only thirty minutes per day on art because they don't know anything about it. Any excuse to skip that one-half hour is also legitimate. Using the concept program, teachers, whether trained or untrained in art, can feel confident that they are giving students awareness and skills and are learning a few themselves while they teach. One such elementary teacher recently reported eagerly, "They GOT it! I'm no artist, but I just taught a concept and they GOT it!'' What he will soon realize is that having grasped the concept, the students will apply it in other areas as well and be ready to build upon that concept with another.

One of the by-products of this program is that students learn to draw. There are many levels of achievement in drawing. Some students develop their drawing skill as a tool for their own ''idea sketching.'' Others will develop, through motivation and arduous practice, great drawing expertise, often excelling their teacher. In these instances, the program uses the basic principle that step one in learning to draw is learning to *see*. Art skills come as a by-product of practicing what is learned from the activities.

There is much discussion of accountability in education today. Rather than spend time on educational jargon such as: this program is individualized, self-directed, reality centered, life relevant, behavior oriented, humanistic, research based, systematically developed, and based on the essential laws that govern human learning — all of which it is — we shall simply point out that the conceptual base allows for accountability in art because the concepts are testable and are built one upon another for continuous progress. Every act of instruction (teaching) should be aimed at changing behavior. This is why we have built lesson plans with measurable and observable behavioral objectives.

How do I use this art program?

This program is structured in such a way that a teacher or parent with no previous art training can teach the art concepts. The program is also helpful to the ''art'' teacher in that it gives sequence to instruction and helps the teacher determine the child's level of perception and skill. It generates new ideas and new instructional approaches for the student.

Placing the Student in the Program
The teacher first finds some way to motivate the student to draw a picture that contains subject matter common to his experience — such as people, buildings, and trees. The teacher must emphasize the need for the student to do his best work and to use paper and media with which he feels most comfortable.

Younger children will respond quickly to an exciting story the teacher reads. Older students might be challenged to show some objects up close and some far away. Telling the student that it is a bright sunny day can help the teacher determine whether the student has had experience with shadow and value concepts.

When the student has finished his picture, the teacher then compares each part of it with the sequence of people, houses, and trees on the diagnostic charts found in this program. The student may well be at different levels in each of the columns on the chart; so a determination must be made as to which level best fits his needs now. Aspects that seem out of context with the rest of the student's picture are best ignored. Once the level has been determined, the diagnostic chart shows where the student should begin in the program (the level and activity number).

The teacher then follows the program as outlined, with these exceptions: Older students beginning at lower levels of perception may skip some activities by virtue of their age and experience. Some lessons may need to be combined to offer sufficient challenge to older students. Students are generally motivated when they are challenged sufficiently by content, and are sufficiently successful at the level in which they are working. Teaching far above or

below the student's level does not bring success or motivation.

Even though subject matter and media are not dictated in any of the lessons, the teacher may want to gear some lessons to holidays or seasonal events; thus certain lessons may be altered in sequence to satisfy this need. The sequence automatically provides the student with media experiences and with skills in crafts and other three-dimensional areas as they tie into his maturation and interest levels in the program. More time is spent in the illusionary aspects of art because the ideas there are more abstract and thus more difficult to comprehend. The three-dimensional processes are inserted periodically at points where the student's age and dexterity make them most appropriate.

In becoming acquainted with the program, the teacher may find it best to work with the entire class at the same level even though an individualized approach is preferred. If the students' pretest drawings are placed in stacks that seem to be at similar levels, one picture in the stack representing a "low-average" can be analyzed with the diagnostic chart and the level determined. Then the whole class could begin at the level of that child.

When the teacher feels confident and comfortable with the program, grouping may be done. Typically, a class might include between two and five different levels.

The Teaching Process

The instructor must make an extensive effort to help the student become well aware of the numerous ways each concept has application in art and in his real-life experience. As the student perceives the multiple applications of concepts dealing with elements such as line, color, value, and texture, his new perceptions will show changes in his art product. Thus the product becomes an essential tool for evaluating the effectiveness of the instruction. For example, a student is at the stage where he typically arranges his subject matter in a line or row across the paper. He then receives instruction on overlapping. The teacher can easily evaluate the learning by the student's verbal responses and by evidence of overlapping found in his drawing.

As each lesson focuses on seeing and thinking processes, a lesson on one concept may trigger perceptual growth in other areas simply because this experience has caused him to look and think more critically.

Lessons and Activities

All of the activities are "sample" lesson plans only. They suggest a variety of ways one might achieve an objective. The teacher may use them as best fits his or her style or method of teaching. The format of this book is such that each lesson page, or activity, becomes a divider, following which the teacher's own ideas and materials relating to that concept may be inserted into a loose-leaf binder, into a folder, or into an 8½" × 11" envelope fashioned by the teacher. The art activities a teacher has used in the past are still relevant to this program. All the teacher needs to do is plug them in at the appropriate spot. (See "A list of common art projects that can be used as devices for teaching a specific concept.")

The program contains two types of lesson plans. One type called "A Note to the Teacher" describes the preschool child in terms of his stages of graphic perception and coordination. It aids the teacher's or the parent's awareness of these stages so that he can suggest activities and encourage further growth of the child. Any of these stages of development could take weeks or even months for the child to pass through. They are not a "one-time" experience.

The other type of lesson plan comprises the balance of the lessons. These are concept-centered and are to be used more on a weekly basis with whatever reinforcement or reteaching seems necessary.

In each instance the focus of instruction must be in the direction of helping the student to *use* the concept in analyzing art, in making art, and in relating the concept to the real world. The art product is used to reinforce and evaluate learning. It must *not* be used to compare one student with another as "artists," nor should the art product become the major goal of the activity.

Suggestions of media and supplementary visual materials are made at the end of each activity. However, none of these is crucial to the experience. Each teacher and school has a vast reservoir of resources that might be used as effectively. The prints suggested with a majority of the lessons are helpful to reinforce the notion that artists through the years have used the same ideas that the student is learning and to introduce the learner to the works of famous artists in the form of visual aids — and this in a rather unobtrusive way. One set of 115 prints may be purchased per school for this purpose.

Contact the publisher for information.

Guidelines for teaching Art is Elementary on a grade level basis

The teacher merely locates his/her grade level in the appropriate column and follows the instructions contained therein.

K	1	2	3	4	5	6
Kindergarten Curriculum includes activities: 12 14 21 23 27 *32 *33	Review activities: 32 33 If they were not taught in kindergarten.	Review activities: 34 35 45 47 49 51 56 If they were not taught in first grade.	Review "Blocking In" concept and activities: 45 51 56 60 61 63 64 65 69 72 If they were not taught in first or second grades	Review "Blocking In" concept and activities: 60 74 61 76 63 77 64 82 65 88 69 92 72 93 95 If they were not taught in second or third grades	Review "Blocking In" concept and activities: 69 92 72 93 74 95 76 99 77 111 82 113 88 120 If they were not taught in second, third, or fourth grades	Review "Blocking In" concept and activities: 74 95 76 99 77 120 82 126 88 129 92 134 93 140 If they were not taught in third, fourth, or fifth grades.
To reinforce basic readiness concepts, teach activities: 19 24 25 26 28 31	The first grade curriculum includes activities: *34 *49 *35 50 37 *51 42 52 43 53 44 54 *45 55 46 *56 *47	The second grade curriculum includes activities: 57 66 58 67 59 68 *60 *69 *61 70 *62 71 *63 *72 64 73 65 Introduce "blocking in" at this level	The third grade curriculum includes activities: *74 86 75 87 *76 *88 *77 *89 78 90 79 91 80 *93 81 *94 *82 95 83 *96 84 97 85	The fourth grade curriculum includes activities: 98 *111 *99 112 100 *113 101 114 102 115 103 116 104 117 105 118 106 119 107 *120 108 121 109 122 110	The fifth grade curriculum includes activities: 123 137 124 138 125 139 *126 *140 127 141 128 142 *129 143 130 144 131 145 132 146 133 147 *134 148 135 149 136	The sixth grade curriculum includes activities: 150 *163 151 *164 *152 *165 153 166 154 *167 155 *168 156 *169 157 170 158 *171 159 *172 *160 *173 *161 174 *162 175
Developmental activities include: 15 17 18 20 22 29 30 Use them when they describe needs or problems evident in your students	Developmental activities include: 36 38 39 40 41 48 Use them when they describe problems evident in your students					Level seven becomes a seventh grade or gifted student's curriculum. Crucial activities include: 178 193 180 195 181 196 182 201 183 202 184 203 186 204

"Blocking In" is an idea used in many "how to draw" books. It helps beginners to avoid many mistakes in learning the skill of drawing. The idea is to look at an object, study it carefully, and try to mentally reduce it to the simplest shape possible. In other words, begin a drawing by lightly "blocking in" the basic shapes of the object. Thus a pine tree may be drawn first as a simple triangle, or a truck as squares, circles, and rectangles.

*Vital Concerns

THE PRESCHOOL LEVEL

THE PRESCHOOL CHILD

Note:

In this program children's drawings are not used as meters of their skill as artists but rather as indicators of their perceptual level. Children use their drawings as an aspect of communication in the early stages of their development, and all students in the United States or in similar cultures will use people, houses, trees, flowers, and animals as the subject matter for their pictures. A sequence may also be noted in the child's awareness as he or she treats illusions of depth and manipulates or gives order to three-dimensional shapes. As the learner has experiences with concepts in this program, awareness will change and perceptions will be altered. The changes in the student's awareness may be evidenced in his drawings — even though his skills may not change very much. Thus a student's pictures are very helpful to a teacher in determining the student's level of perception and in evaluating the effect of any given activity.

MATURITY LEVEL

Developmental stages

This packet of instructional sheets and individual lesson plans for the parent/teacher is designed to help adults motivate and guide children through their developmental stages. The instructional sheets and activities will instruct the parent or teacher concerning the following ideas and activities:

- The early kinesthetic needs of a child
- Ways in which colors influence a child
- Ways in which a variety of experiences in hearing, seeing, and feeling are helpful to a child
- Ways in which verbal skills relate to hearing, seeing, and feeling experiences
- The beginnings of a child's graphic expression (scribbling)
- The beginnings of sculpture and architecture (manipulating shapes)
- A child's early experiences with photography
- The development of a child's imagination
- How a child gives order to the forms he arranges
- How a child arranges his scribbles
- How a child perceives his first two-dimensional shapes or patterns
- The introduction of texture to a child
- The significance of a child's using lines to enclose his scribbles
- A child's ability to name and match colors
- A child's progression in making his first linelike shapes
- How a child creates a simple center of interest in the arranging of objects or forms
- The kinds of things that motivate a child in drawing
- How a child can relate photography to similar life experiences
- A child's introduction to the concept of top, side, and bottom

- A child's first attempts to create symbols that represent people and objects
- A child's first experiences with shaping and modeling pliable materials such as clay
- A child's first attempts to create complex forms by arranging and stacking various objects.

THE DIAGNOSTIC CHART
An explanation

1. Sight (the ability to make visual discriminations) is acquired through experience. At this level (usually between one and two years of age) the child is not really aware of what a marking instrument will do or that it is in fact a marking instrument. Any marks or scribbles that he makes are accidental. He tends to jab and to swing his arm in uncontrolled motions, using the marking instrument as an extension of his hand.

2. Gradually the child, through practice, is able to control his motions. He is aware that his motions have an effect on a marking surface. He can scribble freely and enjoys scribbling with many different types of marking instruments. If he has had opportunities to play with three-dimensional objects like toy blocks, he soon seeks order by lining them up, horizontally or vertically.

3. The ability to see requires mental action. Until the child has had sufficient experiences to build his mental processes, he in effect sees nothing. He is only receiving the *sensation* of light. The gradual orientation to his environment that the child goes through makes him realize the placement of things around him in relation to himself. At this point he tends to place his scribbles selectively. When he scribbles, he tends to place the scribbles in about the same location on the paper and to confine them to one unit. This is an indication that his brain has started to seek order in his scribbles and that he is becoming oriented to the shape of the paper that he scribbles on. He is also able to give further order to manipulatable three-dimensional objects. If there are different sizes of objects available to him, he can arrange them in a line from small to large. It is important to realize that this development comes in sequence. He does not do this before he can place objects in a line, as illustrated on line two. At this level the child will also be able to place items like clothespins around the top of a box. His eye-hand coordination is developed enough to accomplish the movements necessary for this kind of activity.

4. Gradually the *scribbles* of the child will take on the characteristics of specific shapes, such as Xs, circles, squares, or rectangles. For the first time the child is able to make his scribbles look like the basic shapes. This might appear accidental, but it is the outcome of practice and the visual and physical development that comes with practice. These shapes are not to be confused with the stage of purposeful *outlining* of shapes.

PRESCHOOL

DIAGNOSTIC CHART

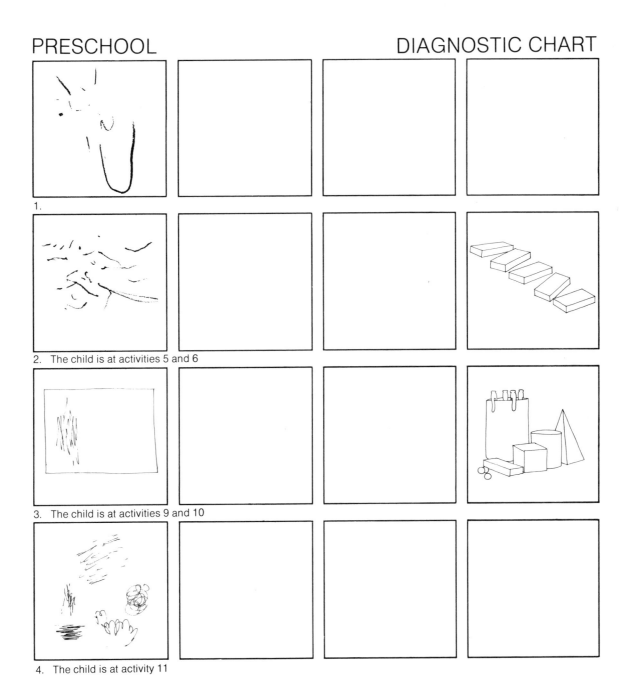

1.

2.   The child is at activities 5 and 6

3.   The child is at activities 9 and 10

4.   The child is at activity 11

5. As the child becomes visually aware that his scribbles are specific shapes, he tends to draw a line around his scribbled shapes. This indicates a rather high degree of visual perception and is an indication that the child is starting to develop a mental system that separates the figure and background; he is able to identify shapes and see them as being different from the background or space around them. This is very important in the process of learning to read, write, and think abstractly.

6. At this level the child does not need to scribble the shapes — to make a mass of scribbles — but rather tends to draw lines that enclose shapes. The shapes start to take on the characteristics of circles, and some even have the appearance of rectangles, squares, and triangles. He can now organize three-dimensional objects in a more complicated order from small to large and back to small again.

7. His shapes now take on the characteristics of people and animals — not readily detectable to the adult, but the child has a tendency to name them as such. The mandala or sunlike shape (a circle with lines drawn through it) is common at this level. He will use the mandala in a variety of ways to symbolize trees, flowers, suns, animals, people, and other familiar things in his environment.

8. The child's symbols of people, houses, trees, and animals are clearly emerging. When he arranges three-dimensional objects, he can arrange big with big, round with round, and square with square. He can now create recognizable objects from pliable materials such as clay, salt, flour, or play dough by jamming them together and pulling, rolling, twisting, and shaping them.

PRESCHOOL   DIAGNOSTIC CHART

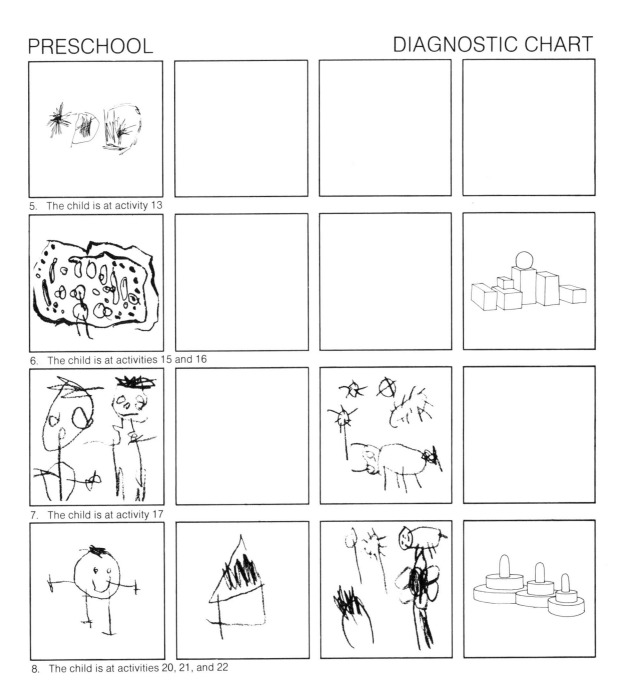

5. The child is at activity 13

6. The child is at activities 15 and 16

7. The child is at activity 17

8. The child is at activities 20, 21, and 22

Art projects that can be used as devices for teaching a specific concept

Drawing
(pencil, crayon, brush, marker, chalk)
Lessons: *5, 8, *10, *11, *13, *15, 17, *20

Murals and friezes
Lesson: 20

Coloring and color mixing
Lessons: 5, 8, 10, 11, 13, 15, 17, 20

Dribble and sponge painting
Lessons: *8, 17

Dioramas
Lessons: 20, 21

Finger painting
Lessons: 5, *8, 10, 11, 13, 15, 17, 20

Blow paint through straws
Lesson: *8

String pull design
Lesson: *8

Water color and tempera painting
Lessons: 8, 10, 11, 13, *14, 15, 17, 20

Collage
Lessons: *12, 14

Sculpture with clay
Lesson: *21

Vegetable prints
Lesson: 8

Gadget prints
Lesson: 8

String and yarn pictures
Lessons: 17, 20

Stitchery (string and yarn)
Lessons: 17, 19, 20

Snow sculpture
Lesson: 21

Photography
Lessons: *7, *18

---

*Key projects for the concept.

A note to the teacher: From birth children instinctively touch and explore materials and objects kinesthetically.

What this means
Even while the child is instinctively pushing into his mouth everything he gets hold of, he begins to handle objects with his own hands — holding onto a finger, his bottle, or an end of a blanket. Apparently the child finds some sort of pleasure in kinesthetic experiences.

How to recognize this level
The child is unable to perceive details of any sort. He is in the earliest stages of "learning to see." By sight he cannot distinguish among members of his family. He cannot follow movement with his eyes. He is frightened by unexpected sounds or movement. He finds security in circumstances simulating the time when he was still being carried by his mother. This developmental level will largely consume the first year of his life and will continue in some aspects on into his kindergarten years.

of his development but are particularly crucial through the primary grades.

What to do, why, how often, and when
Throughout the first year of the child's life or until he takes the initiative, place a variety of textural materials into his hands. Be certain none is harmful or small enough to swallow. Let him hold onto such things as clean fingers, plastic rattles, blankets, diapers, and rubber bones. Place the child in changing environments throughout the day so that he has a variety of visual experiences. Talk to him and play with him throughout his feeding and while you are changing his diapers and clothing. All of these things are as important to the child's early perceptual development as stories are to his reading readiness.

What to look for at the end (evaluation)
Long before a child no longer needs the kinds of experiences described above, a variety of other needs will have developed. Kinesthetic experiences to some degree or another will be important to the child at *all* stages

A note to the teacher: Infants are attracted to bright colors.

What this means

More than 75 percent of all the child learns will come as a result of his visual experiences. Seeing color is a part of his early learning. Visual perception develops in a sequence that is still not completely defined. Apparently children see only dark and light at first, then vague shapes in black and white and shades of gray. Not until the child has learned to recognize people and objects with sight alone will he begin to develop his capacity to see color. Some pediatricians feel that most children are unable to distinguish individual colors until after they are 2½ years old. Even though the small child may not see color and is really attracted to strong contrasts or movement, the experiences he has with bright colors are *still* important.

How to recognize this level

If the child is between the ages of two months and 2½ years, preparatory experiences with color are an important part of his visual development.

What to do, why, how often, and when

Along with providing the child with a variety of kinesthetic experiences, a parent should add to his day-to-day fare slow movement and brightly colored objects. Just as numerous experiences with hearing stories and looking at pictures even before he can talk assist in preparing the child for reading, so do experiences with color begin the development of his visual discrimination. Brightly colored mobiles moving slowly overhead and brilliant red rattles and colorful appliques seen against neutral backgrounds are the kinds of visual experiences the child ought to be having daily.

What to look for at the end (evaluation)

Experiences with color will be a need of the child into adulthood, but the sort of color environment described above will terminate as a need when the child starts to distinguish one color from another. From that point color experiences will become much more specific.

A note to the teacher: Seeing and feeling certain objects or living things can help a child associate noises and functions with their appropriate source, for example, a dog barking, a horn honking, and water running.

What this means
These experiences are part of continually broadening the child's visual experiences. Hearing, feeling, and touching experiences provide important clues that help the child better define what he sees.

How to recognize this level
At the point where the child is beginning to recognize members of his family by sight, he will begin to form other associations that will relate images with sounds and touch sensations. Thus, seeing a faucet with water running from it, turning the faucet on and off, feeling the water, and hearing it run will help the child form a concrete concept of faucet and water.

What to do, why, how often, and when

- Help the child to have daily experiences with (1) familiar objects inside and outside the home, (2) objects and living things that are part of his community, and (3) common things outside his community.
- Make certain that the child encounters the object or living thing in at least three ways: seeing it, touching or handling it (assuming it won't harm the child in any way), and hearing the sound it makes.
- Any time a part of the experience is missing, the child's concept of it will be incomplete. It is very easy for the youngster to develop inaccurate or even false ideas about something. If, for instance, a child's only experience with dogs is with a St. Bernard, he won't likely perceive the "dogness" of a Mexican Chihuahua.
- The teacher or parent should make every effort to keep the child's encounters with things as real as possible. Let's suppose a mother wants her child to learn about ducks. Her first effort should be one of trying to bring ducks to the child or taking the child to a place where ducks can be seen. If neither of these alternatives are available, she should collect a variety of illustrations that show what ducks look like (the variety of their size and color) and how big they are compared with the child and other things he is familiar with.

The child will then need to touch and handle feathers to to know what ducks *feel* like, and he will need to know what they sound like. ("Quack, quack" is not a sufficient imitation of the sound ducks make.)
- Some of the experiences or encounters the child should have include such things as household pets, farm animals, zoo animals (especially those at children's zoos), appliances such as vacuums and blow combs, furnaces, skate boards, bicycles, pots and pans, watches and clocks, tea kettles, car motors, windshield wipers, a car horn, and a variety of musical instruments.
- Remember that the more numerous the child's experiences are, the better his preparation will be in learning to deal with the real world inside and outside his home. When each of the child's experiences are complete in the sense that he sees, hears, and touches, the more *accurate* his concepts will be.

What to look for at the end (evaluation)

This kind of activity will be appropriate for the learner throughout his public school experience but is crucial at the preschool and primary grade levels. Evaluation should be in terms of keeping each experience as real and as relevant as possible and making certain that the child is able to see, hear, and touch each thing he learns about (assuming that the child's protection is always considered).

A note to the teacher: At this stage in his development the child can name familiar objects or forms in his environment, for example, table, chair, window, ball, and book.

What this means

At around the age of two or when the child is learning to talk, he needs to learn the correct name for everything in his environment. Just as in activity 3, he needs the name and the object brought to his attention in a way that will cause him to remember it.

How to recognize this level

If the child is learning to talk — particularly if he's attempting sentences of two or three words — this activity is appropriate.

What to do, why, how often, and when

■ On a daily basis have the child look at and touch common objects both in and out of the home. Just as he is taught to practice saying "mama" and "daddy," he can learn to name such things as tables, chairs, doors, windows, books, steps, and balls.
■ The visual and kinesthetic aspects of this activity have the same impact as they did in the previous activity. With some objects it might even be helpful to let the child see an object upside down or see its working parts.

What to look for at the end (evaluation)

When the child indicates that he knows the name of everything inside and outside his home, the goal of this activity has been reached. The key to the evaluation, however, is a twofold question: (1) Is the child having daily experiences? (2) Are the experiences broad as opposed to superficial — that is, does the child have opportunities to really examine the thing he is learning the name of?

PRESCHOOL

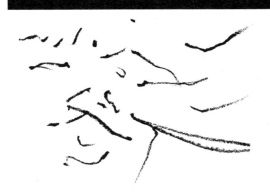

A note to the teacher: When given the opportunity, small children will scribble freely with a marking instrument.

What this means

Around the age of two, small children will begin the development of what eventually will become their drawing skill. Scribbling in its various phases is the beginning stage. When the child is first given an opportunity to use some sort of marking instrument like a pencil, a felt tip pen, or a crayon, he will not scribble freely with it, but he will use it as if it were an extension of himself and will explore with it. It looks as though he is striking at the paper. Later, after the child has had a number of experiences with a drawing instrument, he will begin to scribble quite freely.

How to recognize this level

If the child has never used a marking instrument of any kind — such as a pencil, a crayon, or a felt marker — and he is betwen the ages of 1½ and 2½, he is probably at this level. Show the child what a felt marker or crayon does to paper. If his eyes light up and he reaches for the instrument, he is ready for the experience.

What to do, why, how often, and when

■ Encourage the child to use drawing media and paper between three and seven times a week, making sure that the child sees the experience as fun and interesting. Vary the kinds of paper and the marking instruments. Use crayons, felt markers, chalk, charcoal, ball point pens, and pencils. Offering variety in these things will motivate the child to do more scribbling. Praise his efforts and let him know you are proud of his achievements.

Remember that drawing can develop the child's visual perception (his ability to see and discriminate between things) and that the more experience he has, the better he will develop concepts needed for *all* areas of learning.

■ Don't expect the child to draw images at this point. He needs an attitude of success and motivation. Pressure to draw things he is not capable of handling will only result in discouragement.

■ Recognize that children are inclined to do what their parents do; girls will most likely copy their mothers, and boys will copy their fathers. Thus, if parents want their children to participate in this important activity, they should let the youngsters see them spending time with drawing. (It doesn't matter how *well* the parents draw.)

What to look for at the end (evaluation)

The child will have moved beyond the level of beginning scribbling when he consciously and consistently places scribbles in certain areas of his paper or drawing surface.

PRESCHOOL

ACTIVITY 6

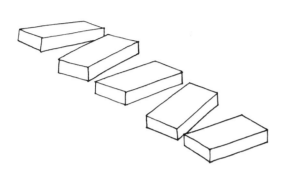

A note to the teacher: When the child is at this stage in his development, he is able to arrange three-dimensional objects, such as wooden blocks, in rows.

What this means

When children are first given a variety of objects such as blocks, wood scraps, tinker toys, or lincoln logs, they will try to give order to them by arranging them. The first kind of order is to arrange the objects in a row.

How to recognize this level

If the child has never had any opportunity to play with three-dimensional objects and he is able to sit up by himself and crawl, he is at this level and is ready for the activity.

What to do, why, how often, and when

- Provide the child with materials to arrange. Don't give him all of them at once. Provide blocks one day, dominoes another, tinker toys the next, and so on.
- Encourage the child and praise his efforts.
- Don't tell the child what to make or ask what he is creating. The natural development is what you are after at first.
- Provide opportunities such as those described two or three times a week. These activities are a forerunner for sculpturing skills, but they are helpful in developing hand-eye coordination, large and small muscle control, and the ability to identify shapes and use them in various arrangements.

What to look for at the end (evaluation)

When the child has been highly motivated, has a feeling of success, and is beginning to arrange objects in other than straight lines, he is ready for the next step (activity 9).

PRESCHOOL

ACTIVITY 7

A note to the teacher: The child is aware that pictures can be taken with a camera and that people use a camera (or cameras) to take pictures. He identifies himself and other people and objects in pictures.

What this means

Since photography is an art form, the child needs some early experiences with the art to develop an awareness of low-level concepts.

How to recognize this level

When the child begins to put words together to form short sentences and to recognize himself in a mirror, he is ready for this activity.

What to do, why, how often, and when

- Show the child one or two varieties of cameras. Talk about what they are called and why they are used. Let the child handle the camera — open and close it, press the shutter, and so on.
- Show him how the film is placed in the camera. Talk about the use of the film. Show him some photographs. Help him to understand the relationship between the camera and the film.
- Show him pictures of himself; see if he knows who the baby or child is.
- Repeat this experience two or three times or until the child seems to comprehend both aspects (cameras and film equal pictures of him and his family).

What to look for at the end (evaluation)

When the child demonstrates an awareness of what cameras are, why they are used, and how film can be made into a picture of himself or someone he loves, the lesson is complete.

PRESCHOOL

A note to the teacher:
Imagination can be
developed.

What this means
Whether or not a child seems to be an imaginative person,
this ability can be developed. It is an important aspect of
his potential for being creative.

How to recognize this level
When the child is talking in sentences and can communicate
simple ideas and feelings verbally, he is ready for this
activity.

What to do, why,
how often, and when

Though most infants are *naturally* imaginative, provide
experiences at least weekly that will encourage his
imagination and develop his abilities in this area of
creativity. These need not be elaborate exercises, but they
are needed on a *regular basis.*
■ Look at clouds and describe what you see in their shapes.
■ Look at pictures of animals and imagine what kinds of
  people they would be most like.
■ Imagine new endings to old familiar stories.
■ Create imaginative characters.
■ Talk about imaginative pets. Some children do this quite
  naturally, playing with imaginary kittens, dogs, or dinosaurs.
■ Read imaginative stories to the child — such as "The Very
  Nice Things" by Jean F. Merrill (Harper and Bros., 1959)
  or any equally appropriate story.
■ Encourage the expression of ideas that are not always the
  same as everyone else's.
■ Reward imaginative thinking or unique ideas with praise.
■ Encourage his naming his scribblelike drawings.
■ Use imagination games for children as prescribed in the
  book *Put Your Mother on the Ceiling,* by Richard De Mille,
  Viking Compass Books.

What to look for at the
end (evaluation)

When the child demonstrates an increased ability to use his
imagination, when activities fostering this ability have been
organized on a weekly basis, the child is profiting from the
experiences. The development of imagination should not
come to an end at *any* point in the child's life; so this is
just a beginning point in this very special kind of activity.
(*See also* level 4, activity 121.)

PRESCHOOL

ACTIVITY 9

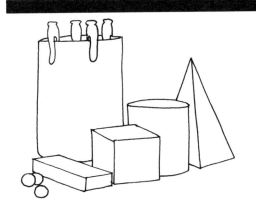

A note to the teacher: The child can now arrange three-dimensional objects in sequential rhythms, for example, short to tall, or around the edge of a box.

What this means
Even when the child is in the crawling stage, he can and should have plenty of manipulative toys around him so that he becomes accustomed to pushing and dividing them. And when he is sitting up by himself, he will gradually become able to arrange manipulative objects, like blocks or dominoes, in a row. He then will give further order to them by taking objects of different sizes and arranging them from small to large, or perhaps he will be able to take objects like clothespins and place them around the top of a box. It is important to realize that this development comes in sequence. It is also important to know that when the child has reached a certain level, he does not disregard the former things he has learned. His including former activities can make it difficult to detect his exact stage, or level, of performance.

How to recognize this level
When the child's only experience in manipulating objects has been to line them up in rows, he is at this level.

What to look for at the end (evaluation)

When the student begins to develop more complex arrangements than are described in this lesson, he has moved to a higher level.

What to do, why, how often, and when

- Follow the same plan described in activity 6. Don't tell the child what to make, and don't comment on what his arrangement looks like; simply encourage the doing. This is merely a low-level experience with form. Success and pleasure are important, but the child also needs to feel a sense of accomplishment.
- Remember, this is the beginning of activity that could lead to the creation of buildings, sculpture, pottery, or any other three-dimensional object. At least weekly experiences are needed. Remember, parental/teacher example helps a great deal. The child should see others manipulating and arranging the same objects he plays with.
- Provide a wide assortment of objects, including small empty boxes, oatmeal box carts, and similar articles.

PRESCHOOL   ACTIVITY 10

A note to the teacher: At this point in his development, the child is consciously placing his scribbles on a drawing surface.

What this means
The child has gone from a random but vigorous form of scribbling to one of consciously placing his scribbles in certain positions on his paper. He still scribbles in a vigorous way and can fill his paper in a very short time, but the placement of his scribbles is no longer arbitrary and the parent/teacher will soon note a pattern developing in what the child does. It should be noted that scribbling includes circular, curved, and wavy lines as well as dots and the very common vertical, horizontal, and diagonal lines.

How to recognize this level
In her book *The Psychology of Children's Art* (Random House, 1967), Rhoda Kellogg identifies seventeen placement patterns that can be recognized in children's scribbling. When one or more of these are used with some consistency, the child is at this level. The seventeen patterns include covering the whole page, using the middle area only, leaving a border, using a vertical or horizontal half only, creating a balanced effect with scribbles on each side, using a diagonal half of the paper (triangular shape), following a diagonal axis, filling two-thirds of the space, filling one-fourth of the space (a corner), filling the space in three different fan shapes, leaving two corners vacant and filling in a pyramid shape, making a band or stripe across the page, and using the bottom of the page to extend fan-like scribbles.

What to do, why, how often, and when

Since scribbling is the foundation experience for children's drawing, encouragement and motivation are prime ingredients the parent/teacher should supply at this level, in addition to a variety of materials to scribble with and scribble on (supplied one at a time on separate occasions).

Encourage daily experiences with scribbling if it's at all feasible and don't worry about verbal responses from the child. He doesn't have to "talk about" his scribbles. The child should see the parent/teacher frequently doing

"drawing-like" things. Children like to do what they see others do, and example by both mother and father will help a great deal.

Accept his work for what it is and reinforce any new things perceived in his scribbling activity.

What to look for at the end (evaluation)

From this point the child will move into a stage of scribbling (activity 11) that represents the beginning of shape formation. As the child begins scribbling lines close together so that a mass or shape is created, he is through with this stage and ready for the experiences described in the next lesson.

PRESCHOOL

ACTIVITY 11

A note to the teacher: At this point the child uses his scribbles to symbolize shapes in his environment. He may scribble lines close together and, from the mass created, perceive two-dimensional shapes or patterns.

What this means

The child is approaching a pictorial stage with his scribbles. He sometimes names his scribbles or describes what they symbolize. He has greater control over his scribbles in placing them on the paper and occasionally scribbles lines close together. The masses of scribbled lines look like shapes — some round, some rectangular, some triangular. At the next level he perceives those masses as shapes just as do older children. (See activity 13.)

How to recognize this level

Watch the child at work and show interest enough to encourage him to verbalize about his pictures. That will give you the information you need to check, then compare his drawings with the illustrations. If they are similar, he is at this level.

What to do, why, how often, and when

See that the child has daily experiences in drawing with crayons, pencils, pens, markers, or paint on any kind of paper available. The child simply needs encouragement and opportunities for him to develop to the point where he can begin building a repertoire of visual symbols. Drawing and painting opportunities will contribute to his growth in all curricular areas and especially in reading readiness. Don't impose ideas on the youngster or expect products beyond his current level of perception. Be accepting and reinforce any indication of change in what he perceives.

What to look for at the end (evaluation)

When the child consistently scribbles at the level described in the "note to the teacher" section, the objective has been achieved.

PRESCHOOL

ACTIVITY 12

Concept taught by this activity: Textures exist, and different objects may have a different feel to them.

Objective: The student demonstrates an awareness that textures exist and that objects may feel different from each other. A sample lesson plan for achieving the objective:

Teacher preparations
- Collect pictures from magazines, photographs, and actual objects — all of which suggest a variety of textures. Look for those kinds of things young children would want to feel and handle.
- Organize or have in mind some kind of short walk where children will come in contact with a variety of surfaces they can touch and describe that are not found only in the classroom.
- Set up a table covered with objects that children will respond to emotionally when they touch them. Label the display, "Touch Me."
- Have several sacks available, each containing a different object for children to describe and eventually identify by their sense of touch.

Teaching suggestions
- Begin the exercise by a discussion that will stimulate students to think about texture. You might ask questions such as the following: "Does anyone know what it means to be blind?" "What are the ways you think it would be like to not ever see anything?" "How could you tell what your mother looked like?" "How would you know who was talking to you?" "How could you tell what you were eating?" "Could you tell the difference between a tomato and an apple?" "Could you do it without tasting them?" "How?" "How would you find your way around your house?" "If it were dark and you got out of bed at night, how would you get to the bathroom without running into

things?" "Could you tell when you walked from carpet to wood or linoleum?" "How could you tell?" "Has anyone ever heard of the word *texture*?" "Who knows what it means?" (Develop the idea that texture is how something feels and tie this to the discussion of the blind finding their way around by feeling things.)
- Tell the story of the six blind men who each felt a different part of an elephant and thought they were describing the whole animal.

Suggested art activity
Have the children cut out pictures of things that have a different feel to them and have them describe what it would be like to touch them. Encourage a variety of descriptions, e.g., hard, prickly, sticky, slimy, bumpy, wrinkled, furry, fuzzy, and icky. They might also try to classify their pictures by placing them under the word that best describes them.

Alternative art activities
- Have the children reach into the sacks and describe how the object inside feels (using just one word). See if they can tell what the object is on the last time around.
- Take a walk and have children try to remember all of the things they felt so that they can describe them when the class gets back to the room.

- See how many ways the children can create textures in clay or some other soft, pliable material. It might even be done with thick finger paint, or by *gluing* sand, feathers, or cotton to paper.
- Look at prints by famous artists and discuss what textures can be found in their pictures and how the different surfaces would probably feel.

Evaluation

When the teacher has observed a heightened awareness on the part of every child in terms of texture and how things feel, the objective has been achieved.

Other things to consider

- Vocabulary: texture, touch, feel, surface.
- Prints needed:
  Bacchus by Caravaggio
  Still Life with Pipe by Chardin
  Cliff of Etretat After Storm by Courbet
  Blue Boy by Gainsborough
  Bandaged Ear by Van Gogh
  My Gems by Harnett
  Man with Golden Helmet by Rembrandt
  Hudson River Logging by Homer

PRESCHOOL

ACTIVITY 13

A note to the teacher: At this stage the child often names his scribbles, and he uses lines to enclose basic shapes, especially when patterns are formed or masses of lines are created.

What this means

The child is in one of the final stages of scribbling. He identifies his scribbles as representatives of people or objects from his experience. He is now doing on a somewhat regular basis the kind of thing he was just beginning to do in activity 11.

How to recognize this level

Encourage the child to talk about his pictures. Look at the contour of the patterns and masses he draws for inferred shapes. Look for instances when geometric shapes — especially lines and circles — are drawn independent of scribbles. This will likely occur but still rather infrequently.

What to do, why, how often, and when

- See that the child has daily experiences in drawing with crayons, pencils, pens, markers, and paint on any kind of paper available. The child simply needs encouragement and opportunities to develop to the point where he can begin building a repertoire of visual symbols. Drawing and painting opportunities will contribute to his growth in all curricular areas and especially in reading readiness. Don't impose ideas on the youngster or expect products beyond his current level of perception.
- Encourage any indications that the child's awareness has changed or that he has perceived a new idea. Reinforce any development of shapes in his scribbles, especially circular shapes. Recognize that the growth of the child's pictorial expression is often quite slow at this level. Use stories with high interest to motivate the child's art production. Keep the experiences short (fifteen to twenty minutes).

What to look for at the end (evaluation)

When the child names his scribbles, either upon request or spontaneously, when his scribbles suggest shapes or patterns, and when he draws independent shapes in some instances, the objective has been achieved.

PRESCHOOL

Concept taught by this activity: The basic colors can be named, then matched.

Objective: The student will be able to match (or group) various shades of a color, then verbally attach one of the eight basic color names to each of them.
A sample lesson plan for achieving the objective:

Teacher preparations
- Collect and display objects or shapes of various colors.
- Obtain desired books, poems, paintings, stories, or records.
- Provide recipe for fingerpaint and prepare it. (See end of this activity.)

Teaching suggestions
Note: This activity sheet outlines numerous activities for helping a child learn colors. They need not all be taught at once. In fact, it is probably more desirable that they be of short duration and stretched over a longer period of time. Additional exercises could be used as part of other subject area activities to reinforce this one further.
- "What are all the red things you can think of?" (List on board.) "Blue things?" etc.
- Show the class the picture of *Sinbad the Sailor* by Klee. Ask questions. "What do you like about this painting?" "What colors are there like colors you are wearing?" "Can anyone name a color they see in this picture?"
- Read story "What is Pink?" Ask questions about it. See if the students can find the color in the room.
- Ask one student, "Are there other boys who have shirts the same color as yours?" Or, "Which of these colors I'm holding is the same color as your dress?" Build on this idea with all eight colors.

- Ask one student what his last name is. "Does everyone in your family have the same last name?" "Does everyone in your family look a little alike?" (Hair, eyes, etc.) Explain that colors are grouped into color families too, such as the red family, the blue family, and so forth, and like people families, they don't look exactly alike. Show table displaying various objects and ask who could come and find all of the members of the blue family, the green family, and so forth.
- Show a set of colored ping-pong balls. Ask the children to close their eyes. Remove one of the balls and see if they can identify which one is missing. (Paint samples or colored paper may be used as well.)
- If available, play the song "Colors" from Hap Palmer's album, *Learning Basic Skills Through Music*. Have children all participate and follow the directions given in the song.

Suggested art activity
The teacher shows the class some large cards of various colors. All are identified by the class. She cuts two (or more) pieces from paper that matches the colors of her cards and hands these papers to various children so that each has a color. She then hides her cards behind her and brings them out one at a time. The children with that color must jump up and show their color quickly. (This can be expanded and varied in many ways.)

Alternative art activities
- Set up table with cups containing various colors of finger paints. Have the children name the color they want to use in their finger painting; give them that color.
- Have the children draw a picture of simple objects readily recognizable to them. Ask them, for example, if they painted trees green. If a child responds that he painted them red, either ignore the response or accept it as the child's right of choice.
- Use a record that tells the child to hop, skip, and jump. The child chooses a color from colored paper cut in different shapes, and everyone that has the color you say does what the record says. The color is held high while the activity is done.
- As you discuss various colors, foods of that color could be provided for the children to taste, e.g., red: cinnamon

bears; blue: blueberries and blue ice; yellow: lemonade; green: green jello; brown: chocolate pudding; black: licorice; purple: grapes; orange: oranges.

- Many things can be done with food coloring in water or colored salt clay.
- You may want to order "Interlocking Concept Train," #304 in Playtime Equipment Co. Catalogue, 808 Harvard Street, Omaha, Nebraska 68102 ($6.00) to teach color discrimination.

Evaluation

When the child can name his basic colors with accuracy and consistency, the objective has been achieved.

Other things to consider

- Vocabulary: name, match, red, yellow, blue, green, orange, purple, black, white, brown.
- Art materials needed: fingerpaints of various colors.
- Books
  Ziggy and His Colors, Maryjane H. Tonn (Ideal, 1975).
  Red Is Never a Mouse, E. Clifford (Bobbs, Merrill Co., 1960).
  David Was Mad, Bill Martin, Jr. (Holt, Rinehart, and Winston).
  What Is Pink, Christina Rosetti (Macmillan, 1959).
- Poem
  "Sensory Impressions" *Instructor,* February 1966 (Deseret Sunday School Union, Salt Lake City, Utah).
- Records
  "Rhythm Time" by Bomar Ed. Records
  "Colors" in Hap Palmer's *Learning Basic Skills Through Music*
- Prints
  Justice and Peace by Overstreet
  Combination Concrete by Davis
  Before the Start by Lapicque
  Bedroom at Arles by Van Gogh
  Water Flowery Mill by Gorky
  Sinbad the Sailor by Klee
  Head of a Man by Klee
  Orange and Yellow by Rothko

Fingerpaint recipes

Recipe #1
½ cup cornstarch or laundry starch
1 quart boiling water
½ cup soap flakes
1 teaspoon of glycerine
(Refer to procedure below for mixing.)

Recipe #2
½ cup cornstarch or laundry starch
1 quart boiling water
1½ cups soap flakes
½ cup talcum powder
1 teaspoon of glycerine

Mixing procedure
Mix starch with enough cold water to make a creamy paste. Add boiling water and cook until it becomes transparent or glossy looking. Stir constantly. If formula includes talcum powder, add it and stir. Let mixture cook awhile; then add soap flakes, stirring until evenly dissolved. Add glycerine and stir. This mixture may spoil if you store it for any length of time. The addition of one of these ingredients will prevent this:

- a teaspoon each of oil of cloves and powdered alum

- two tablespoons of sodium benzoate.
  Color is added from powdered tempera paint mixed with water until creamy. Five tablespoons of tempera is usually enough for the formula. (The formula may be divided into smaller portions of different colors.)

PRESCHOOL

A note to the teacher: The child can now draw the outline of specific shapes or patterns without having to make a mass of scribbles. His drawings still have a scribblelike appearance.

What this means

The child has now reached the point where he frequently draws independent circlelike shapes along with his lines. It is no longer necessary for him to make scribbles first, then enclose them with a line.

How to recognize this level

The example given in "What this means" above is what you look for. The frequency of the kind of drawing he does is the key, since he may be in a transition period, moving from the enclosed scribble to the independent shape.

What to do, why, how often, and when

Provide the child with daily opportunities to draw or paint — even if the period of time is brief. As the child symbolizes objects or people with his circular shapes, reinforce the effort with extra praise. This is the first step in his developing a repertoire of shapes that he will eventually use to represent everything he draws, paints, or sculpts.

What to look for at the end (evaluation)

When the child is frequently drawing shapes independent of scribbled masses, the objective has been achieved and he is moving toward the development described in activities 17 and 20.

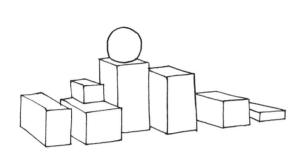

A note to the teacher: Objects can be arranged harmoniously in simple sequences (short to tall to short) with a middle object becoming a simple center of interest.

What this means
If the child has the opportunity and the objects are available for manipulation, he will automatically or intuitively create the simple kinds of arrangements described.

How to recognize this level
When children have opportunities to play with objects such as blocks, tinker toys, dominoes, clothes pins, scraps of wood or plastic, or paper, they are compelled to experiment with them. The first sign of order in their "playing with" objects is to arrange them in rows. The next step in their development will be to arrange objects from short to tall or around the edge of a box if they can be attached. If the child is at this level, he is ready to do what is described in "A note to the teacher".
Step 1. Arrange in rows.
Step 2. Arrange short to tall or tall to short.
Step 3. Arrange short to tall to short with the middle object becoming a simple center of interest.

What to do, why, how often, and when

- Have a variety of objects available for the child. The only requirement is that there be twenty to thirty pieces in each child's set and that they vary in size and height, with some repetition of shapes.
- Provide time for the child to manipulate the objects. The time need not be long, but the activity ought to occur daily.
- Let the child know that you like what he does.
- Recognize that these activities can be the basis for his

  learning what shapes are and how they can be combined to form new shapes. The child's "playing with forms" can lead to the creating of sculptural and other three-dimensional forms and to creating order in his life.
- If the child is *not* at this step, as indicated in B, he may need more frequent experiences to "catch up." Avoid the temptation to ask him what he is making (it might be just

a design to him) and the inclination to show him how to do it. Don't worry that one child takes longer than another to reach the point you are after.

What to look for at the end (evaluation)

When the parent/teacher observes that the child creates a simple center of interest with objects, the objective has been accomplished.

PRESCHOOL

ACTIVITY 17

A note to the teacher: The child now draws basic shapes to symbolize common aspects of his environment. He enjoys his art because of (1) adult approval, (2) tactile sensation, (3) peer acceptance, and (4) personal creation.

What this means

The child at this level has a special need to feel good about the things he does in what we call an art period. The teacher is a symbol of truth and wisdom and thus has a great influence on the kind of beginnings the child will make in his development through art. All children, and adults too, need approval, but it is *especially* crucial for the child at this point.

How to recognize this level

The child is just emerging from the scribble stage. His work will still be very scribblelike, even when he uses lines and basic shapes which seem to represent something.

What to do, why, how often, and when

- Demonstrate approval both verbally and nonverbally. The child's work is a part of *him,* and he needs to know that his parent/teacher likes both.
- Provide daily opportunity for him to express himself in a variety of art media, for example, crayons, pencil, felt-tip pens (water soluble), chalk, water colors, and tempera on large and small sheets of butcher paper, newsprint, manila, or white drawing paper. The child will work quickly; so the art periods need not be lengthy.
- Cater to his tactile needs with experiences in texture, claylike substances, and finger paints.
- Do not exert pressure on the child by expecting him to perform beyond his level, but reinforce any indication that he has perceived something new, for example, scribbles that for the first time resemble what he says they are.

- Parents/teachers should recognize the progress he is making and what it means to the child. It may be helpful for the parent/teacher to know that art (a child's ability to make symbols of what he sees and experiences) will contribute greatly to other aspects of his development, such as his child's reading readiness.

- Recognize that this step leads to the development of a whole series of visual symbols that the child will use for communication purposes.

What to look for at the end (evaluation)

If the child looks forward to his experiences with art media and is reluctant to stop, the objective at this level has been fulfilled. The essence of this activity (or its philosophy) should persist all through levels one and two.

PRESCHOOL

ACTIVITY 18

Concept taught by this activity: The child associates mounted photos with images seen on television or at the movie theater.

Objective: The child demonstrates an ability to recognize that images seen on television or at the movie theater are a form of art and are associated with images captured in snapshots or mounted commercial photographs.

A sample lesson plan for achieving the objective:

Teacher preparations
- Have a number of various kinds of photographs on display, for example, snapshots of family, children, and animals, commercial photographs from a local studio, and photographs from newspapers and magazines.
- Display pictures of various kinds of cameras or of people taking pictures with cameras. Include, if it is possible, pictures of television and motion picture studios and cameras, and have some actual cameras for student examination.

Teaching suggestions
- Refer to the display of photographs and generate a discussion of the concept by asking questions such as: What are these called? Are they pictures or photographs? Could they be both? How? How do we get photographs of ourselves? Have you ever had your picture taken? What is the thing that we take someone's picture with? Was the camera like this? (Refer to a camera or picture of one.) Are there different *kinds* of cameras, then? Are these. all cameras? Have any of you ever been on television? How do they take your picture to show you on TV? Do they use the camera we take snapshots with? How is it different? How max of you like to see movies? Have you ever seen a movie on television? What are ways movies and TV are alike? Different? If we can see movies on TV *or* at the theater, can we see movies in our home? Have you ever been in a movie? How was your picture taken for the movie? Do you suppose they use the same kind of camera for the movies at the theater?
- As the discussion moves along, you may want to clarify words such as *camera, photo, photograph, picture, theater, image, television studio,* and *commercial cameras, large motion picture,* and *color television cameras.*

Suggested art activity
Have children collect photos from home or pictures from magazines that tell a story; relate this quality in individual pictures or groups of pictures to the story-telling capability of television and film.

Alternative art activities
- Where film is available, show children some of the dirrent kinds used, for example, 35 mm film, 120 instamatic, 8 mm movie, 16 mm movie film, and television videotape.
- Take a field trip to a television studio or movie set if possible1
- Have someone who is experienced in filmmaking bring his cameras to demonstrate moviemaking techniques.

Evaluation

Close observation of individual children responding to the experiences should provide ample evidence of whether or not an awareness has been created to fulfill the objective.

Other things to consider

- Vocabulary: camera, film, photo, photograph, picture, moviemaking, videotape, image, lens, and studio.
- Art materials needed: any available paints, crayons, or drawing instruments and two or three types of paper.

PRESCHOOL

ACTIVITY 19

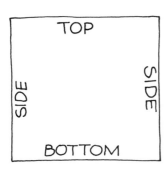

Concept taught by this activity: Labels such as top, sides, and bottom can be assigned to shapes.

Objective: The student will be able to identify the top, bottom, and sides of given shapes.
A sample lesson plan for achieving the objective:

Teacher preparations
Collect pictures and objects that can functionally be oriented to upness and downness — a sense of direction that needs to be present in determining top and bottom: a doll, a bike, a water pitcher and glasses, a box and lid, or pictures of similar items. Place items in a manner of disorientation; that is, place some on their side or upside down. Leave some items correctly oriented to functional use (water pitcher and a glass).

Teaching suggestions
■ Refer to the items on the table. Discuss which ones could or could not be used in the exact positions they are in. "How would you set them so that they would be right?" Have three students hold glasses, one on its side, one upside down, and one right side up. Have a fourth student try to pour water into each glass without turning any of them around. "Who would get the most water?" Do the same with a box, a paper sack, and other items. Trace the shape on the chalk board and mark the top and the bottom. "When children are outside and it starts to rain, how do they keep dry?" "Why do we always hold an open umbrella with the handle down?" Draw an umbrella on the board and have children point to the top of the umbrella and to the bottom of it. Look at a picture of a house. "Doesn't it have a top and a bottom?" "Which part is the roof?"

"We've talked about the top and the bottom of the house — now what are these parts called?" (Point to the sides.) "Does every shape have sides?" Look around the room and identify the top, bottom, and sides of objects. "Does a ball have a top, sides, and a bottom?" "How about a triangle?" "A map?"

■ Discuss a variety of objects in the room. "Where is the top of the sink?" "The bottom of the chair?" "The sides of the file cabinet?" "Where is the top of that car?" "The bottom of the door?"

Suggested art activity
Have students draw an object in the room or outside and label its top, sides, and bottom. If the student can't write, have him merely point out the parts.

Alternative art activities
Have several pictures placed around the room attached to different surfaces. One might be on the wall; one might be on a table top or some other surface. Ask the children to identify the top, bottom, and sides of the pictures. The idea is to help the children orient to a two-dimensional surface that has only height and width and to identify its top, bottom, and sides. This requires abstract thinking. For instance, a piece of paper lying on the top of a table might have two tops — the surface that is up and the top of the picture or written sheet.

Evaluation

Ask students to show or point toward the top, bottom, and sides of several given objects.

Other things to consider

■ Vocabulary: up, down, top, bottom, and sides.
■ Prints:
  Seven a.m. by Hopper
  Cheyt M by Vasarely
  Artist's Mother by Whistler
  Three Flags by Johns

PRESCHOOL

A note to the teacher: At this stage in his drawing the child uses lines plus squares and circular shapes for people and objects. Omitted details and inconsistencies, such as arms attached to the head, are rather common.

What this means

The child is just beginning to represent people and objects with symbols that are recognizable to adults. There is still a scribblelike quality to his pictures in that he does not as yet draw shapes with much assurance. The coloring-in that he does is also scribblish in nature.

How to recognize this level

When his drawings are representative of the descriptions given above, he is at this level.

What to do, why, how often, and when

Continue the practice of having daily art activities in which the child has opportunities to draw what he likes or to react to a story he has heard or to an experience he has had. Encourage the child to think about adding parts or details he currently ignores. Reinforce what he does with praise but *especially* praise any new perceptions you see in his work. The child's symbols are developing now, and he will soon be expanding to additional shapes and added details as he uses art to communicate his thoughts and ideas.

What to look for at the end (evaluation)

When the child consistently uses shapes and lines that give recognizable quality to his pictures and is starting to add or consider additional shapes and details, the teacher has contributed to his perceptual growth.

PRESCHOOL

ACTIVITY 21

A note to the teacher: At this point in his development the child can make forms from pliable materials. The forms will have meaning to the child, but may or may not be recognized by an adult.

How to recognize this level

Provide opportunities for the child to shape and mold clay or some other pliable material. If the product is not even crudely representational or only accidentally resembles a cow or some other figure, the child is at this level.

What this means

The child is at the very beginning in his experiences with pliable materials. When given clay or doughlike substances, he will try shaping them into various things. To the adult, his work will *not* represent what he says it is. It is only a three-dimensional symbol of a bird or a man or whatever. What he does with clay or some other material is similar to the late scribbling stages of his drawing.

What to do, why, how often, and when

- Provide the child with weekly opportunities to manipulate clay and to create forms of his own choice.
- This kind of experience is as beneficial to the child's learning to perceive as any reading readiness or painting activity that is normally a part of the daily curriculum. It is a forerunner of all sculptural experiences and a useful experience in helping the learner relate created forms to objects in life.
- The teacher's only obligation is to provide frequent (at least weekly) opportunities (these need only be fifteen to thirty minutes in length) for children to work with clay or other pliable materials and then to give positive reinforcement to whatever the child creates. At this point the child will *not* profit from formal instruction.

What to look for at the end (evaluation)

If the child has obviously enjoyed the experience and looks forward to future ones, the activity has had value for him, and the teacher's efforts in achieving the objective are realized.

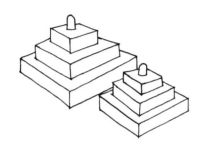

A note to the teacher: At this level a child can arrange objects with a sense of proportion, for example, matching big shapes with big and tiny with tiny as his designs start to grow in size and number of objects.

What this means

The child is now at the beginning of the fourth step in manipulating and arranging objects. His ability to do this is still intuitive, and will become evident when the opportunity is given frequently enough.

How to recognize this level

The child has been creating arrangements with a simple center of interest as described in activity 16.

What to do, why, how often, and when

- Have a variety of objects available that go together in terms of size, for example, a series of large objects, middle-sized objects, small objects, and tiny objects. The variations should be in terms of both height and width. Between twenty and thirty pieces should be available for the child, with some of them fitting together. If there are not parts for the child to combine (big pieces with other big pieces), the child can't achieve what is intended in the lesson.
- Provide frequent experiences as in activity 16, and reinforce his efforts as always.
- Remember to refrain from asking what he is making and from "showing him how."

What to look for at the end (evaluation)

As soon as the child reaches the point that he pairs objects of similar size in his row, like arrangements, he will be moving on to another step. Should he manipulate forms in more *complex* arrangements than stated in this exercise (seemingly skipping this level), it is safe to assume he has already moved on.

- See April issue of *Art Education* magazine, vol. 28, #3, March 1975, National Art Education Assoc., Reston, Va., for article by Robert D. Clements about Frank Lloyd Wright, one of America's greatest architects, and how his mother raised him on theories from "Froebel's Building Blocks."
- Use "Interlocking Concept Train" (#304 in Playtime Equipment Co. Catalogue, 808 Harvard Street, Omaha, Nebraska 68102, $6.00) to teach size/shape discrimination.

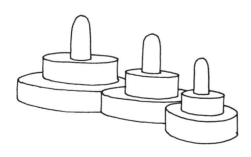

MATURITY LEVEL 1

Developmental stages

In this packet of lesson plans the teacher can provide the child with twenty-five art experiences that are designed to assist the youngster in moving through his developmental stages. The activities will teach how to:

- Identify variations of a given color.
- Properly assign the top, sides, and bottom of geometric shapes.
- Properly identify the middle or center of shapes.
- Correctly identify the sides of a square.
- Identify "alike" and "different."
- Distinguish between "many" and "few."
- Provide opportunities for the child to arrange forms in circular patterns with gates or doors in them.
- Motivate children to give order to arrangements.
- Identify corners on forms.
- Distinguish between rough and smooth textures.
- Pick out geometric shapes or variations of them as they occur in the environment.
- Identify variations in darkness and lightness.
- Identify cast shadows.
- Stack or arrange forms into complex units.
- Compare objects or living things.
- Recognize when children arrange objects with formal and informal balance.
- Recognize when children are attempting illusions of time, space, and depth with lines, dots, and shapes.
- Recognize the basis for the child's inclination for distortion in drawing.
- Recognize the basis for children working primarily in a two-dimensional manner (everything looks flat).
- Assist the child in first experiencing clay and other modeling materials.
- Assist the child in creating texture in form.
- Enrich the child's emotional experience with texture.
- Give expression to the faces of people.
- Help the child recognize the influence of architecture and its related fields on his life.
- Identify repetition in works of art.

THE DIAGNOSTIC CHART

An explanation

9. Consistency is now noted in the student's ability to draw the body as a unit separate from head, arms, and legs. The hand now has fingers, and the eyes, mouth, and sometimes the nose are clearly indicated. Houses, trees, flowers, animals, cars, and other objects may be drawn, but poor motor control is apparent. The coloring of shapes has a scribblelike appearance. The child uses the bottom edge of his picture as a standing line and sets all of his objects on that edge.

10. Arms and legs have thickness to them and shoes (feet) are usually attached to the legs. The nose is now included and the ears (on males) may be shown occasionally. When objects such as blocks are arranged on the floor or on a table, a center of interest may be noted, and gates or doors are created in symmetrical or regular arrangements. Shapes are drawn with more confidence than in line 9. The child often shows the sky as a small strip of blue at the top of the picture.

11. In the arrangement of objects, alternating rhythms may be noted, and numerous parts may be stacked to create rather complex shapes. Pictures may tell a story and are often more detailed than noted above. Attempts to show depth may be observed as the child uses X-ray views, double base lines, folding over, etc. Some parts may be exaggerated in size because of their importance, but pictures look very flat still. Simple forms similar to what he draws may be created from pliable materials such as clay by rolling, squeezing, or patting.

12. The child creates textures by indenting and imprinting into pliable substances. Figures may show action and faces may have expression other than smiles. All shapes are becoming more sophisticated, as the teacher may note by comparing all of the levels on this sheet, e.g., details of hair and costume, and markings on animals.

DIAGNOSTIC CHART

9. The child is at activity #24.

  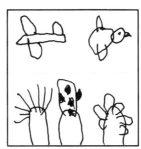 

10. The child is at activity #29.

11. The child is at activities #36, 39, 40, 41, and 42.

12. The child is at activities #43 and 45.

Art projects that can be used as devices for teaching a specific concept

Drawing (pencils, crayon, sticks, pens, markers, brushes, etc.)
Lessons: *35, *39, *40, *41, 45

Posters
Lessons: 45, 47

Murals and friezes
Lessons: 39, 40, 41, 45, 47

Dribble and sponge painting
Lessons: 23, 47

Dioramas
Lessons: 39, 40, 41, 45

Water color and tempera
Lessons: *23, *34, 39, 40, 41, 45

Sculpture with clay (oil, water, salt, flour, etc.)
Lessons: *42, *43, 45

Snow sculpture
Lessons: 43, 45

Vegetable prints
Lesson: *47

Mosaics
Lessons: 45, *47

Stitchery with string or yarn
Lesson: 39

Christmas ornaments
Lesson: 47

Torn paper designs
Lessons: 23, 45, 47

Egg carton crafts
Lessons: 45, 47

Cartooning and/or caricature
Lessons: 40, 41, *45

Rubbings
Lesson: *32

Coloring and color mixing
Lessons: 23, 34, 39, 40, 41

Rock and gourd painting
Lesson: 45

Initial and name design
Lesson: 47

Collage
Lessons: 23, *32, 47

Papier maché
Lessons: 42, 43, 45

Casting and pouring commercial molds or candles
Lesson: 42

Gadget prints
Lessons: 27, 30, *47

String and yarn pictures
Lessons: 39, 45

Puppets (sack, sock, and styrofoam)
Lesson: 45

Paper sack masks
Lesson: 45

Construction paper designs (cut and paste)
Lessons: 45, 47

---

*Key projects for the concept.

LEVEL 1

ACTIVITY 23

LIGHT PINK
PINK
DARK PINK
LIGHT RED
RED
DARK RED
PALE ORANGE
ORANGE
DARK ORANGE

Concept taught by this activity: Variations of a color can be identified.

Objective: The student will correctly identify variations of a given color.

A sample lesson plan for achieving the objective:

Teacher preparations
- Prepare a bulletin board with pictures that are basically done in variation of a single color (monochromatic).
- Have packets of one basic color that include tissue or construction paper and chips from a paint store.
- Have art prints and all materials out and easily accessible.

Teaching suggestions
- Have a student wearing a particular color stand up and ask the class what color it is. Have another student wearing a variation of that color stand and ask what color it is. Repeat at least once more and then ask if all are the same. Or, did they seem a little different to you? Repeat above process with two or more colors. Discuss how a color can be changed or varied.
- Discuss art prints and see how many variations of a given color students can locate.

Suggested art activity
Have students take a sample (paint chip or other object) of their favorite color and then look through magazines for pictures that are almost entirely in that same color. Paste them in a notebook or pamphlet.

Alternative art activities
- Have children experiment with paints to see how many variations of one color they can create by mixing with black, white, or other colors.
- Make concentration games with colors behind the numbers (four rows, with numbers from 1 to 20). The person starting the game has two chances to pick numbers that have the

same color in back of them. He might select number 4, which has a dark blue behind it, and number 17, which might have a dark green behind it. This would mean that the next person would have to remember the numbers selected and what colors were behind them. The second person might then select the number 11, which might have the color orange behind it, and for his second choice the number 13, which is dark blue. The third person, remembering the number 4 and number 13 were both dark blue, would then select those numbers, for which he would be given one point. The game could then be concluded or could continue until all the matching colors had been

discovered.
- Use "interlocking concept train" (#304 in Playtime Equipment Co. Catalogue, 808 Harvard Street, Omaha, Nebraska 68102, $6.00) to teach color discrimination.

Evaluation

View and display student work. Be aware of student responses in discussion periods. Make certain each child has had an opportunity to verbally indicate whether or not he understands the concept.

Other things to consider

- Vocabulary: color, hue, variation, monochromatic, shade, tint.
- Art materials needed: paper, paint, color chips, notebook materials, magazines, scissors, glue.
- Prints:
  Tranquility by Gasser
  Boats at Argenteuil by Monet
  Zebegen by Vasarely
  Head of a Man by Klee
  Quadrille by T. Lautrec
  Water of the Flowery Mill by Gorky
  Mlle. Violette by Redon
  La Grande Jatte by Seurat

LEVEL1   ACTIVITY 24

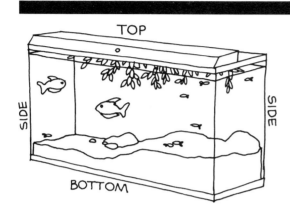

TOP

SIDE

SIDE

BOTTOM

Concept taught by this activity: The top, sides, and bottom of squares, triangles, and rectangles can be assigned or designated.

Objective: The student can indicate the top, two sides, and the bottom of squares, triangles, and rectangles.

A sample lesson plan for achieving the objective:

Teacher preparations
- Have a mental note of actual objects in the room to help clarify the concept such as: doll house, chalkboard, filing cabinet, aquarium, furniture, doors, windows, flannel board, and other objects.
- Have a flannel board with squares, triangles, and rectangles out where students can use them in the classroom.
- Collect and display in prominent places pictures or art prints that contain squares, triangles, and rectangles.
- Have samples of paper triangles, squares, and rectangles available for students to experiment with.

Teaching suggestions
- Review the shapes through a story or by some other exercise.
- Hold up the different shapes and ask children what they are. Elicit from students what is the top, what are the sides, and what is the bottom.
- Can you see things in the room that have the same shapes as these shapes? Where is the top? Where are the sides? Where is the bottom?
- Demonstrate with the students' help where to place side drapes, a valance, and a potted plant in a window shape and have students name the position where they fit in the window arrangement.
- Give each child a square, a triangle, and a rectangle, and tell him to put it on his desk. Have each child indicate where the top is located, also the two sides and the bottom. The

teacher should check to see that each child is doing the activity and that his response is correct. If someone still doesn't understand, try some of the additional activities listed.
- Discuss: Do some things have a top that is always its top (people, houses, chairs, and automobiles)? These can be turned upside down (child doing headstand). The top is then on the _____? Do the sides of things ever become the top or the bottom (squares, circles)?

Suggested art activity
Hand out three sheets of construction paper. Provide each student with a square, a triangle, and a rectangle and have him glue one of those geometric shapes on each sheet of construction paper. Have the student then paste or draw some other object on the top of the shape. Designate other objects to be placed on the two sides, and the bottom.

Alternative art activities
- Give each student a sheet of paper. Direct each one to mark the bottom of the paper (rectangle) with a red crayon. Direct him to mark the sides of the rectangle with a blue crayon. Direct him to mark the top of the rectangle with a green crayon. (This is a good evaluative activity.)
- Make a large square, a large triangle, and a large rectangle to be put on the floor. The teacher will give verbal directions such as: go place this ball at the bottom of the square. Go place this pencil at the top of the triangle. Go place these books on the sides of the rectangle, etc.
- Show art prints and have the students find squares, triangles, and rectangles and tell where the tops, sides, and bottoms are.
- While doing other subjects, continue to refer to the top, bottom, and sides of squares, rectangles, and triangles. (In reading class refer to the shape of the page in the book. Have student point out the top, sides, and bottom.) Try to make the students aware of these shapes in all they do so that they can have continued practice in indicating the top, the two sides, and the bottom.

Evaluation

See if the student can indicate the position requested by the teacher. Refer to activities three and four. Both of these activities would be good for evaluation. See if the students need more work on the concept or if they are ready to go on.

Other things to consider

- Vocabulary: top, sides, bottom, triangle, square, rectangle.
- Art materials needed: construction paper, crayons, scissors, paste.
- Prints:
  Sinbad the Sailor by Klee
  Seven A.M. by Hopper
  Orange and Yellow by Rothko
  Trains du Soir by Delvaux
  The Crucifixion by Dali
  Three Flags by Johns
  Still Music by Shahn
  Young Hare by Durer

LEVEL1

ACTIVITY 25

Concept taught by this activity: The middle of a circle or any other shape is called the center.

Objective: The student will be able to identify the center of any object or shape either verbally or by marking it.

A sample lesson plan for achieving the objective:

Teacher preparations
- Provide pictures of circles and squares.
- Display a wheel and a clock.
- Place an object at a particular point on each child's desk (some centered and some off center).
- Have two jumping ropes handy.
- Provide the class with pencils, scissors, paper, and string.

Teaching suggestions
- Ask questions such as: What does being in the center mean to you? Is this object in the center of the desk? Is the object on *your* desk in the center? (Answers will vary.)
- Look at the clock and the wheel. Ask what point on each is the center. Have a child point to the center. Encourage discussion of wheels. Wheels must be round. It is not much use without a center.
- Give each child a circular piece of paper. Direct each to fold the circle in half. Fold in half again. When the circle is opened, give all children the opportunity to discover that where the folds cross is the center part.

- Continue the folding activity with a square. Fold the square to form a triangle. Fold again to form another triangle. When unfolded, the crossing of the x marks the center.
- Encourage each child to experiment by folding the square different ways to find the center point as: Fold the square in half two times ending with smaller squares.

Suggested art activity
Have each student draw a picture of everything he can think of that has a center point defined (a wheel, a flower . . .).

Alternative art activities
- Make a compass with a pencil and a string (direct each child to tie one end of a particular length of string on a pencil). Have each child hold the free end of the string on the center of the paper with his finger, pull the string tight with the pencil, and move the pencil slowly around his stationary finger. The center point is where he held his finger. A circle is perfectly round. Every point on the circle is the same distance from the center point. "You can draw

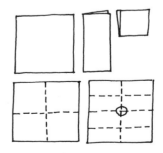

63

a circle by making two holes in a piece of cardboard. Put a pencil in each hole. Hold one pencil still (that point will be the center), and swing the other pencil around like this."

- Arrange many numbered pieces of colored paper (different shapes) on a table. Place an object on each piece of paper, having some centered and some off center. Have each child write in blue the numbers of the papers on which the objects are centered. Have each write in red those that are not centered.
- Have children form circles by joining hands. Have someone guess the center point. Then check by having the children hold jump ropes criss-crossing the center to mark the actual center point.

Evaluation

- Place objects on different surfaces. Ask the children to respond verbally if they are centered.
- Have children place objects on pieces of paper at the center point, first by observation only and then by folding the paper to determine the actual point to see how close they were.
- Or, simply keep track of how students respond to discussion sessions. Check off those who seem to clearly understand.

Other things to consider

- Vocabulary: circle, square, fold, center.
- Art materials: scissors, pencils, paper.
- Prints:
  Apples and Oranges by Cezanne
  I and the Village by Chagall
  Figure Fine in Gold by Demuth
  Virgin Forest by Rousseau
  Three Flags by Johns
  Justice and Peace by Overstreet
  Head of a Man by Klee

LEVEL 1   # ACTIVITY 26

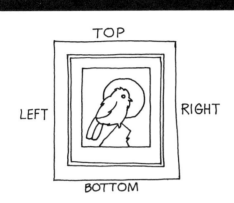

TOP
LEFT   RIGHT
BOTTOM

Concept taught by this activity:
A square has four sides. One
is the top ↑ ; one is the
bottom ↓ ; and the two
remaining sides are right →
and left ←

Objective: The child will be
able to identify a square
object and correctly identify
the right and left sides, the
top, and the bottom.

A sample lesson plan for achieving the objective:

Teacher preparations
- Collect square items to show students. Choose some things that are common and some that are uncommon.
- Cut four pieces of colored paper into equal triangles. Each triangle is a different color. Also, prepare four letters: T, B, L, and R (top, bottom, left, and right).
- Obtain a copy of *The Foot Book* by Dr. Seuss.

Teaching suggestions
- The concept of left and right should be emphasized because of the degree of difficulty children have in learning it. Top and bottom will have been covered by this point. Show items that are square. Ask questions about them. Are all the sides the same size? How many corners are there in a square? Which is the top, bottom, left, and right side?
- Show a picture with square things in it. Have students pick out the squares in the picture.
- Have students line up and march around the room, emphasizing the left and right feet. If they march counter clockwise, their right feet and right arms will be next to the wall. If they march clockwise, their left feet will be next to the wall. Play "Simon Says" to reinforce the right/left, top/bottom concept. Simon Says is a listening game and in this instance could be used to teach the children top, bottom, left, and right as well as to teach them to listen more

accurately. Each child has a square piece of paper on his desk. When the teacher says, "Simon says this is the top of the paper," each child is expected to point to the top of the paper on his desk. When the teacher says, "Simon says point to the left side of the paper," each child is expected to point to the left side of the paper on his desk. If the teacher then says "bottom" (without saying Simon says), and any child points to the bottom, the child is told he lost the game because Simon did not tell him to point to the bottom of his paper. The game is repeated until the interest span of the children has waned or until the children have the concept.

Suggested art activity
Let each child try to fold and cut a square out of a piece of rectangular construction paper. "Paint the top your favorite color, the bottom your least favorite color, the right side red, the left side yellow," and so on.

Alternative art activities
Have each child draw a composition (robot, bug, building) by using six squares of different sizes. Label with T, B, L, R, (the top, bottom, left, and right of each square).

Evaluation

The child who has an awareness of the concept should be able to pick out squares in the room and be able to correctly identify left and right, top and bottom.

Other things to consider

- Vocabulary: square, left, right, top, bottom, equal.
- Art materials needed: construction paper, scissors, crayons, paper cut in squares.
- Book: THE FOOT BOOK by Dr. Seuss
- Prints: *Christina's World* by Wyeth
  Adoration by Botticelli   *Justice and Peace*
  House at Aix by Cezanne   by Overstreet
  6 Day Bicycle Rider by Hopper   *Cheyt M* by Vasarely
  Blue Boy by Gainsborough   *Print Collection* by Daumier

LEVEL 1

ACTIVITY 27

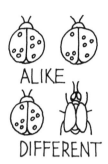

ALIKE

DIFFERENT

Concept taught by this activity: When two things look just the same, we say they are *alike*. When they are not the same we say they are *different*.

Objective: The student will be able to show an awareness that objects or forms of identical nature are *alike* and objects that are not identical are *different*.

A sample lesson plan for achieving the objective:

Teacher preparations
- The room should have many examples of things that look exactly *alike*. This should include objects already existing in the room, as well as pictures of objects hanging on the wall or on bulletin boards and ranging from simple to complex, for example, windows, books, desks, and pencils.
- The teacher should realize that the teaching of this concept involves comparing simple, identical shapes and then moving into more complex things such as colors and objects that are *alike* in some ways but *different* in others.

Teaching suggestions
- It is important for the teacher to use the words *alike* and *different* and to implement the use of these words in the vocabularies of the students for a better understanding of the concept by the children.
- The first explanation of this concept is to show students two identical rhythm or Lummi sticks or other objects of the same length, width, and color. Ask open-ended questions about these sticks and have the students talk about the identical features.
- Next, the teacher can show two triangles (found in the music room). After discussion of identical features, the students should be able to say that these two triangles are *alike*.

- The teacher could now compare one stick used previously and one triangle and ask the question, "Are these two objects *alike*?" When students respond "No," the teacher establishes the concept that if the objects are not *alike*, they must be *different*. The teacher asks the question, "Are these two objects *different*?" (still using the stick and the triangle). If students respond accurately to this question, the teacher can then compare many objects that are *alike* and *different*. (We are still showing objects of the same color here.) Examples: two scissors, two unsharpened identical pencils, two pieces of paper, two identical glasses, two spoons, two forks, two of the students' chairs, two pillows, two identical books, two identical candy bars, and other objects.
- After students show an awareness of various objects, either *alike* or *different,* the teacher can explore the idea of teaching the children that even though some objects have the same shape, they may be *different* in color. For example, the teacher shows two sheets of construction paper the same size but of a *different* color. The students discuss the fact that the name of the object is *paper* and that although some are *different* colors (even *different* shapes) it is still all used for the same purpose; therefore, it is *alike* in some ways. If the students show a keen understanding of the concept, the teacher can branch off into many areas, especially using objects in the children's environments. For example: trees — all trees do not look exactly *alike,* but they are *alike* because of certain characteristics (trunks, branches, leaves); flowers; houses — these are *alike* because of the function or purpose they have (shelter, or for homes). Many other examples exist and can be used here. Also, the teacher can discuss the *difference* between houses and trees. Other subject areas could be used for exploring the concept of *alike* and *different* (characters in *different* stories being *alike* in some ways and *different* in others; musical instruments that look *alike* or sound *alike* in some ways, yet *different* in others).
- Hold up *any* two art prints and ask for *all* the ways they are *alike,* then all the ways they are *different.* Be careful to respond positively to all observations.

Suggested art activity
Make a collage design of objects (or pictures of objects) that are *alike* and *different*.

Alternative art activities
- The teacher and students can take field trips (either in or out of the school building) and discuss various objects existing around them and how they are *alike* and how they are *different*.
- Draw pictures of things that are both *alike* and *different*.

Evaluation

- The students can be evaluated by the teacher in the discussions carried on in the classroom.
- The teacher can ask students to bring from home two objects that are *alike* and two objects that are *different*.

Other things to consider

- Vocabulary:
  Alike: objects or forms that look the same.
  Different: objects or forms that do not look the same.
- Prints:
  Marilyn Monroe by Andy Warhol
  Zebegen by Vasarely
  The Brooklyn Bridge by Stella
  Still Music by Shahn
  Boats at Argenteuil by Monet
  Composition 1963 by Miro
  Bedroom at Arles by Van Gogh
  Dancing Class by Degas

LEVEL1 ACTIVITY 28

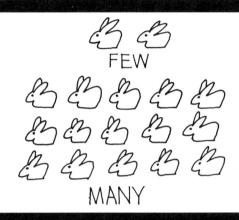

FEW

MANY

Concept taught by this activity: When a space is filled with numerous shapes, we say there are *many*. If we take most of the shapes away, then those which are left are *few*.

Objective: The children will demonstrate an awareness of the meaning of the words *many, most,* and *few.*

A sample lesson plan for achieving the objective:

Teacher preparations

- Arrange two tables (one with *many* blocks, the other with *few*).
- Arrange the desks so that *many* are on one side of the room, *few* on the other.
- Mount cutouts on the windows, doors, and bulletin boards, some *many*, others *few*.
- Arrange pictures in the chalkboard tray showing *many* objects and *few* objects (or people).
- Prepare flannel board cutouts in two colors (to use in demonstrating *many, few,* and *most*).
- Draw two boxes on the chalkboard.
- With masking tape, make two large box shapes on the classroom floor.
- Bring some balance scales to class and marbles or other objects to be weighed.
- Arrange glass jars with colored water at various levels in the jars.
- Provide individual chalkboards and/or flannel boards for each child.
- Prepare popsicle sticks or colored paper strips for each child.

Teaching suggestions

- Begin discussion by asking questions such as:
  - "Count the number of boys and girls in the room. Are *most* of us boys or girls?"
  - "Count the doors and windows, desks, and chairs in the room. Do we have *more* doors or *more* windows?" "Do we have *more* desks or *more* chairs?"
  - "Look at the colored flowers I have put on the windows. Are there *more* red ones or *more* yellow ones?" "Are there *more* daisies or *more* tulips?"
- Divide the class into two obviously unequal teams for a relay. Tell the children they are to go to the chalkboard and draw a ball and return the chalk to the next team member, who must run to the board, draw another ball, and return the chalk to the next team member — until one team finishes. That team will be the winner. Some children will surely protest that it is not fair to have *more* children on one team because the team with *fewer* children will not have to draw as *many* balls to win. Discuss these concepts.
- Choose two children to be the "captains" of the large circles on the floor. Give them the following directions: "Tom, go around the room and bring *many* children back with you to the circle. Dick, go bring a *few* children back to your circle." After this is done: "Tom, take *most* of your children and put them in Dick's circle. Which circle now has just a *few* children?"
- Have the children participate in the following activity:
  - Ask each child to draw a *few* balls on his chalkboard. Have one table at a time line up in front of the room and discuss who has a *few* balls. "Does anyone have *many*?" "How *many* can a *few* be?" "If you have a *few* balls, how many might you have?"
  - Have the children draw *many* balls on their chalkboards. Have them erase *most* of them. "Do we have just a *few* left now?"
- Take the children to the playground. Tell them to pick up as *many* rocks as they can hold in their one hand and bring them to you. After they are all with you, tell them to throw away *most* of the rocks. "Do we have *many* left, or just a *few*?"
- Take a neighborhood walk. Observe a street. "Which side has the *most* houses or buildings?" "Which has the *most* windows?" "Which street has a *few* cars?" "Can you see *many* people?" "Where do you see a *few* people?"

- Have two empty bottles (glass) and a pitcher of colored water. Have children take turns putting various amounts of water in the bottles to show which has the *most*.
- Have children put a *few* marbles or blocks on one side of a balance scale. Put *many* on the other side. "What happens?" "Why?" "If we take *most* of the marbles or blocks off the heavy side, what happens?"
- Give each child a dozen strips of colored paper or popsicle sticks. "Put a *few* sticks at the top of the desk." "Put *many* sticks at the bottom of the desk." "Take *most* of the sticks from the bottom and put them at the top. Where do you now have the *most* sticks?" "Where do you see only a *few* sticks?"
- Have children point out by comparing prints which prints show *many* people and which show just a *few* people (or objects, trees, or whatever).
- Discuss how the terms *many* and *few* are relative. In some cases four may constitute *many,* while the same number may be considered *few* in other instances. For example, "If you eat four times in one week, you have eaten only a *few* meals. If you fall down and break four bones in one week, you have broken *many* bones."

Suggested art activity
Prepare a ditto worksheet with four boxes. Give directions: "Draw *many* things in this box." "Draw a *few* things in this box." "Draw *more* in this box than in that box," and so on.

Alternative art activities
- "Draw a house which has *many* windows." "Draw a house which has just a *few* windows."
- Teacher draws a number of balls on the chalkboard, then says: "Draw *more* than I have on your chalkboard. Erase *most* of them. Do you now have *fewer* than I have?" Do similar things as the teacher draws various numbers of balls and has children draw either *more* or *fewer*.

Evaluation

Compare the child's picture of the houses — one with *many* windows, one with *few*. It will be apparent if the concept is understood. Keep track of individual responses — especially of children who seldom participate. This will also help in evaluating which students are able to fully comprehend the concept.

Other things to consider

- Art materials needed: crayons, paper, tempera, water colors, colored chalk, charcoal.

- Prints:
Bacchus by Caravaggio
Numbering at Bethlehem by Breughel
Allies Day by Hassam
The Bullfight by Goya
View of Toledo by El Greco
Le Moulin de la Galette by Renoir
Marilyn Monroe by Warhol
Young Hare by Durer

LEVEL1   ACTIVITY 29

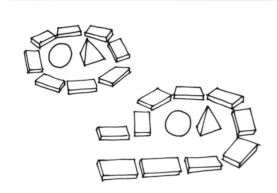

A note to the teacher: Many objects can be arranged with a form in the center of the design. Circular arrangements may have gates or doors in them. (Symmetrical or regular arrangements are preferred at this level.)

What this means

If the child has the opportunity and the objects are available for manipulation, he will automatically place objects that are "different" in the center of circular arrangements, and he will make gates or doors in his symmetrical designs.

How to recognize this level

If the child makes any indication that he is beginning to arrange similar shapes into circular designs, then eventually place the "different" forms available in the center, he is at this level. Check for earlier stages in three-dimensional manipulation. Be familiar with what he has already done with the arranging of objects.

What to do, why, how often, and when

- Have ten to thirty objects such as dominoes available for each child you involve; then provide him with one to three objects that are quite different from the rest.
- Provide time for the child to experiment with the arranging of the object. The time need not be long, but the frequency ought to be weekly until the desired results are achieved. One experience might be sufficient for many children.
- Reinforce the efforts of the child without suggesting any solutions.
- Recognize that these experiences with three-dimensional objects lead the child to a better understanding of all forms and symbols and their relationship to each other. These are also preliminary steps in developing a "feeling" for design and "arranging" of space.

What to look for at the end (evaluation)

When the child, without any assistance, creates arrangements that are similar to the illustrations provided, the objective of the lesson has been achieved.

LEVEL 1   ACTIVITY 30

ORDER

Concept taught by this activity: When things are arranged in a line (or a circle) from large to small or small to large, it can be said that they are in order.

Objective: The student will be able to group a number of objects or people in a line or a circle from large to small or from small to large and recognize that he has created visual order.

A sample lesson plan for achieving the objective:

Teacher preparations
- Have several things available in the classroom for the students to practice putting in order: nesting barrels, nesting cups, blocks in graduating sizes, balls of different sizes, beads, tinker toys (see *Playtime Equipment Co. Catalogue*, 808 Howard St., Omaha, NB 68102).
- Prepare a bulletin board for the science project listed (the last suggestion under "Teaching Suggestions"). This board could show the growth over several weeks' time. It could demonstrate order in nature.
- Make sure there are enough beads or other "stringable" objects for each child to have some, also enough string.

Teaching suggestions
- Review with the class the concepts of order, large, small, line, and circle, to make certain each child understands the key terms being used.
- Start with a number of objects in great disarray. Ask the children if they like the arrangement. "What is wrong with it?" "How could you improve it?" After children have tried to create an orderly arrangement, ask: "Why do these things look better now?"

- Arrange the dramatization of a child's story with a large cast of characters. Choose children who fit the parts (by size). Ask: "Who is the biggest character in the story?" "Who would make a good _____?" "Who is the littlest?" "Who would make a good _____ or _____?" "Line these students up in order and see if we did a good job choosing the right people. Do we have a large child to play the tallest character?" "What different ways can we arrange the characters in order?" "Now dramatize the story."
- During a time when you need a quick activity for just a few minutes, have the students get out a number of objects and put them in some kind of order (metals or plastics or reds, yellows, blues, and so on); then check each one to see if they did it.
- Use the art prints listed at the end of this activity to find different examples of order, such as: *Boats at Argenteuil* by Monet or *Three Flags* by Johns. Ask: "Where do you see examples of order?" "What would they be like if there wasn't any order?" Refer to *The Night Watch* (these are soldiers). "How do they march?" "Is there order in marching?"

- Send five children to the front of the classroom and have a child or a team of students arrange them in order. Do this several times to give more children a chance to use order. If necessary, use questions to get more than one way of arranging the children in order. If there is a disagreement, find out why they disagree and let children come up with the idea that there are different ways of putting things in order.

- Have students line up the entire class in order. Try it first from the largest to the smallest and then from the smallest to the largest. Ask: "How can we decide who would be first?" "How can we check our choices?"

- Discuss with children the existence of order in nature. Start with the fact of the seeds being in rows and growing in an "orderly" manner. Plant seeds each week for about six weeks and label the boxes or pots with the date and type of seed planted.

Suggested art activity

Give the students some triangles (or other shapes) and have them make a design. Have the objects in varying sizes from small to large. The teacher should check to see if the students use the order principle in their designs.

Alternative art activities

- "Draw circles, squares, triangles, and other shapes, using crayon or pencil on construction paper; cut them out, and put these objects in order in some way on your paper."
- As a very simple task, have the students string beads or other objects and see if they can put them in order. This activity would be good to use with the child who did not understand the concept the first few times.
- Have the students team up and put things in order. Give each team some objects to put in order. Sometimes this will help the student who is lagging behind a little. He can watch the first child and put them in order himself. For variation, use a stop watch and time the children to see how long it takes each set to complete the task.
- Go outside and look at things in nature that are in order. Try to make this a good observation time and accept comments a little off the subject if they are using their power of observation to advantage. Look for any kind of grouping that creates order.
- Gather up a group of large boxes and put them in order. Use them also as a tunnel for the children to crawl through, seeing the boxes gradually change from small to large. Also stack them up and build a tower.

Other things to consider

- Vocabulary: order, largest, smallest, shortest, tallest, first, second, third, last, middle-sized.
- Art materials needed: construction paper, paste, scissors, crayons, pencils, tempera paints, brushes, painting paper.

Evaluation

Suggestions for the teacher in determining whether or not *each* student was able to use the concept in the product he created.

- The objective will be met when the child or student can arrange a group of objects in order without help and can recognize order when he sees it. (Verbal responses by children can apprise the teacher.)
- Another way of evaluating the child's use of the concept is to look at his art work during the time the concept is taught and see if he is using order in the designs he creates when he is not specifically directed to do so.

- Prints:
  Boats by Argenteuil by Monet
  Three Flags by Johns
  Zebegen by Vasarely
  Oath of the Horatii by David
  Trains du Soir by Delvaux
  Dancing Class by Degas
  Night Watch by Rembrandt
  The Letter by Vermeer

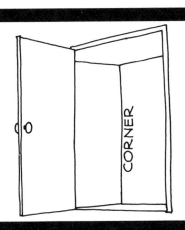

Concept taught by this activity: Any boxlike object has a *corner* where two or more of its sides come together.

Objective: The student will demonstrate an awareness that any boxlike object has a corner where two or more of its sides come together.

A sample lesson plan for achieving the objective:

Teacher preparations
- Display examples of boxlike objects around the room.
- Prepare a bulletin board with pictures containing a collection of boxlike objects.
- Be ready to compare boxlike objects with those that do not have any corners (spheres).
- Have ready any pictures that will bring out this concept.

Teaching suggestions
Following are questions that might initiate a discussion:
- "Call out all of the objects that have corners."
- "Who can tell me what they think a corner is?"
- "Can you see any corners in this room?"
- "How do you think a corner is made?"
- "Can you see anything in the room that doesn't have a corner?"

In the discussion, determine with students what their concept of a corner is.
- Let them demonstrate by showing where corners are in the room.
- Have each student bring from home a boxlike object they think will show a corner. Discuss it with the class and put it on display.
- Have students help make a list of all the boxlike images with corners that they can see in the room or on their way to or from school.

- Compare objects on their list with those that do not have corners.
- Discuss whether or not two-dimensional objects have corners.
- Discuss the following concept in math: Where two lines meet, an angle is formed. By putting two sides together, different shapes can be made that have corners.

Suggested art activity
Create three-dimensional constructions from boxes by gluing or pasting.

Alternative art activities
- Let students work with several strips of paper, putting them together to form corners where two sides come together.
- "Draw pictures of at least five things that have corners."
- On boxlike objects, have students color *only* the part that shows where the two sides come together to form a corner.
- With clay have students create something that has a corner.

Evaluation

Give each child several shapes to cut out and paste on paper. Have him then circle the corners.

Other things to consider

- Vocabulary: triangle, boxlike objects, cube, angle, sphere, corner, square, circle.
- Art materials needed: construction paper, clay, boxlike objects.
- Prints:
  Dempsey and Firpo by Bellows
  Adoration by Botticelli
  Venice by Canaletto
  Notre Dame by Daumier
  Cheyt M by Vasarely

LEVEL 1

ACTIVITY 32

Concept taught by this activity: Some textures are rough and some are smooth.

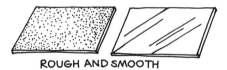

ROUGH AND SMOOTH

Objective: From an assortment of objects the student will identify both by feel and by sight those which are rough and those which are smooth.

A sample lesson plan for achieving the objective:

Teacher preparations
- Display on a table and on the bulletin board wood, fabric, swatches, rocks, varying kinds of sandpaper, plastics, glass, and metal that are examples of rough or smooth surfaces.
- Have prints available or displayed.

Teaching suggestions
- Discuss the meaning of the words *texture, rough, smooth.* "Does anyone know what the word *texture* means?" "Does everything have texture?" (Yes. Smoothness is a textural quality, just as much as roughness.) "Is everything either rough or smooth?" (Some may be a combination or have a nap that when rubbed one way is smooth and the other way is rough.) Ask for all the "smooth things" they can think of. All "rough" ones. Ask for smooth, soft words. For rough, prickly words.
- Divide the class into groups of four-to-six students. Prepare enough sacks or boxes so that there will be one for each group. Put into each sack or box at least eight to ten objects which have rough or smooth surfaces. Instruct students to separate these objects into two groups, one of smooth and one of rough surfaces. Compare findings of each group on the blackboard by having teacher hold up various items and having groups respond with their classification. Ask, "Why do some things appear smooth?" "Why do some appear rough?" "Does everything in the room have a different

'feel' to it?" "Can you tell by just looking whether an object is rough or smooth?" "How can you tell?" "Are there clues to look for?" "Do textures feel any different when you feel them with your toes?" "Or with your face?" "Is there any difference when you feel something with the palm of your hand and then the back of your hand?"
- Identify several rough and smooth surfaces around the room. Show several paintings and ask if the students can look at the painting and see something that is probably smooth. "How did you know that?" "Can you locate a rough surface?" "What leads you to believe it is a rough surface?" "What were some of the visual clues?" Take a mini trip outside and assign groups to find and return with three or four rough items and three or four smooth items. Compare and discuss findings in class. Add the objects to the interest center.

Suggested art activity
Do rubbings of various surfaces with a variety of media (crayon, pencil, colored pencil, chalk, charcoal). Rub these on paper laid on the various surfaces. Identify which rubbings come from rough surfaces and which come from smooth. (Display on a bulletin board or in an interest center in categories of rough and smooth.) Reward students who find *unusual* textures to rub.

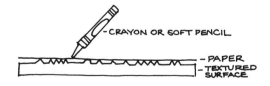

CRAYON OR SOFT PENCIL
- PAPER
- TEXTURED SURFACE

Alternative art activities

- Assign students to make a booklet containing examples of at least five rubbings showing a smooth surface and at least five rubbings showing a rough surface. These rubbings should be labeled as to what the item was and then classified as to whether it is rough or smooth. Also in the booklet may be examples of materials, wood, or plastics, showing rough or smooth surfaces.
- Prepare a bulletin board or chart illustrating several classifications of textures. This could be a small group activity.

Evaluation

On a table place at least fifteen items that are rough and smooth. Number them. Have students go around the table one at a time and classify each numbered item as to rough and smooth. These items may be handled by the student. The verbal responses of students could serve as an adequate evaluation as well, particularly if the teacher has some method for keeping track of them.

Other things to consider

- Vocabulary: rough, smooth, rubbing, texture.
- Art materials needed: paper, crayon, pencil, charcoal, chalk, colored pencils.
- Prints:
  Portrait of Francis I by Clouet
  My Gems by Harnett
  Still Life with Pipe by Chardin
  Bacchus by Caravaggio
  A Bar at the Folies Bergere by Manet
  Christina's World by Wyeth
  Peaceable Kingdom by Hicks
  Women in a Garden by Monet

LEVEL1   ACTIVITY 33

Concept taught by this activity: Four basic geometric shapes (or variations of them) may be found everywhere in the environment.

Objective: The student locates examples of circles, triangles, squares, and rectangles in his environment and demonstrates an awareness that many things are a variation of these shapes.

A sample lesson plan for achieving the objective:

Teacher preparations
■ Locate appropriate prints and pictures and display them.
■ Be prepared to cause students to recognize even the most *subtle* variations of squares, circles, triangles, and rectangles.

Teaching suggestions
■ "What are all of the circular things you can think of?" "Square things?" Review what the student already knows about the four basic shapes. Does he recognize each? Can he pick them out? Does he know what variation means? Students may demonstrate basic shapes by drawing them at the blackboard or at the overhead projector.
■ Discuss the concept itself. "Is it a true statement?" "What does it mean?" "Why is it important to know about it?" "Would it make something easier to draw if I knew that it was a variation of a shape I could easily draw?"
■ Discuss the use of the concept in art prints and other illustrations.
■ Lay thin paper over magazine cutouts and outline the geometric shape of each object found in the pictures.

Suggested art activity
Make a design using geometric shapes cut out of construction paper. With a dark crayon or felt tip pen draw on top of the shapes and turn each one into some familiar form (the circle into a baseball, a wheel, or a flower).

Alternative art activities
■ "Draw a house *without* using any triangular shapes."
■ Take pictures out of magazines and have the children identify the basic shapes in the pictures by outlining them with a dark crayon.
■ Use "Interlocking concept train" (#304 in *Playtime Equipment Co. Catalogue,* 808 Harvard Street, Omaha, Nebraska 68102, $6.00) to teach basic shape discrimination.

Evaluation

When the student can point to a variety of circles, squares, triangles, and rectangles in his environment, the objective has been achieved.

Other things to consider

■ Vocabulary: circle, square, triangle, rectangle, variation.
■ Art materials needed: construction paper, paste, scissors.
■ Prints:
Fighting Horses by Gericault
Artist's Mother by Whistler
Poster-Jan. 18 to Feb. 12 by Shahn
Rebus by Rauschenberg
Moneylender and Wife by Metsys
Virgin with Saints Ines and Tecla by El Greco
City Hall in Rega by Feininger
Sacrament, Last Supper by Dali

LEVEL 1

ACTIVITY 34

Concept taught by this activity: Variations in darkness and lightness exist and can be identified.

Objective: The student is able to verbally identify variations in darkness or lightness (comparing objects or colors and recognizing changes or differences in value).

A sample lesson plan for achieving the objective:

Teacher preparations

■ At the conclusion of this activity, the student should be able to look at two squares (one a lighter version of the color of the first) and correctly identify which is the darker of the two even though the difference is somewhat subtle. The student should further be able to correctly identify the darkest or lightest of two squares of different colors even though they are close in value ("This red is a little darker than that blue.") All instruction should lead to this sort of outcome.

■ From paint stores, collect numerous sheets of color samples and patterns of walltex or wallpaper. If these aren't available in ample supply, look for color automobile advertisements and whatever kinds of illustrations you might find that show colors ranging from very dark to very light shades or tints. Select and display prints that contain numerous variations of two or three basic colors. Have them exhibited prior to the teaching process. Become aware of variations in certain colors both in and out of the room so that you can refer students to them or use them in discussions. Use color wheel in concept #90, Level 4, indicating color values.

Teaching suggestions

■ Discuss the meaning of the word *value* (variation in darkness and lightness ranging from black to white). Be certain that the use of the word in art has nothing to do with cost, price, or ethics. Discuss how any given color is closer in value to either white or black ("Is this yellow more like white or more like black in value?") Compare the relative darkness and lightness of objects in the room. Have all students with blue shirts or red blouses (or other colors) stand up; then see if a student can line everyone up according to whose shirt or blouse is darkest (first) on down to the lightest (last in line). Talk about how the colors of their clothes would look on black and white TV or in a black and white picture. Compare this idea with color blindness and point out that many animals live in a world without color (just like the black and white TV). This would include animals such as horses, dogs, cats, cattle, sheep, and pigs. Emphasize how important it would be for these animals to distinguish differences in darkness and lightness. If your school has black and white and color sets, have the same program going on both TVs and discuss the relative darkness or lightness of the colors your students see.

■ Distribute to each student a variety of color samples and have them arrange the colors in a row from dark to light or light to dark. Then have the students pair up and help each other verify whether or not their judgments have been accurate. Arbitrate where they can't agree. Note that overlapping the colors slightly helps one to see the values more accurately.

■ Discuss artists' prints and see if students can look at two colors (apart from each other in a picture) and tell which is the darkest or lightest.("Is the blue of the guitar darker or lighter than this blue?") Keep pushing each student to see the most subtle changes that it is possible for him to perceive.

Suggested art activity

Paint a picture or create a torn paper design using a variety of value contrasts. Some may be very subtle, while others are highly contrasting.

Alternative art activities

- Do a painting in just one or two colors. Add tiny amounts of black or white to the colors so that there is variety in darkness and lightness.
- Do a paper collage on some subject or feeling and use many variations of one or two colors.

Evaluation

Give everyone an opportunity to respond to the questions and experiences suggested in this outline. The activity arranging color samples from dark to light is probably the most revealing experience for a teaching evaluation. Other activities would substantiate the evaluation.

Other things to consider

- Vocabulary: value, variation, darkness, lightness, sequence, variety, collage.
- Materials needed: color samples, scissors, art paper, glue or paste.
- Prints:
  Absinthe by Degas
  Seven A.M. by Hopper
  Head of a Man by Klee
  The Letter by Vermeer
  The Hay Wain by Constable
  The Box by Renoir
  Notre Dame by Daumier
  Water Flowery Mill by Gorky
  St. Joseph by De La Tour

LEVEL 1

ACTIVITY 35

Concept taught by this activity: People and objects cast shadows.

Objective: The student will demonstrate an awareness that people and objects cast shadows.

A sample lesson plan for achieving the objective:

Teacher preparation

Have a strong light source available as well as a room which can be darkened. Have a white sheet and a variety of objects to show behind the sheet. Trace and cut out the shadow of some individual in the class — preferably in some dark color, but not gray or black. (Shadows are normally a color, but children assume they are all black or gray.) Display pictures that show certain objects or people and their shadows. Have premade silhouettes of several class members available.

Teaching suggestions

■ The concept could be introduced in this manner. "Does anyone remember the story of Peter Pan?" "What happened to Peter Pan's shadow?" (Exhibit the paper shadow of a class member.) "Here's a shadow that someone in this class lost. I wonder who it belongs to?" Have several try to see if they are the shadow's owner. Once the child has been discovered, pursue this idea. "Where should the owner stand on his paper shadow so it is part of him (her)?" "Does *your* shadow look like this?" "Can you roll up your shadow and slip it under your pillow?" "Have you ever lost your shadow?" Bring out the concept that "a shadow is yours because you block out the light and it usually looks like you." Have the children place the shadow where it belongs, not on the back of the child or behind him, but on the floor. Substitute another child for the shadow and ask him to jump. Observe the shadow. Does a shadow move? Why?

■ Involve children in making real shadows. Have two or three children stand behind a bed sheet with a strong light (such as a projector or bedroom lamp with no shade) behind them. Study their shadows and ask if the shadows are different than the area around them. "What causes the shadows?" Continue having other members participate. Have the first child walk towards the sheet, jump up and down, and wave arms. Have the second distort his body shape to that of an animal or monster. Have the third hold up objects and have the class guess what they are (concept: objects have shadows). Have the fourth child show his front, then turn to the side (concept: the outline shadow of a form is called a *silhouette,* particularly referred to as a *profile*).

■ Have several silhouettes of members in the class. Let class members guess who they are.
■ Darken the room and, using a flashlight, let shadows fall around the room. Read the poem, "My Shadow" and observe shadows getting tall, then becoming small by moving the light around. ("My Shadow," Robert Louis Stevenson. *Poems and Rhymes.* Childcraft, vol. 1. Chicago: Field Enterprises Educational Corp., 1975, page 82):

I have a little shadow that goes in and out with me,
And what can be the use of him is more than I can see.
He is very, very like me from the heels up to the head;

83

And I see him jump before me when I jump into my bed.

The funniest thing about him is the way he likes to grow —
Not at all like proper children, which is always very slow;
For he sometimes shoots up taller like an India rubber ball,
And he sometimes gets so little that there's none of him at
     all.

He hasn't got a notion of how children ought to play,
And can only make a fool of me in every sort of way.
He stays so close beside me, he's a coward you can see;
I'd think shame to stick to nursie as that shadow sticks to
     me!

One morning, very early, before the sun was up,
I rose and found the shining dew on every buttercup;
But my lazy little shadow, like an arrant sleepy head,
Had stayed at home behind me and was fast asleep in bed.

- Ask several children to respond to the "as if" idea: "If I were (*any person, student, thing*)'s shadow, I would be . . . ; I would feel . . ."
- "Do you like to watch television with the sound off?" "Why?" "What if we could turn shadows off? What would the world look like?"

Suggested art activity
Discuss prints with the class. Let them pick out the shadows and name what objects cause the shadows. Begin with simple pictures and conclude with more difficult examples.

Alternative art activities
- Have the student draw a picture of something he really likes and show it with its shadow. The student might be allowed to select the drawing media he would like to work with — anything from crayon to charcoal could be used for this activity.
- Cut out pictures from magazines of objects and their shadows and make a display of some sort for the class.

Evaluation

The teacher should be conscious of the student's awareness of shadows as he responds during discussions and as he draws or paints pictures at the close of the activity. Remember that it is only an awareness that the teacher is concerned with at this point.

Other things to consider

- Vocabulary: shadow, light source, silhouette, cast shadow.
- Art materials needed: art prints, drawing materials, magazines, scissors, and paste, flashlight, slide projector, bed sheet, large paper.
- Prints:
  Cliff of Etretat After Storm by Courbet
  The Crucifixion by Dali
  Notre Dame by Daumier
  Oath of the Horatii by David
  6-Day Bicycle Rider by Hopper
  The Gleaners by Millet
  The Scout by Remington

LEVEL1 ACTIVITY 36

A note to the teacher: At this point in his development, the child can arrange objects with alternative rhythms and/or with shapes built upward and outward.

What this means
With at least three kinds of objects (different in shape and size) the child who is given the opportunity and is encouraged along the way will arrange these forms so that they alternate in a rhythmic way or are stacked in an orderly way both upward and outward.

How to recognize this level
When the child first begins to play or experiment with the objects, there should be evidence of the stage which led to this one. As he continues to play, he may move right into this stage or simply indicate an inclination in this direction.

What to do, why, how often, and when

- Provide each child with at least three kinds of objects that differ in size or shape. Furnish five to ten of each type.
- See that the child is free to experiment with the objects so that he can, either quickly or slowly, manipulate them in a variety of arrangements.
- Observe what he does but don't interfere. Simply reinforce his activity with positive comments where appropriate. Don't ask what he is making or suggest that it looks like such and such.
- Remember that this activity is a step toward understanding and perceiving relationships between forms and in developing an intuitive sense of design.
- Since the time the child spends in this activity need not be lengthy (15 to 20 minutes), give him some time at least weekly until the objective is achieved.

What to look for at the end (evaluation)

When the child creates the kind of arrangements described in "A note to the teacher," the objective has been achieved.

LEVEL 1   ACTIVITY 37

Concept taught by this activity: The sizes of objects or living things can be measured by comparing them with such things as a hand or a foot.

Objective: The child will be able to measure the sizes of objects or living things by comparing them with such things as his hand or his foot.

A sample lesson plan for achieving the objective:

Teacher preparations
- Have several objects available for comparison: ribbon, balls, glasses, dishes, baseball bat, broom, as well as students or adults.
- Review the concept and vocabulary.
- Recognize that this is an initial experience in measuring sizes. Children already familiar with rulers and yardsticks would not need this more elementary exercise.
- Have some sequential illustrations available that allow you to show three persons standing next to three tents, in this order:
  (1) Show a man standing by himself.
  (2) Show a man standing next to a small tent with a small opening.
  (3) Show a man standing next to a large tent with a large opening.

Teaching suggestions
- "What are all the *large* things?" (List on board as called out.) "Is a shoe large?" "Compared to an ant?" "What are all the small things?" Review words such as *compare* and *measure*. Be certain that students are aware of their meaning. "Which of these is larger?" "How much larger?" "You are comparing them so you have to visually make a decision without actually measuring them with a ruler or yardstick."

- Take students through a brief exercise of trying to measure objects and pictures of objects by visual estimation. Then ask questions such as the following: "Do you think we can always tell how big or how small something is just by looking at it?" "If you had never seen an elephant before, could you look at a picture of one all by itself and tell how big it was?" "Would it help you if the picture of the elephant had a man standing next to it?" "How would that help?"
- Use your illustrations of the man and the tent. Look at the picture of the man and ask how tall he is. Place him next to the first tent and ask again how tall he is. Repeat the question with the second tent.
- Explore with the children what they have learned from the pictures of the men and the tents. Develop the idea that we need to have something to compare with before we know how tall or how short someone is. Discuss other examples that come to their minds, then move into using them or parts of their body to compare and measure with.
- Relate the idea of measuring to the needs and purposes of artists. Ask, "Would it help you in drawing a picture of something to know how big it was?" "Could you draw a better picture of a horse and cowboy or a fireman and fire engine if you knew how they compared in size?" "How could you tell how big to make the cowboy's or fireman's hat or how long to make his legs compared to his arms?" Pursue this line of questioning until children have an awareness of the importance of measuring and comparing in art.

Suggested art activity
When all of the children have had opportunity to do some comparing or measuring of things in the room, have them also measure parts of things. (How many hands long is their leg? How many feet long is their neighbor's body? How many digits (finger lengths) is their desk top?)

Alternative art activities
- Some artists are concerned with the actual size of things and some are not. Look at the suggested prints and have children discuss which artists were very conscious of measuring and comparing and which were not.
- Motivate children to draw or paint some event that has special interest for them and emphasize their thinking about sizes of things and how they compare.
- Order "Interlocking concept train" (#304 in *Playtime Equipment Co. Catalogue,* $6.00) to teach size discrimination.

Evaluation

Be keenly aware of each student's response in oral discussions, then verify those responses with what changes occur in his drawings or paintings. (Has he done any mental comparing of sizes of things or their parts in relationship to each other?)

Other things to consider

- Vocabulary: measure, compare, longer than, shorter than, higher or taller than, near, far, scale, proportion.
- Art materials: drawing paper, crayons, pencils, water colors or tempera paints (let children choose materials).
- Prints:
  I and the Village by Chagall
  Ville d'Avray by Corot
  Turning the Stake by Eakings
  Autumn by Koryusai
  Harvesters by Breughel
  The Cradle by Morisot
  Young Hare by Durer
  Guernica by Picasso
  Orange and Yellow by Rothko

LEVEL1

ACTIVITY 38

A note to the teacher: The child can instinctively arrange objects with both formal and informal balance occurring together.

What this means
This activity is not one which is taught by the teacher. The teacher's role is to simply make the materials available and to encourage and reinforce the student's use of the three-dimensional materials. If the objects are available for manipulation, the child will intuitively create the kinds of arrangements described in "A note to the teacher."

How to recognize this level
This represents step seven in the child's three-dimensional manipulation development. The two previous steps for comparison are represented in lessons 29 and 35.

What to do, why, how often, and when

■ It would be helpful to have the following kinds of things available: multicolored and multishaped blocks, tinker toys, dominoes, and other assorted objects. Collect small household belongings such as nails, spoons, cookie cutters, and almost anything.

■ Arrange time for every student to have opportunity to work with the objects or materials. Do *not* encourage them to build specific objects or ask what their designs represent. Some children create arrangements that are purely designs and not intended to represent anything. You could make suggestions if the student asks for ideas. Even then it is not wise to suggest designs.

■ Draw attention to those who attempt large arrangements with more numerous objects than children typically use. *Praise the child who is able to balance arrangements which contain objects that are different sizes or shapes and not symmetrical.* Encourage through praise.

■ Recognize that the fulfillment of this objective may require multiple experiences or opportunities for some children or even all of the children. When most of them have achieved the objective, it could become a "special" free time activity for those who still need additional experiences.

■ Display pictures of abstract sculpture of pottery if any are available and refer children to them for ideas if they need

help. Refer to the illustrations in this manner: "Look, Mary is creating designs like artists do!"

What to look for at the end (evaluation)

Since this is a teacher-awareness concept, it will certainly not be gained in one experience. The teacher should be alert during all school activities to see signs of this concept in use. A written record may need to be kept on each child. The teacher may observe the products completed by the children to see which children seem to demonstrate the skill mentioned in the concept.

LEVEL1   ACTIVITY 39

A note to the teacher: Lines, dots, and basic geometric shapes now show objects and living things. More detail and abstraction (X-ray views, double base lines, and folding over) than in lesson 20.

What this means

The child is expressing some of his first concerns (visually) for what he sees as opposed to what he might draw or paint. He has greater confidence in the pictures he makes (firm lines, less scribblelike) and he is concocting ways of showing what he knows to be true of his subject. The child's mental picture of things as they really are is showing some new growth, but he doesn't have sufficient information or maturity to express it well.

How to recognize this level

The child is using "misconcepts" when he bends figures like a hose (and ignores the fact that they have joints), or he uses two standing lines for his objects, or he shows both the inside and the outside of a house all in one. Some of his pictures seem to have been "folded over" and drawn in two states. These and other similar peculiarities represent efforts of the child to create illusions of space and they occur until the individual has internalized concepts that enable him to solve some new problem as artists would. There is also an increased ability to perceive and record detail more accurately. (Compare his work at this level with what he did in lesson 20.)

What to do, why, how often, and when

Be aware of any of the child's attempts to create feelings of depth or space. Avoid any inclination to move into the teaching of perspective concepts but reinforce anything the child does to show depth and details. You can also suggest things the child might look at or think about that would assist him in learning to better handle both problems (depth and details). Subsequent activities will provide sufficient experiences for the child. Just follow the plan. Encourage the child to render pictures of subjects or incidents where depth would be needed. Look at artists' prints where depth has been used and discuss what the artist did to make his picture seem "true to life." Discuss the amount of detail used by the artist and what kinds of things they might consider adding to pictures or sculptures they make.

■ Prints:
Ground Hog Day by Wyeth
Still Life With Pipe by Chardin
Sistine Madonna by Raphael
Hunters In the Snow by Brueghel
The Scout by Remington
Hay Wain by Constable
The Pantry by DeHooch
The Hare by Durer
The Blue Boy by Gainsborough

What to look for at the end (evaluation)

Teacher awareness of the idea expressed in "Note to the teacher" is the only crucial part of the evaluation. Good attitudes and enthusiasm toward art activities on the part of the learner, frequent positive reinforcement by the teacher, and the growth of the child's awareness are also important criteria.

LEVEL 1   ACTIVITY 40

A note to the teacher: At this stage the child sometimes alters the size of things or their parts when he portrays them. Such distortions are the result of a child's experiences with what he is recreating.

What this means

A child shows himself larger than his house or he draws flowers larger than trees because to him flowers are the most important at that moment. He might draw the needles of a tree way out of proportion because he was pricked by them or in a drawing of someone throwing a ball he might draw the throwing arm much larger than the other.

How to recognize this level

When the distortions occur, they are quite evident and are merely a part of the child's communication process.

What to do, why, how often, and when

Art activity should be daily, but the teacher should not make a point of distortion and discourage it. It is a natural thing for children to do and has likely appeared prior to this time. The teacher can help the child in developing an awareness of some natural size relationships or proportions but must not lead the child to feel that he is a failure or that he is inadequate because his pictures are not naturalistic.

- What to look for:
  - *Distortion in size.* A child draws father much smaller than mother or himself larger than anyone else in the family. He draws flowers as tall as trees, exaggerates the size of the hand he throws with, or shows a dog he fears with huge teeth.
  - *Distortion in color.* A child uses colors he enjoys and pays little attention to matching the color of his drawing to the real thing.
  - *Repetition of subjects.* He is captured by themes or subjects that he repeats over and over again in his pictures.
  - *Frequency of subject and media.* The use of these is highly representative of a recent experience with one or the other or both. The more positive his reinforcement the more he repeats their use.

- What to do:
  - Be accepting of what the child has done.
  - Constantly enlarge the child's experience with a great variety of subjects (daily art experiences).
  - Reward the child (verbally) who observes more proper size and color relationships than he has previously.
  - Cause the child to sense your appreciation of his efforts.
  - Keep the emphasis on a great variety of experiences highly motivated and with frequent opportunities to draw and paint.
  - Look at prints and talk about the artists' use of realism and his reasons for distorting or exaggerating. For example, these kinds of questions could be asked:
    - *Dempsey & Firpo* by Bellows: "Why are the people all different sizes?" "Are the colors the artist used like the colors in real life?"
    - *Fur Traders on the Missouri* by Bingham: "How does the cat compare with the men in size?" "Is this picture like a photograph?" "How?"
    - *The Harvesters* by Breughel: "What does this picture tell you about the time and life of the people?" "The artist?"
    - *I and the Village* by Chagall: "Does everything in this picture look real?" "Are the colors real?" "Are the size relationships accurate?" "Chagall was a Russian Jew and often recalled boyhood experiences in his pictures. Do you see any evidence of that in this picture?"

What to look for at the end (evaluation)

An evaluation or culmination for the child is not relevant to this concept. Teacher awareness of what the child is doing and why he does it is sufficient.

LEVEL1

ACTIVITY41

A note to the teacher: At this level, three-dimensional forms are drawn as two-dimensional shapes. (His pictures look flat, but the child's need to create an illusion of depth will grow as subsequent lessons increase his awareness.)

What this means

The child does not have enough information or art ideas to handle the illusion of depth adequately. Everything he draws or paints treats depth in an abstract way. Objects and people stand in rows or "on lines." Houses, swing sets, tables, and animals are drawn with height and width only. Depth is only "hinted at."

How to recognize this level

If the child consistently flattens all of his subjects to the point that he even ignores simple uses of overlapping, it is apparent he is at this level.

What to do, why, how often, and when

- It is natural for children to treat three-dimensional forms as two-dimensional shapes. All children seem to do this at one time or another. Reinforce any attempts to create a feeling of space or depth, but don't attempt the formal teaching of any perspective concepts at this point. At level three he will have experiences with overlapping, and indications of this in his work should certainly be treated very positively. The child's experiences with real shapes and forms are more important now, and the plan you are following has already included these kinds of things. More will come.
- Continue art on a daily basis. Encourage the child to new levels of awareness for his environment, and continue the format of activities suggested in lesson 36.

What to look for at the end (evaluation)

Evaluation in this activity concerns itself with teacher awareness only. Being aware of the child's inability as yet to create illusions of depth and still pursuing a course of daily art experiences for the child (with lots of encouragement) are all that is necessary at this level.

LEVEL 1   # ACTIVITY 42

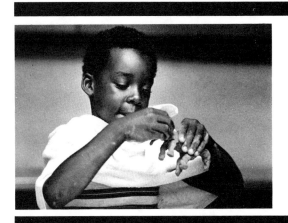

Concept taught by this activity: The child can now create forms of objects, things, and people from pliable materials by rolling, squeezing, and patting. Child should note that some pliable materials become rigid.

Objective: Through manipulation of clay the child will form objects by rolling, squeezing, and patting. He will exhibit an awareness that some pliable materials become rigid.

A sample lesson plan for achieving the objective:

Teacher preparations
■ The teacher should be aware that the child is a natural manipulator. He pats, presses, pokes, pounds, squeezes, rolls, and pinches the moist clay.
■ It is sometimes helpful to start with an oil-base clay which can be used over and over without remixing. This is important in kindergarten and first grade, where the child may be experiencing clay for the first time.
■ The teacher should know how to mix clay and work with it before she uses it with the children. (Water base clay is obtained from ceramics shops in the yellow pages.)
■ Canvas, burlap boards, or papers should be provided for protection of desks and tables. Children should also have smocks or old shirts to protect clothes when water base clay is used.
■ Have pictures of clay objects and some actual examples (when possible) to motivate the children.

Teaching suggestions
To involve the children and stimulate their thinking, ask: "Has anyone ever made things from clay?" "What kinds of things might we make?" "How would we go about it?"

"Can someone show us how we could form a ball of clay and pull legs, arms, tails, and head from the ball?" (This doesn't matter in the oil base clay, but it is essential in the water base clay, since anything added to it breaks easily as it starts to dry. The drier it is the more fragile it becomes.) "Can someone show us how to make the parts of an object' and add it to the biggest part (arms, legs, head to the body?" "Make an imaginary animal or a form you think up — one which no one else in the room will make just like it."

Suggested art activity
"Make an animal that you really like out of clay."
Note: The animal kingdom provides a wealth of inspiration for the child. Four-legged animals such as cows, horses, elephants, bears, hippos, and rhinos are especially recommended because the child can make them stand up with ease. If the advanced children are ready, they might try attaching their figures to a clay background so that they can stand up. Human figures are a little more difficult to model unless the child is guided to construct thick, sturdy legs that will hold the figure erect. They could also have figures lying down and kneeling.

Alternative art activities
■ The teacher may suggest a simple way to make the appendages, such as arms and legs, adhere strongly to the main body. For children who can understand, the process of "scoring" and "welding" might be explained (making surfaces rough by scratching, then scraping wet clay across each joint as a sort of "adhesive").
■ There will always be those who find experimenting with textures exciting. A collection of "found" objects: popsicle sticks, bottle caps, nails, plastic forks, buttons, shells, and beads will help the process. Encourage students to create repeat patterns of textures when they make bowls, cups, or dishes.
Note: Where clay is not available or in plentiful supply, objects can be created utilizing salt dough, papier maché, and sawdust clay.

Evaluation

Observe the finished product. Has the child created an object in some pliable material by patting, squeezing and rolling? Does he recognize that some clay or other pliable materials may dry and become rigid forms? When these are accomplished by each child, you have achieved the objective.

Other things to consider

- Vocabulary: scoring, welding, kiln, wedging, texture, and form.
- Art materials needed: clay, water, found objects, newspaper, burlap boards or canvas, and shirts or smocks.
- Books:
  Clay in the Classroom, George Barford. (Worcester, Mass.: Davis Pub. Inc., 1963).
  Ceramics, Glenn C. Nelson. (New York: Holt Rinehart and Winston, Inc., 1960).
  Creative Clay Design, Ernst Rottger. (New York: Reinhold Publishing Corp., 1963).
- People who might have need for the concept: ceramicists, sculptors, brick industry.

LEVEL1   ACTIVITY43

Concept taught by this activity: At this point in his development the child can create textures in pliable materials by making lines and indentations with fingers, pencils, combs, or other objects or materials.

Objective: The child creates textures in pliable materials by indenting.

A sample lesson plan for achieving the objective:

Teacher preparations
- Have displays set up on a table or on panels to hang on the wall. The display should include a variety of objects that have interesting shapes with which to make patterns or designs in clay or some other soft material as well as to create illusions of texture from imprinting. This display might include pointed dowel sticks, tongue depressors, cookie cutters, combs, hair pins, burlap, coarse wall paper, screen wire, buttons, strainers, straining spoons, bottle openers, bottle caps, and fruits or vegetables — such as cabbage and oranges — cut in half.
- Have clay, plasticene, or other modeling material ready for use.
- Set up the materials in the display so that the child can see what he wants to select when the activity begins. Having everything in a pile tells the child the materials aren't very important, and having minimal numbers of all objects to select from may prove frustrating to the child.
- Display prints or pictures of examples where artists have created textures or patterns in clay.

Teaching suggestions
- Begin by capturing the interest of the child with some demonstration such as: "What is this stuff called that I'm working with?" (Mold, shape, and manipulate the media in a nonpurposeful way.) "Have you ever worked with clay?" "What kinds of things have you made with clay?" "Can I shape it or make designs in it?" "Can I use my fingers as tools?" "What could I use as tools besides my fingers?" (Hold up pointed dowel sticks.) "What could I do with this

tool to make designs or decorate the clay?" "If you will all flatten your clay into a nice flat shape, what kinds of designs can you make with a stick like this?"
- Have the children flatten their clay, then imprint with the stick in many ways, creating a variety of shapes and patterns.
- Have everyone look at each others' designs and caution them not to handle someone else's clay.
- Clays can be obtained from ceramics shops, usually found in the yellow pages of local phone books.

Suggested art activity
- Show the children some of the objects in the work table and draw attention to how they make marks in the clay. Let them know there are many things available and that they will be able to choose two or three to work with.
- Have the children flatten their clay into slabs again and have them come to the display table and select objects to imprint in their clay. Build on the previous experience. Emphasize that sometimes designs and textures make objects more attractive or more beautiful. Encourage them to make designs or decorative patterns with the objects they press into the clay. Help them to be aware that pattern occurs when a shape is repeated in some organized fashion. Refer to pictures on display for ideas, but do not delay the child's opportunity to get into the activity so long that he loses interest.
- For children who work quickly, encourage them to roll up their clay, flatten it out again, and create new textures or patterns with three more objects.

Alternate art activities
- Make a bowl or some other utilitarian object with the idea of imprinting around the outside of them. Encourage the children once again to select two or three objects for their imprinting and caution them not to press too hard; the clay wall can easily be torn or pushed out of shape. Recognize that this may be difficult for some children, and encourage these children to use small objects that they can imprint with more easily. The dowel stick would be especially easy to handle.
- Create textures in animal forms (clay sculpture) by indenting or imprinting.

99

- Other media that might be used: papier maché, sawdust clay, salt and flour.

Evaluation

If the child has imprinted objects in clay or some other soft material and has applied that experience by imprinting a bowl or another form he has created, the objective of the lesson has been achieved.

Other things to consider

- Vocabulary: illusion, texture, imprint, pattern, pliable.
- Art materials needed: tempera paint, clay or some other pliable material, and a variety of papers.
- Photographs of textures and patterns in clay or on paper done by artists.
- People who might have need for the concept: ceramicists, architects, sculptors, engineers.

LEVEL 1   ACTIVITY 44

Concept taught by this activity: The child's awareness is enlarged through textural experiences that affect the emotions (touching a soft spot on a firm apple, or feeling chunks of butter in buttermilk).

Objective: The child demonstrates a heightened awareness of textural experiences that affect the emotions.

A sample lesson plan for achieving the objective:

Teacher preparations
- Collect materials such as an animal skin, buttermilk, vaseline, hand lotion, an avocado pit, spoiled fruit or vegetables, wilted flower, a piece of velvet, polished stones, a raw egg, honey, a rose, ice cream, a peach, a brass instrument, ice, sand, a feather, a brillo pad (dry and soapy), foam rubber, and live things such as crawling insects, a snake, a kitten, a rat, and a hamster.
- Have the materials on several tables in categories or in separate piles on one table with the students in a semicircle out front. See that the materials you use have variety and relate to the child's world or experience.

Teaching suggestions
Review what the students recall about texture — what it is and what kinds there are. (Preceded by Level I, Activity 32.)
- Begin the unit with dialogue such as: "What are all of the icky words?" "Scary words?" "Loving words?" "Today you are all a piece of sandpaper. What are all the ways you feel?" (List them on the board.) "We can feel with our fingers, but also with our heart and mind. I have a lot of different objects for you to touch today. Each has a different feel to it." "Can you think of some different kinds of things you wouldn't want to touch or feel?" "What are they?" "Why wouldn't you want to touch them?" "Is it true then that touching things can affect how we *feel*?" "Who

would like to come up and close their eyes while I put their hand on one of the things I have here?" (Have the child touch one or two things and tell the class how it feels to him.)
- Have the children feel with their fingers, cheeks, mouth, and underside of wrist.
- Recognize which children may be frightened by some of the materials and avoid having them touch those they can't handle emotionally. The child shouldn't be made to feel guilty about not wanting to touch something.
- Discuss how the smell or odor affects the reaction they have to each thing.

Suggested art activity
After all of the objects or living things have been experienced and children have reacted to them emotionally, have them categorize the objects in different ways (neat, scary, icky . . .).

Alternative art activities
- Look at prints or pictures that were created for their emotional effect. Have the children describe the feeling the pictures give them.
- Have the students draw and paint a picture that shows how they felt or responded to a textural experience at home, in the school, or wherever.
- Other media that could be used to teach this concept: assemblage, collage.

Evaluation

Look for any indication of an increased awareness on the part of each individual. When student behavior (verbal or nonverbal) indicates a change in awareness, the objective of the lesson has been achieved for that individual.

Other things to consider

- Vocabulary: texture, awareness, tactile, emotions, and categorize.
- Art materials needed: drawing and painting media as selected by the student.
- Prints:
  The Cradle by Morisot
  Blue Boy by Gainsborough
  Francis I by Clouet
  The Virgin Forest by Rousseau
  Breezing Up by Homer
  The Small Crucifixion by Grunewald
  The Old King by Rouault
  Peaceable Kingdom by Hicks
  The Return by Magritte
- People who might have need for the concept: writers, restaurant owners, artists, architects, interior decorators, advertisers, supermarket managers, T.V. and movie people, zoologists, and cooks.

LEVEL1   ACTIVITY45

Concept taught by this activity: The faces of people may be shown with a variety of different expressions on them.

Objective: The student draws faces of people with expressions reflecting their feelings or circumstances.

A sample lesson plan for achieving the objective:

Teacher preparations
- Collect examples of faces that depict a variety of facial expressions. Display them along with selected prints. (Comic strips may be used.)
- Have examples of children's work — preferably from another class that depict only smiling faces (curved lines). It is typical for children to draw smiley faces regardless of what's happening to the person in the picture.

Teaching suggestions
- Determine whether or not the student knows what facial expressions are: "How do you know how a person feels?" "Can he tell you in ways other than with words?" Explore some of their experiences with facial expression. Cut pictures of faces from magazines. Show only eyes, and ask if they are happy or sad. Then show the rest of the picture. Do the same with mouths.
- Discuss ways in which artists show how people feel: cartoonists, portrait painters, and illustrators of books and magazines. Compare this with how they themselves typically have the same expression on the faces of all the people they draw. Through this discussion try to get the student to come to this conclusion rather than imposing it on him.

Suggested art activity
Think of some story or event in which people show how they feel by the expressions on their faces, then draw or paint some part of the story.

Alternative art activities
- Take pictures from magazines where the heads of people are rather large (three inches or more from the top of the head to the bottom of the chin). Select faces that have different expressions on them. Tear the face in half from top to bottom and paste one half on a piece of drawing paper and then have the children draw in the facial expression for the half that isn't there.
- Have the children make facial expressions with their own faces as you call out words like *sad, happy, hot, cold,* and others, then allow them to make a drawing of a face that has an expression on it. When they are through, display the faces and have the class try to determine what each of the expressions are trying to say.

Evaluation

When the student draws people with facial expressions that reflect what is happening, the objective has been achieved. Each student who discontinues stereotyped facial expressions is *especially* successful.

Other things to consider

- Vocabulary: facial, expression, animated.
- Art materials needed: any drawing and painting materials that are available.
- Prints:
  The Smokers by Brouwer
  Francis I by Clouet
  Absinthe by Degas
  The Small Crucifixion by Grunewald
  Mona Lisa by da Vinci
  Gypsy with Baby by Modigliani
  Man with Helmet by Rembrandt
  The Old King by Rouault
  Mother and Child by Kollwitz

■ People who might have need for the concept: photographer, portrait painter, cartoonist, illustrator, sculptor, puppet maker.

LEVEL1   ACTIVITY46

Concept taught by this activity: The child should develop an awareness of how architecture (buildings) and its related fields influence his life.

Objective: The student is aware of ways in which architecture and its related fields influence his life.

A sample lesson plan for achieving the objective:

Teacher preparations
- Obtain prints to be used.
- Obtain pictures from magazines of houses, buildings, rooms, Igloos, the South Seas.
- Obtain photos and pictures of local architecture (students' own homes, court house, school, churches).
- Obtain story "The Three Bears."

Teaching suggestions
- Hold up a picture of an Igloo, a Polynesian Fale (Faw-Lay), and an American house. Ask, "What are all the reasons for Eskimo children having an Igloo?" "What are all the reasons why Polynesian children and their families have a Fale?" "Why do you have a house?" "Why do buildings and houses have windows?" (Air, to see out, light, to "look nice.") "Why do we have doors?" "How big should they be?" "For a garage?" "For an airplane hanger?" "Why do birds and animals have dens, holes, or nests?" (For shelter, warmth, protection, companionship.)
- Read "The Three Bears," emphasizing how rooms, beds, chairs, and dishes were designed "just right" for each bear. What are all of the things in your house that are "just right" for you? What are all of the things in school that are *not* "just right" for you?
- Have you ever found a drinking fountain that you could reach "just right" without being lifted up or without standing on something? "Can you reach the water in your kitchen?" "Your bathroom?" "Are door knobs ever too high for you?" "For your little brother or sister?" "Draw a picture of a

three-year-old getting a drink at a fountain that is "just right."
- Have students call out what rooms they have in their own homes, and list them or have pictures of those kinds of rooms. Ask them what rooms they would like to have if they could. (Donny Osmond of the Osmond brothers has a bedroom with a bed that raises almost to the ceiling.)
- 1) Hold up an art print *The Scout* by Frederick Remington. Ask "If you were this Indian, how would you feel?" (Lonely, cold?) "Would you want to get into a shelter?" "What kind?" (House, teepe, hogan, wickiup?) "What is in his home that makes him want to be there?" (Warmth, light, food, dryness, family and friends)
  2) Hold up a print of *House at Aix* by Paul Cezanne. Ask if they would like to live in it, and what are all of their reasons? What colors do they see in this print?
  3) Hold up *Boy With A Tire* by Hughie Lee-Smith. Would they like to live in that boy's house? "Which building does he live in?" "What are all of the ways he is feeling?" (Happy, sad, bored, lonely, insignificant, unliked.)
  4) Hold up *Bedroom at Arles* by Vincent Van Gogh. "What are all of the ways this room is like yours?" "All the ways it is different?" "How many of you like this room better than your own?" "Why?"
  5) Hold up a print of *Venice* by Canaletto. "What kind of buildings do you see?" "Any homes like yours?" "Palaces?" "Apartment?" "Churches?" (Point out *dome* on Church of Santa Maria del Salute.)
  6) Hold up *Snap the Whip* by Winslow Homer. "What color is the building?" "Do all those children live here?" "Is it a school?" "Is it like *this* school?" "Why not?" "What shapes do you see in the school?" ($\triangle$, $\square$, etc.)
  7) "Do you have a 'secret space' where you can go and be alone? (By a bush, under a bush, in a tree, or under a table?) "Tell us about *your* secret place." "Why do you like it?"
  8) "If you could build a house — any kind of special secret place — where would it be (under the ocean, in a bed of cactus and sand, behind a rock, on the moon)?"

"What would it be like?" (A cave, small, large, high, low, plastic, colorful, stone.)

Suggested art activity
Draw your special space in its special place.

Alternative art activities
Draw your room. Draw a space house. Draw several squares and put a different shaped roof on each. Build "environments" with large cardboard boxes.

Evaluation

When the student verbally identifies ways in which architecture and its related fields influence his life, the objective has been achieved.

Other things to consider

- Vocabulary: architect, roof, blueprint, builder-contractor, dome, shelter, igloo, Fale.
- Art materials needed: paper, pencils, crayons, paints (optional).
- Media: photographs of local architecture (not absolutely necessary).
- Prints:
  The Scout by Frederick Remington
  House of Aix by Paul Cezanne
  Boy With A Tire by Hughie Lee Smith
  Bedroom At Arles by Vincent Van Gogh
  Venice by Canaletto
  Snap The Whip by Winslow Homer
- Other media using the concept: City planning, architecture, landscape architecture, interior design, art history and analysis, technical-industrial design.
- People who might have need of the concept: architects, interior designers, contractors, the "public," city planners.

LEVEL1   ACTIVITY47

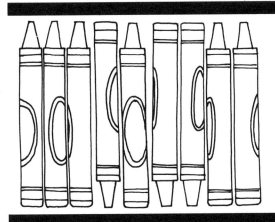

Concept taught by this activity: Repetition is often found in works of art.

Objective: The student points out ways in which repetition is used in works of art.

A sample lesson plan for achieving the objective:

Teacher preparations
- Make note of examples of repetition inside and outside the classroom. (Rhythm as repeated in music, dance, arcades.)
- Collect suggested prints and other appropriate illustrations and have them on display or ready for discussion.

Teacher suggestions
- Review what the student already knows about the word *repetition*. "What does the word mean?" "How is it used in this room?" "Is repetition used in music, math, science, or other subject areas?" "How?" "How many different ways can something be repeated?"
- Discuss the use of repetition in works of art. Discuss repetition in relation to each of the art prints and to other resources collected. "Where is it happening?" "Why does the artist repeat shapes, colors, themes, and textures?" "What if each element only appeared *once* in a picture?"
- Discuss examples of the concept found in the room, in nature, in the students' dress, in books, and in advertising.

Suggested art activity
Create a design, a sculpture, or a picture using repetition. "List every example of repetition you can find in the art you have created."

Alternative art activities
- "Try creating a design or picture in which little or nothing is repeated."
- By using potato prints, have each student create a repeat design by printing the same design all over his paper. When they are finished, display them and talk about the many different ways the designs were organized and how

repetition helps give unity to the designs. Discuss how different they would be and how ununified they might appear if all the prints were different on each sheet of paper. Talk about the different numbers of items that could be used and still have repetition.

Evaluation

When the student demonstrates an understanding of repetition and can evaluate his own use of the concept, the objective has been achieved.

Other things to consider

- Vocabulary: repeat, repetition, pattern, theme.
- Art materials needed: drawing and painting materials or some appropriate medium for sculpture.
- Prints:
  Boy With A Tire by Hughie Lee-Smith
  Le Jour by Braque
  Maas at Dordrecht by Cuyp
  Nude Descending #2 by Duchamp
  Don Manuel Osorio by Goya
  Allies Day May 1917 by Hassam
  Gypsy With Baby by Modigliani
  Snap the Whip by Homer

MATURITY LEVEL 2

Developmental stages

In this packet of lesson plans the teacher can provide the student with twenty-five art experiences that are designed to assist him in moving through his developmental stages. The activities will teach how to:

- Provide the child with elementary experiences in manipulating forms.
- Mix colors to create specific new ones.
- Recognize the influence light has on forms, shapes, values, and colors.
- Use black and white to change the value of any color.
- Develop an awareness of five simple photography ideas.
- Distinguish between photographs, paintings, and drawings.
- Use simple processes in weaving.
- Use simple processes in stitchery and applique.
- Achieve balance.
- Join things together by gluing, pasting, nailing, hinging, sewing, and sticking.
- Show the sky coming down to the earth.
- Place people and objects in positions other than a straight line.
- Show people and objects varying in size.
- Use lines to separate objects or shapes and to create pattern.
- Create the illusion of texture by imprinting.
- Use lines, dots, and shapes to create the illusion of common texture.
- Detect variations in the sizes of people and objects by measuring.
- Use overlapping to create the illusion of depth.
- Build constructions.
- Communicate in nonverbal ways.
- Create the maximum in contrast and reinforce or brighten colors.
- Relate parts of a composition to each other.
- Recognize the relationships of white, black, and gray to other colors.
- Recognize warm or cool characteristics of colors.
- Organize colors and mix specific ones from red, yellow, and blue.

THE DIAGNOSTIC CHART

An explanation

13. The child is able to arrange thirty or more objects into one related unit. Shoulders begin to appear on figures. The subject matter still looks very flat, but changes in awareness are evident, particularly in size relationships and details included. The sky is still a band at the top edge of the picture, but the standing line is beginning to become a horizon line.

14. The student has experiences with weaving and stitchery processes. Shoulders are shown on most figures. Five fingers are on each hand. Fingers come out of the hand rather than the wrist. The eye has an iris, indicated with a small circle inside a larger one. Lashes and eyebrows are often drawn, but hips are still not in evidence (legs come off the outside edge of the body or skirt rather than the hips).

15. The student utilizes simple processes in joining various materials: pasting, nailing, and sewing. The sky is beginning to come down to the ground, illusions of simple textures such as grass and shingles are shown, and over-lapping is used to create depth.

16. Parts of a picture are tied together or related by simple overlapping and repetition. The legs attach to hips, and action is more apparent in figures and animals.

13.   The child is at activity No. 50.

14.   The child is at activities No. 54 and 55.

15.   The child is at activities No. 57, 58, 59, 60, 63, 65, and 66.

Art projects that can be used as devices for teaching a specific concept

Drawing (pencil, crayon, stick, marker, brush, and chalk)
Lessons: 56, *58, *59, *60, *61, *63, *64, *65, 67, *69

Cartooning and/or caricature
Lessons: 56, 58, 59, 60, 61, 63, 64, 65, 67, 69

Rubbings
Lesson: 56

Coloring and color mixing
Lessons: *49, 51, 56, 58, 60, *68, *70, *71, *72

Rock and gourd painting
Lessons: 49, 51, 56, 60, 61, 68

Crayon resist
Lessons: *68, 70

Water color and tempera
Lessons: *49, *51, 56, 58, 60, 63, 64, 65, 67, 69, *70, *71, *72

Toothpick and straw sculpture
Lessons: 56, 57, *66, 69

Whittling and carving
Lessons: 56, 69

Woodcraft
Lessons: 56, 57, 66, 69

Sand bottles
Lessons: 56, 69

Dry flower arranging
Lessons: 56, 69

Vegetable prints
Lessons: 56, 61, *62, 68

Gadget and roll prints
Lessons: 56, *61, *62

Melted crayon painting (encaustic)
Lessons: 56, 69

Perspective
Lessons: *60, 64, *65

Posters
Lessons: 51, 56, 58, 60, 61, 63, 64, 65, *68, 69

Murals and friezes
Lessons: 49, 51, 56, 57, 58, *60, *61, 63, 65, 68, 69

Dribble and sponge painting
Lessons: 56, 61, 62, 63

Dioramas
Lessons: 49, 50, 51, 56, *57, *60, 61, 63, 64, 65, 66, 67, 68, 69

Initial and name designs
Lessons: 49, 56, 68, 70

Collage
Lessons: 56, *57, 68, 69, *70, *71, 72

Wire sculpture
Lessons: 56, 69

Sculpture with clay (oil, water, salt, flour, etc.)
Lessons: 56, *60, 69

Leathercraft
Lessons: 56, 69

Terrariums
Lessons: 56, 69

Photography
Lessons: 50, *52, *53, 56, 65, 69

Stencil prints
Lessons: 56, *62, 68

Copper and foil tooling
Lessons: 56, 69

Batik
Lessons: 56, 69

Tie/dye
Lessons: 56, *68, 69

Starch paper
Lessons: 56, 57, 69

Mosaics
Lessons: 56, 57, 68, 69

Stitchery with string or yarn
Lessons: *55, 56, 61, 69

Applique (sew or glue)
Lessons: *55, 56, 67, 68, *69

Spool knitting
Lessons: 56, 61, 76

Snowflakes
Lesson: *56

Box sculpture
Lessons: 56, 57, *66

Torn paper design
Lessons: 56, *57, 60, *68, *69

Construction paper designs (cut and paste)
Lessons: 56, *57, *60, *68, *69

Mobiles and stabiles
Lessons: *56, 57

Snow sculpture
Lessons: 56, 60

Knitting and crocheting
Lessons: 56, 69

Pin-prick pictures
Lessons: 56, 69

String and yarn pictures
Lessons: 56, *61

Basket weaving
Lessons: 54, 56

Weaving (paper, string, fabric)
Lessons: *54, 56, 69

Puppets (sack, sock, and styrofoam)
Lessons: 56, 57, 61, 63, 67, 68

Christmas ornaments
Lessons: 49, 51, *56, *57, 63

Paper sack masks
Lessons: 49, 51, 56, 57, 61, 63, 67, 68

Paper sculpture (fold, score, roll)
Lessons: 49, 51, 56, 57, 61, 63, 67, 68

Egg carton crafts
Lessons: *56, *57

Papier maché
Lessons: 56, 57, 60

---

*Key projects for the concept.

112

LEVEL 2   ACTIVITY 48

A note to the teacher: At this point the child is able to take multiple objects and arrange thirty or more of them into a single related unit.

What this means

The child can intuitively arrange a variety of shapes into one related unit or design. He simply needs the opportunity to "play" with objects and receive positive reinforcement for his activity.

How to recognize this level

If the child is ready for this activity, the teacher will see this sort of development beginning to take place once the materials are in the youngster's hands. Observation on the part of the teacher to determine what kinds of designs or arrangements are produced by the child, then comparing them with the stages of growth in three-dimensional manipulation are all that is necessary. If the child is below or beyond this level, simply note where he is and then provide additional opportunities only if he is below the level where he should be. Compare what he does with the drawings.

What to do, why, how often, and when

- Have a variety of objects available for the child — variety in size and shape with some duplicates. See that each individual has at least thirty objects to work with.
- Provide ample time for the individual to solve the problem and repeat the time weekly until he is successful.
- Indicate approval in some way. Encourage and motivate but don't compare his efforts with others, don't ask what he is making, and don't "show him how."

What to look for at the end (evaluation)

When the child can organize thirty or more objects that represent a variety of shapes and sizes into one related unit, the objective has been accomplished.

LEVEL 2   ACTIVITY 49

Concept taught by this activity: Colors can be mixed to create specific new colors.

Objective: The student will demonstrate the ability to predict what specific colors will result when he mixes two given colors.

A sample lesson plan for achieving the objective:

Teacher preparations

■ Begin by asking questions such as these: "If all of you had paint boxes containing just red, yellow, and blue, is there any way you could paint pictures containing colors like orange or green without buying some more colors?" (Develop questioning until students recognize that the mixing of colors is the answer.) Then move into a "let's see what happens when we mix colors" phase.

■ Using the overlaps of primary colors, the teacher, along with the students, will demonstrate how red, blue, and yellow, when mixed, yield green, orange, and purple. Ask, "What color will we get when we mix yellow and red?" "What color will we get when we mix yellow and blue?" "What color will we get when we mix blue and red?"

■ With water colors and three petri dishes the children will mix the primary colors with one another to create secondary colors.

■ Using the tray in the water color set, the children will mix the primary colors with one another and create the secondary colors. The children will be given three or more sheets of paper and their water color equipment (paints, brush, paper, newspaper, sponges). "On each paper you will use two primary colors." The two colors will be used in varying intensities. Encourage the children to overlap and inter-mingle, thus creating varying shades of a third new color. (A good technique to use is that of moistening the entire

page before starting.)

Teaching suggestions

■ Display a color chart of the primary and secondary colors (color wheel). Have it contain a triangle forming the primary colors and an inverted triangle forming the secondary colors.

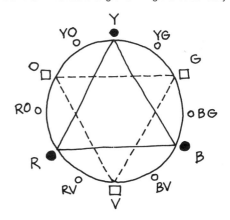

■ Have the overhead projector, transparencies, and overlays that show the mixture of primary colors producing secondary colors. Three petri dishes and liquid food coloring with eye droppers can be used.

■ Pictures should be available of prints of simple primary and secondary colors. Water colors, brushes, a large container of water for each child, crayons, magazines, scissors, and glue should also be on hand.

■ Look at artists' prints and discuss whether or not the artist mixed the colors he used and how one can tell he has: "What did he mix to get this?"

■ Drop four or five drops of light tempera paint on white paper and let a child blow through a straw at an angle, spreading the paint to the edge of the paper. Do as above until several colors have been used, showing how the mixture of the paint will change into other colors. "What new colors did you make?"

- Make a math game with equations for the children to solve. Y = Yellow, B = Blue, R = Red, G = Green, O = Orange, P = Purple. Put these equations on the board and have the children solve them:

  Y + R = ?
  O − R = ?
  B + Y = ?
  Y + ? = R etc.

Suggested art activity

Paint a picture, using just primary colors plus black and white. Encourage a student to try mixing what he has to create what he needs.

Alternative art activities

- Finger paint on the table top, using tempera paint and Stay-Flo liquid starch. Begin with white tempera powder and starch, working it with the finger tips. Add other colors gradually, going from light to dark shades. Discuss what happened. Emphasize what two colors were combined to make each new color.
- Work with frosting and food coloring. Begin with two primary colors to see the color change. Spread the frosting on crackers and eat them. See if the students can predict what new color will result as you mix primary colors.
- Let each child have a piece of clear cellophane food wrap. Place drops of colors on it and pull and stretch the wrap to mix the colors.
- Do a tissue-paper collage. Overlap the tissue to create new colors.

Evaluation

Entitle a bulletin board "Can you make three into seven?" (Primary colors into secondaries?) Display the children's color wheels, collages, and water-color paintings. Observe students individually in this kind of activity, in the discussions and in any of their painting activities. Be able to recognize when the student is able to predict the colors he will get when he mixes them.

Other things to consider

- Vocabulary: primary colors, secondary colors, color wheel, petri dish, color names: red, yellow, blue, green, purple, orange, and transparency.
- Art materials needed: water colors, art paper, pencils, crayons, brushes, tissue, paper, glue.
- Prints:
  Mlle. Violette by Redon
  Women in a Garden by Monet
  Water Flowery Mill by Gorky
  Rebus by Rauschenberg
  Bedroom at Arles by Van Gogh
  La Moulin de la Galette by Renoir
  Orange and Yellow by Rothko
  Justice and Peace by Overstreet
- Filmstrip: "The Yellow Balloon"
- Books:
  Hailstones and Halibut Bones
  The Adventures of the Three Colors
- People who might have need for the concept: puppet makers, batik and tie dye artists, architects, landscape architects, interior designers, art historians, cartoonists, commercial artists, painters, and printmakers.

LEVEL 2

ACTIVITY 50

Concept taught by this activity: Various kinds of light create contrasts in darkness and lightness. At varying levels of brightness, each may influence how clearly forms, shapes, and colors are seen.

Objective: The child will demonstrate an *awareness* of how different kinds of light influence how clearly they see things.

A sample lesson plan for achieving the objective:

Teacher preparations
- Display art prints and photographs showing various degrees of light and darkness. If possible, have two pictures of the same scene — one at night and one in daylight.
- Be aware of light other than sunlight in and out of the room.
- Display pictures of different kinds of lights. These may be obtained from newspapers and magazines or whatever other sources are available. Some of these light sources include: moonlight, spotlights (plain and/or colored), candles, neons, vapor lights, street lights, oil, kerosene (hurricane), matches, fluorescent and black light. Collect whatever of these are available to bring to class.
- Be prepared to darken the room while you use the different lights you have collected.
- Obtain paper bags large enough to cover the child's face; black is preferable, but double brown sacks that won't let light come through are good, too. Attach colored shapes in the bottom of each.
- Use several colored scarves — some opaque and some transparent — to drape over objects to show the effect of filtering light.
- Obtain different varieties and colors of paper such as cellophane and tissue paper to use with the different kinds of lights.

- Have a Polaroid camera and dark glasses ready for experiments (if available).

Teaching suggestions
- The concept should be introduced and taught in some manner similar to this. "If we turned out the lights in this room, would we still be able to see each other?" "Where does light come from?" (The sun.) "Have you ever awakened at night and been able to see without turning on a light?" "Where did the light come from then?" (The moon.) Has anyone ever had his lights go off at night and couldn't get them to come on again?" "What made them go out?" (Electrical storm, etc.) "How did you see?" "Did your mother or father have something else available to make enough light for you to see?" "What else could have been used?" "Do any of you ever go camping?" "What kinds of light do you see by up in the mountains where there isn't any electricity?" "What are some other kinds of light we use?" "How about when you are driving in a car at night?" "Or on a bus?" "What makes these kinds of lights work?" (Batteries.) "Do we need light, then, when the sun has gone down or when the sky is dark and cloudy?" "What are things you can't see to do without light?" "Do lights help us every day?" "How?"
- "Is the light brighter from a flashlight or a match?" The teacher demonstrates this with the light from lighted matches or other dim light sources. "Do we need certain kinds of light to do some jobs?" "Why?" "Compare the differences in the light from a match, a candle, or a flashlight in the room. Students can take turns using a variety of lights (except matches) on various objects in the room.
- Focus colored spotlights (or plain) on a variety of objects. Flash on and off, simulating flashing signs. Let students take part. Discuss the effect of the flashing (dark and light, off and on). "When is this kind of light appropriate?" "Would you like it if the lights in your home went off and on like this all the time?" "Why not?"
- "Do some people use special kinds of lights for very special work?" (Such people as miners, eye and ear specialists, film makers, and others.) "What would they do if only sunlight was available to them?" Refer to pictures of different light sources.

- "How do you use light in your life?" "Would your life change much if you never saw any light?" "If you had only sun and moonlight to see by?"
- Exhibit prints showing different times of day and of night. "Did the artists who painted these pictures use light in any way?" "What would the artists need to know about light to do pictures like these?" "Can you tell where the light is coming from in these pictures?" "How?" (By shadow sides and the direction shadows are cast.)
- Have a child place his face inside a dark sack in a darkened room. Ask what he can see. Then have the child shine a flashlight into the bag. "Now what can he see?"
- Motivate children to visualize fog and its effects by reading *Hide and Seek Fog* by Tressett. Use pictures and children's responses to distinguish between clear, sunny days and foggy, dim days. Use a variety of scarves to screen and "fog out" selected objects. Have children comment on what they can see best and why. Use a variety of papers (for example, cellophane panels) using children as live objects. Have children discern which colors screen out the most light and thus their friends.
- Take two polaroid camera shots of the children — one in a darkened room and one outside. Let the children examine the finished pictures.

Suggested art activity
Make dark glasses, using the student's choice of colored cellophane, then discuss the difference in the ability of each color to filter out light.

Alternative art activities
- Create a drawing, a painting, or a collage suggesting a particular time of day or objects seen in a specified kind of dim light.
- Create an impression of a foggy day, twilight, early morning, or some other time with some art media to show how absence of direct light influences the way a certain subject may appear.
- Other media or projects that could be used to teach this concept:
  - Any type of printmaking or painting processes.
  - A Halloween activity built around darkness could be developed.

Evaluation

Probably the best evaluation is discovering pupil awareness by his interest and participation in discussion (with special focus on the accuracy of his verbal responses).

Other things to consider

- Vocabulary: clear, sunny, misty, foggy, dim, light, transparent, opaque.
- Art materials needed: tempera, water colors, crayons, and chalk with a variety of paper and brushes. (See list of teaching materials under "Teacher Preparations.")
- Prints:
  Dempsey and Firpo by Bellows
  Fur Traders on the Missouri by Bingham
  Rockets and Blue Lights by Turner
  Dancing Class by Degas
  View of Toledo by El Greco
  Night Watch by Rembrandt
  Thatched Cottages by Vlaminck
  Boats at Argentenil by Monet
  The Letter by Vermeer
  St. Joseph by De La Tour
- Books:
  Light and Shadow by Tannebaum
  Teachers' Science Manual Webster McGraw: Experiences in Science Recontext

Hide and Seek Fog by Alvin Tressett
Circus in the Mist by Bruna Munari
- Filmstrip:
  "Look and See," "The Five Senses," Film #1
  "Jam Handy Organization"
- People who might have need for the concept: architects, city planners, interior designers, photographers, painters, printmakers, cartoonists, commercial artists.

Concept taught by this activity: Black or white can be used to change the values of any color, and the value of a color is its darkness or lightness.

Objective: The student demonstrates an awareness that black or white can be used to change the value of any color, and the value of a color is directly related to its relative closeness to black or white.

A sample lesson plan for achieving the objective:

Teacher preparations
■ Acquire prints and other appropriate illustrations. Display for discussion.
■ Acquire paper and tempera paints. Have them ready for use.
■ Require color wheel and value wheel from Activity #90, Level 4.

Teaching suggestions
■ "Before we get into today's concept, what does *value* mean as we use it in art?" (Variations in darkness or lightness.) "Can anything be darker in value than black or lighter in value than white?" (No.) "Imagine my taking a jar of black tempera paint and pouring some of it into a water color cup, then adding one drop of white to it, mixing it in, and painting a strip of the color on a piece of paper. If I kept adding one drop at a time, then mixing it and painting a strip until I finally painted a pure white strip, how many variations or strips of gray do you suppose I would have?" (You may want to demonstrate this part of the discussion or have a

student try it until the point is clearly made that probably hundreds of variations would be possible.)
■ "If there are that many variations of gray possible, are there that many variations of every *color* possible, too?" (None will go as dark as black or as light as white and still retain their identity, but many variations of each color are possible.)
■ "Can we compare the value of colors to each other?" "To black and white?" "To the variations we talked about making?" (Two colors can be the same in value.)
■ Have someone line up all of the people wearing a given color in order of their darkness and lightness. Ask the class, "If we had the colors you see before you as paint in jars and we wanted to make all of the blues (or whatever color everyone is wearing) as dark as the darkest one, what would we mix with each?" (Black.) "Would we add the same amount to each?" (Not if they are different in value to begin with.)
■ Take a black and white Polaroid photograph of students wearing different colors. Show them how the values of some are similar while others are quite different from each other. Have students look at two colors with their eyes partly closed and they will be able to perceive their value differences more accurately.
■ Look at folds in material or curved surfaces and discuss how the lightness and darkness of the object changes from one place to another. "Which is closer to white in value?" "Which is closer to black?" "If I want to lighten a color, what would I mix with it?" (Add white.)
■ "Why would artists need to know about value?" "Why would they need to know how to darken or lighten colors?" Look at suggested prints or photographs available in the library or media center. Reaffirm the concept as used by the artist. Compare values with black and white and with each other.

Suggested art activity
■ Have students experiment by mixing colors with black and then with white. Have them see how many variations they can get.

■ Paint a picture using black and white to make colors darker or lighter. Limit the students to two or three colors and have them create the variety they need by mixing.

Alternative art activity
Have students arrange color chips in order from dark to light.

Evaluation

To determine whether or not each student can clearly use the concept, give everyone an opportunity to respond to the questions and experiences suggested in this outline and the activity in #3 and #46 (arranging and mixing colors from dark to light). These are probably the most revealing experiences for a teaching evaluation.

Other things to consider

■ Vocabulary: lightness, darkness, variations, value, blackness, whiteness, tint, shade.
■ Art materials needed: premixed tempera colors, paper, brushes.
■ Prints:
Bacchus by Caravaggio
Still Life with Pipe by Chardin
Blue Boy by Gainsborough
St. Joseph by De La Tour
Turning the Stake by Eakins
The Night Watch by Rembrandt
Lacemaker by Vermeer
Three Negro Boys by Watteau
■ People who might have need for the concept: paint manufacturers, house painters, artists, dyers, interior decorators, puppeteers, architects, art historians.

LEVEL 2   ACTIVITY 52

Concept taught by this activity: Now the child should be aware of the following photography precepts: loading film into a camera, processing, negatives, enlargements, and how to use a viewfinder.

Objective: The child demonstrates an awareness of how film is loaded into a camera, how film is processed, what negatives and enlargements are and how one looks through a viewfinder.

A sample lesson plan for achieving the objective:

Teacher preparations
- Have photographs on display, along with some story books with large photographs as illustrations.
- Bring a camera, film, and negatives with pictures and enlargements from the negatives. A photo album might also be a good visual aid.
- Try to locate a photographer or a parent proficient in photography who might come and demonstrate some of the precepts in the concept and show a student a number of different cameras. Experiencing the Polaroid camera might be interesting to some students.

Teaching suggestions
- Show the children a photograph and ask them if they know how the picture was made. Discuss the input of the class and then show them a panel containing a picture, its negative, an enlargement, a picture of a camera, and a picture of the viewfinder, the shutter, and film. Ask who can tell us which of these things comes first in creating a photograph?
- When the steps are in order: film, film loaded, look through viewfinder, press shutter, process film (getting a

negative), printing the photograph, and making an enlargement, discuss the role of film in their life.
- "Identify what the negative in a color slide is." (The slide is the negative.) "Why do photographers use a tripod?" "What happens to the negative in a polaroid camera?" (It is the part you throw away.) "Why are photographs important in our lives?" (Permanent records, historical, illustrations in books, TV, newspaper, our driver's license photo for identification, passport photos, mapping the world from satellites, seeing things through a micro photograph and seeing things that are in places we can never get to.)
- Discuss the role of the artist in interpreting subjects that might be photographed, how photographers and artists describe feelings or moods in pictures, why artists distort things, and whether or not photographers can do that too. "How are their roles different?" (The photographer has to deal with tangible things that really exist; whereas the artist can draw from his own mind or imagination.)

Suggested art activity
Let each student participate in some aspect of picture taking: looking through the viewfinder, loading or unloading film, taking a picture with a box camera, a slide camera, or a polaroid.

Alternative art activities
- Take a field trip to some location where there is a photographer's dark room.
- Have a photographer come to class to show the students his equipment and demonstrate as much as he can.

Evaluation

The verbal responses of individual students would be the major source for determining whether or not the objective had been achieved.

Other things to consider

- Vocabulary: viewfinder, film, negative, transparency, enlargement, shutter, lens, tripod, slide, camera, photography, and processing film.
- Books:
  The Little Elephant by Ylla
  I'll Show You Cats by Ylla
  ABC Picture Book by George Adams and Paul Hemming
  The Duck by Margaret Wise Brown
  Micki the Baby Fox by A. Bergman
- People who might have need for the concept: photographers, lay people.

LEVEL 2

ACTIVITY 53

Concept taught by this activity: The child is able to distinguish between a photograph and a painting or drawing.

Objective: The child can distinguish between paintings or drawings and similar subjects in photographs.

A sample lesson plan for achieving the objective:

Teacher preparations

■ Display examples of photographers and paintings of the same subject or the same individual. See if students have had a portrait of themselves drawn or painted that they might bring to school.

■ Have books available either from the list at the end of the activity or from the library and composed in a way similar to the suggested list. Use resources first which allow the child to distinguish easily between photographs and drawings or paintings.

Teaching suggestions

■ Begin with a discussion of how photographs, paintings, and drawings differ from each other: how they are created, the media used, and the tools or equipment needed. "What are the ways they're alike?" "Different?"

■ Discuss which types are easily distinguished from one another and which are more difficult.

■ Discuss how the photographer has to use actual subjects that are already there, while artists can work from their imagination. Students should conclude that when the artist works directly from a model, his product looks more like a photograph.

■ Show students examples of photographs and paintings. Discuss the differences and similarities of each. Have students select from a variety of pictures and decide which are photographs.

■ Help students to recognize that photographs usually have no brush strokes showing or textures that you can feel. They sometimes enable the viewer to see details more sharply.

■ Studying prints: Note that each is a photograph or a painting. Discuss which ones seem most like a photograph and why.

Suggested art activity

Have students look for examples of paintings and photography in magazines and see if they can create displays of each. Discuss the criteria they used for separating the two kinds of art.

Alternative art activities

Have students find examples of photographs of faces in magazines, cut in half vertically. Have them paste half onto a new sheet, then *draw* the missing half by sketching from the part cut off *and* the part saved.

Evaluation

When the student can look closely at a photograph that looks like a painting, or vice versa, and is able to attach the correct label to it, he has achieved the objective.

Other things to consider

- Vocabulary: photograph, painting, drawing, similarities, and categorize.
- Prints:
  Turning the Stake by Eakins
  The Smokers by Brouwer
  Seven AM by Hopper
  The Gleaners by Millet
  Le Moulen de la Galette by Renoir
  The Card Players by Cezanne
  Iliad Study by Ingres
  Self Portrait with Bandaged Ear by Van Gogh
  Fighting Horses by Gericoult
  Still Life Le Jour by Braque
  Mother and Child by Kollwitz
  Man in the Golden Helmet by Rembrandt
- Books:

with drawings and paintings	with photographs
Horton the Elephant by Dr. Suess	*The Little Elephant* by Ylla
The Story of Babar the Little Elephant by Jean de Brunhoff	*Mamba-kan* by Vitold de Golish
Ella the Elephant by Bill Pelt	
Smudge by Clare Newberry	*I'll Show You Cats* by Ylla
Marshmallow by Clare Newberry	*Curious Kittens* by Peggy L. Irwin
Pandora by Clare Newberry	
Green Eyes by A. Birbaum	
Millions of Cats by Wanda	
Hosie's Alphabet by Leonard Baskin and Hosea	*ABC Picture Book* by George Adams and Paul Hemming
Make Way for Ducklings by Robert McCloskey	*The Duck* by Margaret W. Brown
The Tomten and the Fox by Astrid Lindgren	*Micki the Baby Fox* by A. Bergman
Little Fur Family by Margaret Wise Brown	*Two Little Bears* by Ylla
The Biggest Bear by Lynn Ward	
Brian Wildsmith's Circus by Brian Wildsmith	*Here's Jellybean Reilly* by Ylla
Moja Means One by Muriel Feelings	*Primitive and His Dog* by Floria Hoffman
Seashore Story by Taro Yashima	

LEVEL 2   ACTIVITY 54

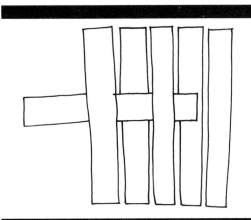

Concept taught by this activity: The student should now have experience with simple processes in weaving.

Objective: The student can utilize simple processes in weaving.

A sample lesson plan for achieving the objective:

Teacher preparations
- Become familiar with the weaving process to be taught.
- Collect materials for the weaving activity.
- Locate illustrations or examples of the kinds of things students might do once the concept has been learned.
- Draw the "weaving" visual as seen under "Teaching suggestions" below.

Teaching suggestions
- "Tell me all of the things you can that have this pattern — or that look like this —"
(Fences, burlap, my shirt, my dress, baskets, hats, etc.)

- "Tell me all of the uses you can think of for knowing how to weave." (Weaving. The harness loom and the power loom are used by technicians and professional weavers but are not at all necessary for the experiences children need to learn in simple weaving processes. The weaving process is simple, one of interlacing threads at right angles to each other. The vertical threads that make the structural "skeleton" for weaving are called the warp and the horizontal fibers that are woven through the warp are called the weft.)

Suggested art activity
Paper Weaving. Simple hand looms can be used by children, but their initial experience requires only paper, scissors, a stapler, and paste.
- Rule a line across a piece of paper about one-half inch down from the top to serve as a margin; then cut strips of equal or unequal widths, stopping at the margin. These strips become the warp. Separate strips of paper are cut to serve as the weft, and they are passed over and under the warp. Alternate strips so that one strip goes over the warp while the other goes under.
- Variations may be created by making all sorts of shapes and patterns with the warp. Here the warp controls the pattern.
- Another variation is to have the weft control the pattern or design. Weave over-and-under different combinations of strips. For example, weave over-one, under-two, over-three, under-two, or over-one and under-three. Weave narrower strips of contrasting colors over previously woven weft.
- Use paint, crayon, yarn, string, or fabric to accent woven areas. Use weaving to add interest to cut out figures of animals.

Alternative art activities
- *Weaving into scrim* (also cotton mesh, burlap, or wire)
  - Weave spontaneously into the scrim material with yarn.
  - Trace a design or picture onto the scrim with a crayon or felt tip pen and weave over and under the scrim fibers to outline the shapes or to fill in solid areas.
- *Weaving on cardboard*
  - Cut a piece of stiff cardboard and notch the top and bottom edges at irregular or regular intervals. Run the warp threads or yarn up and down, passing through the notches. Create the design by weaving over and under with the weft threads. The finished design can either be left on the frame or removed. A number of pieces can be sewed together to make one large piece.
  - Variations
- Use a shoe box or gift box lid for your frame for a shadow-box effect.
- Leave open spaces with the warp.

- Experiment with different loop techniques (loops are formed by lifting the weft or alternate warp threads and inserting a rod, stick, or brush handle).
- Use straight pins to hold the warp rather than notches.

Evaluation

When the student has demonstrated an understanding of simple weaving processes, the objective has been achieved.

Other things to consider

- Vocabulary: weaving, loom, warp, weft, scrim.
- Art materials needed: construction paper, crepe paper, raffia, drinking straws, cardboard looms, string, rug yarn, weeds, and assorted fabrics, crayons, scissors, paste, and stapler.
- People who might have need for the concept: macrame artists, people that work in the textile industry.

LEVEL 2

Concept taught by this activity: The student should now have experiences with simple processes in stitchery and applique.

Objective: The student can utilize simple processes in stitchery and applique.

A sample lesson plan for achieving the objective:

Teacher preparations

■ Read through the entire outline to become familiar with the terms, materials, and processes suggested. Determine which activities will be most appropriate in providing your students with a keen awareness of processes in stitchery and applique.

■ Collect the equipment and materials you will need. Have samples and illustrations of works by both children and professionals that show the learner what has been done by others who used the processes that they are learning about.

■ Six strand embroidery floss or twisted pearl cotton numbers 3, 5, or 8 are good to begin with. Ordinary string or twine is also adequate for the beginner. Fabrics that ravel need a line of strong glue around the edges or fine machine stitching. Metal screen should be taped along the edges to prevent scratches or cuts.

Teaching suggestions

Begin with a discussion of what fabrics or textiles are, what kinds of things are made from them, and how they are decorated. Direct students toward a discussion of terms such as stitchery, applique, knitting, embroidery, needle-point, and weaving. Discuss what experiences they or their family may have had with these processes. Look at and discuss some of the things children and professionals have created with the materials and processes they will be learning about.

Suggested art activity

It is wise for the beginner to learn first to draw with thread and to experiment with different sizes and kinds on a variety

of surfaces. There are dictionaries of stitches and many give explicit instructions which are easy to follow. But before these resources are used, children should have opportunities to take a basic stitch and then experiment with it and all sorts of variations they may wish to try. Activities at the experimental stage might include:

■ Making yarn pictures by pasting yarn to paper or board.

■ Weaving or stitching thread or yarn on some kind of meshwork such as rigid hardware cloth, onion sacking, plastic screen, or other open-weave fabrics.

■ Making a "God's Eye" by twisting yarn around crossed twigs or sticks. (An Indian design in a "plus" shape Note: Applique is the processes of gluing or stitching contrasting paper or fabric to a background. These pieces may represent parts of objects or total objects.

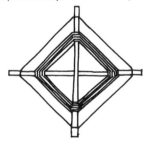

Alternative art activities

■ When the child has learned to thread a large-eyed needle, additional kinds of experiences are advisable. These might include the following activities:
Sewing on paper by outlining drawings or on thin tagboard or railroad board (by first making perforations) are excellent ways of initiating the child to many possibilities of stitching.

When the needle is threaded, tie a knot at one end and bring the needle through the back of the fabric, and you are ready to go. Keep the tension on the thread even so that the fabric doesn't warp, pucker, or sag. Have the thread about twice the length of the child's arm. If you always refer to the process as stitchery rather than embroidery, the boys will enjoy the activity too.

Pull one end of your yarn or string through a box of soft soap to stiffen the thread and make it easier to run through the eye of a needle.
- On a background of burlap or another loosely woven fabric, make a picture or design with crayon. With contrasting yarn, using a large tapestry needle, stitch and applique the design in a variety of stitches.
- Things to make or decorate:
Place mats, hot pads, marble bags, circular mats, purses, baskets, wall hangings, aprons, towels, pillow covers, hats, caps, scarves, rugs, and slippers.

Evaluation

When the student has been able to demonstrate an understanding of stitchery and applique processes, the objective of this lesson has been achieved.

Other things to consider

- Vocabulary: stitchery, applique, sewing, threading a needle, stitches, yarn, thread, needle.
- Art materials needed: papers, fabrics, drapery and curtain materials, scrim, plastic screen, burlap, cheese cloth, oak tag, railroad and tapestry board, thread, string, cord, rug yarn, knitting yarn, twine, found objects, dowel stick or bamboo, crayons, scissors, paste, stapler, felt-tip pens, hoops, felt, pellon, tarletan, daisy mesh, onion sacking, and remnants or scraps. Needles — pointed end: darning 5/0 — 1/0 upholstery or sail (curved) and chenille for finer work; blunt end: tapestry #s 20 to 13 (large eyes)
- Resources:
Dictionary of Embroidery Stitches, 1961
    Women's Day Magazine
    P.O. Box 1000, Dept. WDL
    Greenwich, Conn. 06830
Wall Chart
    Basic Stitches for Creative Stitchery
    Educational Division
    Lily Mills
    Shelby, North Carolina
One Hundred Embroidery Stitches, 1964
    Coats and Blarks Book #105
    Coats and Clarks Sales Corp.
    430 Park Avenue
    New York, New York 10022

LEVEL 2

ACTIVITY 56

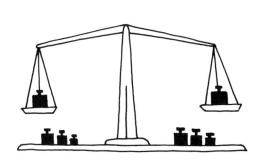

Concept taught by this activity: Balance can be achieved (actual weight).

Objective: The student will demonstrate the ability to balance objects of equal or unequal weight.

A sample lesson plan for achieving the objective:

Teacher preparations
Have access to such things as:
- A playground teeter-totter
- A mobile hanging in the room, along with pictures of mobiles
- A bathroom scale and a balance scale
- Blocks, tinker toys, and other objects of various sizes and weights
- Prints and other pictures as suggested by the concept.

Teaching suggestions
- Hold up two objects, one heavy, one light. Ask: "Which one is heaviest?" "Which one is lightest?"
- If a teeter-totter is available, introduce the concept with questions such as: "How many of you like to play on a teeter-totter (or seesaw)?" "What happens to your fun when someone a lot heavier than you gets on the other end?" "Have you ever been on a teeter-totter with someone who weighed just about the same as you?" (Teeter-totter will balance if no one moves or kicks his feet.)
- "How many of you have ever seen a balance scale or a fulcrum?" "What is it used for?" "If I had a ball (or some other object) on this side and I knew that it weighed one-half pound, and I kept adding buttons (or some other smaller objects) to this side until the scale balanced, what would I know about the weight of the buttons?"

- "Have any of you seen a scale like this used in stores?" (Commonly used to weigh candy, nuts, and other foods.)
- "If I had a large scale or fulcrum and I wanted to balance two things on it, how would I do that?" "What does balance mean then?"
- Let the children try balancing several objects on the scale.
- Discuss how disturbing it is to see pictures hanging crooked on a wall and our natural impulse to straighten or balance them. Discuss prints of artists and what they have done to create balance or a "feeling" of balance. Pictures of buildings and rooms could also be used as part of this kind of discussion.
- Discuss the math concept:
  Both sides of an equation must balance or be equal. 16 oz. = 1 lb.; 5 pennies = 1 nickel

Suggested art activity
Have the children experience balancing by
- Exerimenting with the teeter-totter on their playground and having smaller students try to balance larger ones
- Piling up blocks or tinker toys in various arrangements that look balanced
- Walking a balance beam, or standing on one foot, or standing on a narrow ledge. Discuss the high-wire man of the circus and how he sometimes uses a pole to help him balance.

Alternative art activities
- Discuss the problems of balance that were involved in the designing of a mobile. Refer to an actual one if possible, or a series of pictures. Make a simple mobile. This could even be a small group activity.
- Have cutouts of furniture with the outline of a room. Have children try to create a balanced arrangement.

Evaluation

Be aware of individual student responses to the point that you know when each has developed an awareness of the concept. At this level we are only concerned about the child's awareness. He need not be able to apply the concept in art at this point.

Other things to consider

- Vocabulary: balance, balance scale, balance beam, fulcrum, unbalanced.
- Art materials needed: balance scale or fulcrum, balance beam, photographs of interiors, buildings, nature, and shapes representing articles of furniture scaled to the outline of a room.
- Prints:
  Three Flags by Johns
  Card Players by Cezanne
  The Brooklyn Bridge by Stella
  Adoration of the Magi by Botticelli
  The Small Crucifixion by Grunewald
  Apples and Oranges by Cezanne
  Blindman's Bluff by Fragonard
  Fur Traders on the Missouri by Bingham
  Fox Island by Hartley
- People who might have need for the concept: puppeteers, mosaic artists, fabric designers, architects, interior designers, landscape architects, city planners, sculptors, photographers, painters, commercial artists, printmakers.

LEVEL 2

ACTIVITY 57

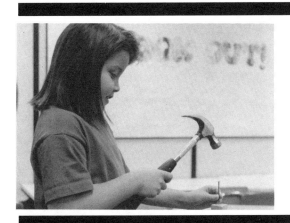

Concept taught by this activity: The child is able to create art objects as part of his experiencing simple processes in gluing, pasting, nailing, hinging, sewing, and sticking.

Objective: The child can utilize simple processes in gluing, pasting, nailing, hinging, sewing, or sticking in creating an art object.

A sample lesson plan for achieving the objective:

Teacher preparations
NOTE: Read through the entire outline to familiarize yourself with the terms, materials, and processes suggested. Determine which materials will be most appropriate for providing your students with a good awareness of the processes involved in gluing, pasting, nailing, hinging, sewing, or sticking.
■ Have available examples by children and professionals, either actual objects or photographs of such.
■ Determine which activities will be best suited for what your students need to know about the processes in this lesson, and assemble everything needed for the experience.
■ Make certain that controls are understood so that order is maintained in the classroom. There should be a system for stationing each adhesive or fastener which the student might wish to use. Some rules may be necessary to protect the floors and desks and the children's clothing. Be certain that children are not limited in what they might make. Encourage great diversity in what they create.

Teaching suggestions
NOTE: The processes involved in this activity are those the child can use to attach or join one material to another. The processes are aimed at the making of collages and constructions (sculpture). The processes involve the use of adhesives such as staples, white glue, wheat paste, school paste, rubber cement, scotch and masking tape,

pins, paper clips, string, brads, fasteners, and nails (all sorts). As part of a discussion, the teacher may wish to list or itemize the kinds of things that can be used to fasten materials together, then inventory students as to which they have used or not used. One major objective of ths activity is to create an awareness of how many different kinds of fasteners or adhesives are used in the child's world.
■ "What are all the ways you could fasten paper to wood?" "What could you use to fasten these toothpicks?" (See "NOTE" above.)
■ "What are all the things you could make with *these* objects?" (Hold up anything you have for them to use, such as straws, toothpicks, paper, balsa wood, cardboard, sticks, all kinds of scraps of any materials.)

Suggested art activity
Paper sack puppets (stuffed or open) that are decorated with hair, lashes, or hats; box and tube animals.

Alternative art activities
■ Toothpick or drinking straw structures
■ Wood scrap structures or designs
■ Cut cardboard constructions or designs
■ Cylinder cities
■ Stick sculpture
■ Collages or paper appliques
With paper, don't teach techniques on folding, scoring, and similar activities that are commonly associated with paper sculpture; this will be accomplished in a subsequent activity.

Make details and decorate objects, sculpture, constructions, or designs by attaching such things as buttons, yarn, cellophane, confetti, seeds, feathers, net, material remnants, fur, rubber scraps, leather scraps, bottle caps, corks, hairpins, pipe cleaners, reeds, sequins, glitter, ribbon, various objects, and crepe or tissue paper. Paint with tempera or watercolor.

Evaluation

When it appears that each learner has had experience with attaching materials together with at least seven of the

thirteen adhesives and fasteners suggested earlier, the
objective has been achieved.

Other things to consider

- Vocabulary: adhesive, join, fasten, attach, hinge,
  construction, sculpture, collage.
- Art materials needed: See list suggested within the outline.
- People who might have need for the concept: sculptors,
  commercial artists of all types, assemblage artists, collage
  artists.

LEVEL 2   ACTIVITY 58

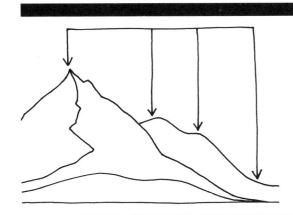

Concept taught by this activity: The sky touches the earth.

Objective: The student will paint or color all the way down to the horizon line where heretofore it was just a strip across the top of the picture.

A sample lesson plan for achieving the objective:

Teacher preparations
■ Pictures showing the horizon line should be ready and displayed.
■ Magazines for the children to find "sky pictures" in should be ready.

Teaching suggestions
■ Introduce discussion about the sky with questions such as the following: "What is the sky made of?" "What color is it?" "Why is it blue?" "Where is the sky?" "Is it both up and down?"
  ● "Take a walk and look at the sky. Discover its shades of blue and how the blue goes all the way down to the earth. "Is there any white space?" "What colors have you seen in the sky?" "Can you see sky through a tree?"
  ● Show and discuss pictures of skies. Show cut-out pictures with the earth only. Put this in front of different pieces of colored construction paper (blue, gray, black, light blue, and white). Discover and discuss why the white doesn't seem natural as a background for the earth.
■ Look at prints and discuss where the artists have sky showing in their pictures. "Is the sky just at the top of the picture?" "Does the sky show through the trees?" "Does it appear to be going behind the mountains?" "Behind the houses?"

Suggested art activity
Give each student some white paper. Have him draw houses, trees, mountains, and whatever on the paper. Then, have him use a sky color. Color the very top of the paper only. Discuss ways the sky may not look right. Color the rest of the way down, using the side of the crayon to cover up the white (except for clouds). Discuss whether or not his sky looks like the sky outside and the sky in artists' paintings.

Alternative art activities
■ Make a science project and create sunsets with dust particles and light rays.
■ Draw the horizon, trees, and objects on top of a blue background. Use black or dark crayons for the drawings.
■ Use a flannel board with the sky and earth painted on and put objects on the flannel in front of the sky and grass. Add some mountains of construction paper; add trees and other objects.
■ Make shoe box diaramas with the sky down the back of the box.
■ Make a booklet showing different skies.

Evaluation

The student's own work is the best source for evaluation. If the student goes back to making sky just at the top of the page, the concept will need to be taught again or reinforced.

Other things to consider

■ Vocabulary: horizon, perspective, ground level, placement, realistic.
■ Art materials needed: magazines, art paper, glue, scissors, paint and crayons.
■ Prints:
  Venice by Canaletto
  Fur Traders Descending the Missouri by Bingham
  Oath of the Horatii by David

Notre Dame by Daumier
La Grande Jatte by Seurat
- People who might have need for the concept: any artists that do drawings, prints, paintings, or illustrations.

LEVEL 2   ACTIVITY 59

Concept taught by this activity: Perpendicular objects can be related to the ground. In creating illusions of depth, figures or objects can be placed in positions other than a straight line.

Objective: The student draws and paints objects perpendicular to the ground line, and he places figures and objects in positions other than just on the base line.

A sample lesson plan for achieving the objective:

Teacher preparations
NOTE: The child at this level typically lines up objects on a base line and draws chimneys perpendicular to the sloped roof. This is a natural stage in the child's development but a misconcept if he wants to show depth in his picture or to describe what he sees or has experienced. Pertinent activities can develop the child's awareness that he has other alternatives in solving his drawing problems.

- Display several pictures showing depth: a grove of trees (overlapping), a city showing buildings far and near, a group of people showing nearness and distance.
- Have some steps available for use, a box with boards slanting down each side at an angle to the floor, and pictures of classroom groups.

- Also have other visual material, such as a farm set and figures to place on peg board sticks or flannel board.

Teaching suggestions
- Have students stand in a straight line before the class and other students on a slanted vertical line. Discuss how they would be drawn. Ask questions such as: "Who is nearest to you?" "Who is the farthest away from you?" "How does your position in the room affect how you see the students?"

- Use a farm set to arrange a scene on the farm. Have children help place the objects in the desired positions. Point out that the animals and buildings are not in a straight line. Ask questions so that the students come to the conclusion.
- Have children arrange a playground scene on a flannel board or peg board and question class about the placement.
- Cover the window with strips of paper and as each is peeled off, have students describe what is seen. Note that what they saw was at all different heights in the window and not in a row across the *bottom*.

- Draw on a window with a water soluble magic marker (that will easily wash off). Show the variety of objects seen outside by tracing their shape on the window pane, pursue the same kinds of questions relative to the positions of things in relation to each other. "How can we make *our* pictures more like this?" is a question that should be asked along the way. Looking at slides or stopping a scene in a movie could serve as another resource for questioning.

- Put a box in the front of the room with two boards slanting to the floor at an angle. Have the children stand on the boards and discuss whether or not they feel a need to stand perpendicular to the earth rather than at an angle away from the board. (A transfer must occur that a chimney has "the same problem.")

- Go outside on a walk and observe buildings, trees, cars, and other objects and have children point out areas of depth and the relationship of the objects to each other and the ground.

- Show pictures of class groups showing everyone standing at a different level in relation to the camera and the floor. Then take a picture of people standing in a straight line at the base of the picture and compare the two by having children point out the specific differences. Ask questions such as: "Can you see the feet of the people on the second row?" "Can you see the feet of the people on the third row?" "Why or why not?" (Bring out the answer that some are standing behind others and cannot be completely seen.)

- Look at art prints and discuss how the impact or feeling of each picture would change should the figures be "lined up" instead of shown in "natural" positions. Why has the artist

  placed this figure here? or here? Why aren't they all the same size? Why aren't they all in the same place?
- Have the children draw or paint the sky or perhaps a minimum amount of background. Then cut people and objects from magazines and paste on paper (collage or montage).

Suggested art activity
Draw or paint a picture that includes a number of people involved in some physical activity. Include mountains with trees on them or houses with chimneys.

Alternative art activities
- With clay build a mountain. Have children place popsicle sticks made to look like trees in the mountain, showing that they are perpendicular to the earth and not growing at an angle.
- Have "contests" (on a tumbling mat or soft surface) to see who can lean the most without falling over. (Make sure

  transfer occurs relative to leaning away from the *vertical*.)

Evaluation

When the student demonstrates a change in his awareness of how objects can be arranged in a picture and draws such things as trees perpendicular to the earth rather than to the slope of a mountain, the objective has been achieved.

Other things to consider

- Vocabulary: depth perception, perpendicular, perspective, diarama, illusion.
- Art materials needed: clay and popsicle sticks, cardboard box, construction paper, tempera paint or water colors, crayons, scissors, and glue.
- Prints:
  The Harvesters by Brueghel
  The Numbering at Bethlehem by Brueghel
  An Afternoon at La Grande Jatte by Seurat
  Christina's World by Wyeth
  Apples and Oranges by Cezanne
  Le Moulin de la Galette by Renoir
  Tranquility by Gasser
  House at Aix by Cezanne

LEVEL 2   ACTIVITY 60

Concept taught by this activity: People and objects vary in size.

Objective: The student will draw people and objects with an indication of their natural size relationship: father taller than child, and other relationships.

A sample lesson plan for achieving the objective:

Teacher preparations
- Collect prints and pictures that illustrate the concept.
- Collect reference and library books helpful in teaching or reinforcing the concept.
- Arrange for film and equipment if desired.
- Acquaint the class with the concept of measuring so that each can compare his height to other things and people.

Teaching suggestions
- Introduce the concept through a question and discussion session. Ask questions such as: "What are all the big things you can think of?" "What are all the tiny things you can think of?"
  - "What does *big* and *little*, or *large* and *small* mean?"
  - "Why aren't all things the same size?" "What would happen if they were?"
  - "How does it make you feel to stand beside someone or something that is much larger than you?"
  - "How can you show how it feels to be as small as an ant?" "As tall as a giraffe?"
  - "How do you compare in size with animals in the zoo?"
  - "Does size have anything to do with what kind of a person you are?" (It is important to teach students that bigness or smallness has nothing to do with "goodness.")

- If available, read and discuss a book such as *Let's Find Out What's Big and What's Small*. (Good introduction for comparing sizes.)
- Read books such as *Animal Babies* / or *The Little Elephant,* and discuss the size relationships of the mothers with their babies.
- Compare sizes of things in the room, such as children, teacher; teacher's desk, children's desks; teacher's chair, children's chairs.
- Go for a walk outside. Let one child stand by the school building and let others see the difference in the size of the child and the building. Then as you walk, compare sizes of buildings, cars, trees, and other people.
- Have a group of students direct others in the class in lining up according to size.
- Show and discuss sizes of things in suggested art prints.
- Discuss these related concepts.
  - The kind and amounts of food eaten affect the size of people during their growing years (health), but not as much as their family history (genetics).
  - Comparison of objects can be used to develop an intuitive feeling for length and size (math).
  - Opposites — big, little; large, small; tall, short (reading).

Suggested art activity
Have the children trace around each other on butcher paper. Invite room mothers or students in to help and draw them also. Compare sizes of children and adults. Put the tracings up around the room and let the children guess who is who.

Alternative art activities
- Read the book *Big Tracks, Little Tracks.* Make children's footprints by dipping their feet in tempera paint. If desired, have them dip their feet in water and have them do outlines with pencil before their feet dry. Do your own feet or another adult's. Compare.
- Read the book, *Little Girl and Her Mother.* Compare sizes. Then give each child two pieces of paper, one 9 × 12", the other 12 × 13", and have them make a 9 × 12" of themselves and a 12 × 18" of one of their parents.

- Have the class respond as the teacher lists on the board *larger* or *smaller* than class members. Make sure the class understands you are referring to the real thing.
- Have the students sketch properly sized silhouettes of the members of his family.

Evaluation

When the student demonstrates an ability to draw the size relationships of common things in his environment more accurately, the objective has been achieved. Verbal responses are additional evidence as to how well the concept has been learned.

Other things to consider

- Vocabulary: size, height, tall, short, big, little, compare.
- Art materials needed: paper, crayons, tempera paint, clay.
- Prints:
  I and the Village by Chagall
  The Life of a Hunter by Currier and Ives
  Three Horses by Marc
  Madame Fourment and her Children by Rubens
  Music at Tuileries by Manet
  Family of Saltimbanques by Picasso
  The Oyster Gatherers of Cancale by Sargent
  Children at the Sea Shore by Renoir
  Ville d'Avry by Corot
  Ballet Encore by Degas
  The Hay Wain by Constable
  La Bachanale by Corot
  The Harvesters by Brueghel
  Ground Hog Day by Wyeth
- Books:
  Big Tracks, Little Tracks by Franklin M. Branley
  Let's Find Out What's Big and What's Small by Martha and
    Charles Shapp
  Little Girl and Her Mother by Beatrice Schenk De Regniers
  Animal Babies by Tony Palazzo
  The Little Elephant by Arthur Greger
  Size, Distance, Weight, a First Look at Measuring by Solveig
    Paulson Russell
- People who might have need for the concept: puppet makers, mosaic artists, architects, interior designers, landscape architects, painters, printmakers.

LEVEL 2

ACTIVITY 61

Concept taught by this activity: Lines can be used to separate one object or shape from another. When shapes are repeated in regular or irregular sequences pattern is created.

Objective: The student uses lines to separate objects or shapes from one another and is able to create patterns by repeating the shapes.

A sample lesson plan for achieving the objective:

Teacher preparations
Recognize that the line is an artistic device that is often used to separate parts or objects in pictures. In reality, lines are really objects such as string and thread, or spaces such as cracks between boards. When some things are seen in the distance, they appear line-like, such as branches of a tree. In this exercise we are assuming the child does not as yet use lines in separating forms and has not yet recognized he can separate parts of objects from each other with lines or can create contrasts with lines as they encircle objects or their parts.
- Collect samples of pattern in clothing, wallpaper, and other figured materials. Display them or have them accessible along with prints. Collect examples of line used as "outline."
- Have materials for drawing and painting available. Provide several choices for children.
- Have a walk planned for outside the school building area. Be certain that the walk will take the students past numerous examples of line and pattern.

Teaching suggestions
- The concept may be introduced in a discussion that might go like this: "Can anyone tell me what a line is?" "How many kinds of lines can you find in this room?" "Outside?" "Are lines used in pictures by artists?" "Are they used in homes, buildings or sculpture?" "What are some examples you can see or that you know about?" "Would you agree

that there are lots of different kinds of lines?" "Is that true of lines in pictures?" "If you took all of the lines out of a picture, what would it do to it?" "Does anyone know what the word *contrast* means?" (Explore the meaning until it is understood.) "If contrast means that one thing is different from another (stands out), do lines ever create contrast?" "How?" "Why would an artist want contrast?"
- "How many know what a *shape* is?" "Is this a shape?" "Is this?" "How about this one?" "Or this one?" (A line can make a shape, but it has to be closed in.) "Are there different shapes in this room?" "How many can we name?" "Are lines needed to make *all* shapes?" "What about your own clothing; are there lines and shapes there?"
- "Which of you knows what a pattern is?" "Does your mother ever do any sewing and use a pattern?" "What does it mean to pattern your life after someone?" "In art, a pattern is like a design — it's usually a shape that is repeated over and over, either in the same way or with differences each time." "Are there any *patterns* in this room?" "Who can name them?"
- "Do artists use pattern in their pictures?" "Did this artist?" Look at suggested prints and discuss patterns they observe. Push them to see more and more pattern. Extend their awareness as far as possible.
- What are patterns used for? (Decoration and protection as in the story of *How the Leopard Got His Spots*)
- Look through a kaleidoscope. See new patterns in the surroundings of the school and classroom.
- Take the children on a walk through and around the building. Discuss whatever patterns they see and draw them to the attention of the group by reinforcing the students' perceptiveness. Discuss the role of line in pattern or in "outlining."

Suggested art activity
Have students draw or paint some subject that contains examples of pattern and of shapes outlined with line. Make a special effort to reward the most *unusual* solutions (not necessarily the "best" ones) — those that are unique.

Alternative art activities

- Arrange colored string on a tack board. Let the children experiment and see how many kinds of lines can be made.
- "Draw an object on paper; see how many kinds of lines you can use inside it." (Straight, circle, curved, wavy, curlicues, zig-zag.)
- "Discuss how artists make your head, ear, arm, legs, body. Discuss how lines seem to separate one part of the body from another."
- Pick out patterns or designs in clothes. Study their detail and discuss how lines separate one shape from another. "What kind of a line made this tree," "house," "doll," "strawberry."
- Tell the story of *The Calico Cat*. Look at samples of pattern in fabric. Have children create their own versions of the Calico Cat.[1]
- Have students trace each other's outlines on large pieces of paper; then have each individual complete a detailed line drawing (portrait) of himself and conclude with patterns created for the different articles of clothing he is wearing.
- Discuss the natural marking of animals and do a picture showing patterns seen on various animals. The student might enjoy mixing odd patterns with animals that are normally rather plain.
- Create patterns by imprinting with gadgets or other objects.

Evaluation

Along with noting the individual verbal responses of students, assess their comprehension by their drawings or paintings highly motivated and generating a use of the concept.

Other things to consider

- Vocabulary: pattern, shape, design, print, printmaking, motif, linear, line, outline, contrast, separate, form.
- Art materials needed: drawing and painting media, other objects and gadgets for imprinting, paper and scissors.
- Stories:
  How the Leopard Got His Spots by Kipling
  The Gingham Dog and Calico Cat
- Prints:
  Jungle Scene with Setting Sun by Rousseau
  Portrait of Frances the 1st by Clouet
  Combination Concrete by Davis
  Still Music by Shahn
  The Letter by Vermeer
  Flowers and Parrots by Matisse
  The Aficionado by Picasso
  Poster — Jan. 18 to Feb. 12 by Shahn
  Cheyt M. by Vasarely

- People who might have need for the concept: puppet makers, mosaic artists, batik and tie-dye artists, fabric designers, craftsmen that work in leather, jewelry, wood, glass, macrame, and weaving; sculptors, architects, interior designers, landscape architects, city planners, painters, commercial artists, printmakers.

---

[1] "The Duel," *Poems and Rhymes* (Childcraft: The How and Why Library, 1975), p. 237.

LEVEL 2   ACTIVITY 62

Concept taught by this activity: The child uses lines, dots, and shapes to create patterns and the illusion of common textures by imprinting.

Objective: The child creates pattern and the illusion of common textures by imprinting.

A sample lesson plan for achieving the objective:

Teacher preparations
- Collect samples of repeat designs and display them.
- Collect a variety of kitchen gadgets that could be used for imprinting interesting shapes. Arrange a display of fruits and vegetables cut in half and thick tempera paint ready for imprinting.
- Have the children in paint shirts and make certain that each individual understands the need to follow good housekeeping rules. Have the dispensing of paint organized and all surfaces covered to protect them. For example, if the paint is mixed, the paper cut, and everything ready before the children arrive, the problems are minimized. Have ready the container for the paint that children dip objects into, and know how the children will use it. When the children arrive go over such rules as the following:
  - Paint shirts must be on and buttoned with sleeves rolled up.
  - Desks and tables must be covered with newspaper.
  - Four desks must be pushed together or a table set up with the paint in the center.

  Be certain the container is large enough to dip the object into, yet low enough not to tip over (a pie tin or pyrex baking dish). Keep the paint shallow and *don't* pour it until they are ready to start.
- If the teacher feels control is a factor, he may limit the activity to one table where the children come one group at a time while the others are involved in some other activity.

- Caution children not to bite or eat the fruit with paint on it.
- Have a damp paper towel for the children to clean their fingers with, and give directions as to what they do with their pictures at the end and that the *teacher* will take care of the paint.

Teaching suggestions
- Review what the children know about the words *repeat* and *print*. Relate the word *print* to *imprint*.
- Talk about their experiences in leaving footprints or handprints in the sand or mud, and such things as a dog leaving footprints on mother's clean floor.
- Begin the activity.

  - Show the children some of the objects that can be used for the imprinting activity and discuss whether or not they can see how the object's pattern might be transferred to paper. Discuss the pattern each object has when it is cut in half or in fourths.
  - Be sure that children know how many they can do and what they do with papers if they make more than one.
  - Encourage the formation of repeat patterns, and allow children to select two or more objects to experiment with.
  - When everyone is ready and properly motivated, pour the paint into the pans, then circulate among the class encouraging and motivating. Let a group start whenever their paint is poured.

- Compare their prints with patterns and textures created by artists (display on walls). Note with children that the textures they have created on paper have not altered the "feel" of the surface and are basically *illusions* of texture.

Suggested art activity
Create a repeat design, using the imprinting method and tools, such as kitchen gadgets or sections of fruit and vegetables.

Alternate art activities

Allow students to create *line* textures by drawing as many different repeat shapes as possible in one-inch squares.

Evaluation

If the child has experienced imprinting on paper that creates illusions of texture and pattern, the objective of the lesson has been achieved. Reward the most *unusual* creations in some way, if only with *attention*.

Other things to consider

- Vocabulary: illusion, texture, imprint, pattern.
- Art materials needed: tempera paint, a variety of papers, and materials for imprinting.
- Prints:
  Le Jour by Braque
  Frances I by Clouet
  Justice and Peace by Overstreet
  Marilyn Monroe by Warhol
  Zebegen by Vasarely
- People who might have need for the concept: printers, graphic artists, printmakers.

LEVEL 2   ACTIVITY 63

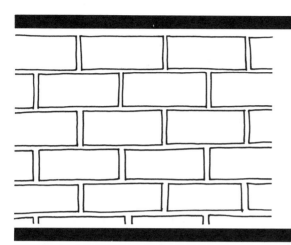

Concept taught by this activity: The illusion of common textures can be created with lines, dots, and shapes: textures such as bricks, grass, shingles, and hair. (Builds on concepts 32, 43, 44, 61, and 62.)

Objective: The student uses a variety of lines or dots, or combinations of both to create the illusion of textures such as brick, grass, shingles, and hair.

A sample lesson plan for achieving the objective:

Teacher preparations

Display art prints and photographs of objects having texture. Use those which "fit" the concept. Have samples of sandpaper and fur of some sort.

Teaching suggestions

■ In reviewing exercises in texture (packet 2), both teacher and student should note that when they were doing rubbings of texture, the rubbings were actually a series of lines and dots. At this level, then, the student will be developing the skill of creating the illusion of familiar textures with just lines and dots. (A magnifying glass can help bring out the dot-line nature of rubbings.)

■ Display art prints and photographs containing a variety of surfaces or textures. Be aware of textural examples in and out of the room. Ask such questions as: "If you were blind, what are all the ways you could tell the difference between this sandpaper and this fur?" "How could you tell the difference if you were *not* blind?" "What can you *see* that is different?" (Any textured objects may be used here.) "Who remembers what the word "texture" means?" "Does everything in this room have a different feel to it?" "Why?" "How can surfaces *feel* the same but *appear* to have entirely different textures?" (This is referring to things like

Alternative art activities

■ Call out the name of an object and have the students quickly render their impression of its texture: porcupine, rabbit, comb, brush, sandpaper, and burlap. (Reward *unusual* responses.)

■ Do a drawing or painting that tells a story. Include textures as a means of telling the story more completely.

two formica tables with one made to look like wood, the other to look like marble.) Have students do a rubbing and compare the appearance of their drawings with pictures of objects having similar textures. Help students to note how lines and dots were instrumental in making those surfaces of texture. Have them look closely at the patterns of texture like the grain of wood or marble or the placement of bricks in relation to one another. Examine objects in the room again; note that wood, ceiling tile, the children's hair, and other items have line and dot qualities about them. Ask what makes grass look like grass in a picture, trees look like trees, and brick look like brick.

■ Discuss several art prints with students, asking questions such as these: "Are these textures real or illusionary?" (illusionary: can't *really* feel them) "What has the artist done to create the appearance of texture?" "How many textures were created with just lines and dots?" "Are you aware of patterns in texture?"

Suggested art activity

Have students make a drawing of some objects that have textures they can recreate with lines and dots: wood, sand, hair, fur, grass, brick, shingles, marble, and ceiling tile.

Evaluation

Any student who has been able to recreate the illusion of the kinds of textures suggested is successful. Other aspects of this picture are of no concern in terms of the concept taught in this activity.

Other things to consider

- Vocabulary: textures, illusion, pattern, impression, render.
- Art materials needed: pencils, white or manila drawing paper, crayons, tempera paint and brushes, and containers of water.
- Prints:
  Still Life: Le Jour by Braque
  Peaceable Kingdom by Hicks
  Allies Day, May 1917 by Hassam
  Christina's World by Wyeth
  Young Hare by Durer
  The Hay Wain by Constable
  Blue Boy by Gainsborough
  Tranquility by Gasser
  Bandaged Ear by Van Gogh
- People who might have need for the concept: painter, industrial designer, illustrator, fashion illustrator, cartoonist, stage set designer, printmaker.

LEVEL 2

ACTIVITY 64

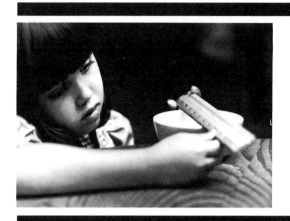

Concept taught by this activity: Variations in the size of people and objects can be determined by measuring them with such things as rulers or other objects.

Objective: The student will be able to compare the size of people and objects in relation to one another as a result of experiences with measuring.

A sample lesson plan for achieving the objective:

Teacher preparations
- Prepare a scale for children to use to make comparisons of objects.
- On a bulletin board show the size relationships of many different objects (dinosaur to lizard, adult to child, tree to plant, bird to bees.)
- Be prepared to examine measurement and measurement terms, or to have the children prepare a chart of common measurements.
- Prearrange for use of measurement equipment (tapes, rulers, yard sticks, large and small desks, chairs in K-6 to compare, and other handy materials).
- Have maps with scales available for study.
- Arrange a display of many different sized bottles or other objects to show size relationships.

Teaching suggestions
- Develop class discussion on the largest and smallest items that they have ever seen; discuss.
  - "What is the biggest thing you can think of?" "How about the tiniest?"
  - "Do things always stay the same size?"
  - "How can you tell how big something is?" (Develop the notion of comparing one thing with another and that an

object can become a tool for measuring.)
  - Show a picture of something they've never seen before and ask, "How big is this?" When they can't guess, hold it next to a picture of something they recognize and can compare it with in scale.
- Have children create their own system of measurement. (Example: "Choose a paper clip; select some object and then measure the height or width of the object in paper clip units.) Use a ruler, tape, or yardstick to measure friends: heads, arms, legs, height. Measure a chair, desks, a ball, a bat, windows, walls, a gym, the wall of school vs. the wall at home.
- On a nature hike, compare the size of grass, trees, leaves, insects, and plants with a selected scale.
- Look at prints or other large illustrations containing people and objects that might be measured and compared. Discuss whether or not the artist has mentally measured what he has painted. Discuss how the student might know if the artist has or hasn't measured his subjects.
- Discuss the need for measurement in each of the following:
  - Math's measurement unit.
  - Science: conversion of measurement to Metric System.
  - Health: growth and individual differences.
  - Social Studies: map study and scale work.
  - Music: size of instrument can influence tone of instrument or thickness and length of a string on a violin, piano, or guitar.

Suggested art activity
From a large list of common things, both living and non-living, have students select several and draw them in the size relationships they now know them to be. (Create visual comparisons.)

Alternative art activities
- Have the children plan a bulletin board of animals, musical instruments, or countries, showing their size relationship by use of a scale.
- Have the children each pick a subject area (lamps, windows, chairs, sports cars, horses), measure it, and report their findings to small groups.

- Have children draw several different objects (fruits, P.E. equipment, pencils, crayons) to scale.
- Have the class collect different sizes of fowl eggs and prepare a display of different sizes.
- Take a field trip to a farm or zoo to see first hand the many sizes of animals. (Measure and compare.)

Evaluation

- Listen to verbal comparison reports of groups.
- See finished art products, noting size relationships of objects drawn.
- List comments made from individuals during nature walk and field-trip discussion.

From all of these resources it should be rather clear which students really comprehend the concept taught.

Other things to consider

- Vocabulary: measurement, compare, relationships, variations, scale, concept, ratio.
- Art materials needed: crayons, charcoal, pencil, drawing paper.
- Teacher choice of display objects for size relationship (eggs, bottles, and a map with a scale).
- Prints:
  I and the Village by Chagall
  Blue Boy by Gainsborough
  The Brooklyn Bridge by Stella
  My Gems by Harnett
  La Grande Jatte by Seurat
  The Letter by Vermeer
  The Cradle by Morisot
  Peaceable Kingdom by Hicks
- People who might have need for the concept: puppet maker, architect, painter, illustrator, sculptor.

LEVEL 2

ACTIVITY 65

Concept taught by this activity: Overlapping objects can be used to create an illusion of depth.

Objective: In creating an illusion of depth, the student will illustrate in his drawings that when objects overlap, the one in front will appear closer.

A sample lesson plan for achieving the objective:

Teacher preparations
■ Collect all material and equipment and have it ready.
■ Display prints and photographs which illustrate the concept.
■ Display advertisements which illustrate the concept.

Teaching suggestions
■ Arrange various sized objects on a tray or desk top in front of the students. First set the objects in a line, side by side. Ask, "Which is closest to you? Farthest?"

■ Overlap the objects and repeat the questions.
■ Repeat above experiences using sheets of paper in places of objects.
■ Show prints of artists and ask:
  ● If large and small shapes are shown side by side, the small ones appear far away, but what happens when the small ones overlap the large ones?
  ● What happens when shapes overlap?

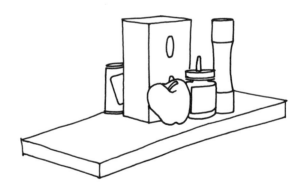

  ● What is depth? Is depth created? (When it is illusionary, how is it created?)
  ● Which things have the greatest influence in creating depth — size? detail? overlapping? color changes? Prove your answer using prints.
  ● Can artists show depth without perspective? How?
■ Have students make line designs with shapes that overlap. Have them change the sizes but keep them two-dimensional. Have some very small shapes in front.

Suggested art activity
Instruct students in making a design by using torn paper to show depth by overlapping. Then trace outlines after they are glued in place.

Alternative art activities

- Paint a background. Then cut out figures or objects to complete picture. Arrange them using the overlapping principle to show depth.
- Have students create an individual picture using the concept taught. Ask: Can you show depth just by overlapping planes? How can you show which shapes are most important? Which objects should be closest, and how can you make them look that way?
- Divide the class into groups and do a mural with each group assigned a different part such as background, mountains, trees, or figures. Each group could do a separate section. Each part should show overlapping. Students may use cut-out objects or choose other media. Detail could be added with crayon, chalk or paint. Ask: What effects are desired in placement of cut-outs on a mural? Try to make small objects look closer than large ones by overlapping. Mural could make use of a holiday theme or illustrate stories or social studies events.
- Have students look outside. Ask: "What overlaps?" Look inside to observe overlapping in the room. Trace shape outlines through a window or from photographs or magazine pictures (not overlapping). Rearrange the shapes, using overlapping and changing size relationships. See if overlapping still gives a feeling of depth.

Evaluation

To determine whether or not each student understands the concept, there should be evidence of this both in his work and in verbal responses.

- Display and discuss their designs and pictures.
- Ask: "Can depth be shown by overlapping linear shapes?"
- "Which pictures show it best and why?"
- "Can an artist show depth in an abstract picture?" Look at Cezanne's *Apples and Oranges*. "How does he show perspective?" Look at Demuth's *Figure Five in Gold*. "Does he show depth?"
- "Do his overlapping planes show depth even though he violates perspective concepts?"

Other things to consider

- Vocabulary: object, overlap, arrange, distance, farther, form, closer, depth, shape, perspective, abstract, influence, linear.
- Art materials needed: art paper, scissors, paste, crayons, chalk, or paint.
- Prints:
  Still Life: Le Jour by Braque
  Apples and Oranges by Cezanne
  Ice Skating Palace by Bonnard
  Numbering at Bethlehem by Brueghel
  Maas at Dordrecht by Cuyp
  Absinthe by Degas
  Combination Concrete by Davis
  I saw the Figure Five in Gold by Demuth
  Don Manuel Osorio by Goya
  Snap the Whip by Homer
  Le Moulin de la Galette by Renoir
  The Brooklyn Bridge by Stella
- Book: *How to Use Perspective* by Ernest Watson
- Film: "Discovering Perspective" by Bailey Film Associates
- People who might have need for the concept: architects, sculptors, photographers; artists that deal with drawing, illustrating, painting; printmaking of all types; mosaic artists; art historians.

LEVEL 2   ACTIVITY 66

Concept taught by this activity: At this point in a child's development, experiences with constructions are appropriate for him.

Objective: The child creates constructions from "found" materials.

A sample lesson plan for achieving the objective:

Teacher preparations
- Collect examples or pictures of constructions made by artists and children: toothpick or straw sculpture, bridges, and welded sculpture.
- Have students bring materials for gluing (found objects or scraps of materials).
- Encourage student curiosity about constructions prior to lesson.

Teaching suggestions
- Develop the idea that some artists have the capacity to take "found" materials and fasten them together in new combinations as sculptural forms. Ask: How many things can you think of that have been glued, pasted, or nailed together? What are all of the things you can think of that you would like to play with by gluing or fastening them together?
- Brainstorm concerning things the students or friends may have made with "found" objects.
- Make a list of things students might bring that would make interesting constructions. (*Construction* is another name for sculpture that is made up of a series of sections, pieces, or parts fastened together to make a "new whole.")
- Discuss the need to select materials which seem to "go together" because of the shape, what they're made of, their use, or some other unifying characteristic.
- Encourage students to sketch their ideas on paper first and to make abstract designs with the materials they choose.
- Emphasize that *patience* is needed in thinking of ideas and waiting for glue to dry before going on constructing. Fast-drying glues are best.

Suggested art activity
Make a toothpick or straw construction, emphasizing design and originality; use other materials that can be used in combination with toothpicks or straws.

Alternative art activities
- Make a construction out of clay, cardboard, straws, or paper.
- Make a construction from scraps of wood.

Evaluation

When the student has created a construction, the objective has been achieved.

Other things to consider

- Vocabulary: construction, found object, design, patience.
- Art materials needed: found objects, glue or paste, toothpicks, and straws.
- Books: Publications are available on making constructions and creating three-dimensional designs. See *Time-Life Series, The World of Art,* volume on Picasso, p. 151 (sculpture using found objects).
- People who might have need for the concept: sculptors, architects, engineers, furniture makers.

LEVEL 2

ACTIVITY 67

Concept taught by this activity: The student develops an awareness of the role of visual communication in his life through experiences in nonverbal communication or "body language."

Objective: The student uses body language and other nonverbal forms of communication to describe his ideas or feelings to others.

A sample lesson plan for achieving the objective:

Teacher preparations
- Display pictures of facial expressions and prints which probably create strong moods or feelings within most observers.
- Have books or stories available that illustrate forms of nonverbal communication.

Teaching suggestions
Stimulate discussion by asking questions such as:
- "How can you tell how someone feels without their saying anything?"
- "Can you tell what kind of mood your mother is in when you get home from school?" "Or your father when he comes home from work?" "How can you tell?"
- "What kinds of feelings do people show by the expressions on their faces?" (List as many as possible.) "What kinds of moods?" (List them.)
- Have students reach into sacks and touch whatever is inside, even though the students don't say anything. From their facial expressions, see if the class members can tell how they felt about what they touched. Have the sacks contain objects that feel good or bad to the touch and some that might prick or feel especially repulsive.
- When a discussion of facial expression has been exhausted investigate aspects of body language: "Can you sometimes tell how people feel without seeing their face?" "Can you

demonstrate things such as hate, joy pain, sadness, strength, or force with your body?"
- Have students work together in small groups to pantomime a variety of ideas that they will practice and demonstrate for the rest of the class. Note that some facial or bodily expressions can represent more than one idea but multiple clues help one to identify expressions more specifically.
- Discuss ways in which people in the arts use facial expression and body language in the dance, drama, and music: singers of rock, folk, and western music; opera singers; ancient Japanese dancers (Kabuki); ballet dancers; actors or actresses in dramatic productions; hula dancers.
- Discuss suggested prints in terms of how aware artists need to be of body language and facial expressions.
- Have students come to the front of the room and "be something" without saying anything; and have the rest of the class try to guess what they are trying to communicate: a rainstorm by wiggling fingers and hands down, and lightening by throwing the fist down and out every so often; a snake; a penguin. Perhaps they could even play charades.

Suggested art activity
Organize the class into groups and let the students choose between these activities:
- Build or make something in groups of four or five without talking — a collage or a house of blocks.
- Act out a play or a scene behind a sheet so that all expression is done by the body. Tape any verbal parts so that students can concentrate on body language.

Alternative art activities
- Write and act out a new version of a familiar story. Tape the spoken parts so that time isn't needed for memorizing. Emphasize the facial and body expressions.
- Do pantomimes or role playing on social situations, fairy tales, or problems of concern to students.
- Do any exercise on ways you can tell people things without talking: how you would tell someone "no" or "yes," "be careful," "don't come near," "come on in," or "let's eat!"
- Observe and/or listen to such things as dance and rhythmic beats in music and discuss what they convey to the viewer.

■ Discuss what clothing tells you about the person wearing it. Look at pictures of people.

Evaluation

When the student demonstrates either verbally or non-verbally that he has an awareness of the concept, the objective has been achieved.

Other things to consider

■ Vocabulary: moods, expressions, communication, verbal, nonverbal, body language, pantomime.
■ Books for the teacher:
Speech Communication/An Interpersonal Approach by Ernest Bormann and Nancy Bormann, Evanston: Harper and Row, 1972.
Reach, Touch and Teach by Terry Borton, New York: McGraw-Hill, 1970.
Non-Verbal Communication by Abne N. Eisenberg and Ralph Smith, Jr., Indianapolis: Bobbs-Merrill, 1971.
Body Language by Julius Fast, New York: Pocket Books, 1971.
The Silent Language by Edward T. Hall, Garden City, N.Y.: Doubleday, 1959.
Non-Verbal Communication in Human Interaction by Mark L. Knapp, New York: Holt, Rinehart and Winston, 1972.
Non-Verbal Communication, a Guide for Teaching by Lois Leubitz, Skokie, Illinois: National Textbook Co., 1973.
■ Prints:
Dempsey and Firpo by Bellows
The Smokers by Brouwer
The Crucifixion by Dali
Dancing Class by Degas
The Small Crucifixion by Grunewald
Autumn by Koryusai
Mona Lisa by da Vinci
Knockout by Morreau
Christina's World by Wyeth
Prodigal Son by Rembrandt
■ People who might have need for the concept: people that deal with drawing, painting, sculpture, commercial art, advertising, puppetry, mosaics, art-history and analysis, photography, and printmaking.

LEVEL 2

ACTIVITY 68

Concept taught by this activity: Black and white areas that overlap create the maximum that can be achieved in contrast. When they surround a color, they reinforce and brighten it.

Objective: The student demonstrates an awareness that black and white are the maximum that can be achieved in contrast and that they can reinforce and brighten colors.

A sample lesson plan for achieving the objective:

Teacher preparations
- Display artist prints, photographs, and other visuals that illustrate the concept.
- Be aware of resources or examples inside the classroom and the school building as well as its surrounding area.
- Assemble materials: crayons, paper, glue, magazines, and scissors.

Teaching suggestions
- Hold up salt and sugar. "In what ways are salt and sugar the same?" "Different?" (They *contrast* in taste.) Hold up a circle and triangle. "How are these shapes different?" (Corners, roundness.) (They *contrast* with each other.)
- Begin discussion by asking questions such as: "Who knows what the word *contrast* means?" "When two things are quite different from each other do we have contrast?" "What are some of the ways two things can contrast with each other?" (Size, shape, color, value, texture, purpose, name, sound, smell, taste, feel, hardness, opaqueness.) "Do you think artists are ever concerned about contrasts?" "Of all the ways things can contrast, which one would an artist be most concerned with?" (Size, shape, color, value,

texture, purpose, feel, hardness, opaqueness.) "Today we're going to talk about just two of these — color and value. There are two colors artists sometimes use. One is the darkest of all colors and one is the lightest of all colors. What colors am I talking about?" (Black and white.) "If I wanted to make a part of my picture really stand out, to have as much contrast as possible, I would have the shape _____ and its background _____?" (The students should fill in the blanks by using white in one and black in the other.) "We've decided, then, that if I wanted the most contrast I could possibly use in a picture, I would use black and white. Are there some things we could do to see if what we've said is really true?" (The teacher and class would then check out several of the best suggestions made.)
- Another line of investigation would be to look at animals that have colorings of black and white and discuss briefly how they contrast with backgrounds of various kinds: the skunk, zebra, penguin, magpie, and panda against green foliage or against snow. You could also look at artist prints and trace shapes of color that appear next to black and cut duplicates out of white that can be set onto the prints and show students how much more white contrasts than the color did.
- Discuss what influence black and white might have on other colors when mixed with them, placed next to them, and used as a background.
- When you have developed the idea that black and white reinforce or brighten another color, have students point out examples in the room and in art prints.
- Ask questions such as the following: "Why did the artist use black (or white) in this way?" "What difference do you see in the way color stands out in this area?" "In this area?" "How do the areas compare?" (Look for colors that are essentially the same but appear different because one is surrounded by black or white and the other is not.)

Suggested art activity
Create designs or pictures in crayon or tempera paint, but have half the class do them without black and white. Those that use black and white should make a special effort to create vivid contrasts even to the point of outlining shapes

or colors with them and using black and white next to each other or as backgrounds for colors.

Display the students' work on a bulletin board, with the work of students who couldn't use black and white on one side, the other students' work on the other side. Discuss whether or not the contrasts achieved with black and white proved their belief that the concept was right.

Alternative art activities
- Have the children make a picture and try different colors of borders on it. Go from pastel colors to darker colors, then to black.
- Do some imprinting with gadgets or found objects. Use white paint or ink on black paper as well as black ink on white paper.
- Create designs with white on black and black on white. Make some imaginary animals cut out of black and white sheets of paper: a zebra pie, panda, or skunkguin.

Evaluation

The teacher needs to be aware of student response and should question directly any who do not seem to grasp the idea. Although the evaluation requires only a verbal awareness, students should demonstrate an increased use of black and white (for creating contrasting areas in their pictures and reinforcing colors).

Other things to consider

- Vocabulary: opposites, contrast, maximum, minimum, reinforce, surround, brighten.
- Materials needed: crayons, water colors, tempera, ink, white and black construction paper, scissors, glue, black markers, and old magazines.
- Prints:
  Combination Concrete by Davis
  Justice and Peace by Overstreet
  The Box by Renoir
  The Old King by Rouault
  The Bullfight by Goya
  View of Toledo by El Greco
  Mural by Pollock
  Composition 1963 by Miro
  Poster-Moulin Rouge by Toulouse-Lautrec

LEVEL 2

ACTIVITY 69

Concept taught by this activity: A design may have one or more shapes, colors, or themes that relate parts of a composition to each other: a tree ties the sky and the ground together.

Objective: The student uses one or more elements to relate parts of a composition to each other.

A sample lesson plan for achieving the objective:

Teacher preparations
- Display pictures (art prints and photographs) that contain examples of overlapping figures or objects which seem to connect the various parts of the illustration.
- Have appropriate art materials available for drawing and painting activities.
- Locate two pictures that can be cut.

Teaching suggestions
Refer to some large pictures that seem to tell a story and that contain overlapping objects. Initiate an understanding of the concept in a discussion session by asking questions such as the following:
- "Does this picture tell a story?" (Allow two or three children to respond.)
- "Does it tell the same story to everyone?" "Why not?"
- "If we took parts of a picture away or covered them up, would it still tell the same story?"
- "Do you think every part of the picture is important, then?" (Somewhere in this dialogue you may wish to use more than one picture to keep interest high.)
- "Does anyone know what overlapping means?" (Discuss and develop the idea that some parts are in front of or behind others.)
- "Can someone show us where overlapping occurs in this picture?"
- "What does it mean when we connect two things?" (Tie them together.)

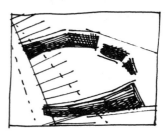

- "Does overlapping *connect* in this picture?" (Show students a photograph that has been cut up so that its parts no longer connect.)
- "When the parts of a picture are no longer connected, what does it do to the picture?"
- "Are the parts related when they aren't connected?" (Be sure students know what related means.) Yes — if a transition by rhythm, shapes, or angles leads the eye across the "gap."
- "When the parts are related, does it lead your eye from one to another?" "Can someone come up and show us the path your eye follows?" "Does anyone see any other paths when the parts in the picture connect?"
- Have a variety of geometric shapes available and have students demonstrate arranging them on a tack board or flannel board. Have students arrange them with no overlapping, then with overlapping parts that "tie" the design together and lead the eye from one to the other.
- Discuss what differences they see in the two kinds of arrangements.

NO OVERLAPPING

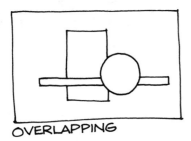

OVERLAPPING

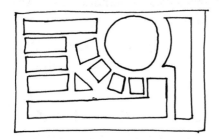

Orange and Yellow by Rothko
Composition 1963 by Miro

■ People who might have need for the concept: people that deal with making and staging puppets, with mosaics, batik and tie dye, hooking rugs, leather crafts, enameling, jewelry making, forging metal for making art objects, wood carving; artists that work with glass, macrame, weaving, stitchery and applique, architecture, city planning, landscape architecture, interior design, ceramics, pottery, sculpture, art history and analysis, photography, drawing, painting, and printmaking.

■ Though objects may *not* overlap or touch, transition or connectedness may be implied by rhythm (repetition), shapes, and angles.

Suggested art activity
Have students draw and paint a subject of their choice and urge them to use the concept as they understand it.

Alternative art activities
■ Bring or take pictures of subjects where "connecting" occurs and where it doesn't. Discuss the good and bad aspects of each approach.
■ Work out two variations of a design or picture; connect parts in one but not in the other. Use the same subject or motif in the two illustrations. Discuss the influence each approach has on the subject.

Evaluation

Use the "art activity" as evidence of whether or not students can use the concept in their own way. Questioning them individually about their picture can further determine their knowledge of the concept. Make sure they haven't achieved the objective simply by chance.

Other things to consider

■ Vocabulary: overlapping, connect, related, repetition.
■ Art materials needed: tempera paints, water colors, or crayons; a variety of art paper and pencils, or other appropriate tools for drawing.
■ Prints:
Dempsey and Firpo by Bellows
Harvesters by Breughel
Still Life with Pipe by Chardin
Dancing Class by Degas
Figure Five in Gold by Demuth
La Grande Jatt by Seurat
The Booklyn Bridge by Stella
Snap the Whip by Homer

In discussion periods discuss the above in contrast with prints such as:
Combination Concrete by Davis
Nude Descending #2 by Duchamp
Head of a Man by Klee
Leisure by Leger

LEVEL 2

ACTIVITY 70

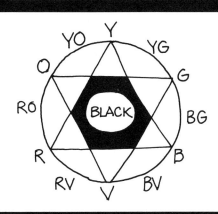

Concept taught by this activity: All colors will harmonize with white, black, and gray.

Objective: Students will be aware that harmony is easier to attain when using black, white, or gray with other colors (because the three are neutral).

A sample lesson plan for achieving the objective:

Teacher preparations
■ Collect and display pictures and prints that illustrate the concept.
■ Prepare visual aids for ideas listed below that might be used.
■ Assemble materials necessary for activities listed below or others that might be used by teacher or students. Some possibilities for needed materials are glue, magazines, paper, brushes, colored paper, colored fabric, fingerpaints, poster paints, and paper sacks.

Teaching suggestions
■ Prepare and display visual aids that demonstrate the concept. A few possibilities are: sets of squares cut from brightly colored paper; squares of black, white and gray.
■ On a sheet of paper, arrange four squares of bright colors. On a separate sheet of paper, arrange one bright colored

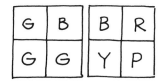

square surrounded by three squares of gray, white, or black. Questions: "Which is more pleasing to the eye?" "What do the brighter colors do?" "Which seem to go together best?" "Why?"
■ Show a large sketch of a white brick fireplace, or white paper rectangles cut to represent bricks: "build" a fireplace on a bulletin board; then through the use of paper floral arrangements and paper art objects, show that all colors will harmonize in this setting.
■ Show how even an ordinarily displeasing color combination can harmonize through the use of black, white, or gray (by mixing either finger paints or poster paints).

Suggested art activity
Make collages of bright colored scraps of tissue paper on a white, black, or gray background, or make paper mosaics of bright colored scraps of paper using strips of black to attain harmony.

Alternative art activities
■ Make paper sack puppets or mannequins, and, using scraps of fabric, prepare aprons, head-scarves, or jackets from colors and black, white, and gray. Ask the students if clothing items harmonize with the use of black, white, and gray.
■ Do a crayon resist on paper. First, with crayons draw brightly colored patterns on colored paper. (Don't use white, black, or gray paper.) Then coat black paint over the crayon patterns. When the paint dries, make a line design or drawing by scraping through the black into the coats of crayon.

Evaluation

There should be evidence in the child's work that he shows some understanding of the concept through his mixing of paints or the addition of white, black, or gray to his pictures.

Other things to consider

- Vocabulary: collage, mosaics, harmony, crayon resist, etching, value, intensity.
- Art materials needed: paper scissors, glue for collages and mosaics, tempera paints, brushes, finger paints, fabric samples, paper sacks, tissue paper, crayons, and art paper of various kinds.
- Prints:
  Absinthe by Degas
  Leisure by Leger
  The Old King by Rouault
  Poster: Moulin Rouge by T. Lautrec
  Hudson River Logging by Homer
  Combination Concrete by Davis
  Quay le Pouliguen by Vuillard
  Interior, Flowers and Parrots by Matisse
  Zebegen by Vasarely
  Composition 1963 by Miro
- People who might have need for the concept: architect, interior designer, painter, art historian, cartoonist, commercial artist, advertising designer, printmaker, technical and industrial illustrator, stage set designer, collage artist.

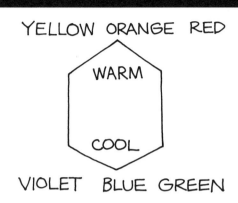

Concept taught by this activity: Color can be used to transmit a feeling of warmth or coolness.

Objective: The student distinguishes colors as warm or cool and demonstrates that color can be used to transmit feelings of warmth or coolness.

A sample lesson plan for achieving the objective:

Teacher preparations
- Have a bulletin board displaying a wide variety of color. Collect and make individual packets of colors (or paint chips).
- Have all materials out and easily accessible (game materials, art prints, and individual color wheels.)
- Have a picture in which the colors of nature have been switched around: red sky, green sun, and blue grass.

Teaching suggestions
Ask several students what their favorite color is. "How does it make you feel?" "What colors do you think are cool?" "What colors do you think are warm?"
- Show and discuss art prints demonstrating this concept. "Did the artist have any reason for using warm or cool colors in these areas?" "What might his reasons have been?" "How would the "feeling" of the pictures change if you reversed the warm and cool?" Discuss how some pictures may have cool colors that seem hot and warm ones that seem cool.

NOTE: *All* colors can take on characteristics of warmness and coolness. In this instance, it is the warmness and coolness of the pure colors found on the standard outer circle of the color wheel.

- Play a color classification game. Divide the class up into equal teams. Have previously made packets containing two color chips for each team member. Give color packets to a team captain, who gives two color chips to each member of his own team. Designate a place on the chalkboard for each team and draw a line down the middle of the area with WARM the heading on the left and COOL the heading on the right of the two areas. Teams line up and race to the board to place their colors under the appropriate heading. Only one color may be placed at a time; so each member runs up twice. First team through with the color chips placed correctly wins. (Put tape on the back of color chips, or give to team captains to hand out.)
- Have students make a collage of warm or cool colors from pictures cut from magazines.
- Pass out many color chips to the students and have them place the warm colors on the left of their desk and the cool colors on the right. Walk around the room to see if the concept is understood.
- In a group discussion, or individually, see if students can pick out the warm and cool colors of art prints, or even illustrations in textbooks.

Suggested art activity
Paint two designs or pictures, one exhibiting a feeling of coolness, the other of warmth, with minimum reliance on objects (ice, refrigerator, fire) as opposed to color.

Alternative art activities
- Students can build a notebook showing warm or cool colors used in various ways (advertisements, illustrations, their own pictures) and listing the colors used as well as placing them under the correct heading.
- Investigate the use of warm and cool colors in clothing and their seasonal differences. Report to the class on findings.
- Investigate the use of warm or cool colors by ethnic groups or by various cultures. Do any patterns of their use emerge? Report to the class on findings.

Evaluation

- The student verbally defining the concept and giving examples, fulfilling an assignment (picture, collage, notebook) correctly using the concept, and displaying and discussing his work, will be a sufficient evaluation for the teacher.

Other things to consider

- Vocabulary: warm and cool colors, variation, color wheel.
- Art materials needed: paints, crayons, magazines, scissors, glue, paper for a collage, paper to complete a small notebook, chips of colored construction paper (or paint chips), paper and tape for game (not all needed in every instance, depending upon which activities are chosen).
- Prints:
  The Artist's Bedroom at Arles by Van Gogh
  Self Portrait with Bandaged Ear by Van Gogh
  Breezing Up by Homer
  Senecio by Klee
  Boats at Argenteuil by Monet
  Orange and Yellow by Rothko
  The Thatched Cottages by Vlaminck
  Before the Start by Lapicque
  Mlle. Violette by Redon
- People who might have need for the concept: architects, interior designers, painters, art historians, cartoonists, commercial artists, print-makers, technical and industrial illustrators, stage set designers.

LEVEL 2 　　　　　　　ACTIVITY 72

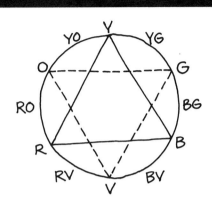

Concept taught by this activity: Color may be organized in many different ways, such as the color wheel. Specific colors can be mixed from red, yellow, and blue.

Objective: The student is aware that colors may be organized in many different ways, and he is able to mix specific colors from red, yellow, and blue.

A sample lesson plan for achieving the objective:

Teacher preparations
■ Prepare materials (including visuals) for discussion of organized color in paint.
■ Have several prints displayed in the room (some possibilities are listed on the back).
■ Have color wheel displayed.
■ Have crayons and paper available.

Teaching suggestions
■ The following questions could be used to explain this concept, as well as to check or evaluate the students' understanding of the concept by the feedback they give you. Discuss the importance of color in everything we do — in nature, in food, in clothes, in homes, even in the way we feel, by asking questions like the following: "How are these colors related?" "How do we find color used in our homes and our clothing?" "Do you feel attractive in certain colors rather than others?" "What color of clothing feels cooler in summer?" "Is it really cooler?" "How could we tell?" (On a hot day, have students touch both a dark and a light colored car and see which feels hotter.) Show two cookies, one baked on a shiny pan and the other on a dark pan. Develop the idea that organizing color in terms of value (darkness and lightness) can affect our physical comfort.

"What values seem to add warmth to us in winter?" "How can we find out if they really do or not?" "What evidence shows us that color is organized in our home, or our yards, or in architecture?" "What colors are found in your kitchen?" "Do they look pleasant together?" "Does the kitchen feel warm or cool?" "Is organized color important in books and magazines?" "Is color an important consideration in preparing a meal?" Discuss a menu for a very colorless meal and ask for suggestions of things to add that would make the meal more colorful and appealing. ("Does the organization of color for a meal affect how the meal tastes?") "What effect does color have on emotions?" "How is color organized in the paint store?" "Why is it done that way?" (To make certain that every time a formula is used the purchaser will have a color that is exactly like the one he wanted.)
■ Bring three students to the front, each one wearing a primary color in his clothing. Explain that every color you can imagine comes from mixing these three colors.
■ Add three more children wearing secondary colors, and actually have them form a color wheel. Repeat and discuss until you are sure they all understand primary and secondary colors.
■ Discuss intermediate colors, tertiary colors. Display your color wheel.
■ Show color chart from paint store to show hundreds of colors available by mixing primary colors.
■ Discuss several prints and have children see if they can find where primary and secondary colors were used.

Experiment with the mixing of primary colors to get secondary and tertiary colors.

Discuss the science concept: All of the colors *in light* mixed together make white, and the absence of color makes black. (Primary colors in light differ from primary colors in pigment.)

Suggested art activity
Paint a picture using nothing but red, yellow, and blue as the source for all colors. (Students may notice that without the use of black or white, *value* gradations are limited.)

Alternative art activities

- Give a sheet of white paper, and a red, yellow, and blue crayon to each child. Have the children make a color wheel, with the primary colors first: yellow at 12 o'clock, blue at 4 o'clock, and red at 8 o'clock.
- Have them add the three secondary colors by blending the primary colors, using the lightest color first.
- Cut circles from red, yellow, and blue tissue paper. Arrange the circles between two sheets of waxed paper with some of the circles overlapping part way. Iron the waxed paper with a warm iron. Hold this up to the light and see that the overlapped primary colors now are secondary colors.
- Make a display showing different ways colors are organized to help the consumer use them more easily and more wisely.
- Create a collage design with all colors being mixtures that resulted from overlapping red, yellow, and blue tissue paper.
- Arrange to have a house painter visit the class to discuss and demonstrate how he mixes and duplicates colors his employers have selected.
- Discuss the need for artists to understand the concept and examine their applications of the idea through art prints.

Evaluation

When the student demonstrates an awareness of the concept (verbal) or an ability to use it (his art work), the objective has been achieved.

Other things to consider

- Vocabulary: color wheel, primary colors, secondary colors, intermediate colors, complementary colors, color scheme, color harmony, tertiary colors.
- Art materials needed: red, yellow, and blue crayons for each child, paper for a color wheel and for pictures (one using primary colors only and one using secondary colors only), water colors, tissue and waxed paper, and a color chart from a paint store to show many available shades and tints of color.
- Prints:
  Composition 1963 by Miro
  Gypsy with Baby by Modigliani
  The Old King by Rouault
  Apples and Oranges by Cezanne
  Virgin Forest by Rousseau
  Before the Start by Lapicque
  Justice and Peace by Overstreet
  Allies Day, May 1917 by Hassam
  Delphic Sibyl by Michelangelo
- People who might have need for the concept: architects, interior designers, painters, art historians, cartoonists, commercial artists, advertisers, printmakers, technical and industrial illustrators, stage set designers, collage artists.

MATURITY LEVEL 3

Developmental stages

In this packet of lesson plans the teacher can provide the student with twenty-five art experiences that are designed to assist the student in moving through his developmental stages. The activities will teach how to:

- Utilize advanced crayon techniques.
- Create a point of emphasis with contrasting colors.
- Create a sense of depth with contrasts in various elements.
- Create the illusion of space by showing people and objects getting smaller as they get farther away.
- Recognize the need to consider all of the space in a given arrangement.
- Recognize ways in which photography is used in the child's society.
- Recognize uses of printing and lettering processes as communication tools.
- Recognize ways in which various commercial printing processes are related to printmaking.
- Recognize a variety of tools artists use in the making of art.
- Draw or paint cast shadows.
- Recognize the linear nature of certain things in the environment.
- Describe the contour or framework of an object and its parts with lines.
- Use clay slip to join clay slabs and coils together.
- Describe differences between works of art.
- Recognize the influence function has on a form.
- Recognize the relationship of the cone, cube, cylinder, sphere, and pyramid to all forms in the environment.
- Create the illusion of space by showing distant objects less detailed and as a mass or combination of forms.
- Take pictures with simple box-type or instamatic cameras.
- Create forms by draping slabs or strips of pliable materials.
- Recognize the role of scale in perceiving proportion.
- Recognize the uses of complementary colors for improving color literacy.
- Recognize ways in which pure colors and bright colors dominate gray or dark ones.
- Recognize the need to consider all views of any three-dimensional form.
- Recognize the relationships of dark and light values to optical weight.
- Vary the darkness or lightness of a hue without using black or white.

THE DIAGNOSTIC CHART

An explanation

17. The student draws the thumb attaching to the hand separate from fingers, hips are defined by leg attachments, trees are more realistic in the proportion of foliage to trunk. Contrasts in value and color are used effectively.
18. Shadows are shown falling away from the light source, attempts to show depth are more evident, and hair styles and clothing details are considered by the student.
19. Clay objects are formed from coils or slabs and joined together with slip. Figures and animals are better proportioned and appear in side or front views. The student can utilize any of the basic forms in creating shapes and symbols for their art. Distant objects are shown as masses or shapes without detail.
20. Clay objects can be made by draping methods. The student demonstrates a greater awareness of size relationships, such as one object to another or parts to a whole.

17. The child is at activity no. 75.

18. The child is at activity no. 82.

19. The child is at activities no. 85, 88, and 89.

20. The child is at activities no. 91 and 92.

Art projects that can be used as devices for teaching a specific concept

Drawing (pencils, crayons, pens, sticks, brushes, and chalk)
Lessons: 73, *76, *77, *82, *83, *84, *89, 92, *96

Perspective
Lessons: *75, *76, *89, 92, *96

Murals and friezes
Lessons: 74, 77, 78, 79, 87, 92, 94

Dribble and sponge painting
Lessons: 81, 97

Crayon resist
Lessons: *73, 74, 77, 81, 94

String pull design
Lessons: *83, *84

Water color and tempera
Lessons: *74, 77, 92, *93, *94, *97

Wire sculpture
Lessons: 77, *83, *84, 87, 88, *92, 95

Sculpture with clay
Lessons: 77, 88, 92, *95

Woodcraft
Lessons: 77, 87, 88, 92, *95

Casting molds and pouring for sculpture and candles
Lessons: 77, 87

Dry flower arrangement
Lessons: *77, 83, 84, 87, 92, 95

Stencil designs
Lesson: 77

Copper and foil tooling
Lesson: 77

Melted crayon painting
Lesson: 77

Cartooning and/or caricature
Lessons: 73, 76, 77, 79, 82, *83, *84, 89, 92, 96

Posters
Lessons: *74, *77, 78, 79, 87, 92, 94

Coloring and color mixing
Lessons: *93, *94, *97

Rock and gourd painting
Lessons: 74, 77, 84

Dioramas
Lessons: *74, 77, 79, 84, 88, 89, 92, *95

Blow paint through a straw
Lessons: 83, 84

Initial and name designs
Lessons: *74, 77, 92

Collage
Lessons: *74, *77, 92, 93, 94

Toothpick or straw sculpture
Lessons: 77, *83, *84, 87, 88, *92, *95

Whittling and carving
Lessons: 77, 88, 92, 95

Soap, wax, and clay carving
Lessons: 77, 88, 91, 92, *95

Leathercraft
Lessons: 77, 87

Sand bottles
Lessons: *77, 92

Terrariums
Lessons: *77, 87, 92

Photography
Lessons: *77, *78, *90, 92

Tie/dye
Lessons: 77, 83, 84, 94

Starch paper
Lesson: 77

Mosaics
Lesson: *77

Stitchery with string
Lessons: 77, *83, *84, 92

Applique (sew or glue)
Lessons: 77, 83, 84, 92

Spool knitting
Lessons: 77, *83, *84

Snowflakes
Lessons: 77, 92

Christmas ornaments
Lessons: 77, 84, 87, 92, *95

Paper-sack masks
Lessons: 77, 87, *92

Paper sculpture (fold, score and roll)
Lessons: 77, 87, 92, 95

Egg-carton crafts
Lesson: 77

Snow sculpture
Lessons: 77, *92, *95

Vegetable prints
Lesson: 77

Gadget prints
Lesson: 77

Batik
Lessons: 77, 94

Knitting and crocheting
Lessons: 77, 84, 87

Pin-prick pictures
Lesson: 77

String and yarn pictures
Lessons: 77, *83, *84

Basket weaving
Lessons: 77, 83, 84, 87, 92, 95

Weaving (paper, string and fabric)
Lessons: 77, 83, 84, 87

Puppets (sack, sock, styrofoam, etc.)
Lessons: 77, 87, 91, *92, 95

Box sculpture
Lessons: 77, 92, *95

Torn-paper designs
Lesson: 77

Construction-paper designs
Lessons: 77, 92

Mobiles and stabiles
Lessons: 77, 83, 84, 87, 92, 95

Papier Mâché
Lessons: 77, *91, 92, *95

*Key projects for the concept.

166

LEVEL 3

ACTIVITY 73

Concept taught by this activity: Experiences with advanced crayon techniques are appropriate for the student.

Objective: The student utilizes some advanced crayon techniques in his art work.

A sample lesson plan for achieving the objective:

Teacher preparations
Develop examples of crayon techniques students might want to experiment with. These could include crayon resist, mixing colors (dark over light), encaustic or melted crayon, blending and shading, and drawing on surfaces to create unusual surfaces (sandpaper, wood, and pebbled mat board).

Teaching suggestions
■ Look at the samples prepared and discuss them with the class. Ask questions such as: "Can anyone tell how any of these were done?" "What materials were used?" "What made this unusual texture?" "What kinds of designs would you want to use these techniques with?" "Would any of them work in some of the drawings or pictures you do all the time?" "How *else* could crayons be used?"
■ One basic crayon technique, often overlooked, is that of using light pressure for light effects, and heavy peessure on the crayon for dark color.

Suggested art activity
Have the student select a crayon technique that is new to him and create a design or picture, using it in one or two areas or throughout his arrangement.

Alternative art activities
■ Combine two or three crayon techniques in a single design or picture.
■ Use crayon on different surfaces and make a collage, using the different effects.

Evaluation
When the student demonstrates an awareness of how two or three crayon techniques might be used to enrich his work, the objective has been achieved.

Other things to consider

■ Vocabulary: technique, encaustic, resist, mixing, blending, shading.
■ Art materials needed: crayons, drawing paper, hot plate (for encaustic) and a variety of textured papers.
■ People who might have need for the concept: painters, teachers, encaustic artist, artists that draw and paint.

LEVEL 3   # ACTIVITY 74

Concept taught by this activity: Contrasting colors can be used to create a point of emphasis.

Objective: The student can use contrasting colors to create a point of emphasis.

A sample lesson plan for achieving the objective:

Teacher preparations
- Collect prints and/or photographs illustrating use of contrasting colors for emphasis (see artists' paintings, home decoration magazine, pictures of nature and wild life, and other publications).
- Collect pieces of cloth and paint color samples.
- Assemble student materials.

Teaching suggestions
Have a plate or tray with many all-day suckers on it (the type without paper wrapping is best). All the suckers should be the same flavor but *one*: a bright-colored alternate flavor. Ask students which sucker they notice. How many want *that* one?
- Develop interest for and an understanding of the concept through a preliminary line of questioning. "Does anyone know what the word *emphasis* means?" (Develop the idea that when something is emphasized it stands out from its surroundings or its background for some reason or another.)
- Discuss the variety of examples of emphasis we see every day. (Flowers against a green background, a man's tie, a ring on one finger, a brightly colored pillow on a sofa.)
- Note that many examples had to do with color; then explore this line of thinking: "Why is color so often used to create emphasis?" "How many different ways can color be used for emphasis?" (When it is different from its background by virtue of size, intensity, or value.)
- Show illustrations that demonstrate a variety of ways in which contrasting colors are used. Use the following kinds

of color examples: (1) light and dark opposition (value contrasts), (2) cold and warm contrast, (3) complementary contrast (green vs. red, blue vs. orange, and violet vs. yellow), (4) contrast in the shape of the color areas, (5) contrast in degrees of saturation or intensity.
- Point out various color combinations in the room or in students' clothing that create emphasis and ask why. "How do you know what needs to be emphasized in a picture or design?" "How could you emphasize a particular spot in a picture or a design?" "Should you make the contrast either very strong or very slight?" "What difference would it make in how the color made you feel?" "What colors are usually associated with Christmas?" "What makes them stand out?" (Complements are used, and they contrast greatly.)

Suggested art activity
Make a simple collage, using contrasting colors cut from magazines to show a point of emphasis.

Alternative art activities
- Design a fabric and paint the design on paper in which color is used for emphasis or for which the fabric itself will serve that purpose.
- Do a repeat design in a process involving color in print-making. Let one of the repeats serve as an area of emphasis in the pattern.
- Use color as a point of emphasis on the decorated part of a ceramic object.
- Bring swatches of fabrics that illustrate this principle and discuss them.
- Design a room setting with contrasting colors making the point of emphasis.

Evaluation

In this instance the student needs to be able to use the concept in his own work; therefore, the evaluation hinges on observation of the student's work. The teacher needs to be aware of whether or not the student has consciously planned areas of emphasis in his art product.

Other things to consider

- Vocabulary: contrast, emphasis, collage, principle, illustrate, swatches, design.
- Art materials needed: swatches of material, colored paper, crayons, scissors, background paper, glue, magazines to cut, and any special materials needed.
- Prints:
  Apples and Oranges by Cezanne
  I and the Village by Chagall
  Zebegen by Vasarely
  The Artist's Bedroom at Arles by Van Gogh
  Sinbad the Sailor by Klee
  Gypsy with Baby by Modigliani
  Virgin Forest by Rousseau
  Breezing Up by Homer
- People who might have need for the concept: puppet makers; mosaic artists; craft designers in batik and tie dye, rug hooking, leather, enameling, jewelry making, forging metal, wood carving, glass, macrame and knotting, weaving, stitchery and applique; architects, landscape architects, interior designers, ceramists, potters, sculptors, art historians, photographers, cartoonists, commercial artists, advertisers, painters, printmakers, collage artists.

LEVEL 3   ACTIVITY 75

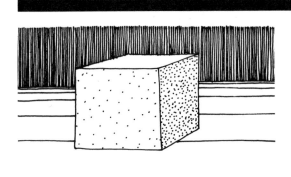

Concept taught by this activity: When shapes contrast with their background, a sense of depth is created. (Contrasts in color, value, shape, texture.)

Objective: The student creates the illusion of depth by using contrasting shapes and backgrounds.

A sample lesson plan for achieving the objective:

Teacher preparations
■ Collect and display prints of art that illustrate the concept. This includes those under "Teaching suggestions" as well as any others that are appropriate.
■ Collect and display photographs that further illustrate the concept.

Teaching suggestions
■ Display the optical-illusion picture of a vase/two faces (see illustration). Ask students, "What do you see?" If they see the vase, ask "Can anyone see two faces?" The background and the foreground in this picture can change places. If some other picture is available for use in demonstrating a changing background, use it also.
■ Display a photograph of objects silhouetted against the sky. Ask, "Which shapes are in the foreground?" "Which shapes are in the background?" Ask, "Is the background far away or close up?" Lead students to identify the idea that when the background appears far away, we say that the picture has depth, and when shapes contrast with their background we see that a sense of depth is created.
■ Display picture of *The Scout* by Remington. Ask questions such as: "Does this picture have depth?" "What are all the reasons you say it has depth?" "How has the *artist* created this feeling of depth?" (Contrast of light and dark between shapes in foreground and background.) Display other prints (see following paragraph) and ask similar questions.

■ Find a suitable picture large enough for the entire class to see and benefit from. With a pair of scissors, cut out the foreground objects and glue them to a sheet of acetate (or other transparent plastic). Put a paper matt or frame around this. Hold different values and colors behind the foreground sheet. Have a class discussion on why certain values and colors create a feeling of depth and others do not.
■ Review the lesson on contrasting colors (concept #74, color) and contrasting values (concept #68).

Suggested art activity
Paint a picture using lighter colors in the background with darker silhouetted objects in the foreground.

Alternative art activities
■ Make a cut or torn paper picture demonstrating the contrast between shapes and their background.
■ Make a diorama in connection with social studies, using colors that contrast to increase the feeling of depth.

- Make linoleum prints and apply the concept.
- The concept could be applied by the students in cartooning.

Evaluation

Note responses of students and ways in which they have already applied the concept in the various activities used.

Other things to consider

- Vocabulary: foreground, background, value, contrast, depth, diorama.
- Art materials needed: colored construction paper, scissors, glue or paste, paper, tempera, and brushes, or paper and crayons, materials for diorama, calendar picture, acetate or overlay transparent plastic, exacto knife.
- Prints:
  The Scout by Remington
  L'Absinthe by Degas
  City Hall In Rega by Feininger
  Seven A.M. by Hopper
  Brooklyn Bridge by Stella
  Bar at the Folies Bergeres by Manet
  La Loge by Renoir
  Gypsy Woman with Child by Modigliani
  The Old King by Rouault
  Man with the Golden Helmet by Rembrandt
  Turning the Stake by Eakins
- People who might have need for the concept: artists that draw, paint, cartoon, do prints of all types, do mosaics, leather craft, woodcarving, interior design, advertising design, and commercial art of many types; and people that deal with art history and analysis.

LEVEL 3

ACTIVITY 76

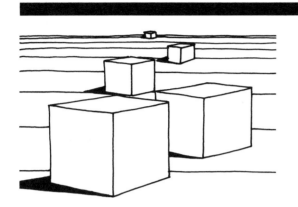

Concept taught by this activity: People and objects appear smaller as they get farther away.

Objective: To create the illusion of depth in a picture, the student will perceive, draw, or paint people and other objects smaller as they get farther away from him.

A sample lesson plan for achieving the objective:

Teacher preparations

- Have visuals available that demonstrate the concept: a pair of similar apples or a pair of shoes. Hold them up to the class with one considerably in front of the other and observe that one appears smaller. An "interest center" could be set up, containing these and other objects for the students to experiment with.
- Arrange the room for mobility (see "Suggested art activity").
- Have artists' prints available or cut pictures from magazines that demonstrate this principle.
- Have measuring devices available: ruler, yardstick, tape measure, for activities below.
- Prepare simple visual aids (find-the-error pictures) and make graduated paper strips for fence-post activity below. Find-the-error pictures are linear diagrams of scenes where some objects get bigger instead of smaller as they get farther away. They can be made by tracing part of a picture with an overhead projector, then changing the focus and tracing some parts in the distance larger than they really appeared. Tracing paper might be placed over a picture and the same sort of thing accomplished. The fence posts could be cutouts made from tracings with copies or sets for each child.

Teaching suggestions

- Discuss the size of an airplane on the ground as compared with the size it appears to be in the air. "Have you ever been on an airplane?" "Was it hard to fit on the airplane?" "Have you ever seen that same type of airplane up in the air?" "Was it very big?" "How could you fit into such a small thing?" "If the plane is big enough for you to fit in, why does it look so small in flight?" "Does it shrink?" Help the children to see their real life experiences involving this concept. Conduct a similar discussion about a car or a bicycle that gets smaller as it moves away from the viewer.
- Discuss the concept as it is revealed in the pictures you have collected for this lesson. Especially discuss the importance of the artist's using this technique to help us see what he saw as he painted the picture. He not only had to put everything in the picture, but he had to show us how near or how far away it was. "How did the artist create the appearance of depth in this picture?" (Referring to one of the pictures.) "It is really just a flat piece of paper?" "Do artists need to know how to make things look real?" "Why do they?" "Do all artists always try to make things look real?"
- Measure the actual height of three children approximately the same size. Take the class outside or to a flight of stairs in the building. Place one child close to the group, one far from the group, and the third one half way between them. Have the children sight-measure with their hand and fingers or a pencil. Bring them back into the room.

Discuss what the students observed. "Which child was the biggest?" "Who was the smallest?" "What about the one in the middle?" "If she was away from you, too, why didn't she appear as small as _____?" Bring out the concept that the things farthest away appear smallest, and the things now so small appear larger but are not largest. Use the discovery approach in all questioning.

- Give each child a set of the graduated fence posts that you prepared earlier. Ask them to arrange them on their desks to show that there is a fence in a field and they are standing right at the beginning of it. Check the students' arrangements. Hold a discussion of which was closest to you or first in the row and which came next, and so on. Show your "what's-wrong-with-this picture" pictures and help the students to discover the errors — to explain in their own words what is wrong and how they would correct it. Your discussion depends on what pictures you have for demonstration. Help the children to understand the concept that things also get thinner and closer together as they get smaller and farther away.

■ What are all of the ways you could use this concept to "fool" people? (Make a statue so *big* that from a distance it looks larger than normal, use a small model airplane in a photograph or movie to look far away because it is little, paint a picture on a flat surface that looks as though you could walk into the picture — as though it has depth.)

Suggested art activity
Draw or paint a picture that illustrates the concept.

Alternative art activities
■ Have the students watch for examples of this concept on their way to and from school. Have a sharing time for discussion of their findings. Make lists.
■ Point out examples of this concept when the class is engaged in outside activities. Ask some fun trick questions to try to get them to use the concept in their thinking. For example, say, "Look at the tiny house over there. It must be a doll house or maybe some very, very little people live there." The children will quickly tell you that you are wrong. Have them draw pictures in which things get larger as they get farther away instead of smaller.
■ A print-making project could be used as a means of teaching the concept.
■ Using the concept in making scenery for a puppet show could be a way of teaching the concept.

Evaluation

■ If the students draw pictures of their choice and emphasize their use of the concept as they understand it, you immediately know how well they achieved the objective.

■ Watch for application of this principle in future work of the students.

Other things to consider

■ Vocabulary: perspective, picture plane, distance, horizon, nearer, appear, farther.
■ Art materials needed: drawing or painting materials (let students select media they feel most comfortable with).
■ Film: "Discovering Perspective," Bailey Film Associates
■ Prints:
 Adoration by Botticelli
 Venice by Canaletto
 La Grande Jatte by Seurat
 The Letter by Vermeer
 The Hay Wain by Constable
 Ville D' Avray by Corot
 Numbering at Bethlehem by Brueghel
 Maas at Dordrecht by Cuyp
 Trains du Soir by Delvaux
 Tranquility by Gasser
■ People who might have need for the concept: any artists that draw, paint, do cartoons, make prints and mosaics, do leather tooling, or woodcarving; people involved in interior design, art history and analysis, advertising design, or commercial art of many types.

LEVEL 3

ACTIVITY 77

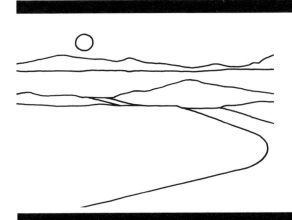

Concept taught by this activity: All of the space in an arrangement should be considered.

Objective: The student demonstrates ways in which all of the space in an arrangement has been considered.

A sample lesson plan for achieving the objective:

Teacher preparations
- Collect and display pictures and prints that illustrate the concept. This includes the list of paintings at the end of this activity as well as any others that seem appropriate.
- Collect and display samples of advertising such as automobiles, famous soft drinks, well-known cosmetics, travel posters, and famous brands of clothing.
- All art communicates an idea of some kind. Some pictures tell a story. Whether or not a picture tells a story or simply communicates an idea, we know that every part of a picture has a role to perform just as actors do in a play. Have a picture available from a magazine that tells a story. Take the picture and cut out individual figures and groups of figures from the background and foreground. Cut them out in a way that they can be reassembled in a sequence that begins with unrelated parts and ends with a complete visual story.

Teaching suggestions
- Take one of the parts of the picture you cut up and display it. Ask such questions as: "What story does this picture tell?" (Add another part.) "Does this second part make the story of the picture more complete?" "How?" (Add the rest of the parts.) "Is the message of the picture quite clear now?" "What is the message?" "Why is it so easy for everyone to see now?" "What would have happened to the

message if the parts were *dropped* on the background and weren't arranged as the artist had them?"
- Cut out one of the key figures or objects from one of the advertisements you selected and place it against a plain background that confuses the message of the ad. Ask such questions as: "What message or story does this picture tell?" "Is it confusing in any way?" "Why?" "How could we improve what the picture might tell us?" (Put figure or object with its original background.) "What is the message of this arrangement now?" "Is every part of it important?"
- Plain or vacant spaces are also important in pictures. Point to an example from the prints or pictures displayed. Ask such questions as: "Can anyone tell us why the artist left this area so plain?" "Would the feeling or the meaning of the picture change if this space were filled with lots of details?" "Can anyone tell us why artists need to *think* about what they want in a picture?" "Does the artist need to worry about every part of his picture?" "Should he have a reason for leaving some parts rather plain or vacant looking?" "Could there be times when he might want parts of his picture to look crowded?" "Do any of these prints have parts that could have been left out without ruining the picture?" (Discuss any that spark student interest. There are few absolutely "right" responses; accept every opinion.)

Suggested art activity
If the concept seems to be clearly implanted in the minds of the students, they can then be led into a drawing or painting activity to implant what has been taught. Motivate the students to choose paper, media, and subjects that appeal to them. Have each student try to tell a story or develop an idea of his own with his picture. Remind each student that every part of his picture is important and must be considered. Encourage the students to "think" about their task.

Alternative art activities
- Make a diorama for science or social studies. Note the importance of the background in relation to the figures and the foreground. Can one tell the whole story without the other?

- Have a committee plan a mural and assign each part to every student involved in the learning of the concept. Work toward a final product that develops a theme or a message and wherein every part, both foreground and background, plays a significant role in the final effect.
- Make a construction from found objects (make wood a primary source) and glue or fasten them together.

Evaluation

To determine whether or not each student clearly understands the concept taught, there should be evidence of thoughtful planning in the picture he drew or painted. If little or none was noted in the process, verbal responses are equally valid indicators of student understanding. A review of the prints might be appropriate for some students to evaluate whether or not they really understood the concept.

Other things to consider

- Vocabulary: background, environment, diorama, commercial artist, style, foreground, detail, space.
- Art materials needed: materials for diorama, water colors or tempera, paint, brushes, paper to paint on, and overlays.
- Prints:
  Harvesters by Breughel
  Hay Wain by Constable
  Lacemaker by Vermeer
  Rockets and Blue Lights by Turner
  The Night Watch by Rembrandt
  The Moneylender and Wife by Metsys
  Print Collector by Daumier
  Oath of Horatti by David
  Snap the Whip by Homer
- People who might have need for the concept: this is a universal art concept; almost any type of artistic process would require it.

LEVEL 3

ACTIVITY 78

Concept taught by this activity: Photography is used to provide information about objects and events in time, such as advertising, illustrations for books, and news items on TV.

Objective: The child demonstrates an awareness of various ways in which photography is used to provide information about objects and events in time through such things as art prints, news and television programs, films, magazines, and advertising.

A sample lesson plan for achieving the objective:

Teacher preparations

■ Have students bring photographs of themselves when they were younger and talk about how it helps them to know or remember what they used to look like or be like. Pictures of a former home might help them to recall the time when they used to live there, or a picture of an old friend could help them to remember events in their own lives.

■ Ask such questions as: "What are other examples of photographs that provide us with information?" "Are photographs used on TV?" "Where are photographs used besides TV?"

■ Collect and display pictures of things that students could discuss. Ask what events the students think the photographs might represent or what they tell us. See if students recognize how much the pictures add to the information they are given verbally or in writing. "Is a picture really worth a thousand *words?*" "Why?"

Teaching suggestions

■ Show art prints and discuss the fact that many art masterpieces would not be seen by the general populace of the world if it weren't for photography. This can be brought out by asking where, if at all, the students have come in contact with famous works of art.

■ Ask students to watch various television programs and observe different ways that photography is used to depict or recreate certain events.

■ Show a wildlife film and ask students to watch for examples in which they were able to see closer and better than they could see in real life. Discuss some events that they might have never seen if it weren't for photography.

● Question students as to how the close-up photography was accomplished.

● Time-lapse photography may also be discussed.

■ Discuss how photography is a "new" art, probably invented during the early 1500's. Some historians say Leonardo da Vinci, the Italian artist, invented it. Making permanent images on film didn't happen until about 1825, when Joseph Niepce made the first photograph. Ask: "What are all of the things, events, or people in history it would be nice to have photographs of?" (List them [cave men, Buddah, Jesus, Moses, the seven wonders of the ancient world, Washington, the Dark Ages].)

Suggested art activity

Have students keep a day-to-day photographic book of newsworthy events from newspapers for a week. They can talk about how some of these photos might be useful to someone twenty years later.

Alternative art activities

■ Have students write an advertisement and shoot their own pictures to use with it. These may be shared in groups or with the entire class. Pictures from magazines or pictures they have drawn can also be used.

■ Have students watch the news on television and report on ways in which photography made the news more interesting and more understandable.

■ Collect pictures that give photographic images of historical events of the past and describe how each picture helps clarify what happened.

■ Collect pictures from magazines and make a slide
presentation to show how well the concept is understood.
(Use sticky-back acetate to make the slides.)

Evaluation

Students may be evaluated through their reports to the
class, their advertisements and photography, and their
verbal responses during the lesson.

Other things to consider

■ Vocabulary: camera, time-lapse photography, events,
masterpieces, advertisements, illustrations.
■ Art materials needed: pictures, newspapers, magazines,
film, scrapbook paper, acetate, pens for labeling, cameras.
■ Prints: Any art print can be used to illustrate how
photography has made it possible for us to see works of
art, even though museums are not easily available.
■ *Films:
"From Blossom to Fruit" (includes microscopic views)
"How Does a Garden Grow" (time-lapse photography);
    Bailey Film Associates
"The World of Animals: Looking at Fishes, Looking at
    Birds" (microscopic views); Encyclopaedia Britannica
    Films
■ People who might have need for the concept: people
involved in commercial art, photography, and technical and
industrial illustration.

---

*Many other films showing close-ups, microscopic views, and
time-lapse photography are as appropriate as these and are likely
available in district film libraries, public libraries, or film
depositories.

LEVEL3   # ACTIVITY 79

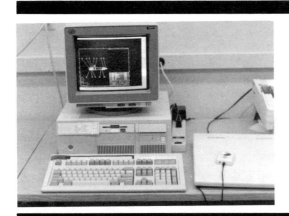

Concept taught by this activity: Printing and lettering processes are communication tools that are used by artists.

Objective: The student demonstrates an awareness of specific ways artists can use printing and lettering processes as communication tools.

A sample lesson plan for achieving the objective:

Teacher preparations
■ Display examples of lettering used in advertising for such media as magazines, newspapers, TV, posters, bulletin boards, and displays.
■ Be prepared to discuss some of the printing processes involved in doing a newspaper, as well as other printing materials, from typewriting, ditto, mimeograph, and xerox to offset, stencil (or silk screen), letter press, and gravure. These need not be discussed in any detail but pictures, examples, or brief descriptions of any would be helpful.
■ Have some commercial illustrations exhibited that contain strong visual messages to sell an idea or product.

Teaching suggestions
■ Begin the discussion by determining how familiar students are with the terms *printing* and *lettering* and then see if any know of their commercial uses: "What is printing?" "Can machines do printing?" "Who can name some machines that print letters?"
■ See if students know that artists use lettering and printing processes in a commercial way. ("Does anyone know what commercial artists do?") Develop the idea that all advertising in all media as well as the illustrations for all published and printed matter began with an artist's bid to do a job for a specified amount of money.

■ Develop the notion that the artist's and his employer's first concern is to attract the viewer's (consumer's) attention and to communicate an idea or to sell a product.
■ Have a commercial printer — a parent or a member of the community — come and discuss printing processes with the children. If possible, take the students to see some of the actual machines used in printing or to a commercial art studio to see artists at work.
■ Have students cut out various types of letters from magazines and letter their names by pasting a variety of letter styles together. Tell them to select styles that they would like to "sell" to other people.

Suggested art activity
Study TV ads and determine which are the most effective and why. Discuss the role of repetition in advertising.

Alternative art activities
■ Have the students look at a number of advertisements and rate their effectiveness in attracting attention and selling or communicating an idea.
■ Assign someone to find out which products in certain kinds of stores attract their attention first and why. Have another group of students determine how long (five minutes — three seconds . . . what?) most people view a sign or advertisement and make some decision about it.
■ Have a group of students find out if the different printing processes have any effect on the appearance of the artists products. ("Are there any advantages of one process over another?")

Evaluation

The student's degree of involvement and his responses in discussion will have to be carefully observed to determine whether or not his awareness of the concept has been enlarged.

Other things to consider

- Vocabulary: printing, lettering, printing process, ditto, mimeograph, xerox, off set, multilith, stencil, silk screen, letter press, gravure, typesetting, typesetter, engraver, commercial art, commercial artist, advertising agency.
- Art materials needed: photographs and advertisements from every available resource.
- Prints:
  Poster — Moulin Rouge by Toulouse-Lautrec
  Poster — Jan. 18 to Feb. 12 by Shahn
  Combination Concrete by Davis
- People who might have need for the concept: people that work for printing companies, advertisers, and commercial artists of all types.

LEVEL 3   # ACTIVITY 80

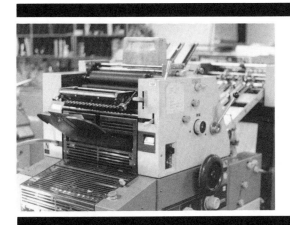

Concept taught by this activity: Much writing the student sees was printed by machines: a typewriter, ditto, mimeograph, offset, and letterpress. These processes relate to the student's own printmaking.

Objective: The student associates printing done on various machines with the experiences he has had with writing and with simple imprinting methods.

A sample lesson plan for achieving the objective:

Teacher preparations
■ If the children have not had an experience in printing or if their experiences in imprinting were some time ago, the concept will have more meaning if it is preceded by an art activity. (Below are preparatory steps for an imprinting experience.)
  ● Lay out paints, clay, fruit, vegetables, or other materials as materials for the children's tables or desks.
  ● Cover tables or desks with paper or some other protective material.
  ● Lay out various sizes, colors, and shapes of paper.
  ● Have all visual aids placed for easy access — hung up, or propped against the chalkboard (include examples of fabric or wallpaper with repeat designs).
  ● Have children wear an old shirt, smock, or other covering to protect their clothing.
■ Display pictures of various equipment used in printing and examples of printing done by each machine.

Teaching suggestions
■ For the imprinting activity the following discussion is suggested:
  ● Show the children examples of repeat designs in fabrics or wall coverings and ask: "Did you know you could

make designs like this?" "How many different designs do you see in this pattern?" "Why do you suppose this is called a repeat pattern?" "Do you know what repeat means?" (Over and over the same way.)
  ● Point to a design motif or shape and say to the class: "If I had the object that made this shape in my hand, I would just stamp it on the material here and here and here, until it covered all the spaces you see it in now. Would I need any paint or ink on my design first?" "Would it show on the material without paint or ink?" ("If soft clay?")
  ● Use a rubber stamp and ink pad or take half an orange, or an art gum eraser, potato, or some other firm object you've cut a design into and dip it into some water soluble printers ink (or a thick mixture of tempera paint) and imprint on a piece of paper. As you demonstrate the process, make the point that anything we put into some liquidlike substance and place on another surface is a form of imprinting or printmaking: bare feet coming out of water and walking across dry pavement, a dog with muddy feet walking across a floor, or a child with dirty hands on a white table top. Therefore, any object with an interesting shape can be dipped in ink or paint and imprinted.
NOTE: Objects for imprinting can include hands, fruits cut in half, sponges, and any kinds of objects or gadgets that have interesting shapes. You can also use vegetables, oil clay, art gum erasers, paraffin wax, and any other material in which a design can be dug or carved. Inks can be made with thick tempera, food coloring, India ink, textile paint, thick instant tea or coffee, finger paint, liquid detergent and tempera, or liquid starch and tempera. Papers can include newsprint, old newspaper, butcher paper, construction paper, vellon, white and colored tissue, or manila paper.
  ● Give several children an opportunity to come up and demonstrate the imprinting process. Note that too much or too little paint on their design can spoil the way it prints. Encourage them to repeat their design and so establish a pattern.
  ● Let all of the children experience the process at their own desks or tables.

- If you include the preceding imprinting experience with this activity, it would be best to start this part the next day. The discussion might go like this:
  - "Can someone tell me any of the ways that imprinting (as you did yesterday) is like the writing you're learning to do?" (They're on paper, they're done with something that makes marks, and they're repeated.)
  - "Did you know that the writing you read in books and see on TV or in movies is also a kind of printmaking?" "Who can tell me some of the ways that they are the same?"
  - "How do you suppose the letters are printed on the pages in your books?" (Draw out the idea of printing being done with machines.) "Do any of you have machines in your home that make letters?" (Typewriter, adding machine, any others.)
  - "Have you seen any machines in our school that make letters?" (Mimeograph, ditto, xerox, and thermofax.) The discussion might lead into mention of a parent who works in a printing shop or for a newspaper or magazine publisher. There might be some student who has seen an offset or other large printing machine in operation. If pictures of any such machines are available, they could add interest to the discussion.
- Discuss how life would change if we didn't have the sophisticated ways of printing.
- Visit a print shop or newspaper company. (This may or may not be possible.)
- Allow the children to make dittos or duplicates on the school equipment.
- Discuss how the machines and our own ways of printing are alike.

Suggested art activity
Set up committees of children to make a bulletin board or display on printmaking illustrating examples of printing that range from samples of their own work (writing and imprinting) to that produced by all the various machines. Pictures might also be included.

Alternative art activities
Paint a mural on printmaking processes and machines. Let each child do a picture of some phase and then put them all together on the bulletin board in a way that tells a visual story. They could also make the letters for any labels that are needed. Many variety stores carry toy lettering stamps made of rubber. The children could use such a tool in learning this concept.

Evaluation

Evaluation will require close observation on the part of the teacher, who will note when each student seems to have acquired an awareness of the concept. Both what the student says and what he does will offer clues to the depth of this understanding.

Other things to consider

- Vocabulary: imprinting, monoprint, mimeograph, ditto, xerox, thermofax, typewriter, offset, letterpress, adding machine, calculator, printmaking, print shop.
- Art materials needed: see "Teaching Suggestions." Also, samples of walltex, wallpaper, or fabrics with a repeat design.
- Prints:
  Le Jour by Braque
  Combination Concrete by Davis (lettering used in painting)
  Autumn by Koryusai (a woodcut print)
  Poster — Moulin Rouge by Lautrec (a colored lithograph print)
  Marilyn Monroe by Warhol (a photo stencil print)
  Poster — Jan. 18 to Feb. 12 by Shahn (colored lithograph)
  Print Collector by Daumier (lithograph)
  Young Hare by Durer (wood engraving)

Prodigal Son by Rembrandt (etching)
- People who might have need for the concept: commercial artists, printers, and artists that make prints of all types.

LEVEL 3   ACTIVITY 81

Concept taught by this activity: Artists use a variety of tools in the making of art.

Objective: The student demonstrates an awareness that artists use a variety of tools in the making of art.

A sample lesson plan for achieving the objective:

Teacher preparations
Draw from the following list of tools artists use in the making of art.

Artist	Tools Used
Painter	brushes, pencils, charcoal, palette, erasers, palette knife
Printmaker	engravers, presses, spoon, limestone, copper plates, pencils
Architect	drafting arm, transit, slide rule, pens, ink, templates, triangles, T-square, rulers
Sculptor	chisels, mallets, welding equipment, carving tools, modeling tools
Ceramist/Potter	pug mill, kiln, potter's wheel, wedging table, sponges, cutting tools, scrapers, turning tools
Interior designer	pencils, fabric samples, catalogs
Package designer	brushes, air brush, pencils, pens, silk screen, squeegee
Illustrator	brushes, pens, pencils, air brush, silk screen, squeegee
Fabric designer	looms, hooking equipment
Jewelry designer	centrifugal caster, crucibles, files, casting equipment
Crafts designer	power saws and drills, glue, paste, hammers, files, sandpaper
Industrial designer	pens, inks, brushes, pencils, air brush

Teaching suggestions
■ Brainstorm on what tools the student has around the house: "How many tools can you name?" "How many uses for a brush?"
■ "What tools do artists use?"
■ Bring a picture of a tool no one else will bring. Be prepared to describe all the ways it could be used in art.
■ "What kinds of tools would be crucial to an artist's success?" "How expensive are his tools?" "Do some artists have a greater investment in tools than others?"
■ "Can you look at an artist's work and tell what tools he used?"

Suggested art activity
Select a tool that artists use and demonstrate its use in an art product. Each student should try to select one they've never tried before.

Alternative art activities
■ Have two or three artists visit the class and demonstrate the use of their tools.
■ Make a display of artists' tools for the classroom.
■ Create tools of your own and make a picture, design, or form using them.
■ Take an ordinary tool and use it in a way that's different from its intended function: using a pencil to shape clay or drawing with a file.
■ Look at artists' prints and describe the tools they used to create them.

Evaluation

When the student demonstrates an awareness of tools used by four or more different artists, the objective has been achieved.

Other things to consider

- Vocabulary: use the list of tools.
- Art materials needed: whatever tools and materials are appropriate to the students' interests.
- Resources: art catalogs and films on art processes.
- Prints:
  The Smokers by Brouwer (oil painting)
  Three Flags by Johns (encaustic painting)
  Autumn by Koryusai (woodcut)
  Delphic Sibyl by Michelangelo (fresco)
  Justice and Peace by Overstreet (hard-edge painting)
  Poster — Moulin Rouge by T. Lautrec (lithography)
  Marilyn Monroe by Warhol (photo silk screen)
  Young Hare by Durer (wood engraving)
  Prodigal Son by Rembrandt (copper etching)
  Hudson River Logging by Homer (water color painting)
- People who might have need for the concept: art critic, art historian, museum director.

LEVEL 3 ACTIVITY 82

Concept taught by this activity: An object in the path of light casts a shadow, and cast shadows fall away from the light source.

Objective: The students will draw or paint the shadow of an object falling away from the light source and will be able to verbally describe what caused the shadow.

A sample lesson plan for achieving the objective:

Teacher preparations
- Collect and display pictures and prints that illustrate the objective and the concept.
- Collect various objects that can be held in front of a direct source of light. Have some objects that will block the light and some that will not so that the children can determine what blocks light and where the shadows go when the light is blocked.
- Make the room as dark as possible. (Close curtains, shut off lights.) Obtain materials for your light source. Flashlights, small globes that can be connected to batteries, spot lights, opaque projector, lighted candles, or the sun may be used.

Teaching suggestions
"How could you tell about what time it is if you were outside on a sunny day without a clock or a watch to look at?" (By observing the sun's position and the length of shadows.)
- Show the students pictures of people or objects with shadows. Discuss which way the shadow is going. (Away from the source of light.) Ask the students where the sun would have to be to make the shadow go in that direction. Demonstrate the formation of shadows with various sources of light. Let the students experiment themselves. Ask them

questions such as the following: "Which way does the shadow fall when you hold the light to the right of the object?" "To the left?" "Above?" "Which way does your shadow fall when your friend holds the light in front of you?" "Behind you?"
- Take the children outdoors at different periods during the day. Let them see the difference in the places their shadow falls on the ground. Have them compare the direction their shadow went to the position of the sun. Look at the shadows cast by bicycles and other interesting objects.
- The children can get the idea that shadows fall away from the light source by using finger puppets. Set up a direct source of light. Have them use their fingers as objects blocking the light. When their fingers come in front of the light, the shadows fall away from the source of light onto the wall, the screen, or whatever you have provided.
- Discuss the relationship of the concept to these in science:
  - The turning of the earth in space brings daytime and nighttime to the earth.
  - We have night and day because the sun shines and the earth turns.
  - The sun is always shining.
  - Objects placed before a direct source of light will cast shadows.
  - Sundials work on this principle.

Suggested art activity
Draw or paint a picture of several objects and their cast shadows. Show where the sun is in the sky.

Alternative art activities
- Ask students to illustrate this question: "Which side of a tree would you stand on to be in its shadow in the morning?" (West.) "In the afternoon?" (East.)
- Students could be responsible for setting up and performing shadow plays. They would need to set up a direct source of light. They would also need a sheet. They would perform behind the sheet but in front of the direct source of light. The audience would be seeing the shadows from the opposite side of the sheet. If the students could set this up by themselves, they would be able to understand the concept.

■ The children could draw self portraits. Take them outside and have them stand with their back against the sun, making a shadow in front of them. Have them draw on a piece of paper what they see in front of them. They might even *trace* the shadow as a warm-up.

Evaluation

Evaluation could be done by reviewing the picture of shadows and having the children tell where the light source is coming from for the picture. Also, through questioning, you could find out if the child could comprehend the concept. Ask questions such as the following: "If I were holding a light directly in front of you, which way would your shadow go?" "If your shadow fell to your left side, where would the light be?" If the child can answer questions like these, he understands the concept.

Other things to consider

■ Vocabulary: shadow, source of light, object, block and blocking, form, shadow side, cast shadow.
■ Art materials needed: drawing and painting materials as selected by the student, a variety of different kinds of lights and objects to use for demonstrations.
■ Prints:
Mona Lisa by Leonardo Da Vinci
The Scout by Remington
Cliff of Etretat After Storm by Courbet
Crucifixion by Dali
Notre Dame by Daumier
The Gleaners by Millet
The Letter by Vermeer
Oath of the Horatii by David
St. Joseph by De La Tour
Tranquility by Gasser
Seven A.M. by Hopper
■ People who might have need for the concept: people who draw, paint, make prints, mosaics, do leather tooling and wood carving; interior designers; people who deal with art history and analysis; cartoonists; commercial artists such as advertising designers and illustrators.

LEVEL 3   ACTIVITY 83

Concept taught by this activity: Some objects have the appearance of lines in space (trees and steel girders). Lines can be implied by the edge of shapes, by a series of points, or by repetition of shapes and movement.

Objective: The student demonstrates an awareness of what a line is, and why some things have a linear appearance.

A sample lesson plan for achieving the objective:

Teacher preparations
■ Have a pin wheel (or some other wheel you can spin) available for discussion plus some of the prints recommended for this activity. It may also be desirable to have whatever art materials that are appropriate ready for any activities that need application.
■ Collect appropriate prints and whatever additional illustrations are available.

Teaching suggestions
Develop a discussion that involves children in a discovery of what lines are and how they perceive lines or linear forms. The following dialogue is a sample of what might be done.
■ "Have you ever seen a 'line' of deer?" "A 'line' of people?" "A 'line' of fence posts?" "What are *all* of the lines you can think of?" (Make note of them; visuals could be drawn of each: a line of telephone poles, a clothesline, a jet airliner, a line of kids [or in a circle], a line of ducks, a line of trees, and others.)
■ "What is a line?" (Field a variety of responses, then draw a line on the board.) "Is this a line?" "Is the chalk a line?" "Is your pencil?" "Is the space between _____ a line?" "Is this string (or thread) a line? "What are some *other* things you think are lines?"

■ "When is a line *not* a line?" (Look out a window or at a picture of something that has a linelike or linear appearance and discuss how things such as trees have branches that look like lines in the distance but are definite shapes or forms when they are near.)
■ Look at a corner. "Is there a line there?" "Is there a line on the corner of a box?" (Help students come to the conclusion that when two edges come together a line is implied. You may need to discuss the word *implied* first.) "Can you find any *other* implied shapes?" "In the room or outside?"
■ Draw a disconnected line on the board and ask, "What is this?" (It is a series of short lines but the eye seems to connect them into one long line.)
■ Spin a wheel and ask, "Can anyone see any implied lines here?" "How about when the wheel stops?" "What if we put some *dots* on the wheel and spin it?"
■ Look at some of the prints and ask: "What shapes are line-like in this picture?" "Are there any implied lines?" "Who can come up and show us some?"
■ "What kinds of art tools can we use to make lines?" "Will a pencil make lots of different kinds of lines?" "What else would you need to make some other kinds of lines that pencils can't make?" (Pens, sticks dipped in ink, magic markers, charcoal, chalk, wide and thin brushes dipped in paint, and crayons both pointed and blunt.)
■ Discuss how a line always goes in some direction, and it may return and touch itself to make a shape. A line can be busy or idle, sitting or standing, thin or fat, fuzzy or smooth. It can take a zigzag walk, or a scalloped one; it can go over a mountain or around a lake. It can even shape a house. (Fun ideas or concepts can be developed from the room and from the children's backgrounds.)
■ A line can express the force of the person or the thing that creates it. Each person is different; the lines we make are also different. Have the students try these ideas as they are discussed.
■ Discuss the concept as it relates to the following:
  ● Geometry: lines, line segments, rays, angles, points, planes, and geometric figures.

- Health: skeletal and circulatory systems.
- Social Studies: lines in map work.

Suggested art activity

Make constructions, using straws or other thin shapes and make interesting linear forms or figures to hang inside the construction.

Alternative art activites

- Make line drawings: simple home and room blueprints, maps of home to school, church, friends' homes, and other familiar places.
- Punch dots on colored paper to express a line.
- Choose a simple lined pattern; place it on art media (tin foil, paper) and outline through both with a pin.
- Make a collage using cord, yarn, cloth scraps, and rick rack.
- Laminate between waxed paper or another medium. Use various lines representing materials: thread, fish line, string, cord, and pipe cleaners.
- Make a line sculpture using coat hangers, wire, and pipe cleaners.
- Invite other children into the class, enough so that each child has two others to whom he must explain and demonstrate what he has learned through the use of his projects and assignments.
- Have several mail order catalogs and let committees find examples of lines used in furniture and other items in the catalog.
- Have children make a list of lines they can find around home.

Evaluation

When the student demonstrates an awareness of what a line is and how some things have a linear or linelike appearance, the objective of the lesson has been achieved.

Other things to consider

- Vocabulary: implied, linear, linelike, repetition, disconnected.
- Pictures needed: skeletons of humans and various animals from science, health, and various textbooks; freeways; a city skyline; the circulatory system of various animals, trees, and woods; steel girders in building construction.
- Art materials needed: a variety of drawing tools and paper of different sizes.
- Prints:
  Numbering at Bethlehem by Breughel
  I and the Village by Chagall
  Frances I by Clouet
  Nude Descending #2 by Duchamp (abstraction)
  Seven A.M. by Hopper
  Mural by Pollock
  Virgin Forest by Rousseau
  Still Music by Shahn
  The Brooklyn Bridge by Stella
  Trains de Soir by Delvaux
  Birds In Bamboo Tree by Koson
- People who might have need for the concept: This is a very universal concept used by almost all areas of art.

LEVEL 3

ACTIVITY 84

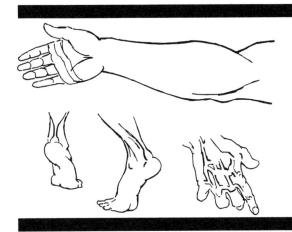

Concept taught by this activity: Lines can be used to describe the contour, or framework, of an object as well as its individual parts.

Objective: The student demonstrates an awareness that lines can be used to describe the contour (outline) or framework (skeleton) of an object as well as its individual parts.

A sample lesson plan for achieving the objective:

Teacher preparations
- Have suggested prints, photographs, and other appropriate illustrations displayed or available for discussion.
- Have media for drawing ready for use and in enough quantity to give students some options in choosing what they would like to work with.

Teaching suggestions
In introducing the concept, make certain students clearly understand the terms used; then move into ways in which artists used the idea.
- "What is a line?" "Where are there lines in this room?" (Help students recognize that most lines they see are actually forms: string and wire, or spaces between forms — the space between ceiling tiles, or sections of cement on a sidewalk.)
- "Could we draw pictures without using lines?" "Is there anything we couldn't draw without lines?"
- "Does anyone know what contour means?" (The outside shape of people or objects.) "Can we draw the contour of something with lines?" "Can we tell who a person is from his contour?" Try it and see.

- "What does the word *framework* mean?" "Have you ever heard of the framework of a building?" (The framework is like the skeleton of the building.) "Could we draw the framework of something with lines?"
- "If we drew the contour of someone in this class and we drew their skeleton inside of it, would we need to do anything more with our picture?" "There are a lot of other parts we can also include with our lines, aren't there? Sometimes these are referred to as *detail*."
- "Would an artist be concerned about all three things we've mentioned — the contour, the framework, and the individual parts that go with them?" "Let's look at some pictures by artists and see if they were really concerned about all three." As different pictures are discussed, students will readily see if the artists drew or painted the contour and the individual parts or details of things in a natural way, but he will need help in recognizing that the artist had to understand the skeleton or framework of such things as animals, plants, and objects too, perceiving bones in the right places and knowing how trees grow.

Suggested art activity
Have students select whatever media they prefer and draw a variety of subjects of their choice, paying special attention to the outside shape, the details inside the contour, and carefully thinking about the framework inside the contour and its influence on what they see.

Alternative art activities
- Do line drawings of the contour of fellow students. See if they recognize one another from the contours. Imagine the individual's contour as being a shadowy form.
- Imagine what the framework of different objects might be like and try drawing just the framework (skeleton).

Evaluation

Students whose awareness has changed should exhibit a greater concern for looking at and more carefully rendering the contour and detail of things they draw.

Other things to consider

- Vocabulary: framework, contour, structure, line, render.
- Film loops:
  "Lines as Structure"
  "Characteristics of Line"
  "Line Techniques"
  "Implied Line and Movement"
  "Texture and Pattern"
  "Line and Space"
  (All by Bailey Film Associates)
- Prints:
  Ice Skating Palace by Bonnard
  Le Jour by Braque
  Birds in Bamboo Tree by Koson
  Leisure by Leger
  Mural by Pollock
  Still Music by Shahn
  The Aficionado by Picasso
  Composition 1963 by Miro
  The Blue Cart by Van Gogh
  Mother and Child by Kollwitz
  Prodigal Son by Rembrandt
- People who might have need for the concept: this is a rather universal concept used by almost all areas of art.

LEVEL 3   ACTIVITY 85

Concept taught by this activity: The child can make clay forms with coils or slabs when he understands the process of joining parts together with slip.

Objective: The student will join coils or slabs of clay together with slip.

A sample lesson plan for achieving the objective:

Teacher preparations
To help eliminate housekeeping problems and to assist the teacher in making adequate preparation prior to the actual teaching process, the following precautions are recommended:
- Have old shirts or smocks available to protect children's clothing. Short sleeves are preferred.
- Have newspaper, butcher paper, pieces of canvas, or burlap-covered boards to protect desks or tables and to serve as a mat-finish surface to work on. (Clay sticks to any hard, slick surface.)
- See that the clay is properly wedged and free of air bubbles. The clay should be moist enough that it doesn't crack when you roll it into a coil, then bend the coil in a circle; neither should it be so moist that it is sticky.
- Have adequate towels and waste baskets for cleanup and a bucket for hardened and unused clay. Children will need to wash thoroughly and be able to get rid of all the paper that was used. See that children do not throw away any clay or wash it down the sink. Any clay not fired can be resoftened, wedged, and used again. Clay washed down the sink in large amounts can plug up drains. You may also need to borrow a broom to sweep afterwards.
- If available, have pictures to display that illustrate processes in clay and clay products. If you are able to display any "real" pots or clay sculpture, so much the better. You will need tools such as thin pieces of wire attached to two clothespins or to short dowel sticks (to cut clay in half) and old combs, pencils, popsicle sticks, or any object that might

be useful for creating textures, carving designs, and cutting, gouging, or smoothing clay.
- Have available an area away from direct heat for drying clay objects after they are made. Plastic bags or sheets are also needed to cover the clay while it dries. Any clay object that dries too quickly (a few hours rather than gradually throughout a week) is in danger of cracking.
- Have containers such as tuna fish cans available for each child to make his own slip in.
- If possible, have rolling pins or sections of pipe available to roll clay into flat slabs. Flat slabs of plaster about four inches thick and somewhere between 9 × 12" and 24 × 36" are also helpful as surfaces for drying or wedging clay on.

Teaching suggestions
To introduce the concept, begin with a discussion and demonstration period. The introduction might include such questions and demonstrations as the following:
- "Here are some objects. What are they made of?" "How were they put together?" "How was this texture made?" OR
- "Who knows what clay is?" "What is clay used for?" "Have any of you ever made something with clay?" "Did the clay you used get dry or hard?" (Some schools use oil base clays that never dry out and can't be fired.) "What can you make out of clay?" "Can you see any clay objects (or pictures of) in this room?"
- You might also discuss clay objects, such as pottery, that some children have in their home.
- Briefly show how clay stretches, and how it will take on the design or surface of anything it is pushed into or onto. Discuss how it will dry out and crack, and present the other information about clay found under "Teacher preparations."
- When motivation has peaked, go into the process of joining clay pieces together. "How can clay pieces be joined together?" (Pinching, pulling, pressing.) "Does anyone know what clay slip is?" (Clay mixed with water for a heavy, creamy consistency.) Demonstrate scoring and joining pieces of clay together with slip. (Use both coils and slabs in the demonstration.) "When you can join clay pieces together like that, what are some of the things you can make that don't work so well when you just press pieces together?" (Joints are more secure.)

Suggested art activity

When all instruction has been given, a range of possible projects have been discussed, the housekeeping rules are understood, and the process concept of this lesson seems clear to everyone, each student should receive about one pound of clay to begin working with. Animals, bowls, pots, bottles, mugs, and vases can be made with the slip process of joining parts together. Offer lots of suggestions, but allow students many alternatives.

Alternative art activities

- Roll out a slab of clay and drape it over a rock until it hardens enough to retain its shape. Remove it from the rock and mount three small legs to its underside with slip. (It will look like a dish with legs.) Let it dry and decorate it with textures, painting, or both.
- Make the same kind of form by draping clay in a small hammock made of burlap or some other coarse material. With slip, add legs or handles.

Evaluation

Any student who successfully joins two pieces of clay together with slip has achieved the lesson objective.

Other things to consider

- Vocabulary: pot, slab, coil, clay, elastic, kiln, firing clay, bisque ware, leather-hard clay, glaze, slip, scoring clay, pinch pot, ceramics, potter, pottery, plaster bat, potter's wheel.
- Art materials needed or helpful (all are not necessary): clay, plaster bats, plastic bags, smocks, aprons or shirts, rolling pins or sections of pipe, pairs of sticks from ¼″ to ¾″ thick (to control the thickness of slabs), a bucket for soaking clay, and paper canvas or burlap to cover desks or tables.
- For textures or designs, the following kinds of things are helpful: popsicle sticks, wire for cutting clay, old combs, pencils, broken saw blades, rope, burlap, cheese cloth, corrugated cardboard, chains, keys, wire of all kinds, machine parts, bolts and nuts, radio parts, sponges, springs, and containers for water.
- People who might have need for the concept: sculptors, ceramists, potters.

LEVEL 3

ACTIVITY 86

Concept taught by this activity: Given appropriate terms to use, students can describe differences among works of art.

Objective: The student describes differences among works of art as he identifies subject matter, color usage, the feeling or mood the works portray, the age of the works, and what is happening in them.

A sample lesson plan for achieving the objective:

Teacher preparations
Collect and display a variety of prints and pictures of works of art. Where possible, original works might be displayed. Try to include art representing a variety of media and similar types, categories, or styles.

Teaching suggestions
To get students thinking comparatively, descriptively:
- "Can you make up a simile about this painting?" (Hold up any print.) Sample similes: The mood is as quiet as time passing. The leaves are as restless as the bobbles on mother's necklace. (The teacher may have to start the similes, such as: "The shadows (in the painting) are as long as _____.") Strive for unusual comparisons.
- Simile and metaphor are almost the same. The difference is that a metaphor is more implicit and a simile is more explicit. For example, "The Renaissance was like the opening of a flower" is a simile. "The Renaissance blossomed" is a metaphor. Flowers and Renaissance are

not really alike. The likeness is hidden, obscure. "Can you make up metaphors about this painting?" The students can generate ideas for a metaphor by fluency exercises like these: "What things are not at all like color?" (Snow, coal, paper, book pages, darkness, gray.) Example composed from brainstorming: "The snow spilt its palette." (The hidden analogy: white is the reflection of all colors — the palette is the artist's tray of colors.) Other example metaphors: "the evening of life," for a painting of an old man in a rocking chair, possibly at sunset. The beauty of a metaphor is in the surprise, the dissimilarity of the ideas expressed by the metaphor.
- "Think up appropriate titles for these prints, then I'll tell you what the artist called it."
- "Do artists always work in exactly the same way?" (No.) "Why not?" When artists work in their own special way, they are becoming creative. Before they can be creative they have to know all about seeing and all about their craft. They must have knowledge, as well as imagination.
- Develop some headings that the class can use to describe differences among works of art. Keep it simple and at the level of the student. More sophisticated terms will be used later in the child's experience (activity #109). Include with the heading suggested by students the following:
  - Subject matter
  - Color usage (What kinds of colors are used primarily, warm, cool)
  - Feeling or mood portrayed (lovely, weird, busy, happy)
  - The age of the work (recent, when dad was little, very old). Students will not likely know the age of the works but let them speculate, then supply the information at the end of the discussion.
  - What's happening? (Describe what is happening in the painting, what people are doing, how colors, textures, or patterns lead the eye.)
  - Is it real-looking or abstract?
- In the discussion, all the students' ideas are appropriate if they help them differentiate among works of art. The major purpose of this activity is to encourage students to begin looking at and thinking about works of art.

- Keep the student from knowing the names of the art work or any other facts until *after* their discussion, when they *ask* for further information.

Suggested art activity
Have the student take two pictures or pieces of sculpture that have one basic similarity. Have him chart all the differences he can see.

Alternative art activities
- "Look at a print or a picture of art and write a story about it. Speculate as to what happened and why the artist created it."
- "Look at two or three examples of art that are by the same artist. Write an imaginative story about the artist — what he was like, when he lived, and the kind of life he must have lived. Draw a picture of what you think he looked like." If the student is so inclined, he may want to find out more about the artist and see how close his imaginative description was to the truth.
- The above suggestions could also be done with other forms of art, such as architecture or sculpture.

Evaluation

When the student is able to describe differences among works of art and gives some indication that he has looked at works of art in a discerning way, the objective has been achieved.

Other things to consider

- Vocabulary: mood, feeling, subject matter, portray, usage, metaphor.
- Art materials needed: drawing and painting materials as selected by the student.
- Prints:
  (Portraits) *Bacchus* by Caravaggio
  　　　　　 Bandaged Ear by Van Gogh
  　　　　　 Artists Mother by Whistler
  　　　　　 Mother and Child by Kollwitz
  (Places)　 *Fox Island* by Hartley
  　　　　　 View of Toledo by El Greco
  　　　　　 Venice by Canaletto
  　　　　　 Ville d'Avray by Corot
  (Events)　 *Guernica* by Picasso
  　　　　　 Rockets and Blue Lights by Turner
  　　　　　 Sacrament, Last Supper by Dali
  　　　　　 Knockout by Morreau
- People who might have need for the concept: art historians, museum curators, gallery directors, teachers.

LEVEL 3   ACTIVITY 87

Concept taught by this
activity: The function of an
object influences its form.

Objective: The student can describe ways in which the function of an object influenced its form.

A sample lesson plan for achieving the objective:

Teacher preparations
■ Have magazines available for examination later. Collect household items, such as spoons, forks, glasses, bowls, and pans, which illustrate the principle "form follows function."
■ Have available pictures of buildings and other functional designs for display and discussion.

Teaching suggestions
■ Discuss the meaning of the word *function,* and show illustrations of familiar objects that have had parts altered so that they are nonfunctional: a pencil sharpener without the basket, a tape dispenser without tape, a toothbrush with no bristles, and magazine ads altered by scissors (such as cars without wheels). Instruct children in this manner: "Look carefully at these pictures. Each object has something unusual about it. Who can tell what I mean?" After children discover each error, follow this line of discussion: "Would you like to have these kinds of things in *your* home?" "Even if you think they are funny, would you want to use them the way they are and not have the kind you are familiar with?" "Why not?" (Develop the idea that the objects they are discussing would be very hard to use — that they aren't *functional.*) "Do any of you have little brothers and sisters?" "Do they ever have trouble going up or down stairs?" "Getting a drink at a drinking fountain?" "Why do they?" (These things aren't designed for people their size and therefore aren't very functional for them.)

■ "A great architect (Frank Lloyd Wright or Louis Sullivan) once said that everything we use — cars, tables, desks, vacuum cleaners, bicycles — all of these things should look nice but that they should *first* be able to do what they were made for. Do you think that's true?" "Remember the story of *The Three Bears* and how everything was 'just right'?"
■ "Would you like a chair if it were terribly hard to sit in and yet very nice to look at?" "What if you lived in a world where you were the first man there, and you had to invent all of the things we use in our homes, at work, and in our communities?" "What if in designing all of these things you could see them through Frank Lloyd Wright's eyes and with his philosophy, would some of them look different than they do today?" (Form committees and have children work in groups to discuss different categories of familiar objects and see if they can think of objects whose shapes ought to be changed.)
■ Emphasize the idea that what something is used for helps determine what it will look like. ("Would you move a bed on bicycle wheels rather than on casters?" "Should a glass have the size and shape of a pitcher?")
■ Take a walk or research magazines to collect examples of forms that incorporate the concept and forms that violate the concept.
■ Look at pictures, photographs, and artists' prints that use the concept and discuss them. "If artists are also people who design and make ordinary things such as we have in and around our homes, how would an understanding of function help them?"
■ Discuss how the materials an object is made of might also influence its appearance. ("Why not make pillows out of steel or bicycles out of foam rubber or shoes out of paper?")

Suggested art activity
Create imaginary machines that have no function (such as an electric fork) or try to create a more functional design for some common object or machine. Improve some product.

Alternative art activities
Have a discussion of how sometimes we change the function of an object, such as making a flower pot out of an

old stove, a lamp out of a vase, and mailboxes out of plows. To use an object for something other than for what it was designed can be very much like using a melody with words that were written for a different tune. Generally it is *not* beautiful.

Evaluation

Through teacher awareness and through classroom discussion and activities the teacher should be able to determine if the students understand the concept and have an awareness that objects we use everyday look the way they do because their intended use influenced the way an artist had to design them.

Other things to consider

- Vocabulary: form, structure, designer, function, practical, useful.
- Art materials needed: drawing and painting materials and construction media if desired.
- Books: *An American Architecture* by Frank Lloyd Wright
- Prints:
  My Gems by Harnett
  Six Day Bicycle Rider by Hopper
  Numbering at Bethlehem by Brueghel
  Still Life with Pipe by Chardin
  The Brooklyn Bridge by Stella
  Man with Helmet by Rembrandt
  Trains du Soir by Delvaux
  Mass at Dordrecht by Cuyp
  Bedroom at Arles by Van Gogh
- People who might have need for the concept: artists that make such things as puppets, leather work, macrame, buildings, jewelry; design interiors of buildings and use metal, wood, glass; make weavings, stitchery and applique; plan cities, landscapes, and stage sets.

LEVEL 3 ACTIVITY 88

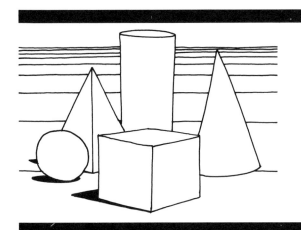

Concept taught by this activity: All forms are variations of the cone, cube, cylinder, sphere, and pyramid.

Objective: By naming the basic forms or combinations of forms in a number of items, the student will be led to recognize that all forms are variations of the cone, cube, cylinder, sphere and pyramid.

A sample lesson plan for achieving the objective:

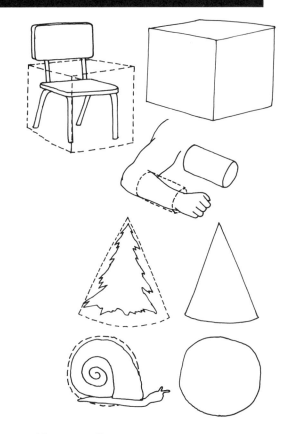

Teacher preparations
Determine materials and plans in advance.
- Collect materials beforehand that are suitable for this lesson.
- Select items that are easy to perceive: a box for a cube, a rolling pin for a cylinder.
- Choose several objects that are a combination of shapes. Choose those that will challenge students at their level of understanding and awareness.
- Have all items hidden in a box or some place ready for action.
- Pre-identify shapes in the room. Plan to point out the more simple shapes, but be aware of the more complex in the event students mention them.
- Have a chart or some plan for a review on basic shapes changing to basic forms: square to cube, circle to sphere.
- Select famous prints with questions for each one emphasizing the objective.
- Make available a variety of appropriate art materials for activities.

Teaching suggestions
- In the initial discussions, begin with what students already know and move from there into increasingly more subtle applications of the concept. The following dialogue is one way this might be achieved. Draw a square on the blackboard or show a picture of one. Review what it is called;

then add the other geometric shapes (circle, triangle, and rectangle). Pull each of the basic forms from a box or some place where students cannot see them until you want them to. Discuss what each form is called and how it relates to the shapes you have discussed. Have students quickly draw each of the forms: a cone, a cube, a cylinder, a sphere, and a pyramid. Then ask: "Looking at the forms you have drawn, are there any like them in this room?" (The desk a cube, the basketball a sphere, and others.)

- "Can you find some of these forms on you or your neighbor?" (The head a sphere, the arm a cylinder, and so forth.) Discuss how each is a variation of the basic forms. A Halloween pumpkin (Jack-o-lantern) is an example of facial forms.
- "Can you see or think of anything outside that is not one of the five basic shapes we've talked about (or a variation of one)?"
- "Is there any shape any place in the world that is not a variation of either the cone, the cube, the sphere, the cylinder or the pyramid?" "Are some living things combinations of the basic forms?" "What are some of the ones you have seen?"
- "Why would artists need to know about the five basic forms?" "Could he draw things like people and mountains and trees by simplifying them first?" "What does *simplify* mean?" "If we simplified our view of mountains, which of the five basic forms would we be using? (The pyramid.) "Would the pyramids all be the same size?" (Mountains are a series of pyramids in all sizes and in all positions.)
- Discuss rockets and space travel: earth is the shape of a sphere; rockets have a cylindrical shape; missiles, in certain areas, are triangular.
- Discuss the bodies of living plants and animals and what forms the parts of their structure, or body, relate to.

Suggested art activity

Look at some of the prints recommended and have students identify the artists' use of the basic forms. Lay tracing paper or acetate over one and show what the forms would look like when simplified as cones, cubes, etc.

Alternative art activities

- Have students experiment with drawing familiar objects by starting them out as basic forms or a combination of basic forms.
- "Take a field trip around the school area. Identify basic forms and draw them."
- Have the students lay tracing paper over a photograph of some complex subject and outline all of the basic forms he sees.
- Distribute a variety of shapes in many sizes and colors representing the five basic forms. Have each student select at least twenty pieces and create a picture by gluing the shapes onto a piece of paper.

Evaluation

The student is able to point out the different forms in art prints, in shapes in the room, or in forms outside the room. If some record is kept of student responses in normal discussion, those who haven't participated can be questioned further.

Other things to consider

- Vocabulary: cone, cube, cylinder, sphere, pyramid, variation, combination.
- Art materials needed:
  (1) Objects brought to class to demonstrate forms and variations of forms; (2) Tracing paper or acetate; (3) Paper, pencils, paste, water colors, tempera, construction paper, and any other materials appropriate for the activities.

- Prints:
  Cheyt M by Vasarely
  Sinbad the Sailor by Klee
  Virgin with Saints Ines and Tecla by El Greco
  Trains du Soir by Delvaux
  Delphic Sibyl by Michelangelo
  Flowers and Parrots by Matisse
  My Gems by Harnett
  I and my Village by Chagell
- People who might have need for the concept: architects, painters, interior designers, industrial designers, jewelry designers, sculptors.

LEVEL 3

ACTIVITY 89

Concept taught by this activity: Distant objects appear as a mass or as combinations of forms as their detail seems to diminish.

Objective: The student draws or paints distant objects as a single mass or as combinations of forms as their details seem to diminish.

A sample lesson plan for achieving the objective:

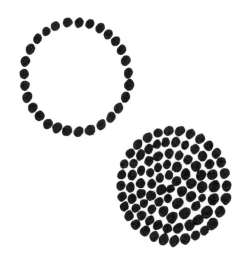

Teacher preparations

Display art prints and photographs containing objects or people (both near and far) showing decreased detail with increased distance. Make an assessment of available comparisons in the outside area.

Teaching suggestions

■ "What are all the reasons you can't see the craters on the moon?" "What are all the things that happen to an airplane as you watch it leave the terminal, taxi down the runway, take off and fly away?" "What happens to windows?" "People inside?" "Can you see them up in the sky?"

■ Use these dot diagrams. Hold them up as far away from the class as your room allows and ask what they see. (Circles.) "What is making the circles?" (lines, shading) Move nearer and nearer the class until they can see the individual dots. At a distance they looked like one mass, but up close the details are visible. The same is true of trees, people, everything.

■ Develop an awareness of the concept by asking questions such as this: "Does anyone have any idea what this art concept is all about?" (Have it on the board.) "What about some of the words in the concept — *detail, diminish, mass*?" "Does anyone know what those words refer to?" After the words are defined, pursue the students' awareness of the concept in the school area and in prints or photographs that are on display: "Have any of you ever been unable to recognize a friend at a distance — then realized who it was as he got closer to you?" "Why did that happen?" "Where would a tree have to be in relation to you before you could count every leaf on a branch?" "How does the same tree limb seem to change when it is across the street or when it is a block away?" "Can you think of some other examples?"

■ Take the class outside and have students compare such things as people, automobiles, buses, trees, and mountains that are both near and far away. "How does the detail differ in each case?"

- Use binoculars and achieve the same effect by looking at things first through the end that magnifies, then through the end that makes everything look very small.

  How artists use the concept:

  Look at prints of paintings or drawings by artists and discuss how well they have followed the concept. Note that some have modified the concept (*Mont. St. Victoire* by Cezanne) and some have ignored it (*Three Flags* by Jasper Johns). "Why would the artist need the concept?" "Why would he choose to ignore it?" "Would he need to know the concept before he could modify it or ignore it?" (Build on the idea that he would need to know it in both cases in order for him to be consistent with his distortions of reality.)

Suggested art activity

Have the students paint or draw a picture with objects or people both near and far away. Allow them their own choice of subject and media. Emphasize their proving they understand the concept by using it in their picture.

Alternative art activities

- Make a collage of pictures out of magazines that illustrate the concept.
- Have a contest in which the students look for and bring to school a picture that best illustrates the concept.
- Put up a display in the hall that would explain the concept.

Evaluation

If the student has been able to apply the concept in a picture of his own making, he has been successful. Those who use it in future work and when the concept is not emphasized are doubly successful.

Other things to consider

- Vocabulary: foliage, mass, distinct, diminish, detail.
- Art materials needed: paper, paints, crayons, pencils.
- Binoculars
- Prints:
  The Gleaners by Millet
  The Hay Wain by Constable
  Le Moulin De La Galette by Renoir
  Hunters in the Snow by Brueghel
  Mont Ste. Victoire by Cezanne
  Dancing Class by Degas
  Three Flags by Johns
  Iron Bridge by Van Gogh
- People who might have need of the concept: painters, printmakers, illustrators.

LEVEL 3   ACTIVITY 90

Concept taught by this activity: The student is able to use a simple box camera or Kodak instamatic type to take pictures of subjects he likes.

Objective: The student takes pictures with a simple box camera or Kodak instamatic.

A sample lesson plan for achieving the objective:

Teacher preparations
- Plan the activity for a day when sunlight is available.
- Have available two or three simple cameras with flash attachments. Students can buy additional ones for their own use. Have sufficient black and white film and flash cubes for each child to take at least two pictures.
- Have in mind a number of good subjects that are available to take pictures of.
- Have a display of numerous examples of photography illustrating a variety of subjects. Have some poor but typical snapshots to compare with the professional work, such as subjects too far away and heads cut off.
- Have students bring examples of snapshots or photographs that they feel are both good and bad. Display them on a bulletin board.

Teaching suggestions
- Review what the students know about the camera — its parts, the film used, how the film is loaded, and what they have to do to take a picture (mechanical aspects).
- You may wish to work with students in small groups rather than as a total class. If the class is working at several levels, the size of the group may already be limited suitably.
- Discuss the basic requirements for good photographs:
  - Where the sun must be in relation to you as photographer.
  - Making sure shadows aren't in the picture in a distracting way.
  - Making certain parts of the subject aren't left out or cut in two at illogical places (head cut off at neck).
  - Determining your center of interest and having it just *off* center.
  - The necessity of holding the camera still and not standing too close or far away for the camera's limitations in taking pictures.

- When a flash is used, making certain that reflections are eliminated.
- Holding the camera firmly and keeping fingers away from the front of the lens. Not jabbing at the shutter release but pressing firmly and gently.
- Make a view finder with a 3 × 5″ card to practice framing pictures.
- Bring in a resource person who can provide additional examples, answer questions, and give more specific advice.
- Discuss the angles from which they might take pictures for unusual effects. "When are distortions good or bad?"
- Discuss what made the pictures on display good or bad. "How can you avoid such problems?"
- Discuss formal and informal shots and the benefits of each. "Are candid shots generally more interesting?" "Why?"

Suggested art activity
Relate the activity to language arts by taking pictures to illustrate a poem or story, or write a story about a picture they've taken. This could be a group activity rather than an individual one.

Alternative art activities
- Display and discuss the photographs taken by the group.
- Make a scrapbook of the photographs they have taken.
- Relate the activity to a social-studies unit (characteristics of their community or social structure).
- Hold a photography contest.
  - Have the winner be the official photographer for the next field trip.
  - Determine beforehand what the judge or judges will be looking for in picking a winner.

Evaluation

If the student can take a picture with some success or at least have an awareness of what caused the blunders he made, he has achieved the objective.

Other things to consider

- Vocabulary: focus, framing, shutter, loading, candid shot, formal and informal shots, composition, focal point, center of interest.
- Art materials needed:
  Two or three cameras; sufficient black and white film for each student to take at least two pictures; a flash cube for each student; examples of good photography and bad photography.
- People who might have need for the concept: general public, photographer, commercial artist.

LEVEL 3

ACTIVITY 91

Concept taught by this activity: The student is aware that objects can be made with pliable slabs or strips by draping them over other forms.

Objective: The student creates objects by draping pliable slabs or strips over other forms.

A sample lesson plan for achieving the objective:

Teacher preparations
- Secure quantities of newspapers for students to work on and with. Have wheat paste, balloons, rocks, or other forms such as bowls or blocks available. Paper towels will also be useful.
- Be sure there is adequate space for storage of student projects.
- Use smocks or old shirts to protect students' clothing.
- Have clay, rolling pins (or some other object that will serve the same purpose) and sticks for controlling the thickness of slabs if the concept is taught as a ceramic activity.
- Collect and display examples of forms created by draping (either pictures or objects).

Teaching suggestions
Have students cover various forms with wet paper or cloth towels.
- "How do the forms change?"
- "Can the forms be made more graceful?" "lumpy?" "jagged?"
- "What 'feelings' do the various forms give the viewer?"
- "What would happen to the new form if the form it is draped over were removed?" "What could be done to alter the reaction?"
- "Are there ways the new form could be preserved?"

Suggested art activity
Have students create masks or piñatas by draping papier

mâché strips or clay slabs over an inflated balloon, or over combinations of two or more balloons.

Alternative art activities
- Have the students create a diorama with mountains and/or hills, by draping papier mâché strips over blocks of wood, rocks, or crumpled paper.
- Create forms by draping ceramic clay slabs over rocks or preassembled wooden frames. They can also be draped on some cloth suspended in hammocklike fashion.
- Create papier mâché figures over wooden or wire frameworks.

Evaluation

Have students display and discuss the completed projects and explain how they achieved the various forms. If they were done by draping, the learners were successful.

Other things to consider

- Vocabulary: pliable, drape, form, papier mâché, ceramic.
- Art materials needed: newsprint or old newspaper, wheat paste, ceramic clay, modeling clay, wire, wood rocks and/or other forms that can be draped, burlap or other materials that can be hung like a hammock with clay slabs draped inside, paper towels.
- People who might have need for the concept: sculptors and ceramists.

LEVEL 3   ACTIVITY 92

Concept taught by this activity: Scale is the size relationships of two things or of parts to a whole.

Objective: The student demonstrates an awareness of scale.

A sample lesson plan for achieving the objective:

Teacher preparations
Collect pictures that illustrate the concept and display them along with the suggested prints. Science and social studies pictures filed in the media center or library make excellent resources for this activity. Recognize that this exercise is an enlargement of #60 in Level 2.

Teaching suggestions
■ Brainstorm with the students to determine the extent of their understanding of scale. Ask questions such as: "How big is a dinosaur?" (They range in size from Brachiosaurus, who was as long as five big elephants standing in a line and so tall he could look over the top of a five-story building, to another kind that was no larger than a chicken.) "What are the biggest and the smallest mammals, birds, reptiles, amphibians, and fish, living today?" "How do they compare with dinosaurs?" "With each other?" "What animal has the longest tail?" "How does the length of an animal's tail compare to its body size?" (Stress the great differences that exist from one to another.)
■ Talk about the word *scale*: "How many uses are there for the word?" "What does it have to do with measurement?" "What do *we* need to know about things to compare their size relationships?" "What kinds of professions would be concerned with scale?"
■ "Compare the scale of man's parts (feet, legs, arms, trunk, head, and hands) with other primates." "How do the differences in size relationships affect what each species does?"

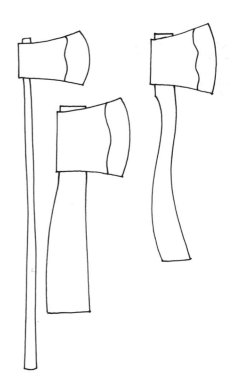

MAMMALS	Etruscan shrew: 1″	blue whale: as long as eight elephants in a row
BIRDS	bee hummingbird: 2″	ostrich: 8′ tall
REPTILES	West Indian gecko: 2″	Anaconda: 30′ or six bicycles
AMPHIBIANS	Cuban arrow-poison frog: size of dime	giant salamander: as long as a bicycle
FISH	dwarf pigmy goby: 1/2″	whale shark: longer than a boxcar

- Develop the idea that a unit of measurement is needed before one can determine if something is larger or smaller than another or if its parts are out of proportion.
- Discuss the scale of furniture to a room ("Why does one style of furniture look out of place in a room while another kind looks alright?"), of parts of furniture to each other.
- Discuss scale as it relates to the prints recommended.
- Discuss the use of scale in making a grid and transferring a small picture to a much larger surface.
- Discuss which professions in the arts would require a keen sense of scale.

"The Three Bears and Goldilocks" teaches scale: furniture that is the right scale to people.)
- Prints:
  Still Life with Pipe by Chardin
  Notre Dame by Daumier
  Blind Man's Bluff by Fragonard
  Birds In Bamboo Tree by Koson
  Women In a Garden by Monet
  The Brooklyn Bridge by Stella
  Fighting Horses by Gericault
- People who might have need for the concept: architects, city planners, interior decorators, engineers, zoologists, scientists, painters, sculptors.

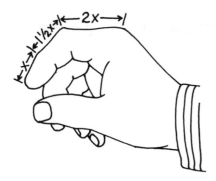

Suggested art activity
Working in small groups, have each take an animal family or a group of some sort and make a display illustrating differences in scale between members of the family or the group and between the various parts of the subject.

Alternative art activities
- Draw or paint a favorite plant or animal to scale.
- Draw or paint some geometric objects to scale.
- Design a piece of sculpture to scale.
- Design a building or floor plan to scale.
- Collect pictures of home and family products designed "out of scale."

Evaluation

When the student describes ways in which objects may be "to scale" or "out of scale" and his work reflects new concerns about scale, the objective has been achieved.

Other things to consider

- Vocabulary: scale, proportion, unit of measurement.
- Art materials needed: any drawing or painting materials that are available could be used along with some sculpture materials commonly used in construction. (The story of

LEVEL 3 ACTIVITY 93

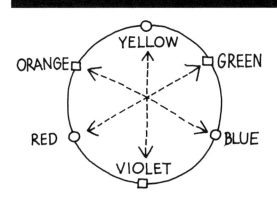

Concept taught by this activity: Complementary colors are directly opposite each other on the traditional color wheel. (The afterimage is an illusionary way of experiencing complements.)

Objective: The student describes complementary colors as being opposites on the traditional color wheel.

A sample lesson plan for achieving the objective:

Teacher preparations
- Have a large color wheel on display to use for discussion.
- Collect and display prints that exemplify the use of complementary colors.
- Check the library or media center for useful films or filmstrips.
- Collect art materials appropriate for the activities planned.
- Collect samples of complementary colors used in advertising or package design.
- Have a large sheet of white paper and squares of two bright colors to use in an experiment with the afterimage.

Teaching suggestions
- Begin by asking such questions as: "What are all of the 'opposites' you can think of?" "Are you *opposite* someone on a teeter-totter?" "What does the word *complement* mean?" "What are colors that complement each other?" (Other color combinations may qualify under a "broad" definition.) Look at the color wheel and ask: "Are there colors on this color wheel that are commonly called complementary colors?" "Which ones are they?" "How can we remember which ones they are?" (Red and green, blue and orange, yellow and violet, and so forth.) "Why do you suppose complementary colors are used in color blind tests?" (Have someone check this out if no one knows the answer.) (Color blind people cannot see the

difference between complements.) "Why are complementary colors used so often in advertising?" Mentally substitute colors for those used in ads and discuss the difference it makes in "eye appeal."
- Review whatever films or filmstrips are available dealing with complementary colors.
- Have experiences with such things as: Looking at prints and finding complementary colors; breaking into groups and brainstorming for a list of things using complementary colors: nature and manmade things (roses = red, green, Christmas cards = red, green, and others).
- See if students know what the word *afterimage* means.
- Then ask questions such as: "What happens when you look up at the sun?" "What do you see when you look away?" "What happens when you have your picture taken and the flash cube goes off?" "If you were to stare at a bright color for awhile and then turn away, what color would you see?" ("We'll see if _____ is right in a minute.") "What do you see on the snow when the sun is shining?" "Some people say that complementary colors placed next to each other seem to vibrate. Is that true?" "Why?" (You may want to try it.) "Could this phenomenon be used in fruit markets or meat markets?" "What for?" "Could an 'afterimage' explain the 'ghost' that someone might see after retiring to bed for the night?" "What color do you see when you stare at one of the circles on display for one or two minutes and then look at the white paper?" "Is the color the complement of the circles you stared at?" (It should be.)

Suggested art activity
Have students wear complementary colors. Break into groups of four or five and have each group select a pair of complementary colors. When they go home, have them find examples of those colors that could be used in a collage. Back at school, combine the examples and put them all together in one collage per group.

Alternative art activities
- Make a construction-paper design using complementary colors.
- Make a mosaic in complementary colors.

- Paint a picture in complementary colors. The same thing would be appropriate in crayon or some other art media.
- Design and build a model room decorated in complementary colors.
- Make three designs or pictures using a different set of complementary colors in each.
- Paint a picture or design representing a season or holiday. Have complementary colors dominate the color scheme.
- Other media or projects that could be used to teach this concept: puppets, cartooning, printmaking.

Evaluation

When the student demonstrates an awareness of the concept, the objective has been achieved.

Other things to consider

- Vocabulary: opposite, complementary, color wheel, collage, adjacent, mosaic, color composition, color scheme, afterimage, vibrate, psychedelic.
- Art materials needed: construction paper, scissors, paste, colored macaroni or tissue paper, crayons, and art paper.
- Prints:
  I and the Village by Chagall
  Harvest Scene by Gauguin
  Zebegen by Vasarely
  Figure Five in Gold by Demuth
  The Small Crucifixion by Grunewald
  Leisure by Leger
  Mlle. Violette by Redon
  Thatched Cottages by Vlaminck
  Lacemaker by Vermeer
- Film Loop: "Basic Color Schemes" by Bailey Film Associates
- Book: *Principles of Harmony and Contrast of Colors* by M. E. Chevreul, Reinhold Book Corporation.
- People who might have need for the concept: optometrists, painters, paint manufacturers, printers, scientists, architects, interior designers, art historians, commercial artists, print makers.

LEVEL 3

ACTIVITY 94

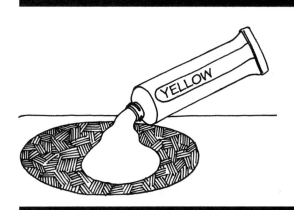

Concept taught by this activity: Pure colors dominate gray, and bright colors dominate dark ones.

Objective: The student can describe ways in which pure colors seem to dominate grays and bright colors dominate dark ones.

A sample lesson plan for achieving the objective:

Teacher preparations
- Set up materials for activity selected.
- Collect examples of the concept and display them: a colored piece of material with a small piece of gray attached, prints of sculpture, interior designs, and paintings.
- Collect colored swatches of paper and cloth.

Teaching suggestions
Getting at the meaning of *dominate, intensity, harmony, advancing,* and *receding:*
- "What are the feelings you have if you wrestle with someone who is not so strong as you?" "If he or she is stronger?" (The "winner" is said to *dominate.*) "What are the reasons fire engines are painted red or sometimes yellow, and not gray or black?"
- "If it were just getting dark and you saw two people a long way down the street, one wearing yellow and the other dark brown, which one would you be able to see better?"
- "Does an artist need to know anything special about color before he can put any two colors together in a harmonious way?" "What kinds of things would he need to know?" (Develop the notion of altering the value and intensity of one or both.) Harmony may be taught at a piano.
- "Do some colors demand more attention than others?" "Why?" "What makes a color dominant over another?"

- "Which is dominant, a bright color or a dark one?" (Dark purple vs. yellow orange, or a black vs. crimson red.) "Does one seem to come forward?" "Which one?" "Can we say then that a dominant color seems to advance, and a less dominant color seems to recede or go into the background?" (Use visuals as you go through this part of the exercise.) Do the same sort of questioning and compare pure colors with grays.
- "How can or how does the artist use this information in landscaping, architecture, pottery, interior decorating, fashion design, painting and sculpture?" "Is the problem basically the same in each art form?" "Why?" (Explore each art area independently.)
- Examine some of the prints suggested at the end of the activity sheet; discuss ways in which artists have utilized the concept in their paintings and how the effect of each painting would have changed if dark colors were more dominant than bright ones. Ask which colors the students see first. "Why?" "What would happen to the feeling the picture has if the dark colors stood out the most?"
- Ask such questions as these: "How can this idea be used in your dress?" "In your home?" "Do artists understand it?" "Do they apply it?" "What are some examples?" "What is the concept in force in this room?" "Outside?" "What happens to a picture if we add nothing but a color and gray?" "Does the gray become more dominant or more submissive?" "Can it be used to make something stand out?" "How can gray be used to change the color or value of other colors?" Discuss the effects of gray being added to a red piece of paper. "Does it alter the feeling or mood of the picture?" Pictures of birds show use of bright colors against neutral grays.

Suggested art activity
Give students a black sheet of paper and let them develop a chart illustrating the concept. This could be done with chalk, colored paper, or tempera. Produce a tissue collage demonstrating the concept.

Alternative art activities
- With tempera paint or chalk, create a design with bright

colors set off by a field of dark colors. Include gray areas
as well.
- Create a stained-glass window design, using tissue paper
  or cellophane with black cardboard.
- Create a design in applique or stitchery, using dark, gray,
  and bright colors.
- Analyze the ratio of pure colors used in nature as compared
  with grayed tones. Show what might happen if the reverse
  were true by illustrating it.
- Other media or projects that might be used to teach this
  concept: puppets, all painting media, any type of
  printmaking.

Evaluation

Any strong indication of an understanding of the concept
either in response to discussion questions or in the
fulfillment of an activity is sufficient to determine if the
objective of the lesson has been achieved.

Other things to consider

- Vocabulary: dominant, submissive, mood, feeling,
  intensity, overpower, and advancing color.
- Art materials needed: pictures for display, material on
  color swatches, painting materials as needed.
- Audiovisual materials needed: pictures of painted
  sculpture and interior designs.
- Film Loops:
  "Color and Space" by Bailey Film Associates
  "Value and Intensity" by Bailey Film Associates
- Film: "Discovering Color" by Bailey Film Associates
- Prints:
  Sinbad the Sailor by Klee
  Interior with Eggplants by Matisse
  Virgin Forest by Rousseau
  Mural by Pollock
  Harvest Scene by Gauguin
  Thatched Cottages by Vlaminck
  The Old King by Rouault
  Bar, Folies Bergere by Manet
- People who might have need for the concept: architects,
  interior designers, painters, art historians, cartoonists,
  commercial artists, printmakers, stage-set designers.

LEVEL 3

ACTIVITY 95

Concept taught by this activity: All views of any three-dimensional forms should be considered.

Objective: The student will create forms in which all views appear related or thoughtfully considered.

A sample lesson plan for achieving the objective:

Teacher preparations
- Collect and have the students bring a number of three-dimensional forms to be observed from various angles. Examples: sculptures, figurines, puppets, wood carvings, pottery, mobiles, vases, wall plaques, toys.
- Arrange a field trip around the school neighborhood to observe and discuss examples of three-dimensional forms (buildings, cars, and other objects).
- Have the students bring empty condiment bottles of different shapes that can be used to create colorful vases by adding strips and panels of red, yellow, blue, and black self-stick vinyl tape.

Teaching suggestions
- Review and discussion: Arrange for students to observe and handle (where permissible) the three-dimensional material collected. Discuss the meaning of *three-dimensional*. Ask such questions as the following: "How do three-dimensional forms differ from two-dimensional forms?" "How do they make you feel?" "How can you tell which they are?"

Which objects in the room are three-dimensional? Which are two-dimensional?" "Which objects outside our room are three-dimensional?" "What parts of a building are three-dimensional?" "What parts are flat?"

"What toys do you have that are three-dimensional?" "Where would you use three-dimensional art in the home?"

"In or around buildings?" "What kinds of three-dimensional objects are found in museums?" "For what purpose" "What about the museum building?" "What is it?"

"How do all three sides of a three-dimensional object relate or go together?" "What feeling would you have if they did not go together?" "In creating a three-dimensional object, should one try to perceive it from every possible angle?" "Why?"

"Must the total composition of the wall on this building go with the composition of other planes in this three-dimensional whole?" "Why?' "Is the scale of a three-dimensional object important?" (Size relationships of one part to another.)

- How artists use the concept: *Time* is the principle that artists are concerned with in considering all views of an object; time allows a person to progress (walk) around, in, or through his work. Architects always think of someone moving through his building and what his experiences will be at different points within the building.

Suggested art activity
Model an object of clay or of papier mâché, or create one by gluing of nailing pieces of things together.
- Have the students observe that all views of any three-dimensional form should be related.
- Involve students in a discussion of possibilities.
- "Should shapes, textures, colors, and other such things relate to each other or *go* together?" "Why?" "What happens if they don't?"
- Have students constantly turn the forms as they work on them, examining the relationships of all parts from all views to see that they relate or go together as a single whole. Parts should not appear "added on" or poorly considered.

Alternative art activities
Create three-dimensional forms from bottles, clay, soap, wax, wood, papier mâché, salt-flour mix, plaster blocks, paper, plaster of Paris, three-inch plastic foam balls or four-inch by twelve-inch plastic cones. Students can create puppets, mobiles, paper sculpture, bottle art, wall plaques,

figurines, or seed-encrusted ornaments made with assorted seeds.

Evaluation

■ To determine whether or not each student clearly under-stands the concept, give everyone an opportunity to respond to the questions and experiences suggested in this outline and evaluate their responses.
■ Have the students decorate their bottles into vases by using self-stick vinyl tape.

Other things to consider

■ Vocabulary: three-dimensional design and two-dimensional design form, sculpture, architecture, figurine, mobile, wood carvings, puppets, pottery, wall plaques, vase, cone, condiment bottle, plane, composition.
■ Art materials needed: fabric, fine wire, scissors, carving tools, poster and acrylic paints, clear lacquer, turpentine, brushes, balloons, white glue, assorted seeds, masking tape, foil pie tins, a mold, protective coverings for tables and students, sawdust and wheat paste, and self-stick vinyl tape.
■ Books:
  Crafts for Fun and Profit by Eleanor Van Zandt
  Pottery Without a Wheel by Carlton and Lovoos
  Adventures with Clay by C. C. Payne
  Creative Clay Design by Rottger
  Sculpture with Simple Materials by Robert and Joan Dawson
  Modeling and Sculpturing by Manttil
  Paper Sculpture by Johnson
  Papier Mâché by Johnson
  Original Creations in Papier Mâché by Anderson-Sterling Col.
■ Magazines:
  "Ceramics Monthly"
  "Crafts Horizons"
■ Resource people: Sculptors, architects, hobbyists, art supervisors, ceramics teachers, potter artists.
■ People who might have need for the concept: puppet makers; sculptors; jewelry designers; craftsmen in metal, wood, plastics, macrame; architects; city planners; interior designers; artists that do ceramics, mobiles and stabiles; art historians; technical and industrial designers; and stage-set designers, to mention a few.

LEVEL 3

ACTIVITY 96

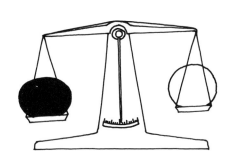

Concept taught by this activity: Forms and shapes have optical "weight" and dark values seem optically "heavier" than light values.

Objective: The student will verbally demonstrate an awareness that forms and shapes have optical weight, and dark values appear heavier than light values.

A sample lesson plan for achieving the objective:

Teacher preparations
- Display swatches of colored paper having both dark values and light values in each color.
- Display various objects for comparison of weights — such as feathers, cotton, fur, sponge, sawdust, granite rock and lava rock, popcorn, plain and printed materials, opaque and transparent glass, aluminum and iron, and a variety of woods.
- Display pairs of objects, each of different color, but of equal size — such as white and red balls, a red and yellow apple, and black and white boxes.
- Collect and display pictures and prints that illustrate the concept.
- Obtain scales to determine the correct weights.

Teaching suggestions
- Have students observe and compare objects and discuss why some appear heavier than others. Compare the following kinds of objects: (a) granite rock and lava rock, (b) light colored cloth and dark colored cloth (also colored paper), (c) plain water and colored water, (d) opaque and transparent glass, (e) aluminum and iron, (f) black and white boxes of the same size, (g) red and yellow apples, (h) red and white balls, (i) variety of woods. Have students

record weights and draw their own conclusions as to why some things may appear heavier but will either weigh less or the same.
- Have students observe pictures and discuss how the artist used optical weight in color, texture, shape, and size to create optical balance.
- Have students take swatches of colored paper and cloth that have both dark and light values of the same color; discuss which appears heavier and why. In pursuing these activities, work at the development of awareness in each student by posing numerous questions. "What factors influence the optical weight of something?" "Does our eye sometimes deceive us?" "Why do shapes that vary only in value and color appear different in size and weight?" "How can the artist use this knowledge in his art?" "What are some examples of this?"

Suggested art activity
Students do a collage of any paper or other materials, and balance the right side on their design against the left side

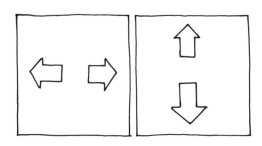

and also the top to the bottom. They should use optical weights of the materials in their collage.

Alternative art activities
- Students could obtain objects or pictures of objects with optical weight and have other students guess the weight and tell why some appeared heavier or lighter than they really were.

- Students could paint several (three or so) designs on one piece of paper , making different illusions of textures in them and thinking of the different aspects of balance, such as: The painting could be with a media chosen by the student.

Evaluation

Students proved the concept that forms and shapes have optical weight by comparing and weighing objects and materials that appeared to be the same weight but were deceptive because of the mass that formed them. Verify or keep records on those who have this awareness. The awareness may be demonstrated either verbally or through the students' art activities.

Other things to consider

- Vocabulary: form, weight, mass, heavy, light, compare, identify, line value, contrast, texture, opaque, transparent, optical illusion, optically heavy.
- Art materials needed: scales, swatches of colored paper or cloth having dark value and light value of the same color.
- Prints:
  Boats at Argenteuil by Monet
  Le Jour by Braque
  Dancing Class by Degas
  Fur Traders Descending the Mississippi by Bingham
  Absinthe by Degas
  Poster — Moulin Rouge by Toulouse-Lautrec
  Mlle. Violette by Redon
  Cheyt M by Vasarely
- People who might have need for the concept: painters, interior decorators, architects. This is a general art concept that would be of use to any type of artist.

LEVEL 3

ACTIVITY 97

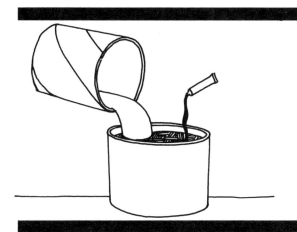

Concept taught by this activity: Small amounts of one hue can be used to vary the darkness or lightness of another hue.

Objective: The student will demonstrate that colors can be used to vary the darkness and lightness of other colors.

A sample lesson plan for achieving the objective:

Teacher preparations
- Obtain materials needed: paints and paper selection.
- Obtain various prints showing dark and light shades.
- Plan a field trip to a museum or art gallery.
- Set up demonstration and exhibit samples.
- Display prints or other pictures that illustrate the concept.

Teaching suggestions
- Show pictures that the artist has darkened or lightened by using another color.
- Discuss the concept that colors can be made darker or lighter by using small amounts of another color and not by just adding black or white.
- Ask such questions as the following: "Why do artists use so many different values in a picture?" "How do we lighten or darken a color?" "Do we ever use anything but white and black to change values?"

  "If we had orange and we wanted to make it darker, what color could we use?" "If we wanted to make it lighter, what color would we add to blue?" "How much can we add before it becomes a different color?"
- Demonstrate by the use of an overhead projector and the cellophane sheets how, by adding one color over another, the colors get darker or lighter.
- Make an issue of the need to use *small* amounts of a color to darken or lighten another.

Suggested art activity
Paint a picture that contains shades of light and dark values created *without* the use of black or white. Try it with variations of one or two colors.

Alternative art activities
- By using three colors, construct a color scale that will show how a color can become lighter or darker by adding another color to it.
- Using water soluble paints, add one color to a container of water and a few drops at a time add another color; then check to see if the original color has become darker or lighter. First use light colors and add only dark colors; then use dark color and add only light colors.
- Mix crayons in an overlapping manner to lighten or darken an original hue.
- Use cellophane paper to demonstrate combinations of hues by overlapping.
- Use cake frosting, food coloring, and artificial flavorings for mixing colors with other hues.

Evaluation

- Display pictures and discuss their relative success with the concept.
- At another time have the student paint a picture of this concept without any refresher course. (This might not be necessary.)
- Take note of the student's verbal responses as an indication of his awareness of the concept.

Other things to consider

- Vocabulary: hue, blending, overlapping, shade, tint, intensity.
- Art materials needed: tempera paints, food coloring, containers, paper, brushes, cellophane paper, frosting, flavorings, overhead projector.

- Prints:
  Apples and Oranges by Cezanne
  Before the Start by Lapicque
  LeGrande Jatte by Seurat
  Flowers and Parrots by Matisse
  House at Aix by Cezanne
  Women In a Garden by Monet
  Room at Arles by Van Gogh
  Harvest Scene by Gauguin
- People who might have need for the concept: painters, house painters, interior designers, illustrators, commercial artists, cartoonists, technical and industrial illustrators, artists who work with collages, serigraphs, and printmaking.

MATURITY LEVEL 4

Developing awareness

In this packet of lesson plans the teacher can provide the student with twenty-seven art experiences that develop his awareness of how to:

- Recognize the ways in which areas of a picture plane tend to influence the weight of the shape or form placed there.
- Create the illusion of movement in a design by repeating colors.
- Indicate the time of day in a drawing or painting with cast shadows.
- Recognize ways in which a shadow outside a shape can differ from the shape casting it.
- Add interest to a form or an arrangement.
- Recognize basic kinds of forms sculptors create.
- Distinguish differences or recognize similarities in the styles of works of art.
- Recognize the importance detailed drawings can play in the development of one's visual awareness.
- Detect the abstract nature of things.
- Add decorative texture to clay or paper forms.
- Utilize simple processes in jewelry making.
- Describe works of art.
- Recognize the role experimentation plays in artists' lives.
- Alter the intensity of a given color with gray.
- Recognize warm aspects of cool colors and cool aspects of warm colors.
- Give form to an object by showing a shadow side.
- Recognize the influence color keys have on moods or feelings in a work of art.
- Recognize the nature of space.
- Create shallow space.
- Identify the theme or themes of works of art.
- Recognize the convex and concave nature of forms.
- Recognize ways in which shapes can appear to escape the boundaries of a picture plane.
- Make space divisions more interesting.
- Recognize some of the sources artists use for their ideas.
- Express moods, feelings, and ideas in a symbolic way.
- Recognize some of the relationships of distortion to abstraction and stylized things.
- Recognize ways in which some forms appear distorted.

THE DIAGNOSTIC CHART

An explanation

21. The student draws more distant objects higher in the picture. He is able to use shadows to illustrate the time of day and shows composite shadows when objects are close to each other. The student creates both in-relief and in-the-round forms of sculpture.
22. The student is able to perceive intricate details and record some of them in his art. He sometimes draws objects from unusual angles and demonstrates an awareness of the abstract elements of nature.
23. The student creates simple jewelry and decorates forms by imprinting, adding texture, or embossing techniques. He draws objects with a light side and a shadow side, thus indicating a light source direction. Depth as adults commonly perceive it is now evidenced in the student's pictures. The student is able to create either shallow or almost limitless space.
24. Convex and concave shapes are recognized and utilized in sculpture. Illusions of various textures are created. Shapes sometimes escape the borders of the student's picture. Space divisions are less symmetrical and less monotonous. The student demonstrates an awareness of how distortion exists in nature and is able to create simple forms in stylized or distorted modes.

LEVEL 4

DIAGNOSTIC CHART

21. The child is at activities #98, 100, 101, and 103

22. The child is at activities #105 and 106

23. The child is at activities #107, 108, 113, 115, and 116

24. The child is at activities #118, 119, 120, and 124

Art projects that can be used as devices for teaching a specific concept

Drawing (pencils, crayon, pens, sticks, markers, brushes)
Lessons: *98, *100, *101, *105, *106, 110, *113, *119, *120, 121, *122, *123, *124

Perspective
Lessons: *98, 110, 113, 115

Murals and friezes
Lessons: *98, 99, *100, 101, 106, 110, 111, 113, 114, *115, *116, 117, 119, 121, 122, 123, 124

Dribble and sponge painting
Lessons: *110, 119

Dioramas
Lessons: 98, 99, 100, 101, 102, *103, 106, 107, 110, 111, 113, 114, *115, 116, 117, 118, 119, 120, 121, *122, *123

Water color and tempera
Lessons: 98, 99, 106, 110, *111, *112, 113, *114, 115, 119, 120, 121, *122

Wire sculpture
Lessons: 103, 110, 115, 120, 122

Sculpture with clay
Lessons: 102, *103, *107, 110, 115, *118, 120, 121

Woodcraft
Lessons: *102, 103, 107, 108, 110, 115, 118, 120, 122

Casting and pouring commercial molds and candles
Lessons: *102, 110, 118

Dry flower arranging
Lessons: 99, 110, 112, *114, 115, 120

Stencil designs
Lessons: *99, 110, 112, 120, 122

Cartooning and/or caricature
Lessons: 110, 101, 105, 106, *110, 113, 114, 115, 117, 118, 121, *122, *123

Posters
Lessons: 98, 99, 100, 101, 106, 111, 112, 113, *114, 116, 117, 119, *120, 121, 123

Coloring and color mixing
Lessons: 110, *111, 122, 123

Rock and gourd painting
Lessons: *102, 110, 111, 118, 119, 123

Crayon resist
Lessons: 110, 119, 120, 122

Collage
Lessons: 99, 107, *110, 112, *114, 115, *116, 120, 121, 122

Toothpick or straw sculpture
Lessons: 103, 110, 115, 120, 121, 122

Whittling and carving
Lessons: *103, 107, *108, 110, 115, 116, *118, 120, 122

Soap, wax, and clay carving
Lessons: 102, *103, *107, 110, 115, *116, *118, 120, 122, 123

Leathercraft
Lessons: *102, 107, *108, 110, 116, 119, 120, 122

Terrariums
Lessons: 110, 115

Photography
Lessons: 98, 99, 106, 110, 113, 114, 115, 117, 119, 120, 123, 124

Gadget prints and roll prints
Lessons: *99, 110, 112, *120, 122

Copper and foil tooling
Lessons: *103, 110, 115, *116, 120, 122

Batik
Lessons: 99, *110, 112, *114, 120, 121, 122

Knitting and crocheting
Lessons: 99, 110, 114, 120, 122

Stitchery with string
Lessons: 99, 110, 114, 116, 120

Applique (sew or glue)
Lessons: 99, 107, 110, 114, 115, *116, 119, 120, 121, 122

Puppets (Sack, sock, styrofoam)
Lessons: 103, 107, 110, 114, 117, 122

Christmas ornaments
Lessons: 99, 107, *110, 111, *118, 120

Torn paper designs
Lessons: *99, 107, 110, 112, 114, 116, 120

Construction paper designs
Lessons: 99, 107, 110, 112, 114, *116, 120

Mobiles and stabiles
Lessons: 99, 102, 103, 107, 110, 115, 118, 120, 122

Snow sculpture
Lessons: 107, 110, 115, 117

Melted crayon painting (encaustic)
Lessons: 99, 110, 112, 121, 122

Tie/dye
Lessons: 99, *110, 112, 114, 120, 121, 122

Mosaics
Lessons: 98, 99, 103, 110, 114, 119, *120, 121, 122

Basket weaving
Lessons: 110, 118, 120

Weaving (paper, string, fabric)
Lessons: 99, 107, *110, 114, 116, 120, 121, 122

Snowflakes
Lessons: 110, *120

Box sculpture
Lessons: 107, 110, *115

Paper sculpture (fold, score, roll)
Lessons: 107, *110, 114, *115, 120, 122

Egg carton crafts
Lessons: 107, 110, 115, 120

Papier maché
Lessons: *102, *107, 110, 114, 116, 118, 120, 122

---

*Key projects for the concept.

LEVEL 4

ACTIVITY 98

Concept taught by this activity: Realistic forms located in the lower half of a picture area appear slightly heavier and nearer to the viewer than they do when placed in the upper half of the picture.

Objective: The student demonstrates an awareness of how placement in a picture can affect how heavy and how near to the viewer forms may appear.

A sample lesson plan for achieving the objective:

Teacher preparations

Note: When experiments are performed, this concept will *tend* to be true when geometric shapes are used but will become obvious when realistic shapes are substituted. This is because we associate things like dogs, trees, or people with the ground and with a horizon line.

■ Make up two cards identical in size and color. Have some sort of background of cardboard that you can attach circles or squares to in a temporary fashion. Have two identical pictures of some living thing to replace the circles or squares in the discussion period.

■ Collect prints, pictures, or illustrations showing that large shapes or spaces are generally placed in the lower half of a picture or arrangement.

■ Be aware that examples of colors located near the base of a picture appear nearer to you than the same colors in the upper half of the picture.

Teaching suggestions

■ Arrange the circles or square on the selected background. Ask: "Which circle (or square) appears heaviest?" "Which appears closest?" Some students will think the lower one is slightly larger and nearer to them than the upper one; others will not.

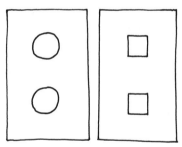

■ Replace the circles or squares with identical pictures of a tree or a dog or some other realistic object. When the same question is asked, the responses should be more uniform, and most students should think the lower one looks heavier and closer to them. Develop a discussion around why this is so when both are identical. Use the single vanishing point as an example of our typical orientation. Note that the tree trunks start higher up in the picture as they get further back.

■ Discuss how the placement of heavy objects or wider spaces is commonly associated with the base of pictures. "What happens if you place heavy objects in the top part?" "How does it make you feel?" "Which seems more comfortable?" "Why?"

■ Look at artists' prints. "Where do they commonly place large or heavier objects?" "Does something appear heavier and nearer to you when it is in the lower part of an

arrangement because we are used to seeing it there?''
''Is it because of our sense of balance?'' ''Do we *know* the reason?'' (There need not be any conclusion in this discussion except that the condition does exist.)
- Extend discussion to examples in the room, in other parts of the building, and to the outside of the building.
- Discuss the reason for having a wider space on the bottom side of the mat used to frame drawings or water colors.

Suggested art activity
Utilize the concept in a construction paper design. Try revising the idea of the concept in the picture or design by placing larger and heavier objects high in the arrangement. Report to the class how this sort of arrangement and the feeling it creates can be appropriate.

Alternative art activities
- Have the students go to a window and observe several similar objects, such as two trees, one that is near and one that is a little in the distance. Have them chart with a sliver of soap, perhaps, the location of each of the trees on the window glass. The base of the one in the distance will be much higher on the glass than the one that is nearest.
- The students could use some thin transparent paper to make tracings of pictures out of magazines to check the concept. They might try to find a condition in which there would be an exception to the concept.

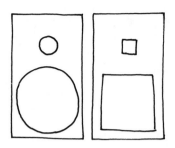

Evaluation

Suggestions for the teacher in determining whether or not *each* student was able to use the concept in the product he created. Verbal awareness as well as the ability to use the concept in an arrangement are both adequate in evaluating the students' ability to use the concept taught. Remember, however, that the evaluation serves primarily as an indicator of how effectively you have taught an idea.

Other things to consider

- Vocabulary: arrangement, balance, space, psychological.
- Art materials needed: construction paper, scissors, paste or glue, and paper and materials appropriate for painting.
- Prints:
  Breezing Up by Homer
  Bar at the Folies Bergere by Manet
  The Cradle by Morisot
  Poster: Moulin Rouge by Lautrec
  Sacrament of the Last Supper by Dali
  6-Day Bicycle Rider by Hopper
  Moneylender and Wife by Metsys
  Don Manuel Osorio by Goya

LEVEL 4

ACTIVITY 99

Concept taught by this activity: Repetitions of color can create the illusion of movement in a design. (The human eye, following the repetition in the design, helps to create the feeling of movement or rhythm.)

Objective: The student creates the illusion of movement by repeating colors in a design.

A sample lesson plan for achieving the objective:

Teacher preparations
- Collect art prints and display them. Refer to the section "Other things to consider."
- Set up record player and have records ready to play.
- Display border print material, painted china plate, and wall paper with a repeating design.
- Select colored construction paper to be used in the game. Make sure one color is brighter or more dominant, and have several sheets of this color. The other color should be more subdued. Have pins ready to pin a paper on each child.
- Prepare drawing materials for children's use.

Teaching suggestions
- Play music that contains a theme or phrase that is repeated. The teacher might suggest the following: "There is something that the music and the displays have in common, can you suggest what it is?" Discuss the word *repetition* and what it means generally. Show repetition in rooms and halls: bricks, ceiling tiles, lights, desks, chairs, windows, and children. Discuss the art prints. Show how color that is repeated creates an illusion of movement (how it leads the eye). Show and discuss other display items. "What do they have in common?"
- Select several children to do some role playing. Pin a large colored construction paper sheet on each child. Choose three or four more children to position the ones with the colored paper in such a manner as to create a design. Discuss. It might take several times before they can see

that the repetition of the brighter or more dominant color created an illusion of movement. Switch the children; let the ones who had the paper pinned on them create the designs.
- Take a nature walk. Observe trees, shrubs, fences, light posts, or power lines. Discuss and make a conclusion as to the concept.
- The students will be able to identify the concept of repetition by comparing the musical phrases and the border print material, the painted china, and the wall paper. By switching the groups of children used in role playing, the teacher will be able to determine the children who understand the concept.

Suggested art activity
Let the children choose materials to create a picture to show that they have learned the concept. They can choose to make their pictures from water colors, crayons, or colored chalk; or they can tear or cut colored construction paper to create a design showing movement by the repetition of certain colors.

Alternative art activities
- Using "rhythm" instruments, assign colors to each instrument. When a student hears the drum, they should paint some *brown* patches. When they hear the symbol, they should paint some *orange* shapes, when they hear a triangle, they should paint *yellow*. The sound of a horn might trigger experimentation in blues. (Do not let the

223

students "overwork" their paintings; only a few minutes are required for this activity.)
- Have a team of children paint a mural that illustrates the concept. The mural might be done as a large collage from pictures in magazines displayed on swatches of color that lead the eye from one to the other. (The mural might also be built around another subject in the curriculum, such as science or social studies.)

Evaluation

During each activity, the teacher will draw responses from each child to help determine whether or not he understands the concept. The children's creating of repetition and movement will complete the teacher's understanding of which students really understand the concept.

Other things to consider

- Vocabulary: repetition, movement, design, illustration.
- Art materials needed: colored construction paper, white art paper, water colors, colored chalk, crayons, scissors, paste or glue.
- Records:
  "On the Trail" from the Grand Canyon Suite
  "William Tell Overture"
  "Peter and the Wolf"
- Media: painted china plate or cup with border design, border print material, wall paper with design that will illustrate the concept.
- Prints:
  Zebegen by Vasarely
  Combination Concrete by Davis
  Harvest Scene by Gauguin
  Sinbad the Sailor by Klee
  Apples and Oranges by Cezanne
  Figure Five in Gold by Demuth
  Water Flowery Mill by Gorky
  Before the Start by Lapicque
  Justice and Peace by Overstreet
- People who might have need for the concept: painters; interior decorators; illustrators; landscape architects; artists that do mosaics, batiks, hookrugs, enameling, and jewelry, who are involved in crafts such as glass, weaving, stitchery, and applique; artists that design buildings and plan cities; artists that make pottery and ceramics of all types; sculptors; photographers; cartoonists; artists that do all types of commercial art and drawings, who make prints, serigraphs, and woodcuts.

LEVEL 4

ACTIVITY 100

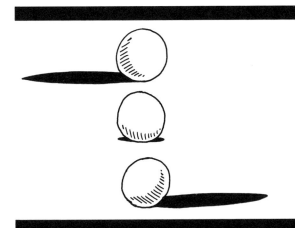

Concept taught by this activity: Shadows help us to observe the passage of time.

Objective: The student will demonstrate an awareness that shadows can assist him in determining what time it is.

A sample lesson plan for achieving the objective:

Teacher preparations
- Display shadows of a child taken or traced at various times during the day.
- Display familiar scenes showing various lengths and shapes of shadows at different times of the day.
- Display the poem entitled, "Runny Day, Sunny Day," by Aileen Fisher (illustrations of shadows).
- Have a sun lamp or flashlight for demonstration purposes. Have facilities to darken the classroom, or have a dark room reserved.

Teaching suggestions
- Discuss with students the possibility of being in a deserted area without a clock, and try to determine the time of day from the placement of your shadow. "Could you tell when a day had passed?" "Is there any way you could tell what time it was during the day?" "If it was a cloudy day, could you still estimate the time of day?" "How?" "Are there shadows on overcast days?" "How does a shadow help you to tell what time it is?" "How could we find out?" Have students get into small groups, go outside in sunshine, and trace each other's shadow. This should be done three times during the day — morning, noon and afternoon. They should compare the length and shape of the shadows. Have the students draw their own conclusions concerning the concept. Have students draw with chalk the outline of shadows on the ground of objects such as basketball standards and others. Periodically have them notice the

change of the shadows as the sun moves. Keep records of the changes and draw conclusions about the concept. Read the poem, "Runny Day, Sunny Day" by Aileen Fisher. Have students go outside and act out the poem by making shadows resembling animals.
- Darken the room. Shine a sun lamp on various objects from different positions. Let the students record their observations and draw conclusions about the concept.
- Questions to motivate thinking concerning the concept: "If your shadow is short and squatty, what time of the day is it?" "If your shadow is long and thin, what time would it be?" "Is your shadow ever longer than your body?" "When?" "If you stood under the shade tree in the morning to get out of the sun, would the shade be there in the afternoon?" "Why not?" "If you parked a car in a shady place in the morning, would it still be in the shade in the afternoon?" "Why not?" "How could you use this concept in a picture or a design?" "How have some artists used this concept?"
- Have students analyze pictures to determine the approximate time of day by the shadows in the picture.

Suggested art activity
Have students draw a picture with a shadow, designating a certain time of day by the length and the size of the shadows.

Alternative art activities
Study a sundial. How does it function? How is it adjusted seasonally? Build your own sundial with cardboard and a popsicle stick.

Evaluation

The student's work, his verbal responses to questions, and the contribution he makes to general discussions are all ample evidence that the objective has been achieved.

Other things to consider

- Vocabulary: Shadows, time length, angles, stretched, silhouettes.
- Art materials needed: pictures showing shadows cast at different times of day, sun lamp or flashlight, chalk and paper for tracing students' shadows, paper and art media for each student to portray his knowledge of the concept by drawing shadows and the time of day.
- Poems:
  "Runny Days, Sunny Days" by Aileen Fisher
  "My Shadow" by Robert Louis Stevenson
- Prints:
  Snap the Whip by Homer
  The Scout by Remington
  Notre Dame by Daumier
  The Cliff of Entretat by Courbet
  Venice by Canaletto
  Turning the Stake by Eakins
  Hay Wain by Constable
  Boy with a Tire by Lee-Smith
- People who might have need for the concept: artists that do painting, cartoons, illustrations.

LEVEL 4

ACTIVITY 101

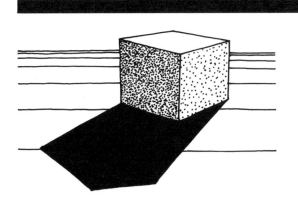

Concept taught by this activity: The shape of shadows can appear to be different from the shape of the objects casting them.

Objective: The student demonstrates an awareness that the shape of shadows can appear to be different from the shape of the objects casting them.

A sample lesson plan for achieving the objective:

Teacher preparations

Obtain any examples of sundials, either actual or in books, or create a model of one for demonstration.

Collect pictures, prints, and photographs of objects casting shadows at various times of day. Have photographs of the school building taken at various times of the day, illustrating the size of the building and the shadow. Have a good light source: a lamp, a flashlight, or a projector for making shadows. Have a way of darkening the room.

Teaching suggestions

■ Develop a discussion and review of what the student already knows by asking such questions as the following: "Does anyone recall what causes shadows?" (Concept #82.) "You have also learned that shadows change length at different times of the day. How did that information help you?" (Concept #100.) "Today we are going to take the idea of shadow length a little bit further. Does a shadow always look just like the person or the object that is blocking out the light?" "What kinds of things will cause the shape of a shadow to seem different than the thing that is making it?" (Light source angle or whatever.)
■ Take several kinds of lights such as a spotlight or a flashlight and the light of a filmstrip projector into a darkened

room and have the students determine what they need to do to distort the shape of a shadow.
■ Students should note that the shape appears to change when it is lengthened or shortened as in concept #100, but it also appears to change when the object is in such a position in relation to the light that the viewer sees the shadow as an abstraction.
■ Students should also note that the shadows of three-dimensional forms are always two-dimensional and without detail; thus when the shadow of something like a file cabinet

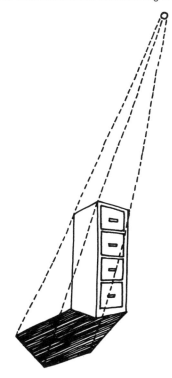

casts a shadow showing three of its corners at once, it appears distorted or abstract. The distortion is increased when the file cabinet's shadow is longer or shorter than the file cabinet.

- Have children make hand shadows. Discuss ways in which the shadows appear different from the actual hand and what caused the distortions.
- Study artists' prints and photographs containing shadows and discuss individual perceptions of the concept and the conditions responsible for its happening.
- Analogies:
  - A shadow is to light as lightning is to _____. (Causation principle: rain, electricity, air masses, clouds, static.)
  - Color is to paint (pigment) as an object is to its _____. (Shadow, reflection.) (*Light* is a ''common denominator'' in this analogy.)

Suggested art activity
Draw or paint a picture of some sort of group activity or a landscape with groupings of trees or buildings. Make it represent a sunny day so that there are strong shadows.

Alternative art activities
- The students could do a cartoon strip with the story built around a cartoon character and his shadow.
- A collage could be developed with the theme built around objects and their shadows.
- A display for the room or hall could be developed by a small committee illustrating the concept.

Evaluation

The individual's awareness can be determined by his oral responses to the discussion and analysis. Some record may be necessary to keep track of each student's reactions in order that none will be missed. (The student may discuss what has been attempted in the drawing or painting and how shadow is shown.)

Other things to consider

- Vocabulary: shadow, long, short, silhouette, sundial, distortion, abstraction.
- Art materials needed: magazine pictures, paper, glue, scissors, pencils, silhouettes, black paper, white chalk.
- Stories
  A Most Delightful Bone (Have students make up a story about dogs and shadows.)
  Bee, Who Used to Be Scared of the Dark
- Prints:
  Boy with a Tire by Smith
  The Scout by Remington
  Ville d'Avray by Corot
  The Return by Magritte
  Breezing Up by Homer
  Birds in Bamboo Tree by Koson
  Fox Island by Hartley
  Blindman's Bluff by Fragonard
  Harvesters by Brueghel

LEVEL4

Concept taught by this activity: Value changes can be used to add interest to a form or an arrangement: changes in planes, staining, coloring, and adding texture.

Objective: The student demonstrates an awareness that value changes can be used to add interest to a form by changing planes, by staining and coloring, or by adding texture.

A sample lesson plan for achieving the objective:

Teacher preparations
- Prepare bulletin boards or a table with examples of texture, staining, coloring, and changes in plane.
- Prepare word strips as needed.
- Collect prints or other examples where artists have utilized the concept in their work.

Teaching suggestions
Select several ways in which the concept can be taught, from the simple and obvious to the more subtle applications of the idea. Suggest open-ended questions, experiments, ways of involving children and demonstrations. This process should result in each student's being able to use the concept in his own unique way.
- To draw attention to the concept, the teacher — or parent — might use the following demonstration as a review:
  - Turn lights out.
  - Turn lights on.
  - Discuss blackness and whiteness (darkness is black and lightness is white).
  - Use dimmer switch, if your room has one, to show *degrees* of darkness.

- Review the concept *value* (discussion).
  "What is value?" "How are value changes created?" "Is each color closer to black or to white in darkness or lightness?" Looking around the room and outside, discuss ways in which such things as paint, changes in plane, and texture add interest to forms or arrangements.
- Discuss the paintings found in reference books.
  "Where is value shown in the pictures?" "How does an artist use value?" "How can we use value?" Discuss the value change of clothing on the students. Discuss the value change of the eyes of the students. (Look around at your neighbors and find the value of their clothing and their eyes.)

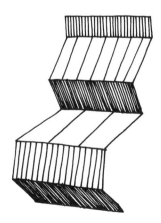

- Discussion forms to add interest:
  "Look at this piece of clay. How can I change the value?" (Dramatic change by bending.) "How can I change the value of this piece of paper?" Notice that bending and folding create shadows. (Bending, folding, crushing, changing color, adding a different texture.)
- Discuss the use of decoration on simple forms: "Why do we add decoration to simple forms?" "What are some ways

that can be used to make forms more interesting?'' (Adding texture.) ''What is texture?'' ''How many different types of texture are there?'' ''How does an interior decorator use value change and texture in decorating a room or a school?''

- Show and discuss the value and texture of such things as the following:
  - a found object
  - a tree (green value change)
  - an animal
  - a picture

Suggested art activity

- Make a relief design using corrugated cardboard and laying the pattern in different directions.
- Make a relief form of plywood, heavy cardboard, or maché, where layers are superimposed on layers, varying the depth. This may be a design or a map.

Alternative art activities

- Make a simple clay form and make it more interesting by adding indentions or convexities.
- Make paper sculpture designs, folding and changing planes to make forms more interesting.
- Do a wood sculpture by gluing scrap pieces of wood together. Textures could be cut or filed into selected pieces to change the value and to create more interest.

Evaluation

From the student's responses in discussion and from his use of the information in whatever activities he participates in, the teacher can evaluate whether or not his awareness has changed.

Other things to consider

- Resources:
  Childcraft, Volume 9
  The Encyclopedia of Art (Golden Press)
- Vocabulary: plane, value, texture, decorative, value change.
- Art materials needed: paper, crayons, clay, found objects, string, yarn, paint; different textured materials and such things as construction paper, buttons, paper sacks, tin foil, felt, glue, scissors, cards, cardboard, and magazines.
- Prints:
  Bacchus by Caravaggio
  Man In The Golden Helmet by Rembrandt
  La Loge by Renoir
  The Virgin Forest by Rousseau
  Le Jour by Braque
  The Letter by Vermeer
- People who might have need for the concept: artists that make mosaics, do batiks and tie-dye work; artists that hook rugs, tool leather, make jewelry, forge metal, work in glass; artists that do macrame, weaving, stitchery and applique; architects; interior designers; sculptors; potters; ceramists; painters; cartoonists; commercial artists of all types; printmakers; and artists that do collages.

LEVEL 4   ACTIVITY 103

Concept taught by this activity: Forms can be in the round (3-D, free-standing, or free-hanging) or in-relief, or they may be one shape or combinations of several.

Objective: The student is able to distinguish between forms that are in the round and forms that are in-relief and is able to demonstrate an awareness that a form can be one shape or a combination of several.

A sample lesson plan for achieving the objective:

Teacher preparations
■ Collect and display pictures and prints that illustrate the concept.
■ Have plastic or wooden geometric forms available to use in demonstrations. Other objects which have these shapes are equally helpful.
■ Assemble a basket of fruit that includes a banana, a pear, an apple, an orange, and grapes. (If this is not possible, some other display could be made.)
■ Display a plaster of Paris or papier-maché relief map of a topographical area to show the concept of "relief." Coins or other examples are equally useful.
■ Assemble and display pictures of architecture of homes and buildings (in-the-round forms).
■ Display actual samples of four types of sculpture such as plaques, coins, figures, and embossed paper.
Note: It must be recognized that each teacher's situation is different from another's, and substitutions for any suggestions made in these lessons may not only be appropriate but may often be better.

Teaching suggestions
■ Discuss the meaning of terms such as *relief, in-the-round, embossed, low relief,* and *high relief.*
■ Start with a simple coin. Ask: "Why don't we use in-the-round sculpture to decorate coins?" (Discuss the types of coins used by primitive people and other money forms.) Ask: "How is a footprint like a map?"
■ Show examples of each type of sculpture. Discuss differences in the various types. Ask: "How are the forms made?" "Why do you think it is called a _____?" "Which material would be best for each type of form?" "Which type of sculpture is most common?" "What is 'relief' sculpture used for?" (Answers will vary: "decorations," "columns," "buildings," and others.) Use pictures and filmstrips at this point for examples. "Does it make any difference if you use different materials?"
■ Show examples of simple and complex forms and discuss the following questions: "Why is this form simple?" "What makes this form complex?" "How would you make a simple form into a complex form?" Name some complex forms and use pictures to demonstrate. Compare simple forms such as blocks with more complex forms such as model cars. Demonstrate with clay a simple form, then make it complex by adding features to it (animal forms and others). Have students make a relief map of a mountain range with rivers which is located in the immediate area. Discuss advantages of using maps in relief.

Suggested art activity
Make a relief sculpture and an in-the-round kind of sculpture. It might even be helpful to use the same subject in both examples. Clay, soap, wax, or a flour-and-salt dough are appropriate media for this activity.

Alternative art activities
■ Make a construction, gluing a variety of forms together to create a new one.
■ Prepare a bulletin board containing a variety of examples of the concept.
■ Lay a piece of tracing paper on top of a print and locate every shape or form that appears to be in-the-round or a combination of several shapes.

Evaluation

When the student gives evidence either verbal or nonverbal, that he can recognize and distinguish between relief and in-the-round forms, the objective has been achieved.

Other things to consider

- Vocabulary needed: in-the-round, in-relief, embossed, coin, plaque, primitive, simple, complex, geometric, block, circle, cylinder, incised.
- Conduct a discussion for the purpose of (1) clarification of vocabulary, (2) discovering how a circle becomes a sphere and a rectangle a cylinder, and (3) discovering that many forms can be combinations of two or more basic forms.
- Art materials needed: pencils, papier maché materials, drawing paper, crayons, tempera paint and brushes, water containers, paste, and glue.
- Prints:
  Apples and Oranges by Cezanne
  Guernica by Picasso
  Le Moulin de la Galette by Renoir
  An Afternoon at La Grande Jatte by Seurat
  My Gems by Harnett
  Still Life with Pipe by Chardin
  Francis I by Clouet
  Lacemaker by Vermeer
  Moneylender and Wife by Metsys
  Delphic Sibyl by Michelangelo
- People who might have need for the concept: sculptors, art historians, art critics, engravers, teachers.

LEVEL 4

Paintings photographed with permission of BYU Art Galleries.

Concept taught by this activity: Works of art may be either similar or different in style.

Objective: The student identifies similarities and differences in the style of works of art.

A sample lesson plan for achieving the objective:

Teacher preparations

■ Collect examples of works of art, suggested prints, and/or photographs of these for display and discussion.
■ Note that style and period are two different things. Two artists associated with the same period may have somewhat different styles. For instance, Toulouse-Lautrec and Degas are both Post Impressionists, and they painted in a similar style. Van Gogh, Cezanne, and Gauguin are also Post Impressionists, but their style was very different from each other's and from the styles of Degas and Toulouse-Lautrec. An artist's style is his mode of working. When he matures as an artist, he adopts peculiar characteristics that enable us to identify his work or to distinguish it from the works of other artists. The more familiar a student becomes with a particular artist's style, the more easily he can identify other works by that artist. A similar thing occurs as we develop our longhand, cursive writing. Everyone develops his personal style in writing each letter.

Teaching suggestions

■ Brainstorm with students regarding their understanding and experience with the word *style*: "Name ten different things you associate with the word *style*." "What similarities and differences are there in styles of clothing, writing, lettering, and ways of life (lifestyles)?"
■ "How are we able to distinguish among styles of dress or automobile designs?" "What do we need to know about any given thing to recognize it and tell how its style is

different from another?" (The materials the artist used, his intent, his training, forms used, his way of using colors, and other means.)
■ Look at the prints and have students describe characteristics of the artists' styles and tell how they differ from other artists'.

Compare the prints listed in column one with each other and identify their individual characteristics, then see if students can pick out the work of the same artist from list 2. (Be sure the artists' names are covered.)

Column One
Harvesters by Breughel
House at Aix by Cezanne
Sacrament, Last Supper by Dali
Dancing Class by Degas
Bedroom at Arles by Van Gogh
Snap the Whip by Homer
Head of a Man by Klee
View of Toledo by El Greco
The Box by Renoir
6-Day Bicycle Rider by Hopper
Man with Helmet by Rembrandt
Poster: Moulin Rouge by T. Lautrec

Column Two
The Crucifixion by Dali
Absinthe by Degas
Virgin with Saint Ines & Tecla by El Greco
Numbering at Bethlehem by Brueghel
Seven A.M. by Hopper
The Card Players by Cezanne
Bandaged Ear by Van Gogh
Breezing Up by Homer
Quadrille by Toulouse-Lautrec
Night Watch by Rembrandt
Le Moulin de la Galette by Renoir
Sinbad the Sailor by Klee

Suggested art activity

Have students form small groups and try to locate artists with styles similar to those they have already studied or similar to each other's. Have them report to the class (written or oral reports) on their findings. They may use the art prints, magazines, newspapers (including the "funnies" or "comics"), art books, or original work.

Alternative art activities

■ Create a painting or sculpture in the style of an artist you like. (This requires considerable research to duplicate materials used as well as the technique.)

- Have the students try to develop a technique of painting of their own that has never been done before. A lot of brainstorming should proceed this activity so that each student will have enough ideas to start with. Thought could be given not only to using new and different kinds of tools to produce a different technique but also to new and unusual surfaces or paints.

Evaluation

When the student demonstrates an increased capacity to identify an artist's style (what an artist does differently from other artists working with the same media) and to discuss the characteristics of a style, the objective has been achieved.

Other things to consider

- Vocabulary: style, stylish, technique, period.
- Art materials needed: art materials as suggested in alternative activities.
- Prints: see the list included in this activity.
- People who might have need of the concept: art critics, docents (docent: conductor of groups through an art gallery), museum directors, teachers, art historians, psychologists.

LEVEL 4

ACTIVITY 105

Painting photographed with permission of BYU Art Galleries.

Concept taught by this activity: Drawing details of objects or people will enhance the students' awareness.

Objective: The student demonstrates a heightened awareness of detail in his environment as he graphically describes some of the subtle differences between the parts of living things — by visually comparing such things as feet, leaves, trunks, or skin coverings.

A sample lesson plan for achieving the objective:

Teacher preparations
- Arrange a field trip to a zoo or a museum of natural history.
- Collect pictures of many kinds of animals and plants and groups of similar types.
- Have slides, filmstrips, or other illustrations of animal life available to look at.
- Provide an opportunity for students to study mammals, birds, and other living things to observe firsthand what kind of skin, feet, claws, beaks, eyes, ears, fur, and other parts they have. Use a field trip or filmstrips and films about animals in their natural habitat. Have students observe the way they move and survive in their environment.
- Arrange the room so that bulletin boards have displays of animal pictures and even pictures of humans so that the

student can observe the differences and similarities in all living things. Have lists for them to write in differences and similarities they discover. See who can make the longest list.
- Set up book displays about animals and other living creatures you wish to introduce into the visual-discrimination unit being taught. Encourage students to study them.
- If available, arrange for a taxidermist or a science teacher to bring subjects for the students to examine more closely and to study details of animal and plant parts and coverings. Bring the real thing whenever possible.

Teaching suggestions
- As part of the activity, intense discussions should ensue regarding such things as: "What similarities do you find in these two animals?" "What differences?" "How are the animals different and similar to the student himself?"
- Develop *comparisons* in your questioning. "How is an ape like a car?" (After brainstorming this, show Picasso's ape with a car head. Found in *Time-Life Art Series,* World of Art, Picasso, p. 151.)

  If you had pictures of a skunk, squirrel, and a rabbit, you might ask: "What might happen if the squirrel had a tail like the rabbit?" "How would he survive?" "Could he survive?" "Why?" "Would he be able to change the way he lives?" "What would the rabbit do if he had the squirrel's or the skunk's long, heavy tail?" "Do you think it would make any difference if the skunk had long ears like the rabbit?" "Or feet?"
- Look at animals from a broader view and discuss such things as the following: "What are some of the strangest looking animals you know of?" "Why couldn't all animals be alike?" "Would they survive if they were?" "Why have some animals become extinct?" "Would they have died if their bodies had been constructed differently?" "Do things that aren't alike need to be functional?" "Which ones?" "Why are animals certain colors?" "Why are they marked the way they are?"

- Describe ways in which shape, size, or coloring are directly related to animals' functions: beaks and claws of birds, elephants' trunks, kangaroos' legs, polar bears' coats, and others.
- Discuss the scientific concept that the structure and/or coloring helps animals adapt to their environment.

Suggested art activity
Study an animal carefully, then draw it from memory. Score one point for each major characteristic you remember.

Alternative art activities
- Create imaginary animals that lack functional parts, such as a giraffe with a zebra's neck and an elephant with a parrot's beak.
- Make a chart illustrating subtle differences between similarly shaped plants or animals and dramatizing some of the unique characteristics of each. Illustrations could be drawn or cut from magazines.
- Other art media or projects that might be used to teach this concept: photography, cartoons, collage, printmaking.

Evaluation

When the student exhibits a heightened awareness of plant and animal life, their similarities and differences, the objective has been achieved. Some mental or written record of each student's oral response should be kept.

Other things to consider

- Pictures of animals (SVE study prints, encyclopedias, animal books, science books); Audobon pictures and others that are appropriate. Films may also be available.
- Vocabulary: function, functional, form, structure, extinct, survive.
- Art materials needed: drawing and painting media.
- Prints:
  Francis I by Clouet
  Night Watch by Rembrandt
  View of Toledo by El Greco
  My Gems by Harnett
  Birds in Bamboo Tree by Koson
  Young Hare by Durer
  The Blue Cart by Van Gogh
- People who might have need for the concept: artists that draw and do paintings and illustrations of all sorts and prints of all types.

LEVEL 4

ACTIVITY 106

Concept taught by this activity: Artists may detect the abstract nature of things by recognizing that objects appear surprisingly different when seen in part, viewed from a new or unusual angle, seen up close, or magnified.

Objective: The child will develop a visual and aesthetic awareness of the world he lives in. (Sub-Objective: The student will be able to detect the abstract nature of an object by showing this concept in his work.)

A sample lesson plan for achieving the objective:

Teacher preparations
Prepare the room with a variety of objects (many can be natural objects such as tree bark, shells, weeds, seed pods, and other things). Hang a variety of pictures in the room that contain objects viewed from unusual angles and/or those seen very near or magnified a great deal. Science pictures may be helpful.

Teaching suggestions
- "List all the uses you can for a magnifying glass." "What are all of the ways an *artist* could use one?" Show close ups or magnified portions or sections of an object and have students guess what it is. "What makes it look interesting?" "Is it color, the texture, line, shape, space, or the angle?"
- Point out that in order to make an abstract drawing the artist "takes out" and uses those things that he finds the most important, meaningful, and interesting to him. It is, therefore, important to know and learn as much about the

object one draws as possible. Discuss pictures by various artists who used this idea.
- Invite students to examine objects closely. By using rolled-up paper to form a tube or by using a cardboard tube, look through it at different objects. Using this as a view-finder (much like looking through a camera) move the tube so that just portions of the object or picture show. Have students try to find and create interesting shapes and patterns through your viewfinders.
- Take two L-shaped strips of paper. Form a square or rectangle from them. Using the two L shapes, have the students find a portion of a magazine picture that they find interesting. Have them draw this design on a large scale to create a very interesting piece of art work. When the class is finished, post all of the work and let the class guess what everyone has drawn. (Slide mounts may be used as viewfinders if available.)

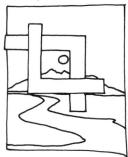

- Talk about an ant's eye view. Have the students sit or lay their heads on the floor and look at the desks or chairs from underneath. Have them find patterns of light or other interesting patterns from this view.
- Have students observe their world as they walk to and from school. Have them bring a thing (object) to class and discuss what and why they like it.
- Give students a portion of a picture you have previously cut up. Have each student draw it on a large scale. Assemble them and let them see what picture they have

helped to draw.

- Show a slide that is completely out of focus. Little by little put it into focus, discussing with each refocus what the slide could be. Students might like to draw the picture on the slide with each focusing. They would have to change their drawings with each focusing. It might be easier to use charcoal for drawing.

Suggested art activity
Draw fragments of objects magnified to the extent that they no longer resemble their natural appearance. Paint them in color schemes that are also unrelated to their natural appearance.

Alternative art activities
- Do a photo study of complicated objects, such as a train engine or a road grader. Look for views and parts up close that have an abstract appearance. Display the photos or make a film strip or slide presentation.
- Draw figures on ladders or in unusual positions where fore-shortening (a visual distortion of forms) takes place.

Evaluation

Student work and oral response are the criteria used to evaluate this assignment. What is it that the student is trying to bring out or express? Is it the texture he found most interesting or the line, color, form, whatever? Talk with the student about it. Is he learning to look for abstraction in seeing familiar objects from a new or unusual angle? From viewing them in part or in a new environment? When he has this kind of awareness, the objective has been achieved.

Other things to consider

- Vocabulary: magnifying glass, aesthetic (compared with unaesthetic), abstract, viewfinder, foreshortening.
- Art materials needed: pastels, colored chalk, crayons, poster paint, large paper.
- Prints:
  The Brooklyn Bridge by Joseph Stella
  The Crucifixion by Dali
  Dempsey and Firpo by Bellows
  I and the Village by Chagall
  Allies Day, May 1917 by Hassam
  The Letter by Vermeer
  Marilyn Monroe by Warhol
  Christina's World by Wyeth
  Knockout by Morreau
  The Return by Magritte
- Books: Any science books showing microscopic pictures of crystals, cells, flowers, or other interesting detail.
- People who might have need for the concept: sculptors, painters, printmakers, illustrators, photographers, interior designers, display designers, set designers.

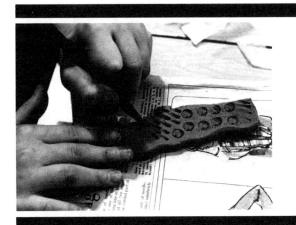

Concept taught by this activity: Decorative texture can be added to improve art: imprinting in clay, attaching strips, adding grog or sand to clay, and attaching string or yarn to papier mâché forms.

Objective: The student adds decorative texture to clay forms or papier mâché forms with such things as grog, sand, imprinting strips and pieces of clay, or string and yarn.

A sample lesson plan for achieving the objective:

Teacher preparations

■ Where possible display samples of decorated clay forms, such as Indian and Greek pottery, and pictures of clay objects in home magazines. Displays of papier mâché forms decorated with materials attached to the surface may also be helpful.

■ Check local department stores for pottery and the decorations used on them. Some stores may be willing to lend pieces or send their specialist to the school. Look for papier mâché figures, too, if clay isn't available.

■ Check with any nearby college, university, or high school that might have a potter willing to bring some of his or her work to display and discuss.

Teaching suggestions

"What are all of the ways this square on this paper could be made more interesting?" (Colors, marking it, cutting it; in other words, it needs *decoration*. It needs other shapes and lines on it.)

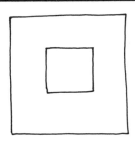

■ Discuss the need for decoration and ask such questions as the following: "What experience have you had with decorating clay?" "Where does the decoration work best on a form?" "How is texture a kind of decoration?" "How can decoration be kept from interfering with function?"

■ Discuss how moist the clay body should be for certain modes of decoration. Introduce the idea that decoration can be added to the surface as well as carved or cut into the clay. (If the clay is too dry, pieces fall off, or it cracks.)

■ Discuss ways in which clay could be added to a surface. For example:
  ● Long coils used as a line to make figure or faces
  ● Balls of clay attached in patterns
  ● Pieces of coils attached in patterns to represent, for example, the spines of a hedgehog or a porcupine
  ● Pieces of slabs attached with slip for raised areas on a turtle's shell
  ● Pieces cut out with cookie cutters, bottle caps, or thimbles to attach in patterns
  ● Grog pressed into the surface in certain areas for textured patterns

■ Stress with whatever shapes are used that it is necessary to arrange them in patterns (simple, repeat, or others).

■ Make certain that students score (roughen) both surfaces that are joined together with slip. This is especially necessary if you attach large pieces, one square inch or bigger.

Suggested art activity

Have the students create objects out of clay with the

239

objective of decorating them. The objects could be anything from dots to animal sculpture. Make certain students have the concept well in mind, because there is a tendency for them to forget the goal when the activity takes a fairly long period of time.

Alternative art activities

If clay is not available, the same principle can be applied to papier mâché forms, and the decoration can be added by attaching such things as yarn, string, hair, fabric, or a different kind of paper that has a contrasting surface. Painting and varnishing the surface adds further decorative notes.

Evaluation

Suggestions for the teacher in determining whether or not *each* student has been able to use the concept in the product he created. The form that the student decorates or attempts to decorate will serve as an evaluative instrument and will tell the teacher how effective he has been in guiding the student.

Other things to consider

- Vocabulary: slip, scoring, texture, pattern, decoration, pottery, functional.
- Art materials needed: water base clay (or a substitution of an oil base clay or papier mâché if the former isn't available); tools for cutting, trimming, and attaching; containers for water and slip.
- Pictures of pottery and ceramics, and papier mâché figures.
- People who might have need for the concept: ceramists, sculptors, craft designers.

LEVEL 4   ACTIVITY 108

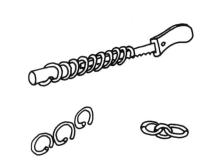

Concept taught by this activity: To enhance the student's awareness of decoration, he should now have experiences with simple processes in jewelry making.

Objective: The student utilizes simple processes in jewelry making to create an ornament for himself or someone else.

A sample lesson plan for achieving the objective:

Teacher preparations
Locate and collect examples of jewelry and any illustrations available. Display them for discussion. Have students bring examples.

Teaching suggestions
- Brainstorm with the students on their understanding of decoration and ways in which people decorate themselves in different parts of the world. Ask such questions as: "What does the word *decoration* mean?" "How many kinds of things can you list that people decorate?" Lead up to the idea that people decorate themselves and then see how many different ways can be listed. Bring decoration as experiences in primitive and ancient civilizations into the discussion: scarring, painting, and tatooing; hair styles; beads, bracelets and necklaces; nose and ear ornaments; hair ornaments; reshaping parts of the body; and decorating clothing. Present the idea that many artists believe the human body is decorated "just right" by nature — that any change ruins it. They disapprove of tatooing, reshaping, and even piercing the ears.
- Discuss the kinds of jewelry they or their parents may have made. "What materials were used?" "What kinds did they like best?" "What would primitive people use today?" "Could they likely see value in things we might throw away?"
- List every conceivable thing that might be used in some way to decorate either the human body or objects in the home.

- Discuss ways in which jewelry may or may not be aesthetic or beautiful. (Shapes don't go well together; materials or colors are unrelated.)

Suggested art activity
Make some simple form of jewelry. Necklaces are easily made by threading small pieces onto string or some tough thread. Use pieces such as shells, beads, eyelets, fired pieces of clay with tiny openings left through them, seeds, and seed pods, hollow weed, or nuts and shells, pieces of bone and driftwood (for pendants), leather pieces, all different kinds of pasta (dry macaroni, spaghetti, and such things made from paste), bottle tops, and the rings out of aluminum soft-drink cans.

Alternative art activities
- Fashion bracelets, chains, hair ornaments, and earrings out of wire. Chains can be made by wrapping wire around a piece of dowel, then sawing through each wire along one side of the dowel. With a pair of pliers you can pinch each C-shaped piece of wire into a link of the chain.
- Decorate a jewelry box with found objects.
- Decorate a belt by punching different sizes of holes in it. (Use a leather punch or bullet casings and a hammer.)
- Use a hacksaw to cut aluminum or copper pipe into small sections; use spacers between them to make necklaces and bracelets.
- Make bolo tie slips out of bone, leather, or boondoggle.

Evaluation

When the student has created some sort of simple jewelry, the objective has been achieved. If some attempt has been made to keep it aesthetic, the teacher has been especially successful.

Other things to consider

- Vocabulary: ornament, ornamentation, decoration, jewelry, primitive, aesthetic.
- Art materials needed: Whatever found materials selected by the student are used in his jewelry could be the basis of this list.

241

■ People who might have need for the concept: jewelry
  designer, designer, craftsman.

LEVEL 4   ACTIVITY 109

Concept taught by this activity: A variety of terms can be used to describe works of art: *portrait* or *landscape, abstract* or *realistic, painting* or *sculpture, drawing* or *print.*

Objective: The student describes works of art with terms such as *portrait* or *landscape, abstract* or *realistic, painting* or *sculpture,* and *drawing* or *print.*

A sample lesson plan for achieving the objective:

Teacher preparations
Collect prints and other illustrations for display and discussion.

Teaching suggestions
■ Review what was learned in activity #86 (describing works of art according to subject, activity, color usage, mood or feeling, and other criteria).
■ Warmup activities useful to this concept: "What are all the ways a horse and a car are alike?" "Different?" "Think up a title for this painting." "How is a footprint like a map?" "How are these two paintings alike?"
■ Look over the selected prints and place them according to these descriptive headings.

Other categories might include: cityscape, still life, weaving, ceramics, pottery, nonobjective (totally abstract), impressionistic (giving the *impression* of realism, but more free in strokes and use of color).
■ Complete this analogy: "Realism is to abstraction as an object is to _____." (Its form, its structure, its ideas.)

Picture	Artist	Descriptive Terms
Harvesters	Breughel	Landscape; realistic;
The Hay Wain	Constable	a painting
Tranquility	Gasser	
Breezing Up	Homer	Seascape; realistic;
Maas at Dordrecht	Cuyp	a painting
Bacchus	Caravaggio	Portrait; realistic; a
Blue Boy	Gainsborough	painting
I and the Village	Chagall	Figurative; abstract;
Sinbad the Sailor	Klee	a painting
Mother and Child	Kollwitz	Figurative; realistic; a drawing
Young Hare	Durer	Animal; realistic; a print

Suggested art activity
Have students collect examples of works of art including sculpture, ceramics, weaving, architecture, and other art forms that can be easily located. Classify them in a display for the class.

Alternative art activities
■ Paint a picture that represents at least three descriptive categories.
■ Have a scrapbook of art pieces done with different media and with different techniques.

Evaluation

When the student is able to utilize all of the suggested categories found in this lesson to describe works of art, the objective has been achieved.

Other things to consider

■ Vocabulary: abstract, realistic, landscape, seascape, figurative, portrait, print, painting, drawing, sculpture, weaving, ceramics, pottery, cityscape, still life, nonobjective.
■ Art materials needed: drawing and painting materials.
■ Prints: see list in this activity.

243

■ People who might have need for the concept: docents, art
critics, teachers, art historians, museum or gallery directors,
and artists of all different types.

Abstract
Print
Sculpture
Portrait
Landscape
Realistic

LEVEL 4   ACTIVITY 110

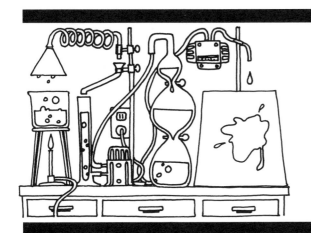

Concept taught by this activity: Experimentation as an outgrowth of imagination and knowledge plays an important role in the creative output of artists.

Objective: The student demonstrates an awareness of how experimentation is an outgrowth of imagination and knowledge and how it plays an important role in creativity.

A sample lesson plan for achieving the objective:

Teacher preparations
- Collect and display pictures and prints that are examples of experimentation in art.
- Fill two clear glasses or beakers with water. Have food coloring, Clorox (bleach), salt, and sugar ready to use.
- Think about the role of imagination and knowledge in experimentation. Be prepared to discuss them. Remember that *creativity* itself is a function of knowledge, imagination, and evaluation.

Teaching suggestions
"What are all the ways you have tried out a new idea you have had?" "Perhaps such things as riding your bicycle with one hand, licking an ice cream cone a different way, changing the furniture in your bedroom, or making up a new game with your friends." Encourage as many responses as possible. "When you tried out these new ideas, you were experimenting."
- Show the students a glass or beaker of water. Tell them you want to *experiment* and see what will happen if you put a drop of yellow food coloring into the water. Drop it in. Ask students what might happen if you put a drop of blue food

coloring into the glass. Drop it in with the yellow. Point: It is *knowledge* telling us that if blue is mixed with yellow it might make green. Tell students that you would like to see if you can make the water clear again without dumping out the green water and starting over. "Would sugar help?" (Try it.) "Will salt do it?" (Try it.) "Would this liquid do it?" (Pour in some Clorox or bleach and let it clear the green out.) Explain that *knowledge* indicated that a bleach can get rid of color. "We only *imagined* salt and sugar could do it." (Caution: Do NOT let children experiment with the Clorox. Explain that it could burn or poison them.) Summarize that both *knowledge* and *imagination* were used in doing the experiment.
- Artists try out new ideas and experiment too. Look at these prints by Klee and Rembrandt. Klee was experimenting with new ways to draw or paint a face. As you can see, his way was very different from that of Rembrandt. (Use *Head of a Man* by Klee, and *Man with Helmet* by Rembrandt.) Hold up a print by Watteau, *Three Negro Boys,* and comment that Watteau was experimenting with several possible views of boys by drawing different views of them. He was making a drawing *experiment.* Hold up print by Ingres, *Study of Iliad,* and comment that Ingres is also doing drawing experiments for a painting he wants to do later. He is experimenting with various positions and ways to handle the clothing. Hold up the print by Pollock, *Mural,* and ask what the students think this artist might have been experimenting with. (Color relationships, getting his own movements or gestures into his art, ways to paint without touching the canvas with his hand or brush.) Hold up a print by Seurat, *La Grande Jatte,* and explain that Seurat was experimenting by painting with little dots of pure color, using no color mixing or blending by brush strokes. He wanted people's eyes to mix the color by seeing a blue dot next to a yellow and seeing their "mix," green. Hold up a print by Rothko, *Orange and Yellow,* and comment that Rothko wanted to see what these two colors looked like on that background and next to each other. He was experimenting to see whether one color would look nearer or farther back in the painting and to get a sort of

vibration of colors. Vasarely did the same sort of thing, using form as well as color in *Zebegen*.

Suggested art activity

Ask students to *imagine* an animal that doesn't really exist. Ask if they can see it in their minds. Ask if it is smiling or growling. Tell them to make it have a tail. To make it pink. Make it purple. "Can you *see* it?" "What color are his eyes?" "Make the animal pink again." "What do its ears look like?" Now ask the students to *draw* their imaginary animal. (They might use crayons, paint, or just pencils.) Tell them: "Your *experiment* is to see if you can *imagine* it clearly enough to *draw* it. You will have to use your *knowledge* of other animals and things to draw it."

Alternative art activities (Experiments)

- "What would happen if you mixed red, black, and yellow?" "Try it." (Brown.)
- "Could you mix black from the primary colors of red, yellow, and blue?" (No, those colors are not really enough to get black.)
- "Is there an art idea you would like to experiment with?" "A collage?" "Paper sculpture?" "Clay?" "Weaving?" "Go ahead and plan an experiment, then try it."
- "Do a sculpture of your imaginary animal, using clay, wood, or plaster."

Evaluation

- Oral feedback can be analyzed to see if students understand what an experiment is and how knowledge and imagination are used in formulating and trying.
- Observe each student's working process; see if he draws upon knowledge or experience and his own imagination. (Reward the most unusual, imaginative, and successful experiments.)

Other things to consider

- Vocabulary: imagination, knowledge, experiment, idea, discovery, creativity.
- Art materials needed: Two beakers (or glasses), water, food coloring, salt, sugar, Clorox (bleach), paper for each student, paint or crayons, and pencils.
- Prints:
  Head of a Man by Klee
  Man With a Helmet by Rembrandt
  Three Negro Boys by Watteau
  Study of Iliad by Ingres
  Mural by Pollock
  La Grande Jatte by Seurat
  Orange and Yellow by Rothko
  Zebegen by Vasarely
- People who might have need for the concept: besides the artists that use this concept in every type of art possible, the people who deal with art history and analysis.

LEVEL 4   # ACTIVITY 111

GREY

Concept taught by this activity: The intensity of any color can be changed by adding gray.

Objective: The children will demonstrate that by adding gray the intensity of any color will change.

A sample lesson plan for achieving the objective:

Teacher preparations
- Bring magazine pictures of interior decors (be aware of the grayed colors).
- Construct a value scale by using found objects or swatches cut from photographic reproductions in magazines (nine steps graduated from white to black).
- Using grayed colors, try to relate them to the scale, and experiment with one color, gradually adding amounts of gray to the pigment. Use as a visual for the lesson.

Teaching suggestions
- Have several reproductions of artists' paintings and a color wheel or some paint chips of pure hues. Begin discussions by asking such questions as: "How is the color in the pictures different from these?" "Why do artists mix colors?" "Why not just use all of your colors just as they are in the paint sets?" "Why don't we paint the walls and ceilings of our homes with bright colors?"
- "What happens to a color if gray is added?" Show numerous examples of a color in various stages of grayness and ask which has no gray in it. "What has the most?" "Can you place each color in a sequential degree of grayness?" "How do grayed colors make you feel in contrast to bright colors?" "How does a bright day make you feel in contrast to a dull, grayish day?" "How would an artist use grayed colors?" "What would happen if our sidewalks were changed from a gray color to a bright color?" "Or our buildings?" "What color would you like the playground to be?" "Would you use grayed colors or bright, clear colors if you could plan a room for yourself?"

"If you are buying clothes for yourself?" "Why are most colors in a home grayish colors rather than strong, bright colors?"

Suggested art activity
Have the children make a picture from construction paper, using only the very bright colors for sidewalks, sky, houses, and other objects. Discuss the effect the picture has on members of the class. Compare it with other pictures containing grayed colors.

Alternative art activities
- Have the children make a collection of pictures with all one color they have chosen and make a collage showing the different grayed tones of one color.
- Have the children water-color a picture, using grayed tones.
- Make an abstract design using greenish grays, reddish grays, yellowish grays, and other colors.
- Make an abstract design of value contrasts (light to dark) or a combination of hue contrast and value contrast (a pale pink next to a dark olive green).

Evaluation
The teacher will examine the pictures the children create and examine them for grayed color. Also be aware of what progress the student has made in discussions of graying color.

Other things to consider
- Vocabulary needed: grayness, intensity, abstract, design, numerous, sequential, degree of intensity.
- Art materials needed: colored paper, art paper, water colors, tempera.
- Prints:
  Portrait of the Artist's Mother by Whistler
  Sinbad the Sailor by Klee
  The Scout by Remington
  The Last Supper by Dali
  The Card Players by Cazanne
  Ville d'Avray by Corot
  Quadrille by Toulouse-Lautrec
  Christina's World by Wyeth
  Hudson River Logging by Homer
- Film: "Color and Pigment in Art" by Coronet Films

■ People who might have need for the concept: painter; interior decorator; illustrator; advertising designer; artists that do batik, tie-dye, enameling, collages, serigraphs, cartoons, and prints.

LEVEL 4

ACTIVITY 112

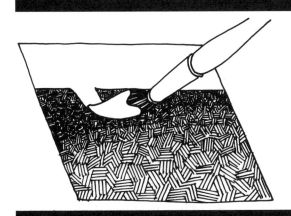

Concept taught by this activity: Warm colors may have aspects of coolness just as cool colors may have aspects of warmth.

Objective: The student demonstrates an awareness that warm colors can appear both warm and cool and that cool colors can appear both cool and warm.

A sample lesson plan for achieving the objective:

Teacher preparations
- Collect examples of many colors, both warm and cool (large). Include samples of warm and cool greens, reds, and others. Have both obvious and subtle examples.
- Exhibit prints in which artists have used both warm and cool colors for specific purposes.
- Make mental notes of warm and cool greens, reds, and other colors in and around the school environment.

Teaching suggestions
- Review what warm and cool colors are.
- Discuss how warm and cool colors make us feel (cool vs. warm). Suggest examples of how colors influence the behavior and activity of people, such as workers in industry. Discuss wearing colors as they fit one's mood or personality. Discuss how color affects how appetizing food is.
- Break the class into groups. Give each group a stack of colors (paint chips, fabric samples, or others) to divide into piles of warm and cool. Then determine whether or not each stack of the cool ones contains colors that are warmer than others. ("Which blues are the warmest and which are the coolest?" "Which reds are coolest and which are warmest?")

- Gather the students together to discuss what they have learned in their groups. If any incorrect decisions have been made, see if the total group can correct them. There may be some ideas that no one can totally agree on.
- Look at pictures in books commonly used to see how the warm or cool feeling of them relates to the story or the poem.
- Read or tell a story (or poem) and have the children take color notes so that at certain points they have to describe what color would be used to illustrate what was happening and whether it was a cool or warm version of the color.
- Create a "color metaphor": "The *orange* sun remained *cool* in the crisis of the white hot fire that day," or "The storm spread a warm blanket of snow over the field." The steps to create a metaphor:
  - Write or tell all of the *cold* words (then the *warm* words).
    - Synonyms: cool, chilly, brisk, brrr, crisp, frosty, shivery, freezing, icy.
    - Suggestive words: snow, ice, sleet, hail, wind, freeze, popsicle.
  - Use any color and transfer it from an object it usually designates or relates to, to an object it may designate only by analogy and comparison: The violets became a *flaming* bouquet midst the white and blue-gray snow, or the violets had an *icy* stare from the midst of the red roses.

Suggested art activity
- Take some painting media and have students see if they can make their cool colors slightly warm and their warm colors slightly cool by mixing.
- Do the same thing with overlapping colored cellophane or tissue paper.
- Do the same thing with an overhead and colored acetate or with petri dishes and food coloring.

Alternative art activities
- Do a picture with several versions of some subject that is typically associated with warmness or coolness. For example, paint several versions of a snow scene, starting it in shades of red, then a cooler red, then a reddish violet,

then a violet and a blue or blue-violet. ''At what point does the snow really look like snow?''

- At some future time, take the students out of doors, and as they look at the variety of greens, blues, and other hues, see if they can pick out the variations in warmness and coolness of each.
- Play music and have the students make the color of the mood created by each passage. Emphasize that they need to be looking for whether or not each color should be a warm or cool version. Music such as *The Grand Canyon Suite*, Ravel's *Bolero*, Debussey's *Claire de Lune*, Smetna's *The Moldeau* or Stravinsky's *Rite of Spring*.

Evaluation

Suggestions for the teacher in determining whether or not *each* student was able to use the concept in the product he created. Make mental notes of those who responded in a way that their awareness of the concept had been indicated. Observe the individual's ability to use the information in the suggested activities.

Other things to consider

- Vocabulary: warm, cool, intensity, hue, value, chroma, mixture, mood, psychology of color (the reaction to color).
- Art materials needed: paint chips, fabric, wall covering samples, or colored paper.
- Stories on color, such as *Hailstones and Halibut Bones* but check to see if the book has been used in a previous activity.
- Prints:
  The Artist's Bedroom at Arles by Van Gogh
  Sinbad the Sailor by Klee
  Combination Concrete by Davis
  Justice and Peace by Overstreet
  Rebus by Rauschenberg
  Composition 1963 by Miro
  Women in a Garden by Monet
  The Card Players by Cezanne
- People who might have need for the concept: painters, interior designers, illustrators, art historians, and those who analyze works of art.

LEVEL 4

ACTIVITY 113

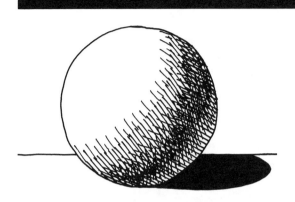

Concept taught by this activity: Objects can be drawn with a light side and a shadow side.

Objective: The student will draw objects or people with a light side and a shadow side.

A sample lesson plan for achieving the objective:

Teacher preparations
- Arrange the classroom so that light is coming from just one window or from just one direction. (Could use artificial lights such as a flood, a spot or projector, or a flashlight in a darkened room.)
- Have numerous prints or pictures that show the shadows and the dark and light sides of objects.
- If you are a female teacher, you could wear either a pleated skirt or a full skirt.
- Place objects such as a can, globe, ball, box, or cone around the room for children to see and to study lighting variations.
- Place chairs so that several students can sit in various places that would cast light and shadow on them for the class to view.
- Open the door and compare light hitting the door from the hallway or to the outside.
- Be prepared to study shadows on a face, a shadow from the nose, and other effects from the light.

Teaching suggestions
- Start by asking such questions as the following: "I've asked two students to sit in certain places (one in the dark and the other in bright light). Why does Linda look lighter than Johnny?" "How is Mary different from either one of the others?" (Have Mary sitting with shadow on her in a middle light.) "Do people have some part in the dark nearly all of the time?" "Why?" "Now look at this can and see if you

can find a part that is dark." "Tell me what parts of the room are in darker areas than others." "Why are some parts of the room in more darkness than other parts?" "What makes the difference?" "How is it helpful to an artist for his subject to have some parts dark and some in the light?" "Why do you think we might need to put some dark in our drawings?" Shine a light on one object, such as a cone, and move around behind it and near it. Ask for observations from the students. Let the students discover most of the answers you are seeking. Redirect and ask additional questions when the students' thoughts move in the wrong direction.
- Use whatever media is available on value (variations in darkness and lightness) or shadow.
  - Show pictures of objects and people with shadows on them. Examine the value scale showing gradations from white to black.
  - Discuss each of the visuals in the same manner as before. Focus the development of student awareness on how light influences what they see and on the fact that when light comes from just one direction and is not diffused, everything has a light side and a dark side.
- Have students put a light on objects in the room to see where the light hits and where it doesn't hit.
  - Use questions to discuss the way the sun moves and the way shadows change position, shape, and value.
  - Look at pictures that show a dark shadow and ask why things look deeper in some pictures than others.
  - Take the students outside to look at the school building and at houses near the school and have them look for shadows. Notice the sun's position. Have them note telephone poles, playground equipment, and their own shadows.
- Relate this concept to the sun and the way it creates the light and dark sides of the earth and the moon. Discuss the astronauts' traveling to the moon and the fact that they have to time their landing between the light and shadow side.

Suggested art activity
- Have students select one or two objects to draw in a controlled lighting environment. Have them discuss the

lighting and check each other on this first attempt to see if they can tell where the light is coming from.

■ Pass out paper to the children and ask them to draw an object other than the one they did. They may do several objects or people. Every student who has developed an awareness of the concept should now draw or paint this object with a light side and a shadow side.

Alternative art activities

■ Have the students do a drawing of whatever subject they choose, using white chalk and charcoal on a gray paper. The chalk will create all light values and the charcoal all shadow areas (the dark side).

■ Make a diagram showing the influence of light on a form.

Evaluation

When the student draws or paints an object with a light side and a shadow side and completes his picture without help, the objective has been achieved. The student who utilizes the concept at a later date without teacher input has the kind of awareness this lesson would hopefully generate.

Other things to consider

■ Vocabulary: light, shadow, dark, source, depth, multiple, single, value, intense, direct, indirect, reflection.
■ Art materials needed: found objects, cans, balls, bottles, cones, boxes, colored chalk, art paper, charcoal, gray paper, white chalk.
■ Prints:
Dempsey and Firpo by Bellows
Venice by Canaletto
Cliff of Etretat After Storm by Courbet
The Crucifixion by Dali
Absinthe by Degas
Seven A.M. by Hopper
St. Joseph by De La Tour
Man With Helmet by Rembrandt
Lacemaker by Vermeer
■ Materials: photographs taken in black and white showing shadows, flashlight, projector, lamp, paper, pencils, value chart, filmstrip, projector, dark room.
■ People who might have need for the concept: artists that draw, paint, do illustrations and prints.

LEVEL4

ACTIVITY 114

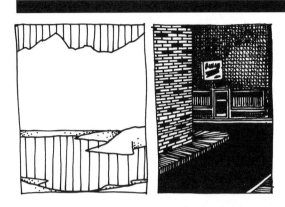

Concept taught by this activity: The keying of color (low, middle, or high keys) greatly influences the mood or feeling of a work of art.

Objective: The student will paint a picture of his own choosing, depicting a mood or a feeling through appropriate value keys.

A sample lesson plan for achieving the objective:

Teacher preparations
- Collect pictures, objects, and materials depicting moods or feelings.
- Arrange bulletin boards and lighting so that the two sides of the room depict contrasting moods.
- Select appropriate media and have a projector and other necessary equipment ready in an easily darkened area.
- Have a value scale in front of the room.

Teaching suggestions
- Hold up something brown and ask: "What are all the brown things you can think of?" Hold up a red orange painting or paper and ask: "How does this make you feel?"
- Show colors depicting gaiety, such as the colors of carnivals, circuses, or balloons. Ask such questions as the following: "What do these colors make you think of?" "Why do you suppose they cause you to have such feelings?" "Which colors do you feel might be called heavy colors?" "Which colors cause you to feel airy?" "Can you relate any colors to events such as death, marriage, rainy days, sales, or other incidents?" "Do you feel different when you wear various colors of clothing?" (A red shirt or dress as opposed to a white or gray one.) "Why do colors affect how we feel?" "Does the darkness or lightness of a color affect how we react to it?" (A light pink versus a deep red, or a pale yellow green versus a dark brownish green.)

- Look at some of the prints suggested and discuss the feeling or mood of each. "How does the lightness or darkness of the colors affect the mood or feeling of the picture?"
Note: Look at a value scale of shades of black and white (nine graduated steps in value ranging from white at the top to black at the bottom with a middle gray in between).

1	White	
2	High Light	High Key
3	Light	
4	Low Light	
5	Middle Value	Middle Key
6	High Dark	
7	Dark	
8	Low Dark	Low Key
9	Black	

If a picture is said to be in a high key, most of the colors are in the value range of steps 1, 2, and 3. If it is in a middle key, the colors are in the value range of steps 4, 5, and 6. If it is in a low key, the colors range in steps 7, 8, and 9.

In any of the three keys, colors can be at any level; however, the largest area or the greatest number of shapes in a print will be primarily in one. For example, *The Boats at Argenteuil* are in a high key; *Christina's World* by Wyeth is in a middle key; and Rembrandt's *Man With the Golden Helmet* is in a low key.
- Talk about happy experiences and relate them to color keys.
- Have small groups select color keys that represent the personality of people they know or people who are famous.
- "What feelings do you get when you enter some homes, and how do color keys affect this feeling?"
- "Visual antonyms": Ask the students to tell the class the opposite-feeling colors that you hold up. (Allow discussion of *why* they see the opposition.)
- "Visual similes": Ask the students to create similes using color moods, such as "The *fire* on the hearth was like a shimmering *bouquet* of orange and yellow," or "The soft blue was like time passing quietly."

Suggested art activity
Paint a picture in a specific key. Try to create a mood or a feeling with the value range you use.

Alternative art activities
- Write a haiku poem (see dictionary for precise definition) using color keying and moods of color as the subject.

Illustrate it.
- Write and tell stories relating to mood and color. Illustrate one.
- Locate and sing a number of songs about color that depict mood. Illustrate one.

Evaluation

Be aware of each student's responses and oral contributions for some of the evaluation, and reinforce it by how well the student applies the concept in a painting.

Other things to consider

- Vocabulary: color, value, mood, feeling, color keys.
- Art materials needed: paper, water colors, crayons, pencils, water containers.
- Prints:
  View of Toledo by El Greco
  Boats at Argenteuil by Monet
  Man With Helmet by Rembrandt
  Christina's World by Wyeth
  St. Joseph by De La Tour
  Head of a Man by Klee
  Portrait of the Artist's Mother by Whistler
  Mlle. Violette by Redon
  Quadrille by Toulouse-Lautrec
  Mona Lisa by da Vinci
  Water Flowery Mill by Gorky
  Iliad Study by Ingres
- People who might have need for the concept: those who deal with art history and analysis as well as artisans of all types.

LEVEL 4   ACTIVITY 115

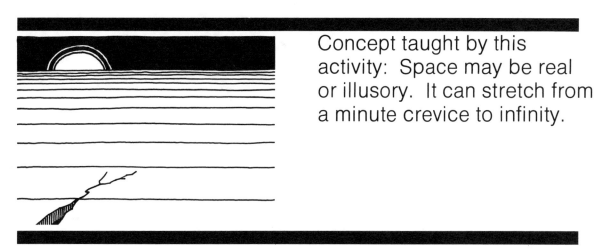

Concept taught by this activity: Space may be real or illusory. It can stretch from a minute crevice to infinity.

Objective: The student recognizes the limitless nature of space, both real and illusory.

A sample lesson plan for achieving the objective:

Teacher preparations
- Display appropriate photographs and prints for discussion period.
- Have materials such as painting and sculpturing materials available for both two- and three-dimensional activities.

Teaching suggestions
- "What are all of the words that come to your minds if I say 'depth'?" (*Distance, deep, far, wide, long, lake, ocean, sky, space*) "How far away is the house in *Christina's World* by Wyeth?" "What is between the house and the girl?" (Space. And the space is an obstacle.) Review the term *space* and the student's experience with arranging things in a picture.
- Discuss some of the broad uses of the term *space:* paper as space, wall space, room space, purse space, space as atmosphere, space between buildings or between a person's neck and his collar.
- Refer to the concept and discuss whether or not it is a true concept. Have the students give further examples of the concept, such as space between fibers of cloth as seen through a magnifying glass in contrast with the space between here and the farthest star.
- Ask such questions as: "Why would artists be concerned about space?" "What would be the space concerns of a painter, a potter, an interior decorator, or a landscape architect?" Define common concerns as well as other concerns. "When would space be an illusion?" "Does anyone know what illusion means?" "In looking at these

pictures how has the artist been able to make us think the picture has space in it?"

Suggested art activity
Make a sculpture from clay, wood, or paper and pay particular attention to the spacial relationships between forms. If you have time, do a *drawing* of your sculpture.

Alternative art activities
- Draw or paint a picture that contains the illusion of space or depth.
- Do a drawing of "make believe" space. Try to make the space on the paper appear as though it has many different depths and many different kinds of spaces.

Evaluation

When the student demonstrates an awareness of the concept, the objective has been achieved.

Other things to consider

- Vocabulary: space, illusory, infinite.
- Art materials needed: painting and sculpturing materials as available.
- Prints:
  Dempsey and Firpo by Bellows
  Numbering at Bethlehem by Brueghel
  Ville d'Avray by Corot
  Bedroom at Arles by Van Gogh
  Delphic Sibyl by Michelangelo
  The Scout by Remington
  The Letter by Vermeer
  Christina's World by Wyeth
  This is the first of a series of four lessons dealing with space. Number 115 defines, #116 deals with flattening space.
- People who might have need for the concept: artists of almost every type. This is a very universal concept for artists.

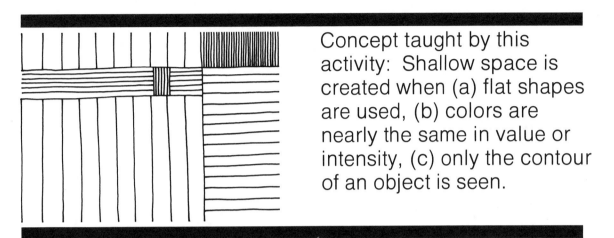

Concept taught by this activity: Shallow space is created when (a) flat shapes are used, (b) colors are nearly the same in value or intensity, (c) only the contour of an object is seen.

Objective: The student minimizes the feeling of space in a design or picture by (a) using flat shapes, (b) keeping colors nearly the same in value or intensity, or (c) allowing only the contour of objects to be seen.

A sample lesson plan for achieving the objective:

Teacher preparations
- Display several pictures having little or no depth in them.
- Cut flat shapes out of construction paper and arrange them in a picture or a design on a tack board. Some should be recognizable silhouettes.
- Have pictures available that contain the illusion of great depth.

Teaching suggestions
- Discuss this notion briefly: Some artists want to show depth in their pictures because it suits their style or method of working and helps them in expressing their ideas. Other artists, however, like to keep everything flat looking. They believe that a picture should be seen as a part of the wall where it hangs and that perspective in a picture "digs" holes in the wall, and in the flat canvas.
- Show some of the pictures containing obvious illusions of depth and space. Compare them with the pictures where everything looks quite flat. Use Cezanne's and Gauguin's pictures as good examples of the point at which the artist

first started to minimize illusions of depth in his paintings.
- Ask questions. Look at pictures with depth: "Why was depth necessary in these pictures?" Look at pictures that seem flat: "Why does this picture look so flat?" "What did the artists do to the perspective in his picture?" "What kinds of shapes did he use to keep things flat?"

See if students notice that when an artist doesn't shade his subject or use gradations in value this helps him to maintain a flat appearance.

The artist may make distant objects larger in size and warmer in color, too. Discuss whether or not these changes in size or color influence the appearance of depth.

See if the students can tell whether or not all of the pictures have at least *some* depth in them. (If there is any overlapping at all or any colors that seem to advance or recede, *some* depth *is* created.)
- Explore the students' understanding of *contour*.

"What does the word *contour* mean?" (The outside outline of an object.)
"What conditions would we need to have if only the basic shape of something was clearly visible?" (Darkened room, early morning or late evening, foggy or rainy day.)

"Do the objects *really* become flatter?" (They only *appear* to.)

"How does the idea of fewer details relate to our being able to see only the contour of an object?" (If you can't see anything but the outside shape, you certainly won't see details.)

"Why do distant objects appear flat and less detailed?"

"When are the contours of a distant object visible?" (When it's a *long* way away.)

Review the idea that the object is visible when the amount of light is reduced sufficiently or when objects are far away.
- The student should come to recognize that contrast in the value or intensity of any two colors affects the depth or feeling of space in a design or picture. Use a variety of

photographs, prints, or paintings as examples and discuss each in relation to the following statements: "Does the picture have any feeling of depth in it?" (Recall experiences with lesson #115.)

"Let's look at each picture in terms of the effect contrasts in value and intensity of colors have on depth or space." (Discuss one at a time and do it with the pictures you have decided on.) *Example:* "Does the print have much depth?"

"How about contrasts in value?" "Are these contrasts in the intensity of colors?" "How does each affect the feeling of space in the picture?" "If the colors were more nearly the same intensity, would the picture seem more flat?" "If the colors had little difference in value, would the picture seem more flat?"

- Look at objects inside the room in a very dim light. Help students to observe that the lack of light influences contrasts in value and intensity so that all colors seem grayer and more neutral; then ask the question: "Do objects seem to flatten out when the contrasts disappear?" (They do.) "Why?"
- Discuss what some of the reason might have been that caused each artist to make his picture look flat. Discuss what he did to accomplish this goal: how he changed or distorted shapes, colors, and textures. Refer to the design or picture made from construction paper. "Is it flat looking?" "Why?"

Suggested art activity
Make a picture representing whatever subject you choose but one that has little or no depth. Shapes may overlap, but do everything else you can to destroy all feeling of space in your picture.

Alternative art activities
- Cut shapes out of cloth, wallpaper, or construction paper — with or without patterns — and arrange them into a very flat-looking two-dimensional design.
- Take a series of slides, colored photos, or black and white pictures that illustrate the concept. Use a variety of subjects in a number of different lighting or climatic situations.
- Paint a picture in which the color contrasts in value and in intensity are minimal to see how flat-looking you can make a design. If you want to illustrate this concept even *more* clearly, do the same picture twice — once with contrasts in value and intensity and once without.

Evaluation

The picture or pictures the student renders should be ample evidence of whether or not the concept was understood. If there is some question about the legitimacy of either the student's use of the concept or his understanding (did he copy from someone?), the teacher may wish to ask further questions.

Other things to consider

- Vocabulary: space, depth, value, intensity, two-dimensional, three-dimensional, detail, climatic conditions, contour, silhouette, distance, value.
- Art materials needed: crayons or painting media, brushes, and art paper in two or three sizes.
- Prints:
  - Pictures with greath depth:
    The Harvester by Breughel
    The Gleaners by Millet
    The Blue Cart by Van Gogh
  - Pictures with depth minimized:
    House at Aix by Cezanne
    Harvest Scene by Gauguin
  - Example of contour (silhouettes) flattening space:
    Fur Traders on the Missouri by Bingham

    Fox Island by Hartley
  - Examples of flat shapes minimizing space:
    Ice-Skating Palace by Bonnard
    Guernica by Picasso
  - Examples of flat space created with colors nearly the same in value:
    The Bullfight by Goya
    Allies Day, May 1917 by Hassam
- People who might have need for the concept: painters, printmakers, commercial artists, craft designers of all types, stage set designers, architects, interior designers, and artists that do collages.

LEVEL 4

Concept taught by this activity: Many works of art have themes that are easily identified. Artists may treat given themes either in a similar way or in a quite different way.

Objective: The student identifies themes in works of art and describes ways in which artists treat themes in either similar ways or in quite different ways.

A sample lesson plan for achieving the objective:

Teacher preparations
- *Theme* as used in this lesson is an idea or point of view expanded on in a work of art. It is the underlying or essential subject of an artist's creation.
- Works of art may, therefore, contain *more* than one theme. An examination of this chart may be helpful in developing a better understanding of the concept and in teaching it to the student. Some themes are even psychological manifestations that occur over and over.

Print	Theme
Bacchus by Caravaggio	Mythology
The Rhine Maidens by Ryder	
*Numbering at Bethlehem** by Brueghel	
Harvest Scene by Gauguin	Genre (Scenes of
Snap the Whip by Homer	everyday life)
*Quadrille** by Toulouse-Lautrec	
*Guernica** by Picasso	Social Protest
Les Miserables by Picasso	

Print	Theme
*Prodigal Son** by Rembrandt	
Peaceable Kingdom by Hicks (lamb & lion idea)	Christianity
*Small Crucifixion** by Grunewald	
*The Crucifixion** by Dali	
Breezing Up by Homer	
Fox Island by Hartley	The Sea
Maas at Dordrecht by Cuyp	

- There are many more themes than the five in the chart, and additional examples for each of the categories can be found in the prints suggested for this overall program.
- Display suggested prints and whatever visual aids are available and usable for this concept.

   Teaching suggestions (To get at the recognition of various themes or motifs, a discussion about *categorizing* is useful.)
- ● Separate students into small groups, each group with a papersack full of "odds and ends." Their task is to take turns putting the *objects* in categories, such as the red objects, the blue ones, the plastic ones, and so forth; or: tools, pointed objects, flammable objects, and any other categories they can think of.
   - Do some general brainstorming, such as "uses for a brick"; then practice putting lists into categories.
- Review the meaning of the concept. "What does the word *theme* mean?" "How many different kinds of themes can you think of?" Paintings may be categorized by themes.
- Have students look at the prints, identify the theme or themes, then itemize prints with similar themes in columns.
- Discuss pictures or works of art that use the same theme in very different ways, and discuss artists who have treated a given theme in very similar ways.

   Suggested art activity
   Select one or two themes and find all of the titles of works of art you can locate that follow the given theme.

Alternative art activities
- As a group activity locate examples of several themes and make a display for the room or school.
- Draw or paint a picture that illustrates a given theme. (A sculpturing activity would be equally appropriate.)

Evaluation

When the student can point out the theme of a given work of art and tell how other artists treat a similar theme, the objective has been achieved.

Other things to consider

- Vocabulary: theme, subject, idea, motif, genre.
- Art materials needed: drawing, painting, or sculpturing materials as selected by the student.
- Prints: See the listing under "Teacher Preparations."
- People who might have need for the concept: docents, art historians, gallery directors, painters.

---

*Prints that might also be grouped under a historical theme or an event theme.

LEVEL 4   ACTIVITY 118

Concept taught by this activity: Forms may be convex or concave. They occupy space, and space can be created within them.

Objective: The student demonstrates an awareness of the differences between convex and concave shapes. He is able to show how forms occupy space and that space can be created within them.

A sample lesson plan for achieving the objective:

Teacher preparations
- Collect materials needed for discussion and projects.
- Obtain concrete examples.
- Collect pictures illustrating examples of concept.
- Research the importance of convex and concave forms in relation to the microscope, telescope, eye glasses, contact lenses, and the lens of the eye.
- Collect examples of concave and convex forms.

Teaching suggestions
Discuss *convex* and *concave*.
- Ask questions such as the following: "Who had cereal for breakfast?" "From what did you eat it?" "What was the shape of the bowl?" "Why did it have to be that kind of shape?" "What would we call that form?" "What form would it be if we inverted it?" (Use rounded, deep bowl.)
- Find examples of convex and concave. "Are there examples in the room?" "In your desk?" "Outside our building?" "In our homes?"
- Discuss the various uses of convex and concave forms. "Are some merely decorative?" "Are all concave forms utilitarian?" "What would our world be missing if there were no concave or convex forms?"
- Discuss the variety of forms artists (architects, potters, jewelry makers, and sculptors) have created that are both convex and concave.
- "Let's go outside and observe some concave and convex forms. What do you see out here that have such forms?" "Is the apparent surface of the heavens a half sphere or concave form as we see it?" "Is it a dome of the visible sky?" "Is the inside of this drinking fountain a concave or convex form?" "Can you form these two forms in any way, using your two hands?"

"Which wooden figures in a geometric figure kit would you say demonstrate the concept of concave and convex forms?"

"Do engineers, manufacturers, and builders use these words and have an awareness of their meaning in their work?" "How?"

"Do you think the early Indian pottery makers were aware of this concept, even though they had had no formal training about it?" "What Indians or other people fashioned their homes in this manner?" "How could you make a flat piece of paper concave?" "Which object would be stronger, a flat or convex form?"

"What are some objects with concave form in the room?" (Clock face, wash basin, door knobs) "Out-of-doors?"

"Name some convex shapes." "Are some forms combinations of both?" "Name some."

Discuss *space*.
- Identify various forms within the room or refer to the convex and concave shapes discussed. Look at them in terms of the following kinds of questions: "Is space part of our everyday life and world?" "Is there form in our everyday life and world?" "What do you think of when you hear of space?" "Is all form solid or can it have space within it?" "Can we create form?" "Do all forms occupy space?" "What would be some good materials to use to demonstrate this?" "What kinds of artists are concerned with space

problems?'' ''How does each use space?'' (Discuss the architect's concern about public buildings and homes, the painter's concern about creating or destroying the illusion of space, the interior decorator's concern with making rooms look large or small — arranging space.)

■ Demonstrate concept of space in form by showing common objects such as bottles, cups, and cans. (These are forms, but within each is space.)

■ Demonstrate the concept of form in space by passing a hand or arm over the desk. Place a block of wood or a book on the desk and again pass a hand over the desk, showing that some of the space is now occupied by a form.

Discuss how this concept applies to their experience with the following.

■ Convex mirrors cause rays to come to a point; concave mirrors spread the rays out; a flat lens doesn't affect transmission.

■ Concave mirrors enlarge an image, and convex mirrors reduce the image.

■ Lenses are used in microscopes, telescopes, and eye glasses to bend and focus light rays and to magnify images.

■ Air is a real substance that has weight and takes up space. Objects placed in water take up space.

■ A material is anything that takes up room (occupies space) and has weight.

■ Objects of the same weight may take up different amounts of space. Geometry is the study of space and of the figure in space.

Involve students in the following experiences.

■ Have students team up and test each other as to whether certain objects are convex, concave, or both.

■ Discuss ways in which artists have created an illusion of convex and concave forms or have created the actual form.

■ Discuss aspects of the eye (its shape) and the camera lens and its focal length.

Suggested art activity
Roll clay into a ball. Using a fine, taut wire, cut the sphere in half. Round and hollow out the center of one half the ball with your thumbs and fingers to concavity. Do the same with the other half. Invert the finished piece to show a convex shape. Create something out of them by combining them in some way.

Alternative art activities
■ Use small pieces of copper foil. With a pointed yet dull instrument such as an inkless ballpoint pen, draw some circles on the foil. With the foil now on a pad of several thicknesses of newspaper, and using a popsicle stick or other round-ended wooden tool, press inwardly to form a concave indention. Reverse the foil and do the same with another circle. Attractive patterns may be formed by arranging the circles in petal form to make flowers. Abstract pictures can be made by combining convex and concave figures with lines.

■ Use inflated balloons as forms to form papier maché around. When the forms are dry, cut them in half to show both concave and convex concepts as well as space within forms.

■ Make concave and convex forms out of clay, soap, or some other modeling material.

■ Pour plaster of Paris block into a milk carton. Color by pouring tempera into it while still wet and mixing it with a stick. After the plaster of Paris is dry, peel off the carton. Students can now make designs by scraping and gouging with a stick or other instrument. If this is done while the plaster of Paris is newly dried, it will carve more easily.

■ Do a balsa wood carving.

■ Investigate ways in which artists (painters, sculptors, architects, and interior designers) create illusion of space and ''real'' space.

■ Create a three-dimensional form that has both convex and concave shapes in it. Is space automatically created? Do the forms occupy space?

■ Make an abstract sculpture, using the concept.

■ Draw a picture of a concave form, using shading.

Evaluation

Evaluation is based on the teacher's observations of how the individual student's awareness seems to have changed in relation to the concept.

Other things to consider

■ Vocabulary needed: convex, concave, lens, focus, refraction, grinding, lenses, sphere, hemisphere, space, transmission of light, image.

■ Art materials needed: plasticine clay, fine wire, copper foil, newspapers, popsicle sticks, orange sticks, inkless ballpoint pens, steel wool and tincture of benzine, round balloons, strips of newsprint or paper toweling, wheat paste, bowls for paste, plaster of Paris, balsa wood, bars of soap, newspaper to cover working area, tempera, milk cartons, wax, clay, construction paper and glue. (The materials you select from this list will be determined by the activities the students participate in for implementing the concept.)

■ Audiovisual materials that might be used:
Film Loops:
''Line and Space,'' Bailey Film Associates
''Form and Space,'' Bailey Film Associates
Films:
''Space'' by ACI Films Incorporated
''Space and Creating with Clay,'' Bailey Film Associates
Magazines and pictures, a globe, a geometric figure kit.

■ Prints:
Autumn by Koryusai
Bacchus by Caravaggio
Venice by Canaletto
Don Manuel Osorio by Goya
My Gems by Harnett
The Return by Magritte
Man with Helmet by Rembrandt

■ People who might have need for the concept: architects, sculptors, ceramists.

Concept taught by this activity: Shapes (top, bottom, sides, and surface) can appear to escape the boundaries of a picture plane.

Objective: The student identifies situations when shapes in a design escape or move past the boundaries of the picture plane.

A sample lesson plan for achieving the objective:

Teacher preparations
- Display suggested prints and other pictures illustrating the concept.
- Discuss terminology with the students. Be certain that they know that a *plane* is any flat or nearly flat surface such as a desk top, the bridge of the nose, or the edge of a door. A *picture plane* is the surface the artist draws or paints on, and in the case of art prints, it is the surface bounded by the white border.
- You may want to discuss the word *boundary,* too. With pictures, either the frame, the border, or the matt constitutes the boundaries.

Teaching suggestions
- Discuss some of the reasons why artists use this concept.

Note: Some artists, especially those of the past, believed in some rather rigid rules regarding this concept. They tried to avoid having *any* part of their main subject go out of the picture plane or appear cut off by the frame. Even now one needs to be careful about *where* you cut a shape with the frame. For example, it would seldom be wise to have the head of a person rest on the bottom edge of a picture. The artist needs to be very much aware of the fact that when objects or shapes seem to escape the boundaries of the picture or seem to move beyond the frame line, the eye is led *out* of the picture. This gives the picture a feeling of

greater dimension or space — as if it never ended. Some shapes lead the eye in and out of the picture plane, too. It is interesting to look at pictures with these elements in them, to discuss why the artist did what he did, and to imagine how different the picture would seem if *none* of the major shapes left the picture plane.

Paintings photographed with permission of BYU Art Galleries.

- Have the students lay tracing paper or acetate over the top of a picture or print and trace the outlines of the major shapes, using directional arrows, as in the illustration. The outlines and arrows can show the effect of shapes that escape the boundaries of a picture plane.

Suggested art activity

Have the students purposely create small drawings or pictures in which they have parts of animals, plants, or objects cut off by the edge of the picture, at a point where it looks strange or distracting: cutting off the head, waist, or knees of people or animals, or the trunks of trees.

Evaluation

When it is evident that each student's awareness has been influenced by the experience with this lesson, the objective has been achieved.

Other things to consider

- Vocabulary: boundary, picture plane, plane.
- Art materials needed: tracing paper or acetate, and drawing materials.
- Prints:
  Escaping the boundaries:
  Dempsey and Firpo by Bellows
  Absinthe by Degas
  Allies Day, May 1917 by Hassam
  Seven A.M. by Hopper
  Breezing Up by Homer
  The Card Players by Cezanne
  Main subjects kept inside the frame:
  The Crucifixion by Dali
  The Scout by Remington
  Fur Traders on the Missouri by Bingham
  Three Flags by Johns
  Composition 1963 by Miro
  Poster: Jan. 18 to Feb. 12 by Shahn
- People who might have need for the concept: painters, illustrators, interior designers.

LEVEL 4

ACTIVITY 120

Concept taught by this activity: Variations in the elements can make space divisions more interesting.

Objective: The student demonstrates an awareness that variations in the elements of any arrangement can make the space divisions more interesting.

A sample lesson plan for achieving the objective:

Teacher preparations
- Obtain visual examples of the concept, both pro and con.
- Set up art materials needed for the activity or application part.
- Arrange for a field trip inside and outside the building to look for actual examples of the concept.

Teaching suggestions
- Ask such questions as the following: "What does variety mean?" "Why do we need variety in our life?" "What does its opposite, monotony, do to us?" "What makes a picture look monotonous?" "Can the same thing happen to a room?" "To sculpture?" Compare similar arrangements. "Which are most interesting?" "Why?" "Can our dress or our home become monotonous?" "How?" "Can a picture be made interesting by varying just one element of it, such as color or value?" "What happens if you vary all of the elements in a picture?" (Chaos.) "How have artists like Van Der Rohe, Mondrian, Albers, Pollock, and Warhol used variety?" "Can a design be interesting without variation in any of the elements used?" "Why?"

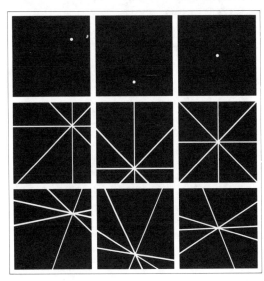

- Collect some object from nature and discuss ways in which there is a variety in that object. ("Could anyone find an object in nature that had no variations?")
- Discuss how artists may sometimes refer to all things in their environment as shapes and how the shapes are organized by the artist in a specific way for specific reasons. (Examine several prints from this view.) Do the same thing with the work of other kinds of artists, such as architects, interior decorators, and fashion designers.
- Discuss ways in which variety helps make pictures interesting and how lack of variety helps create monotony or a static condition.

Suggested art activity
Select a shape for the environment and compose a picture, repeating that shape with whatever variation seems necessary, such as height or width. Glue the shapes to a background in an appropriate arrangement. (This can be

done with any element or combination of elements.)
Compare the variety in elements used in your picture with
the variety in elements used by well-known artists. Compare
with the work of other students.

Alternative art activities
Trace a simple shape in a monotonous repeating pattern
arrangement until you have ten or twenty all the same. Have
each student paint most of the shapes all the same color,
but paint one to three either a different color, a different
shape, or a different texture. Discuss how important it was
to alter at least one object or shape in some way. (Have
one student make his design completely monotonous so
that the rest of the class will have something to compare
theirs with.)

Evaluation

Keeping some sort of record of each student's responses
that indicate an awareness of the concept along with the
product he makes should combine for an easily assessed
evaluation of how well the objective has been achieved.

Other things to consider

- Vocabulary: monotony, shape, variety, organize, interesting, environment.
- Art materials needed: painting media and paper, materials for gluing and cutting.
- Films:
  "Discovering Composition in Art"
  "Expressionism"
  "Cubism"
  "Non-Objective Art" (all Bailey Film Associates)
- Prints:
  Figure Five in Gold by Demuth
  Apples and Oranges by Cezanne
  I and the Village by Chagall
  The Bullfight by Goya
  Head of a Man by Klee
  Mural by Pollock
  Nude Descending #2 by Duchamp
  Zebegen by Vasarely
  Marilyn Monroe by Warhol
- Matisse was a master of spatial arrangement. Your library may have the July/August 1975 issue of "Art in America" that shows much of Matisse's work.
- People who might have need for the concept: painters, illustrators, commercial artists, sculptors, printmakers, fabric designers, architects, city planners, landscape architects, interior designers.

LEVEL 4

ACTIVITY 121

Concept taught by this activity: Artists get ideas from sources such as nature, other people, imagination, experimentation, and events.

Objective: The student demonstrates an awareness that artists get ideas from sources such as nature, other people, imagination, experimentation, and events.

A sample lesson plan for achieving the objective:

Teacher preparations
- Locate appropriate prints and sculpture reproductions for display.
- Plan appropriate field trips for collecting things from nature.
- Collect art materials and equipment needed for activities.
  Teaching suggestions (How to get an idea)
- Imagination games:
  - *Put the Melon on the Ceiling* (developing inner imagery): "What color is a watermelon?" "How big is a melon?" "Using your imagination, put a watermelon in this room — in that corner, right over there. Can you *see* it?" "Does it have stripes?" "Make your melon *not* have stripes — just a dark green one." "Can you *see* it?" "Make it be pink." "Let dark pink stripes be on it." "Can you *see* your pink striped watermelon in the corner?" "Make it green-striped now." "Make it pink-striped again." "Now make the melon float up to the ceiling like a balloon." "Make it stick to the ceiling." "Can you see a pink striped watermelon up there?" "When I say, *"now,"* let it fall down to the floor and break into pieces. Now can you see the broken melon?" "Make the inside of the pink melon green colored, with white seeds." "Make it reverse now, with green *outside* and pink *inside*." "Make it go back together so that it isn't broken." "Tell the

green melon goodbye. Have it disappear. No melon is in the corner now." (Idea from "Put Your Mother on the Ceiling" by Richard De Mille [Children's imagination games] Viking-Compass Books)
  - *Fortunately-Unfortunately*. Read story "Fortunately-Unfortunately" by Remy Charlip (published by Parents Magazine Press, N.Y. 1964 Library Congress catalog card number: 64-103-64).

    Begin a sentence of an imaginary story. Each student must pick up where the other leaves off and build the story from there. Here is an example: "Once there was a shiny new penny who was given as change to a little boy named Benny. Unfortunately, as he ran to the store where there was a gum ball machine, the penny dropped out of his pocket. . . ." The first student then says, "Fortunately the penny started to roll down the hill toward the store." The next student might say, "But *un*fortunately he rolled right into a sewer grate" . . . and so on.

    Discuss how imagination can make strange and fun things happen and that the unique, surprising parts of the story were most *imaginative*.
- Ideas. Artists get ideas from many sources. "What are five things you would like to draw?" "Why did you choose those five things?" (You had seen one, you own one, you like them, they're interesting.)

    "How could you use this roll of tape if you were an artist?" (To draw from as a model for a cylinder, to tape onto the paper to keep paint off that spot, to hang things or attach things.)

Artists often turn to nature for ideas — watching animals, people, rocks, the ocean, trees, the sky, water, insects, shells, and so on. In *The Smokers,* Brouwer had an idea from watching people. In *Cliff of Etretat* by Courbet we see sky, rocks, building, boats, and water. In *Apples and Oranges,* Cezanne used fruit for inspiration. The *Figure Five in Gold* by Demuth shows how numbers, shapes, and color can be an idea. In Pollock's *Mural,* he had an idea of painting without touching the canvas, just by dripping paint.
- Discuss the art prints in terms of where the artist might have obtained the idea for the painting.

Suggested art activities
- Collect things in nature (seeds, pods, flowers, toads, bugs, lizards). Observe interesting combinations of texture, color, line, and patterns. Suggest a design or picture that these things bring to mind.
- Think of an experience or a special event that happened to you or your family. Draw, paint, or use clay to express what you felt, saw, or heard.
- Examine an animal or a plant closely. Try to draw it from memory.

Alternative art activities
- Make a mural or chart showing different kinds of artists and their skills.
- Make a collection of fabrics with patterns. Guess or suggest from where the designer might have obtained his ideas for the design.
- "Design a line border that could be used to put around a certain mural, painting, or drawing." "Where did you get the idea for it?"
- "Play the role of an artist." "What do you do well that you could share with others to make their lives more interesting, more pleasant, or easier?" "How would an artist do it?"
- Briefly sketch ideas the students can develop from other people or events, or can arrive at through imagination and experimentation. Keep the emphasis on motivation and not on what they draw or paint or how they do it.
- Create an original design for a book cover by using a line or a pattern observed from nature. All activities and options should be open-ended for individual expression of ideas and for providing opportunities for numerous choices of paper and media.

Evaluation

The student's oral responses that indicate some success in analyzing the source for artists' ideas as well as the need for hard work, experience, and perceptual sensitivity to human needs will determine how well the objective has been achieved.

Other things to consider

- Vocabulary: industrial artist (dishes, furniture, trains, irons), commercial artist (displays, posters, shops, buildings), fabrics, wood, metal, plastic designers, ceramics, glass, photography, printing, painting, sculpture, architecture, city planner, musician, poet, nature, imagination, experimentation, aesthetic, fanciful, fantastic, visionary, and critique.
- Art materials needed: varied size and textured papers, paint, crayons, charcoal, fabrics, clay, rulers, pencils.
- Resource people: sculptor, architect, city planner, landscape architect, potter, art teacher, art critic or art historian, curator.
- Books:
  Your Creative Power by Alex Osborne
  Put Your Mother on the Ceiling by Richard DeMille
  Fortunately — Unfortunately by Remy Charlip
- Audiovisual materials needed: pictures of *Chicago Prairie Houses* by Frank Lloyd Wright, rose stained glass windows in churches and animal or plant pictures.
  Films:
  "Animals in Motion"
  "Artists at Work"
- Prints:
  - *From Nature*
    Cliff of Etretat After Storm* by Courbet
    Rocky Mountains by Bierstadt
    The Snow Storm by Turner
    Lion Attacking a Horse by Stubbs
    Apples & Oranges* by Cezanne
    Figure Five in Gold* by Demuth
    Ville d'Avray* by Corot
  - *From Other People*
    Fur Traders Descending the Missouri* by Bingham
    The Smokers by Brouwer
    Bacchus* by Caravaggio
    Sinbad the Sailor* by Klee
  - *From Imagination*
    Senecio* by Klee
    The Virgin Forest* by Rousseau
    Composition 1963* by Miro
  - *From Experimentation*
    Mural* by Pollock
    Nude Descending a Staircase #2* by Duchamp
    La Grande Jatte* by Seurat
    Rebus* by Rauschenberg
  - *From Events*
    Dempsey and Firpo* by Bellows
    The Raft of the Medusa by Gericault
    The Third of May by Goya
    The Small Crucifixion* by Gruenwald
- People who might have need for the concept: art historian, museum director, curator, art critic, docent, teacher.

*Prints suggested as part of the total program.

LEVEL 4   ACTIVITY 122

Concept taught by this activity: Elements such as color, texture, line, shape, and form can be used symbolically by artists to express moods, feelings, and ideas. Forms, therefore, can have symbolic meanings.

Objective: The student demonstrates that the symbols of artists can be perceived.

A sample lesson plan for achieving the objective:

Teacher preparations
■ Become familiar with background information.
■ Display illustrations, prints, and examples.
■ Collect magazines and other materials for selected activities.

Teaching suggestions
■ Identify symbols in the classroom or school. Ask the children, "How are they used?" "Do they mean the same thing to everyone?" "Do their meanings change?" (flag and its parts, crosswalks, signs, and other symbols)
■ Discuss how writing started as picture symbols. (Egyptians, Indians, and Orientals)
■ Discuss the universal meaning of symbols like those at the left.
■ Discuss the symbolism of native dances and ceremonies, and of Indian sand paintings. (Others for discussion could be Zodiac symbols, seals, coats of arms, pictographs.)
■ Lead the class in a discussion of lines and shapes. Have various students draw on the board lines and shapes reflecting different emotions. (anger, fear, happiness, sadness, for example)

Questions: "How are lines used in a room?" (Low horizontal lines in furniture create repose. High stately lines of windows add dignity.)

"Would you draw a beach scene or picnic with tall stately lines?" "What kind of a picture would you draw with tall stately lines?"

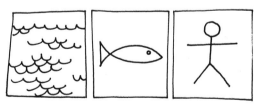

■ Discuss the symbolism of colors. "Which colors make you feel warm?" "Cool?" "Happy?" "Sad?" "Why would you want to wear gay colors sometimes and subdued colors other times?" "What colors are predominant in your home?" "What colors would you change in your home?" "Why?" "What colors would you use to paint a jungle scene?" "Why?" "A desert scene?" "Why?" "An Alaskan scene?" "Why?" "Would you like a Halloween picture in a dainty pink or blue?" "Why not?"
■ Early Christian artists often filled their paintings with symbols. Discuss those used in *The Virgin with Saint Ines and Saint Tecla* by El Greco, *The Small Crucifixion* by Grunewald, and *Flemish Proverbs* by Brueghel. "What do

different animals or plants symbolize?'' (bear, bull, eagle, lion, dove, pine tree, ant, sheep, ''lamb of God,'' snake, dragon, beehive, bee, and other common symbols) ''How would artists use these symbols?'' ''Could you?''
- ■ Discuss personal symbols and trademarks that some artists or businesses use over and over.
- ■ Discuss these related concepts: In math, numbers can be compared through the use of symbols. Music, literature and communications all make use of symbols.

Suggested art activity
Select several symbols used by artists and combine them in a picture or design of your own.

Alternative art activities
- ■ Make a class scrapbook of symbols commonly used in our society and symbols used by artists.
- ■ Make a bulletin board or mural. Investigate the creation of trademarks and the use of symbolism by artists.
- ■ Play a record such as ''Peter and the Wolf'' in segments, stopping where a particular mood is pronounced. In color and line drawings, have children depict their emotions and feelings at this segment of the record. (Nonrepresentational drawings are more emotive.)
- ■ Have the children draw a picture of buildings or trees or other forms that suggest dignity in their placing (straight up and down). Change the drawing so that the buildings or trees are tilted toward the middle or are at various angles. Note the change in feeling.
- ■ Have the children draw two designs using two different color schemes — a warm one, a cool one, an aggressive one, or a retiring one. Discuss in terms of mood or feelings.
- ■ Create forms that seem frivolous and gay, and others that seem solemn or dignified. Try to discover why this is so.

Evaluation

When the student is able to identify ways in which elements of art have been given symbolic meanings by the artist then the objective has been achieved.

Other things to consider

- ■ Vocabulary: symbols, brand, trademark, zodiac, hieroglyphics, Egyptian, Oriental, mood, feeling, nonrepresentational, expression.
- ■ Art materials needed: painting materials, scissors, paste or glue, and a variety of papers.
- ■ Resource person: someone representing a different culture — one which has symbols we know little of.
- ■ Audiovisual materials needed: books on heraldry, encyclopedia for symbolism, Scout books, films on Indian sand painting.
- ■ Prints:
  The Virgin with Saint Ines and Saint Tecla by El Greco
  The Small Crucifixion by Grunewald
  Leisure by Leger
  Guernica by Picasso
  Rockets and Blue Lights by Turner
  Room at Arles by Van Gogh
  The Crucifixion by Dali
  View of Toledo by El Greco
  Still Music by Shahn
  Sinbad the Sailor by Klee
  Three Flags by Johns
  Gypsy with Baby by Modigliani
  Combination Concrete by Davis
  Other good prints available from other sources include:
  Sunny Midi: Arles by Van Gogh
  Fishing in Spring by Van Gogh
  The Madonna with Holy Child and Maidens by Master of the Lucy Legend

The Marriage of Giovanni Arnolfini and Geovanna Cenami by Van Eyck
Adoration of the Shepherds by Van Der Goes
The Annunciation with Donors and Saint Joseph by Campin
The Van Eyck Alter Piece by Hubert and Jan Van Eyck
- ■ Books:
  Memorial — Symbolism, Epitaphs and Design Types, American Monument Association, Inc.
- ■ *Picasso's Guernica — The Genesis of a Painting* by Rudolf Arnheim, University of California Press, Berkeley and Los Angeles, 1962.
  Signs and Symbols in Christian Art by George Ferguson, Oxford University Press, New York.
  Signs of Life — A Pictorial Dictionary of Symbols by H. M. Raphaelian.
  Symbolic Mythology by John M. Woolsey, New York, 1917.
  The Symbolic Language of Vincent Van Gogh by H. R. Graetz, McGraw-Hill Book Co., Inc., New York.
- ■ Films:
  ''Color Associations,'' Associated Film Associates.
  ''Characteristics of Curved, Vertical, Diagonal, and Horizontal Lines,'' Bailey Film Associates.
- ■ People who might have need for the concept: painter, illustrator, commercial artist, art critic, art historian, teacher, docent.

LEVEL 4

ACTIVITY 123

Concept taught by this activity: Distortion in art is a form of abstraction. Artists distort or stylize things for various reasons.

Objective: The student demonstrates an awareness of ways in which he can better express himself by distorting or stylizing his subject.

A sample lesson plan for achieving the objective:

Teacher preparations
- Collect examples of concept and display them.
- Set up materials for activity selected.
- Review terminology and the suggested procedures.
- The discussion and teaching of the concept is done from the view that stylized figures are those which are slightly distorted or abstracted, for example, cartoon figures and illustrations in many popular children's books. The term *distortion* has a broader connotation which may range from the stylized figure to the highly abstract or expressionistic figure. It would not include such things as "pure abstraction," "hard edge," "nonobjective art," "minimal art," and "abstract expressionisms."

Teaching suggestions
- Relate drama or acting to the idea of distortion. Drama is another way to express feelings, moods, attitudes, or concepts which are to be "projected."
- Both teacher and students collect illustrations of examples of distortion in art: caricatures, cartoons, book illustrations. (Dr. Seuss and Brian Wildsmith, for example.)
- Have a cartoonist demonstrate and explain the reasons for his distortions. "How are cartoon figures different from 'real' people?"
- Discuss distortions in illustrations found in many books. "Why do the artists distort there?"
- Look at paintings by Michelangelo, Picasso, El Greco, fashion illustrators, Chagall, and Feininger. "How have they used distortions?" (Michelangelo and El Greco made figures longer, taller than reality. Picasso showed front and profile at same time and distorted figures for the sake of design.) Which elements are not true to life? Why do you suppose they're distorted in this way?
- Look at pictures and discuss ways in which the children's feelings would change if there was no distortion. (Consider color, texture, proportion, size.)
- "Are cartoons simplified characters?" "stylized?" "distorted?" "How about fashion drawings?" "fabric patterns?" "building decoration?"
- "How many different ways can one form be interpreted?" (Look at Picasso's drawings of bulls.)
- "Do sculptors stylize forms?" (Yes) "Are sculptors artists?" (Yes — so are many architects.)
- "Does stylizing a form give it a new feeling?" "How?" "Why?"
- "Why are some ideas better expressed through simplification?" "Or *are* they?"
- "Do you ever distort the truth in your speech?" "Your writing?" "Why?" "Do writers?" "Do speakers?" "Why?" "Do writers and speakers try to simplify?" "Why?"
- "Look at and discuss examples of stylized painting and then three-dimensional forms."
- "What has the artist simplified that makes it stylized?" "Has he been consistent in his distortion?" "Why did he simplify?"

- "How does the simplification make you feel?" "Can feelings be described better with simplifying?"

Suggested art activity
- Choose words and illustrate their meaning through drawings of people. Distort shape, size, color, and other characteristics to make the interpretation of the word as clear as possible. Use words like *angry, terrified, starving, happy-go-lucky, lonely, sore, painful, thirsty, content, hero, sleepy, shivering, hot, surprised, old, bashful, crippled, hippy, killer, teacher, principal, burglar.* Consider color, position of body, expression of hands and other parts of the body — not just facial expression.
- Make a mural or bulletin board on distortion and its uses in advertising and illustrating.

Alternative art activities
- Have the children draw two pictures. Make the first as realistic as possible and the second stylized. Use objects for models.
- Discuss differences between the terms *realistic, abstract, stylized,* and *nonobjective.* Show examples of *realistic* (photographic rerepresentation), *abstract* (the broad term for any more away from realism), *stylized* (a form that is abstract but still recognizable in terms of what it represents or distorts), *nonobjective* (abstract to the point that it does not resemble any actual form of combinations of pure elements — complete distortion).
- Take an object and see how much it can be simplified and still be recognized for what it is.
- Put abstract, stylized, and actual (natural) forms in piles and separate them into three groups correctly.

Evaluation

- If the student is able to stylize or distort some subject of his choice in a way that it communicates an idea more fully then the objective of the lesson has been realized.
- Verbal expressions may be additional indicators of how the students' awareness has been affected.

Other things to consider

- Vocabulary: realistic, abstract, stylized, nonobjective, distortion, distort, simplification, exaggeration, interpretation, emphasis, proportion, caricature, cartoon, illustration, natural.
- Art materials needed: drawing and painting materials for selected activities, paper, scissors, and glue.
- Audiovisual materials needed: children's books such as those by Dr. Seuss, Brian Wildsmith, and Maurice Sendak; fashion illustrations; cartoon strips; caricatures; animated cartoons; political cartoons.
- Prints:
  Guernica by Picasso
  Les Miserables by Picasso
  The Rhine Maidens by Ryder
  Sinbad the Sailor by Klee
  The Crucifixion by Dali
  The Small Crucifixion by Grunewald
  Autumn by Koryusai
  The Delphic Sibyl by Michelangelo
  City Hall in Rega by Feininger
  Le Jour by Braque
  I and the Village by Chagall
  The Old King by Rouault
  Poster — Moulin Rouge by T. Lautrec
- People who might have need for the concept: art critic, art historian, teacher, commercial artist.

LEVEL 4

ACTIVITY 124

Concept taught by this activity: Distortion occurs when forms appear warped, softened, or otherwise altered, for example, reflections on water, rubbery forms, and melting or deflating objects.

Objective: The student demonstrates a broad awareness of what the word *distortion* infers and sees application in such things as reflections, rubbery forms, and melting or deflating objects.

A sample lesson plan for achieving the objective:

Teacher preparations
Have examples of distortion readily available, both actual and in print or photograph forms. Use them in the discussions which follow.

Teacher suggestions
■ Review what the word *distortion* means. It might be helpful for students to discuss the relationship between distortion in art, distortion in sound (music or poetry), vision, touch ("Can you be fooled trying to guess what things are just by the sense of touch?"), and taste. The terms *stylize, abstract,* and *symbolic* are related in meaning and might be discussed along with distortion.
Conclude your discussion with a definition of distortion which is broad enough to include anything that is altered or appears twisted out of its natural, normal, or original shape. "How do the elements or things in nature distort what we see, for example, water, rain, tornados, hurricanes, fog, mist, snow storms?" "How does size contribute to the feeling of distortion in pictures or sculpture?"
■ Some contemporary artists have been intrigued with the idea of creating replicas of objects with unrelated materials, for example, hamburgers and pastries made from inflatable substances or from painted clay. Ask how and when a balloon appears distorted. How about wax when it melts, or plaster when it hardens? What happens to a glass bottle in a kiln? (Melted and stretched pop bottles are a good visual aid here.)

Suggested art activity
Have students create pictures, designs, or sculpture that are either illustrations of distortions they have discovered or are made of materials which are very unlike the thing they represent, for example, a coke bottle made of melted wax, or a man made of balloons tied together.

Alternative art activities
■ Have students do a series of photographs on distortion.
■ Have students research information about artists such as Marcel Duchamp, Clae, S. Oldenburg, Robert Watts, and Jasper Johns (pop art and dada art). Show how they used the concept in the work they created.
■ Have students trace or draw interesting objects (cans, dogs, people) and then stretch, inflate, squash, or break them up into distortions.

Evaluation

When the student evidences a heightened awareness of what distortion means and identifies a variety of examples in his environment and in the working of artists, then the objective of the lesson has been achieved.

Other things to consider

- Vocabulary: distort, distorted, abstract, stylize, symbolize, alter, proportions.
- Art materials needed: drawing and painting materials as selected by the student plus whatever three-dimensional materials some students may wish to work with, such as wax or rubber.
- Prints:
  Maas at Dordrecht by Cuyp
  Ville D'Avray by Corot
  Nude Descending #2 by Duchamp
  Turning the Stake by Eakins
  Virgin with St. Ines and Tecla by El Greco
  Bar, Folies Bergere by Manet
  The Return by Magritte
  Zebegen by Vasarely
  Cheyt M by Vasarely
- Books and Films: Films and books on modern or pop art.
- People who might have need for the concept: painter, sculptor, cartoonist, printmaker, illustrator.

MATURITY LEVEL 5

Developmental stages

In this packet of lesson plans the teacher can provide the student with twenty-five art experiences that develop his awareness of how to:

- Recognize relationships between stylized and naturalistic shapes or forms.
- Create the illusion of common textures such as marble, wood, and sand.
- Weave baskets and create simple wire sculpture.
- Use water color washes.
- Measure proportions or ratios with the thumb or a pencil.
- Recognize the developmental potential for art skills that comes from a study of plant and animal families.
- Recognize the relationships of materials and function to the shape or appearance of forms.
- Strengthen structures or designs with triangular shapes.
- Utilize the embossed method of printmaking.
- Recognize the positive/negative aspects of art forms.
- Recognize the influence that advertising design and its related fields play in his life.
- Recognize the relationship of a contour to one's ability to identify a given shape.
- Recognize the relationship of the human eye to a camera lens.
- Create photograms.
- Make a pin hole camera and use it.
- Balance space both formally and informally.
- Use symmetry in creating balance.
- Make an object or figure appear in suspension.
- Identify five basic reasons for the creating of art.
- Categorize all art forms.
- Make a press mold.
- Make mosaics with grout as a filler.
- Create and pour molds.
- Recognize ways in which artists can utilize both accidental and intentional processes in the creating of art.
- Create paper sculpture.

An explanation of level 5

This program is *not* designed for potential art students only; art skills are treated simply as a by-product of instruction.

Up through level 4, the drawings of the student are relatively accurate meters of his perceptual level. But as the learner develops the ability to portray his experience in greater detail, it becomes increasingly difficult for the teacher to evaluate the student's work by measuring his perceptions. By the time he has reached this level, the student is receiving inputs that move him into both two and three dimensional areas of art and into forms of abstraction. This complexity in his perceptual level makes analysis rather impractical.

At stages above level 4, currently beyond the experience of most students and adults in our society, all the teacher needs to do is note the number of the activity the student has completed and then pass that information on to the next teacher. Those who are sufficiently interested in art to develop skills in drawing or to specialize in some specific discipline would move beyond this "core" program and become art specialists at higher levels.

Art projects that can be used as devices for teaching a specific concept

Drawing (pencils, crayons, pens, sticks, markers, brushes, etc.)
Lessons: *125, *126, *129, *130, 134, *140, 141, *142, *143, *148

Perspective
Lesson: 142

Murals and Friezes
Lessons: 125, 126, 140, 141, *143

Crayon Resist
Lesson: 148

Collage
Lessons: 134, 140, 148

Wire Sculpture
Lessons: *127, 131, 132, 134, *140, 143, 144

Sculpture with Clay (oil or water base clay, salt and flour clay)
Lessons: 129, 131, 132, 140, 141, 143, 144, *145, 147

Woodcraft
Lessons: *131, 132, 140, 141, *143, 144

Casting and Pouring Commercial Molds (candles, ceramics, etc.)
Lessons: *131, *143, *147

Dry Flower Arranging
Lessons: 134, *140, *141, *143

Stencil Designs
Lessons: *134, 140, 141, 143

Copper and Foil Tooling
Lessons: 131, 140, 141, *143

Batik
Lessons: 131, *134, 140, 148

Knitting and Crocheting
Lessons: 131, 140, 141

Cartooning and/or Caricature
Lessons: *125, *126, 129, 130, 136, 140, 141, 142, 143

Posters
Lessons: 125, 126, *135, 140, 141, 143

Dioramas
Lessons: 125, 126, 129, 130, *140, 141, *143

Water Color and Tempera
Lessons: *128, 134, 140, 142, *143, *148

Toothpick or Straw Sculpture
Lessons: *131, *132, *134, *140, 141, 143, 144

Whittling and Carving
Lessons: 131, 132, 140, 141, 143, 144

Soap, Wax, and Clay Carving
Lessons: *131, 132, 140, 141, 143, 144

Leathercraft
Lessons: 131, 140, 141, *143

Terrariums
Lessons: 131, 140, 141, *143

Photography
Lessons: 134, *137, *138, *139, 140, 141, 143, 144, 148

Gadget and Roll Prints
Lessons: *134, 140, 141, 143, 144, 148

Melted Crayon Painting (encaustic)
Lessons: 131, 140, 148

Tie-Dye
Lessons: 131, *134, 140, 148

Basket Weaving
Lessons: *127, 131, 141, 143, 144

Weaving (paper, string, and fabric)
Lesson: *131, 134, 140, 141, 143, 144

Snowflakes
Lessons: *134, 140

Box Sculpture
Lessons: 131, 132, 134, 140, 149

Construction Paper Designs (cut and paste heart people
for valentines and other paper constructions)
Lessons: 134, 140

Papier Mâché
Lessons: 131, 140, 143, *145

Mosaics
Lessons: 134, 140, 141, 143, *146

Applique (sew or glue)
Lessons: 131, 134, 140, 141, 143, 144

Puppets (sack, sock, styrofoam)
Lessons: *140, 143

Christmas Ornaments
Lessons: 140, 143

Paper Sculpture (fold, score, roll)
Lessons: *131, 132, 134, 140, 141, 143, *149

Mobiles and Stabiles
Lessons: 131, 132, *134, 140, 141, 143, 144

Snow Sculpture
Lessons: *131, *140, 143

---

*Key projects for the concept.

LEVEL 5 ACTIVITY 125

Concept taught by this activity: Stylized forms can have a representational or naturalistic appearance, for example, Michelangelo's *Pieta* or El Greco's figures.

Objective: The student demonstrates an awareness that a form which the artist has rendered in a stylized manner can have a representational or naturalistic appearance because he has become used to that particular style.

A sample lesson plan for achieving the objective:

Teacher preparations
- Obtain photographs and corresponding subjects in drawings and paintings.
- Assemble a group of toys and art objects which have counterparts in actual life.
- Obtain two movies—one with real people and a similar film with cartoon characters or a series of pictures which serve the same purpose.

Teaching suggestions
- Bring actual photographs or photographs from magazines of people, animals, and objects which are somehow stylized. Discuss them. Bring drawings and paintings which will correspond with the photographs and compare them. For example, discuss the similarities between a photograph of a lion and a drawing of one.
- Show toys and art objects. Discuss how they are like the actual thing and how they are unlike it. For example, go outside and look at an actual car. Compare it to a toy car.
- If possible, obtain a movie which utilizes real people. Then show another movie of the same story, but in cartoon form. Prior to looking at these kinds of things prepare the student by asking the following questions: "What does it mean when we say something is natural?" "What does the word *realistic* mean?" "Can you give an example of something which is not realistic?" "Name something which might not look like anything you are familiar with at all." "Are small children fooled by puppets?" "Do they think they're real?" "Think of something which isn't exactly like the real thing but that you can recognize right away." "What makes this thing *like* the real thing?" "What makes this thing *unlike* the real thing?"
- Carefully examine each of the following prints and discuss ways in which the artist has stylized aspects of his picture. *The Artist's Bedroom at Arles* by Van Gogh (distorted perspective, childlike drawing), *The Delphic Sibyl* by Michelangelo (masculine characteristics, small head), *The Virgin with Saint Ines and Saint Tecla* by El Greco (elongated figures 10 to 12 heads tall, normal figure 7½), *The Virgin Forest* by Rousseau (childlike character of jungle), *Gypsy with Baby* by Modigliani (elongated parts, simplified facial characteristics), *Prodigal Son* by Rembrandt (distortion of figure to give a look of protection and grief), *Pieta* by Michelangelo (Christ smaller than Mary; Mary has a face of a 16-year-old girl), *Les Miserables* by Picasso (distortion of color and body position to create a feeling of misery and discouragement).

Suggested art activity
Draw or paint a picture in which slight distortions are used to better communicate an idea or feeling.

Additional art activities
- Analyze the distortions used in *The Small Crucifixion* by Grunewald. The student should be able to uncover at least eight to ten different examples of distortion in this print.
- Have a small group of students do a mural around the theme of stylization or
- Some students might want to put up a display in the hall built around the concept—using their own work, masters'

prints and verbal explanation so that the rest of the students in the school would also learn the concept.

Evaluation

The ability of the student to detect subtle distortions by the artist should indicate a good awareness of the concept.

Other things to consider

- Vocabulary: natural, realistic, unrealistic, stylized, representation.
- Art materials needed: photographs, drawings and paintings, toys, art objects, paper, paint, and films representing the cartoon form of distortion and realism.
- Prints:
  The Artist's Bedroom at Arles by Van Gogh
  The Delphic Sibyl by Michelangelo
  The Virgin with Saint Ines and Saint Tecla by El Greco
  Pieta by Michelangelo
  The Small Crucifixion by Grunewald
  Gypsy with Baby by Modigliani
  The Virgin Forest by Rousseau
  Les Miserables by Picasso
  The Prodigal Son by Rembrandt
- People who might have need for the concept: art critic, art historian, teacher, museum director, docent.

LEVEL 5 ACTIVITY 126

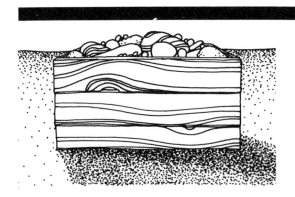

Concept taught by this activity: The student creates illusions of marble, wood, and sand textures with lines, dots, shapes, and value controls.

Objective: The student creates illusions of common textures with lines, dots, shapes, and value contrasts.

A sample lesson plan for achieving the objective:

Teacher preparations
- Collect appropriate prints along with available pictures which graphically illustrate a variety of common textures. Large colored photographs commonly used in many school libraries or media centers are an excellent resource.
- In your discussions, talking about actual textures can be an appropriate activity but remember that the objective of the lesson is for the student to create *illusions* of texture.

Teaching suggestions
- Review what the student already knows about texture and the "illusion" of texture. Review experiences with rubbings and how that led to student's first experiences in creating illusions of texture. (Activities 12, 32, 43, and 63.)
- Ask questions such as: "How many different textures can you create with just straight lines?" "How many textures can you find in the room that could be drawn using nothing but lines and dots?" "How many textures are patterns?" "Is it possible to create textures by making tiny shapes and repeating them in some sort of pattern?" "Can you find or name examples of texture that are nothing more than shapes arranged in a pattern?"
- Review the terms *value* and *value contrasts*. Relate them to pattern and illusions of texture by leading the student to recognize how some kinds of texture can't be drawn very well without value contrasts. (This is particularly true when the student has a need to be more accurate in his drawing.

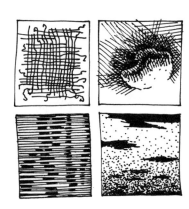

At this point such things as bark and wood, shiny surfaces, and illusions of glass require more detail, along with changes in value, to render them accurately.)
- Encourage the student to start with those things he feels will be easiest. Students should establish the line and shape parts first, then the pattern, and finally the value contrasts.
- Visual fluency in textural illusions can be developed by having each student work in one-inch squares creating as many illusions of texture as possible; for example, reward the student with the most samples and the one with the most unusual textural illusion.

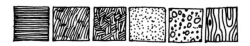

Suggested art activity
Draw or paint a picture of some familiar subject containing textures that the student hasn't dealt with before. Pencil, charcoal, ink, crayon, or paint are all appropriate media.

Alternative art activities
- Make a chart illustrating the texture (illusions) of at least ten common objects or living things. (See last teaching suggestion, above.)
- Try to paint as realistic an illusion of *grass* as possible (or sand, or rock and gravel, or fur, or other common textured object).

Evaluation

When the student creates the illusion of textures such as marble, wood, and sand then the objective has been achieved.

Other things to consider

- Vocabulary: value contrasts, illusion, illusionary, render.
- Art materials needed: any drawing or painting materials selected by the student would be appropriate for the activity.
- Prints:
  Le Jour by Braque
  Bandaged Ear by Van Gogh
  Don Manuel Osorio by Goya
  Man with Helmet by Rembrandt
  The Blue Cart by Van Gogh
  Cliff of Etretat After the Storm by Courbet
  Oath of the Horatii by David
  My Gems by Harnett
  Bar, Folies Bergere by Manet
- People who might have need for the concept: painter, illustrator, commercial artist, industrial designer, printmaker, sculptor, artists that draw and cartoon.

LEVEL 5

ACTIVITY 127

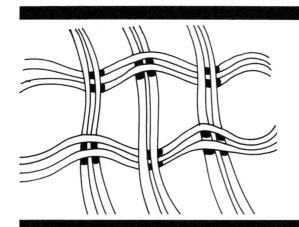

Concept taught by this activity: The processes involved in simple wire sculpture and basket weaving are appropriate for kinesthetic development at this level.

Objective: The student will create forms by bending, twisting, and shaping wire and by weaving pieces of cane or raffia.

A sample lesson plan for achieving the objective:

Teacher preparations
Note: This concept actually covers two entirely different processes, either of which would be appropriate for children at this level. Read through the two and choose whichever experience suits your students' interests and the materials you have available.
- Planning
  - Assemble materials.
  - Get pictures from magazines, art books, or brochures to show line drawings of wire mobiles, stabiles, and other sculpture.

Teaching suggestions
Show pictures of wire sculpture and ask questions such as: "What could be done to wire to make it more interesting?" "Where have you seen wire used in an artistic way?" "What decorative uses can you think of for using wire?" "Why do you think artists would use wire?" "Do you think heating the wire would make it easier to handle?" "Why?" (Too hot to handle, makes it more pliable or tempered.) "What properties of wire make it a desirable material to use?" "Undesirable?" "In what ways is wire used commercially?" (telephones, television sets, radios, lights, paper clips, spring clothes pegs, bed springs) "What other materials might you use with wire in creating a form?" (paper, papier mâché, wire screen, sequins, glass jewels, beads, sculp

metal, paper, metallic papers, pipe cleaners) "In what ways can wire, a thin flexible material, be used to suggest space?" "What importance has enclosed space when working with wire?" "In what ways can wire be used like a line to create mood?" "Describe a gesture?" "A contour?"

Suggested art activity
Create a stabile of wire using one or more of the above processes (free form).

Alternative art activities
- Create a mobile of wire using one or more of the above processes (three or four forms).
- Create a simple piece of jewelry.
- Create wire figures of people in various activities or of other animals which interest the individual student.

Evaluation

If the student is able to bend, twist, and shape wire into some recognizable form or acceptable design, then the objective for wire sculpture has been achieved.

Other things to consider

- Vocabulary: free form, pliable, mobile, stabile, contour, gesture, flux, welding, soldering.
- Materials needed: wire (aluminum, copper, or steel), various gauges, materials for base or foundation, soldering iron and flux, tools for bending, twisting, and cutting, for example, hammer and pliers.
- Audiovisual materials needed: films, books, magazines.
- Books:
  Model Making in Paper, Cardboard, and Metal by George Aspden
  Sculpture and Ideas by Michael Andrews
  The Art of Three-Dimensional Design by Louis Wolchonock
- People who might have need for the concept: wire sculptor.

Weaving cane or raffia

Teacher preparations

- Become familiar with materials and process types—round
reed comes from the core of the rattan palm, a tropical
climbing plant with thorny shoots that can grow to a length
of five hundred feet. The inner pulp of these shoots is
composed of long fibers. The heavier winding reed is
always flat on one surface and convex on the other and is
used for weaving and particularly for wrapping around
handles. Round reed is available in thicknesses from nos.
00 to 10; winding reed comes in narrow (approx. 1/8")
and wide (from 3/16" to 1/4"). Some hobby shops carry
only one size of winding reed. If you are going to make
several baskets it is cheaper to buy round reed by the
pound. Winding reed is sold in 500-feet bundles or hanks
and you will profit by buying the best quality. Prepared kits,
with all the necessary material included, are also widely
available at hobby shops.
- Basic materials: sponge—to dampen reed and take up
excess water; pan for water—to soak reed; pincers or
pliers—to hold or bend curved areas; scissors; ruler or tape
measure—to measure lengths of reed; pencil—to mark
measurements, sandpaper—to smooth rough areas when
finished and dry; pen knife; round and flat reed.
- Optional materials: rattan, raffia, cords, strings, and twines.
- Native materials: twigs, vines, grasses, pine needles, corn
husks, cattails, mosses, stems, leaves, bark.
- Papers: crepe paper, tissue paper, cellophane.
- Materials used by American Indians: white oak and river
reed.

Teaching suggestions

Procedure: While natural plant reed is exciting as material
for weaving, commercial reed is usually more easily
available and may be purchased in the form of round or flat
strands of various diameters and widths. Commercial reed
often comes in skeins and is usually dry and brittle, but
soaking in water for a short time will make it pliable for
cutting and manipulating. When used for handles or spokes,
reed can be cut to specific lengths before soaking. To
prepare for soaking, roll the reed into a loose coil and
fasten its end by twisting. Since reed is most pliable while
damp, wrap it in soft material such as terry cloth to keep it
moist until needed.

It will be helpful to know some basketry techniques when
experimenting with reed weaving. First of all a tight, firm
base is essential to the entire form. The reeds of the base,
called spokes, lie flat. Some spokes are inserted through
slits of other spokes and all radiate from the center. They
may be cut to the length needed for the base size, or long
enough for weaving the entire form.

- Round base. Using reed made pliable by soaking, select
four spokes and cut a slit lengthwise in the middle of
each. (a) Make these slits large enough so that four
additional spokes may be pushed through them. Lay the
four spokes closely side by side. Place the four additional
spokes, also close together, perpendicular to the first four
and push them through the slits in the first four to form a
symmetrical cross. (b) The weaving proceeds around the
center of this four-armed cross. To begin the weaving,
use a thinner reed than that used for spokes and bend it
at its midpoint to form a loop around one of the four
arms of the cross. (c) Fit the reed close to the center of
the cross and keep its two loose ends of equal length.
Cross these ends and weave them around the second
arm of the crosses. (d) Cross the ends again and weave
them around the third arm. Repeat with the fourth arm
and continue to weave the two reed ends around the
center of the cross. This is known as the *pairing*
technique. (e) Next, separate the spokes of the cross,

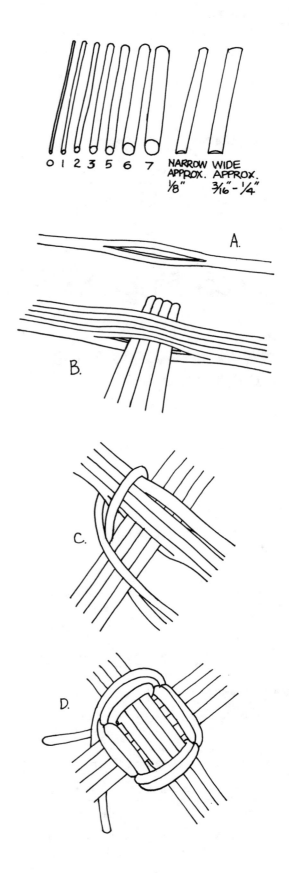

0 1 2 3 5 6 7   NARROW   WIDE
               APPROX.   APPROX.
               1/8"   3/16" - 1/4"

A.

B.

C.

D.

making them pairs of adjacent reeds. Weave reed-ends over and under these pairs often enough to hold the spokes firmly in place (f) Once more, separate the cross arms, this time making single spokes. Weave in and around each individual spoke until the base attains the desired circular shape and size. The base may be strengthened by using larger reed around the edge. A variation of the simple round base is made by weaving a finish around the edge of the base, continuing to use the same pairing weave. First, decide on the diameter of the base; cut the base spokes at least six inches longer than the diameter. Continue weaving the base previously described, using the pairing weave for the largest part of the base. When the desired size of base is reached, weave the extra length of the spokes into one another to form a finished edge.

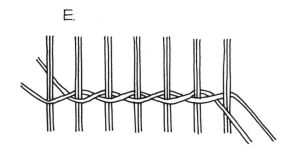

E.

- Oval base. The oval base is a variation of the round base. Decide upon the number of base spokes, then cut half of them to one length and the other half slightly shorter. Cut slits in the centers of the shorter group of spokes. Push the long spokes through these center slits. Space the short spokes some distance apart. Begin weaving with the pairing techniques as explained previously. Continue to twist the thin reed around all the side, or shorter spokes, then again around the whole group of spokes, and so on for at least two cycles.
- Wooden base. A wooden base can be of any shape or size. Commercial bases usually come with holes drilled for the reed. However, a wood base may be cut and holes drilled to the size needed for the reeds. Decide upon the length of reed necessary for constructing the sides. When the reed stands in a vertical position, it is called a stake. The basic stakes are those that fit into the holes and stand perpendicular to the base. Around these, the shape is woven.

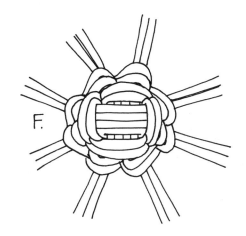

F.

To vary the design and give the ends that stick through the bottom a finished appearance, extend the stakes a few inches on the underside. Bend one stake end down, weaving in and out around the following three stakes. Continue this process until all stake-ends are woven in front and back of one another on the underside. Clip off the excess reed.

For variety, extend the basic stakes through the wood bottom and drive wooden beads onto the reed. This not only holds the reed securely, but also produces an interesting base. If the beads are loose, because their holes are larger than the reeds, cut additional pieces of reed and stuff into each bead hole. This will hold the bead in place.

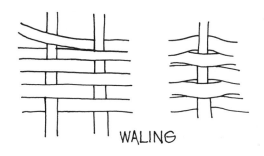

WALING

- Sides. The sides of the basket are an integral part of the base and rise from it. There are many ways of weaving the sides. After becoming familiar with one method, experiment with others. Begin bending the ends of the base reeds slightly upward. If the original base spokes are too stiff for easy bending, cut them off close to the woven base and insert more pliable reed between the original base spokes. Another method is to insert vertical stakes through the spaces in the woven edging. These verticals provide a structure through which the form is woven. It is important to remember that unless the spokes are damp, they will not bend, and may break,
- The next step involves a fairly easy type of weaving which is called waling. Waling is used to strengthen the form as the side takes shape. To do waling weave, use three strands of reed. Place two strands on opposite sides of a vertical stake; cross them and then pass them around the next stake, etc. The third strand is then twined into the previous weave by weaving it over the top of the two crossed strands, then in front of the next two stakes and under the next cross.
- Side variations. To achieve interest in spacing and accenting designs, use leather strips, wooden balls,

bamboo bits, or beads as decorations. Combine round and flat reed. Vary the size of the round reed and the width of the flat reed. Insert extra stakes. Place round reed next to flat reed and alternate.

- Edges. Whatever form is created, the final edge gives it a finished appearance. Experiment to develop interesting and unusual edges.

■ Trimming round and winding reeds should be done so that the ends rest against a stake on the wrong side of the work and are long enough so that they will not slip through to the front.

Small plastic clothespins are practical for fastening the corners while setting-up the base. Because of their smaller size they are preferable to ordinary wood clothespins, and since these come in bright colors you may use them in a particular color as markers for counting.

Winding reed for handles should be rolled into a coil and fastened with a few clothespins. It is then much easier to handle, curling readily, when you are winding with it.

If it is necessary to join the winding reed while winding a handle, it can be done by letting it lie doubled for about 5/16″ on the back. Fasten the joint with a clothespin, and later, glue it into place.

To join winding reed while weaving, double it over two stakes to hold it tightly pressed at two points.

To join with round reed, when your round reed weaver runs out before the project is finished, pick up a new piece and begin weaving with it, letting the new one cross in front of the old one behind a stake or pair of stakes at the back of the work, leaving the remaining ends resting against a stake. When the work is finished you can then trim off the extra ends.

Suggested art activity
Make a basket by weaving or raffia.

Alternative art activities
- Make baskets or purses out of rattan, cord, string, or twine.
- Weave cellophane or tissue paper.

Evaluation

When the student is able to weave a basket with any of the suggested material the objective has been achieved.

Other things to consider

- Vocabulary: reed, cane, raffia, winding reed, round reed, basketry, weaving, warp, weft, vertical stakes, winding reed stakes, joining, pairing, wood-based basket.
- Art materials needed: (See list within activity.)
- Books:
  Weaving with Cane and Reed by Kroncke, A Reinhold Publication, 1968.
  Weaving without a Loom by Rainey, A Davis Publication, 1971, (6th printing).
- People who might have need for the concept: (basket weaving) sculptor, craft designer.

LEVEL 5

ACTIVITY 128

Concept taught by this activity: The student uses a variety of washes in painting with water base media.

Objective: The student can do a wash that is even over the whole area that is painted as well as a wash that is graded from dark to light in an even gradual way.

A sample lesson plan for achieving the objective:

Teacher preparations
- A collection of watercolor paintings or prints of watercolors could be made showing examples of the two kinds of washes. A display could be made with the pictures gathered.
- One of the things that should be considered in this activity is to help the students be able to tell when it is appropriate to use the different types of washes. Students should be able to identify the different washes as they were used in the paintings displayed,
- An eight-color watercolor set would be adequate for this activity. The brush that comes in the set would be the only brush needed.
- About two sheets of 50-pound white drawing paper should be provided for each student. If 50-pound paper is not available, then 40-pound paper will do. Manila paper might be used as a last resort.
- A container for water (such as a plastic cottage cheese container) should be available for each student. The water should be tepid or cold because hot water tends to dissolve the glue in the ferrule of the brush.

Teaching suggestions
- The student should be instructed to treat the brush with

care. A brush should not be left standing in the water because this also tends to dissolve the glue in the ferrule and causes the brush to lose its shape. The brush should always be washed off when not in use.
- Have the student place a drop or two of water in each of the colors in the watercolor set to soften them.
- Have students tear their paper into four pieces each. This activity is only for practice of technique, not for doing a painting.
- It is helpful for the students to now realize that the watercolors can be controlled by the wetness of the paper. If the paper has a wash of clear water placed on it, the paint will only run where the paper is wet. This property can be used to control the watercolors while doing a painting.
- Have the students take one of their small pieces of paper and wash about half of it with clear water. The wash is done by laying the paper flat on the desk and then loading the brush with water. Apply the water on the paper by using the side of the brush, rather than the point, so that a broad stroke is applied. Move the brush back and forth until the paper is covered with a smooth, even application of water.
- The brush is now dipped into one of the colors and the paint is applied the same way the water was.
- The objective in this instance is to have one even coat of color. By picking the paper up and tilting it, the student will get the color to run more evenly.
- When the paper is tilted, a bead of water and color might form at the bottom of the wet area. If the student washes the brush out and squeezes the bristles of the brush between the index finger and the thumb until the brush is dry, the brush can be used much like a blotter to pick up the excess water.
- By following the same steps a gradated wash can be done. With the gradated wash, though, the paint is applied at the top of the area to be painted and the brush is moved back and forth across the paper, left to right, top to bottom, as the paper is tilted, causing the paint to go from dark to light in an even smooth fashion as it runs down the paper.
- Now, by leaving some dry patches (in the shape of clouds), the student should be able to paint an area that looks very much like a cloudy sky. Practice is important to be able to

get the control that would be needed to do a painting.

- Because watercolor is a transparent media, it is possible to cover a light color with a dark color, but a light color will not cover a darker color. Therefore, it is most helpful to the student in doing a watercolor painting to work from the light colored areas to the dark, for example, put light colors on first, then allow them to dry. If light colors are applied first, a great deal of correcting can take place.

- Cleaning and pointing the brush when the student has finished painting is a very important habit to develop. To clean the brush, the student should use tepid or cold water, rinse the color out of the brush, and with a little soap on the fingers, wash all the color out of the brush. The brush should then be pinched dry with the fingers, pointed to a fine even point, and allowed to dry without the bristles of the brush being bent or altered from the point position.

Additional suggestions for helping the student

- Remember that no value can be whiter than the paper. Because watercolor is transparent (you can see through it), the paper itself is the white part of your picture.

- When the student attempts to show detail, it is helpful to know of the dry brush technique: putting rather thick paint on dry paper. The dry brush technique is helpful in adding detail and textures in watercolor. For instance, the bristles of the brush can be spread out by squeezing them between the thumb and finger so that grasslike effects can be painted. By pushing or making a scrubbing motion, foliage and other texture effects can be created.

  Have the students take one of their small sheets of paper and practice the dry brush method to see how many ways they can use their brush and how many textures they can create.

- As a general rule, it is good to remember to use brighter and darker colors in watercolor than seems necessary, because they get lighter and less bright as they dry.

- Taping or tacking the paper onto a board of some sort is very helpful to keep the paper from rolling or warping.

- Calligraphy or outlining a watercolor composition's detail in ink or dark colors can help the appearance of a watercolor if the colors or values are weak.

Suggested art activity

Paint a landscape using the wash techniques that have been taught and discussed, emphasizing washes in sky, ground, or buildings.

Alternative art activities

- Make a collection of watercolor paintings from magazines, calendars, and other sources for a display on a bulletin board. Indicate on the display where the two types of washes have been used.

- Invite a local watercolor painter to come to class and spend a few minutes demonstrating the two wash techniques. Make certain that the artist does not stay too long and does not cover more material than would be needed.

Evaluation

When the students are able to do the several types of washes that have been taught in this activity, you know you have met the objective of the lesson.

Other things to consider

- Vocabulary: transparent, opaque, wash, ferrule, bead of water.

- Art materials needed: eight-color watercolor sets, 50- or 40-pound white drawing paper, cottage cheese containers for water, sponges, cotton, and other tools.

- Prints:
  Fighting Horses by Gericault
  Hudson River Logging by Homer
  Quay Le Pouliguen by Vuillard
  Many art books contain water color paintings of Marian, Homer, Kingman, Wyeth, and Chen Chi.

- Books:
  Watercolor Technique by Brandt
  Watercolor, a Challenge by Brooks
  Master of Pencil and Watercolor by Kautzky
  Making Watercolor Behave by O'Hara
  Watercolor Made Easy by Olson

- People who might have need for the concept: painters, illustrators, commercial artists.

LEVEL 5 ACTIVITY 129

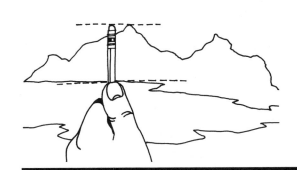

Concept taught by this activity: Proportions or ratios exist between and within natural and manmade forms. Relationships can be measured with such things as the thumb or a pencil.

Objective: The student can measure and describe the ratio between two given objects or a part to its whole.

A sample lesson plan for achieving the objective:

Teacher preparations

- Collect illustrations and display them. Select objects in the room which students can easily measure.
- Review the vocabulary associated with the activity.

Proportion: Proportion is a law of relationships or a plan of organization. It has to do with the relationships of space, length, value, height, shapes, colors, and other properties. Each relationship can vary in its beauty according to how properties relate to each other—how length relates to height, how sizes or shapes relate to each other, and so on.

Scale: Scale is a principle of proportion and has to do with the relationship of one object to another and parts to a whole. It deals primarily with *size* relationships. A lamp shade that appeared too large for the base would be out of scale. Large massive furniture in a small room would be out of scale.

Ratios: In art, ratio is the relationship of quantity, amount or *size* between two or more things.

Proportion is always of major concern to the majority of artists. Errors in proportion are most easily seen in nature or with objects with which we are most familiar. When a child draws himself much larger than his mother or father, or he draws himself with a head larger than his body and with arms which won't reach below his waist, these errors in proportion are obvious.

Teaching suggestions

- Discuss the importance of good proportion in areas such as drawing, sculpture, architecture, and interior decoration. Locate pictures of common objects which are poorly proportioned. It's easy to find illustrations of such things as poorly proportioned lamps, TV sets with tiny thin legs (which look as if they'll collapse at any minute), houses with huge dormers or tiny chimneys, divisions which cut objects into equal and thus uninteresting parts, objects with monotonous repetitions of shapes or colors, and objects containing a hodge podge of shapes and textures, none of which seem to go together. Even home decoration magazines will usually contain pictures of furnishings which are out of scale with a room.
- Once the notion of what proportion is and why it's important is established, the student can then concentrate on the real task of this lesson. That task is learning to measure proportions and determine ratios. The student should have had prior experiences with measuring proportions (activity #37, comparing the sizes of things with himself; and activity #61, measuring with yardsticks and rulers), but some review or mention of the activities might be helpful.
- The student can now learn to measure objects in the same manner artists do. Simply hold a pencil or brush at arm's length and line up the top of the object to be measured. Then place your thumb on the pencil or brush at the point where you see the base of the object.
- Note that the measurer must *always* keep his arm straight. Bending the arm changes the measurement and destroys accuracy. It is helpful to squint or close one eye when measuring. The purpose for measuring is to become more accurate in perceiving size relationships. The eye or what we know often deceives us as we look at objects and try to draw them realistically. Measuring will be very helpful in trying to determine such things as how tall Mary is compared with her father or compared to her desk, how many heads shorter a person is sitting down than when he is standing, how many heads wide are someone's shoulders, how big the handle on the pitcher is in comparison with its total height or its spout.

- Remind the student that he is measuring *size relationships* (scale or ratio) and not *actual* sizes. If Bill measures Jimmy and finds that he is 5 1/2 heads tall, he can then use that scale in drawing Jimmy, and he can do it accurately regardless of the size he decides to make Jimmy or how large a sheet of paper he uses.
- Measure objects with pencils or brushes to get ratios and then have someone measure the same objects with a yardstick or tape. Discuss why some people may not have been accurate with their measuring (bending arm, turning hand over, getting in too much of a hurry).

Suggested art activity

Do a before and after picture. Have students choose a subject that might be difficult to draw in proportion and render it first without *any* measuring and then again *with* measuring. Encourage the student to be very thorough in the measuring he does and emphasize the fact that careful measurement alone will automatically improve the accuracy of his work significantly.

Alternative art activities

- Set up additional activities which require measuring, or let the student decide on his own exercises or means for implementing the concept. A variety of experiences which don't require a lot of time would probably be more helpful to the student than one or two long term experiences which require a ''finished'' drawing.
- Look at artists' work and discuss how and why proportions were important to the artist in the completion of each work. Measure parts of the pictures and compare results with other students.

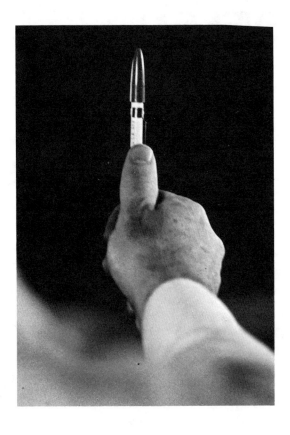

Evaluation

When the student is able to measure the scale or ratio of a variety of objects and living things, he can use the information he gathers to improve his art skills. Then his awareness of the concept is sufficiently developed.

Other things to consider

- Vocabulary: proportion, scale, ratio, measuring, measurement.
- Art materials needed: drawing paper and pencils.
- Book:
  Art in Everyday Life by Goldstein
- Prints:
  Young Hare by Durer
  Poster—Jan. 18 to Feb. 12 by Shahn
  Gypsy With Baby by Modigliani
  Delphic Sibyl by Michelangelo
  Still Life With Pipe by Chardin
  Blue Boy by Gainsborough
  Artist's Mother by Whistler
  Lacemaker by Vermeer
- People who might have need for the concept: painters, draftsmen, printmakers, interior designers, art teachers, any artist that draws, does sculpture, or arranges space.

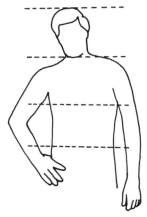

LEVEL 5

ACTIVITY 130

Concept taught by this activity: An analysis of how plant and animal families develop, each in its own unique way, assists the learner in rendering impressions of them.

Objective: To demonstrate that exercises which deeply involve the student in looking at and thinking about plants and animals enable him to render them more accurately.

A sample lesson plan for achieving the objective:

Teacher preparations

Note: This lesson is designed to help the student learn to observe more carefully—to see discriminatly and to think about things he sees. The plants and animals are merely a tool for shaping of the learner's visual perception.

■ Select a series of plants and animals which are available in either a live form, as stuffed models, or in full color pictures. Students need to examine the plants and animals quite closely and carefully.

■ Have a system which will allow all students to handle at least one of the plants or animals discussed.

■ Have visuals or display and art materials for painting and drawing activities.

Teaching suggestions

■ Have the students draw a plant or an animal the very best they can. (Have students select their subject from a list of examples you have collected for them to study and draw from later.)

■ Compare animals in all sorts of ways by asking questions but never answering them. Force the students to *find* the

answers and report their findings. Much of the discovery process will be almost immediate, but some may require outside research. Look for both similarities and differences in all of the comparisons made. The following list is intended as a resource for ideas. You may wish to use all of the ideas, part of them, or make up a list that is completely different.

■ Animals
  ● Compare gerbils, hamsters, and kangaroo rats or field mice.
  ● Compare primates with humans.
  ● Compare reptiles with amphibians.
  ● Compare amphibians with fish.
  ● Compare a variety of tropical fish with each other. The similarities may be more difficult to determine than the differences. Look at shapes, coloring, patterns, size, how they eat, what part of the aquarium they stay in, how their young are born (live or from eggs), whether or not they eat the young or fish of others, how hostile they are with other fish, and how they change as they grow.
  ● Discuss how some animals change radically in appearance as they grow to adulthood while others change very little, for example, the frog and the horse. Discuss the reasons for their changing or not changing.
  ● Compare how well some can take care of themselves at birth and how poorly others do. (Compare a pheasant chick one day old with a one-day-old bear or kangaroo.) "Which are born live or which from eggs?" "Which kinds are similar at birth like poultry but very different as adults?" (chickens, turkeys, and ducks)
  ● Compare the eggs of birds. Discuss why there are certain sizes, colors and shapes.
■ Plants
  ● Compare the shapes of trees—the coloring, change in color, color and texture of bark, kinds of leaves and seeds.
  ● Discuss the parts of plants we eat—compare roots, seeds, flowers, and leaves.
  ● Discuss the characteristics of unusual plants such as the venus fly trap.
  ● Discuss the varying needs of plants for water (cactus compared with ivy or ferns).

- Discuss the variety of color, shape, and role of aquarium plants.
- Compare plants at various stages of growth—how they change and why—from seed to maturity, for example, radishes and peas, cucumbers and watermelons, corn and bamboo, pumpkins, and gourds.
- "How do trees like the spruce, fir, and pine differ from each other?" "Or the fig, date, and palm trees?"
- Compare the trunks, limbs, and branches of plants like a mushroom, a shrub, a tree, and seaweed.

■ Assign students problems individually or in groups. Have them do their research and report to the class.
■ Discuss the following science concepts:
Animals and plants, because of their structure and/or coloring, are able to adapt to their environment. (safety, food gathering, other characteristics)

The *drawing* of something improves a student's retention of form and structure of the thing, and conversely, the perception of the form and structure enhances one's ability to draw the thing.

Suggested art activity
Do before and after pictures. Have students draw the best picture they can of a specific plant or animal. This is done at the *beginning* of this activity. Next *re-draw* the plant or animal *after* comparisons and analogies. Then discuss the difference between the two drawings.

Alternative art activities
■ Make a mural illustrating the interesting things that the class has discovered about the similarities and differences of plants and animals.
■ Make charts or friezes which describe similarities or differences noted in specific plants or animals.

Evaluation

When the student demonstrates a new awareness of what certain plants or animals are really like, then the objective has been achieved. The verbal comments of the learner and his before and after picture would be major indicators of any change in awareness.

Other things to consider

■ Vocabulary: similarity, difference, compare, characteristics, identify, classify, perceive, awareness.
■ Art materials needed: drawing or painting media and a selection of paper.
■ Pictures and models of plants and animals appropriate for the lesson.
■ People who might have need for the concept: scientists, biologists, painters, illiustrators, artists that are printmakers, designers of all types.

LEVEL 5   ACTIVITY 131

Concept taught by this activity: In man-made things, materials and function directly control the structure of a form and influence its shape or appearance.

Objective: The student demonstrates an awareness of how the function and materials that a form is made of influence its structure, shape, and appearance.

A sample lesson plan for achieving the objective:

Teacher preparations
- Plan to have plenty of pictures of home furnishings on hand by providing them or having the students bring them from home.
- Review Frank Lloyd Wright's statement about form following function and have his meaning well in mind.
- Prepare to discuss the materials used in the construction of common objects in and out of the room.

Teaching suggestions
- Discuss objects in the home and ways the function of each has influenced its shape by asking the following questions: "What is meant when we say something is functional?" "Should a chair be functional?" "What would you do to the design of a chair to keep it from being functional?" "Does the function of a clock, or a bed, or a light switch or a pair of scissors influence how it will look?" "Why?" "What are some other examples?" Discuss numerous examples allowing students an opportunity to really explore the relationship between how things look and how they are used. Explore equally the role of the materials used in various objects.
- Give each child the assignment of bringing an object to class. In class, divide the children into groups and have

each group discuss how the function of their objects relates to their shape or appearance and how the materials they are made of have influenced the appearance. Let each group choose a spokesman to report their discussion and findings to the rest of the class.
- Collect examples of home furnishings which are both well designed and poorly designed in terms of appearing functional as well as beautiful, for example, chairs which look comfortable and cheap toys which "look" good but wear out too quickly . Have the students defend their judgments before the class. Examine the standard heights of tables, chairs and countertops and discuss the effect slight changes in their size would have on us, for example, lower or higher.
- Discuss Frank Lloyd Wright's application of his thesis "Form Follows Function." Ask questions such as: "Are artists ever concerned with function in design?" "When?" "What concerns about function would an architect have?" "A potter?" "An industrial designer?" "Landscape architect?" "A city planner?"
- Ask the following questions: "Have you noticed the objects we have around our playground?" "Do all of these objects (such as the play equipment) look as though they are made of the same materials?" "Why are certain materials used for this purpose and not others?" "What are all the ways you could improve a playground swing, or slide, or tricky bar?" "Draw it with the improvements."

"Notice the pictures we have up around our classroom. They are pictures of different objects or forms. Why were certain materials selected for each of them?"
"Are all forms beautiful?" "Do they add to their surroundings?" "Why not?"

"Are all forms suited to their purpose?" "Why not?" "Can you name some?"
- Discuss these related concepts:
  - Chemistry—the chemical makeup of the materials directly controls the structure of a form,
  - Conservation—the structure or shape of a form is affected by the elements,

- Ecology—the surroundings or the environment in which a form is located has a certain effect on the form,
- Mathematics—the weight of a form in relation to the size of the base and the height of the form directly controls the structure of the form.
- Construction—skyscrapers were made possible by the development of the steel girder (beam) system often called a "skeleton" because the lighter construction allows greater height, as opposed to stone masonry, for example.

Suggested art activity

In magazines or newspapers, locate examples of objects which do *not* appear well proportioned, functional, or practical in their design. Lay tracing paper over the top of the pictures and show by outline what you would change to restore the functional aspect of the design. (Poor fashion and home furnishing designs are especially easy to locate for this assignment.)

Alternative art activities

- Look at a number of common objects and discuss each in terms of what alternative materials might have been used in their construction and how each change would affect the life and function of the object.
- What would happen to a satellite if it were made of a less durable material? Draw some common or well known objects as they would appear if they were made of "impractical" materials or if they ceased being functional.
- Design a functional kitchen plan.
- Design a paper bridge that will support a glass of water.
- Redesign a clothing style so that it will go well on someone with an entirely different figure than the typical model. Do the same thing with some other design.

Evaluation

When the learner is able to list reasons why certain forms are made of certain materials and how their function relates to their shapes or appearance, the objective has been achieved. Some materials are not strong enough or flexible enough to be used for certain forms. Some materials may not add either to the beauty or the purpose of the form. Note how each student responds and contributes to the class thoughts in these areas.

Other things to consider

- Vocabulary: function, structure, purposeful, practical, and well-proportioned.
- Art materials needed: drawing and painting materials plus scissors, glue, and tracing paper.
- Books:
  Art in Everyday Life by Goldstein
  An American Architecture by Frank Lloyd Wright
- People who might have need for the concept: architects, industrial designers, interior designers, city planners, people who tool leather, make puppets, hookrugs, jewelry, things in metal, wood, glass, do macrame, weaving, stitchery, and applique, landscape architecture, ceramics, pottery, sculpture, castings, mobiles and stabiles, and assemblages.

LEVEL 5

ACTIVITY 132

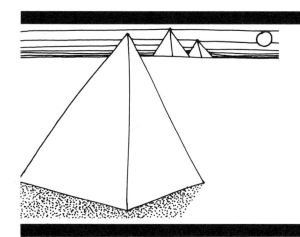

Concept taught by this activity: Structures are strengthened with triangular shapes. The triangle gives a feeling of rigidity to designs. Even when the triangle is only inferred, the arrangement seems more solid.

Objective: The student demonstrates an awareness of how artists have used triangular shapes to strengthen their designs. He is able to utilize his awareness to strengthen his own designs when the need arises.

A sample lesson plan for achieving the objective:

Teacher preparations
Locate and display such things as a pyramid, a sphere, prints containing triangular shapes, and pictures of buildings containing triangular shapes which strengthen or support their basic structure.

Teaching suggestions
■ Ask the following questions: "What are all of the things which have triangle shapes?" (roofs [gables], superman's emblem) "What shapes can you draw with several triangles?" (⊠ , ☆ , pine trees, mountains)
■ Have students assess what *they* know about triangles. Discuss the triangle as a solid form. The concept says this is the most rigid of all forms. Does it have to be in any certain position to appear rigid?
■ Discuss the words *infer* and *inferred* in relation to triangle-like.

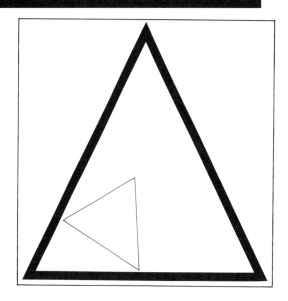

■ Examine a series of prints and discuss the role of the triangle in creating stability.
■ Have the students identify every visible use of the concept within the classroom and outside the building. List them, point them out, and draw them.
■ Discuss the reasoning behind artists sometimes using triangles in stable or rigid ways and sometimes in dynamic or active ways. "Does the artist's use of the triangle harmonize with the feeling, mood, or idea behind his creation?" Both Leonardo Da Vinci and Salvador Dali did paintings of "The Last Supper" and used the inferred triangle with Christ at the apex.
■ The triangle controls eye-movement, almost like an arrow, leading the eye to its most prominent angles.

Suggested art activity
Draw or paint a picture that contains inferred triangles

which give the picture a feeling of solidity or rigidity.

Alternative art activities
- Weaving could be done using the triangle as the motif.
- Stitchery and applique could also be projects used to teach this concept.
- Other media or projects that could be used to teach this concept: architectural constructions (perhaps with tooth picks), sculptural creations, mobiles and stabiles, collages, prints.

Evaluation

When the student is able to use triangles or inferred triangles to give rigidity to his design and point out instances where the concept has been used, then the objective has been achieved.

Other things to consider

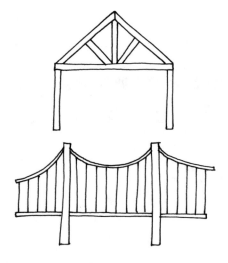

- Vocabulary: triangular, inferred, rigid, rigidity, structure, solidity.
- Art materials needed: use whatever drawing and painting materials are easily available and familiar to the students.
- Prints:
  Last Supper by Dali
  Christina's World by Wyeth
  Dempsey and Firpo by Bellows
  I and The Village by Chagall
  Bandaged Ear by Van Gogh
  The Cradle by Morisot
  Artist's Mother by Whistler
  Guernica by Picasso
  Night Watch by Rembrandt
  The Box by Renoir
  Brooklyn Bridge by Stella
  Oath of the Horatii by David
  Les Miserables by Picasso
- People who might have need for the concept: painters, architects, commercial artists, sculptors, jewelry makers, artists that work with glass, landscape architects.

LEVEL 5

ACTIVITY 133

Concept taught by this activity: Printmaking designs can be created by attaching parts of a composition to a stiff background. Ink the raised pieces; print either as a picture or part of a repeat pattern.

Objective: The student creates designs in print-making with the applique process of making prints.

A sample lesson plan for achieving the objective:

Teacher preparations

Note: When the term applique is used in printmaking, it simply describes a process for creating the design you print with. The design may be made from materials such as felt, leather, rubber, cardboard, and string. The materials are cut into shapes and then the shapes are glued to another material. The raised portion of the design which was fastened to a backing with glue is then inked or painted and then printed on paper or some other surface.

■ Collect and have ready a variety of materials that students can use to cut out their shapes and create designs or pictures.

■ Use materials such as cardboard, oak tag, masonite, upson board, and plywood as background for the students to fasten their designs.

■ Thick tempera paint, colored liquid starch, water soluble printer's ink, india ink, fingerpaint, a detergent and tempera paint mixture, and thick instant tea or coffee can be used to ink the designs.

■ Have brushes or rollers (brayers) available for the inking process and spoons for transferring the design to the paper or printing surface. Printmakers usually ink their designs with printer's ink and roll it on the surface they've created with a brayer. (See illustration.)

In most classroom situations some sort of paint will probably be used in place of ink and that goes on best with a brush. When a printing press is not available, the transfer of paint (or ink) to paper is best accomplished with a spoon or some hard, smooth object. (See illustration.)

Note: When students get ready to cut out shapes for a design or picture, make sure they use materials that have the same thickness. The lower parts of a design won't print.

■ Some system should be devised where the teacher can control the potential "messiness" of this activity. For example, students may need to wear some sort of protective clothing since tempera and other paints can stain their clothes. Two or more areas might be identified where students would do all of their painting and their printing. Materials can be dispensed in an orderly way and areas for drying the prints might be established so pictures don't stick together, for example, hanging them on a line with clothes pins or paper clips.

Teaching suggestions

Prepare the students for the activity by identifying some of the reasons artists use the process they are about to learn. For example, the teacher may wish to review a previous concept in perspective or some other area and reinforce it with the pictures students make through this applique process.

You could review the role printmaking plays in the students' lives since almost every design they see on walltex, wallpaper, and fabrics of all sorts originated in some sort of printmaking process. You could also discuss the aspect of original art being made available to the consumer at much reduced prices when the artist is able to create a large number of prints from one design. The artist always records the number of each issue on the print and the value or cost of the print is determined by the reputation of the artist and how low the edition and issue numbers are. For example: The artist might have ten editions of an etching with twenty issues in each edition. Each print in an edition would be the same price but the higher the edition number gets, the lower the price of each print. Whether or not the artist signs the print also affects its value.

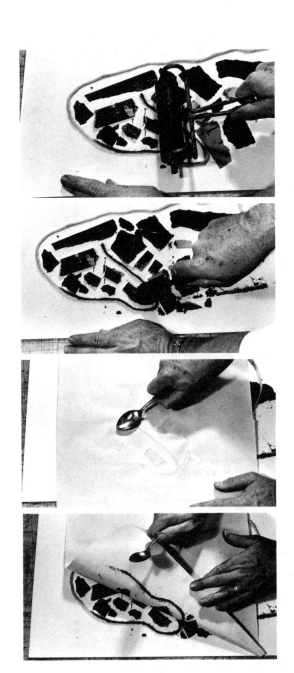

After the discussions and students acknowledge an understanding of the process, each individual needs to create a design for his applique print.

Suggested art activity
Do a series of small sketches with some sort of theme in mind, for example, insects, animals, or fruit. Select the best design and cut out the shapes used in it. Glue them to a stiff background and print.

Alternative art activities
- Have the students create designs for some specific use or area of the building where the repetition of shapes or a theme is needed. For example: Use prints to create the background for murals or use print designs for decorating windows during holidays.
- Cut out a number of related shapes and arrange them into an aesthetic design. Glue them in place and make prints.

Evaluation

When the student is able to utilize the process described in the concept and create an applique design for printmaking, then the objective has been achieved.

Other things to consider

- Vocabulary: applique, relief, printmaking, print, brayer, water soluble ink, edition, issue, printmaker.
- Art materials needed: a great variety of options are available to the student. See suggestions already noted under sample lesson plan.
- Prints:
  Autumn by Koryusai (woodcut)
  Marilyn Monroe by Warhol (silk screen)
  Poster--Moulin Rouge by T. Lautrec (lithograph)

  Use wallpaper or walltex samples and fabric samples with patterns on them.

  You may also refer to etchings and lithographs of Durer, Rembrandt, and Kollwitz or some contemporary printmakers.
- People who might have need for the concept: printmakers, teachers, artists that do woodcuts, and art historians.

LEVEL 5

ACTIVITY 134

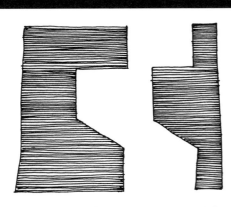

Concept taught by this activity: Shapes or spaces are either positive or negative.

Objective: The student can distinguish between positive and negative shapes.

A sample lesson plan for achieving the objective:

Teacher preparations
■ Obtain pictures that can be used to identify positive and negative space.
■ Develop transparencies showing the positive and negative areas of prints or photographs.
■ Obtain transparent paper and drawing media.
■ Be aware that positive space is basically the foreground objects in a picture or arrangement and the negative space represents the background. For example, in a room arrangement the furniture and fixtures would represent the positive space and the walls, ceiling, and floor the negative space.

Teaching suggestions
■ Establish the notion that whenever artists of any kind develop their product or creation, they have great concern that everything they do in the process of its completion will play a contributing role at the end. If any one part is over emphasized to the point that it dominates too much and takes away from the desired result, then that apsect of their design *has* to be changed. Thus the background spaces (negative) are just as important as the foreground (positive) shapes.
■ Look at negatives from photographs and discuss the black-white relationship to positive and negative space.
■ Look at transparencies where the positive and negative spaces have been simplified as foreground and background shapes. Ask, "What things in this room would then be positive and which would be negative?"
■ Play "ANALOGIES": A doughnut is to its hole as

_____." (A printed word is to the page, a picture is to the wall, the skyline is to the sky) Have students create their own analogy.
■ Have pictures of a variety of art products that include such things as room interiors, fashion designs, paintings, buildings, and their environment, and pieces of sculpture. Have students identify the positive and negative shapes in each.
■ Discuss and identify the positive and negative space in the prints or pictures that you have obtained. Ask questions such as: "Why do artists concern themselves with positive and negative spaces?" "Is it sometimes difficult to tell which is which?" "Does it give a picture greater unity to consider both?" "How?" "Could you draw the positive space by just concentrating on the drawing of the negative space, or the shape of each space you see between and inside of things?" Have someone try it briefly.
■ Develop the discussion to the point that students recognize that one only needs to make a mark on a piece of paper and a positive and negative space relationship is developed. Artists also call this a figure-ground relationship, the mark or line being the figure and the paper being the ground.
■ Develop the idea that in an arrangement some objects may be more positive than others just as some spaces may be more negative than others. Thus the least positive shapes and the least negative shapes may be almost one and the same.

Suggested art activity

Cut out colored shapes and arrange them on a plain background, taking care that the negative spaces are as interesting and as varied as the positive spaces.

Alternative art activities

- Paint a picture with shapes viewed as simple silhouettes and taking considerable care in making sure that the negative shapes are just as varied and as interesting as the positive ones.
- Take a common object, like a car, and discuss how important the negative spaces are, and how many variations could be made and still have a car. Have the students sculpt, out of oil-based clay, some imaginary object that would have positive and negative space. Discuss the objects.

Evaluation

When the student is consistently able to distinguish between positive and negative shapes and indicates some increased awareness of the negative shapes in his pictures or designs, then the objective has been achieved.

Other things to consider

- Vocabulary: positive space, negative space, harmony, figure-ground, unity and variety.
- Art materials needed: drawing and painting media, art paper, construction paper, scissors, and glue.
- Prints:
  Dempsey and Firpo by Bellows
  I and the Village by Chagall
  Absinthe by Degas
  Ice Skating Palace by Bonnard
  Head of a Man by Klee
  Birds in Bamboo Tree by Koson
  The Old King by Rouault
  Poster—Moulin Rouge by Lautrec
- Books: *Form, Space, and Vision* by Graham Collier, Prentice Hall. (See Chapter 2 on space and the figure-ground relationship.)
- People who might have need for the concept: painters, illustrators, commercial artists, sculptors.

LEVEL 5   ACTIVITY 135

Concept taught by this activity: The student should develop an awareness of how advertising design and its related fields influence his life.

Objective: The student describes ways in which advertising design and its related fields influence his life.

A sample lesson plan for achieving the objective:

Teacher preparations
■ Collect examples of effective advertisements: packages, boxes, or containers which catch the eye, advertisements which entice the viewer to buy the product, and other appropriate examples of visual propaganda.
■ Select some of the most familiar radio or TV advertisements for discussion purposes.

Teaching suggestions
■ Ask the class what the best kind of car or the best kind of detergent (or other common product) is. Probe to see how much of their opinion came from experience and how much came from effective advertising (even vicariously through their parents).
■ P. T. Barnum, the great circus promoter and freak show specialist, said, "There's a sucker born every minute." Discuss the implications of his statement. The Morton Salt Company always said, "When *it* rains, it pours." What do they mean by their slogan?

Advertising and propaganda experts say that it is possible to get people to believe *anything* if it is said often enough and long enough. What are the implications of *that* statement?
■ A local businessman was asked if radio and TV advertising helped his business much and he replied that it changed his business from a local affair to a statewide endeavor.

Discuss the reasons behind such a statement. "Why is it that a business will pay $250,000 or more for space on the inside cover of a magazine or for a few minutes of prime time on television?"
■ "What would happen to your book sales if you as an author were invited to appear for a few minutes on a famous television talk show?" "Why would sales increase so much?" (double, triple or quadruple)
■ Help the student in becoming familiar with the following concepts of advertising.
  ● The types of advertising
    National, retail, mail order, lead (addressed to occupant), trade (to a specific clientele, for example, retail outlet), industrial, professional (specific profession that won't recall it).
  ● The advertising spiral
    (a) Pioneer level (first of its kind). Tell why people need a product.
    (b) Competitive advertising. Tell how yours is better than others.
    (c) Retentive. The clientele is used up so you broaden your market to a new group.
  ● The purposes of advertising
    (a) To increase use of the product.
      (1) frequency of use
      (2) frequency of replacement
      (3) variety of use
      (4) units of purchase (two boxes instead of one)
      (5) length of buying season.
    (b) To attract a new generaton of consumers.
    (c) To present a specific offer.
    (d) To bring a family of products together.
    (e) To make known an organization behind a product (one product sells in a company and its other products are boosted too).
    (f) To offer the public a service.
    (g) To dispel wrong impressions.
    (h) To combat substitution.
    (i) To reach the power behind the throne (making breakfast cereals appeal to children so they'll influence the purchaser parent).

(j) To secure acceptance of a subordinate product.
(k) To increase the strength of an entire industry (dairy or steel, for example).
- The ways to advertise
  (a) Mass media (magazines, movie, TV, radio, newspaper).
  (b) Mail.
  (c) Outdoor.
  (d) Transportation (buses, taxi cabs).
  (e) Point of sale displays.
  (f) Premium and specialties (gifts).
- The means of delivering advertisement
  (a) Zone. Company works as one unit.
  (b) Cream. Advertise only to the actual user.
  (c) National. Blanket coverage.
- The propaganda principles in advertisement
  This promotes one side of an argument and ignores the other. It appeals to vanity, greed, and fear. The devices are:
  (a) name calling
  (b) glittering generalities
  (c) transfer
  (d) testimonial devices
  (e) plain folk pose
  (f) card stacking
  (g) band wagon
- The propagandist uses the power of suggestion
  Catchy phrases that people will repeat are key ingredients: fill-er up, vote democratic, party of the people, and others. Ten psychological forms of propaganda are:
  (a) The atmosphere effect. (Setting a mood or feeling for the product, idea, or person.)
  (b) The together device. ("This is what they're wearing.")
  (c) Common ground. (Creating the impression we're all in this together.)
  (d) Rationalization. (Induce you to go in debt for a new car you don't need.)
  (e) Repetition.
  (f) Prestige.
  (g) Scapegoat. (Someone else takes the blame.)
  (h) Big lie. (It would have to be true or they'd be sued!)
  (i) Strategy of terror. (Using fear to sell a product.)
  (j) Word manipulation. (Use of words such as *freedom, home, mother*. Words with loaded meanings.)

Suggested art activity
From a store or magazine select a product and its mode of advertisement. Identify the characteristics that make it sell and who it appeals to as an audience. Make a verbal or written report and display the presentation with other analytical papers, and a new or revised art image (new lettering or new logo, for example). Tracing is appropriate if needed to aid student's accomplishment of goal.

Alternative art activities
- Take any given advertisement and analyze the information in it by posing questions such as: "On what facts is the information based?" "What motives do they reveal?" "How do the motives concern me?" "What information has been left out?" "Who is giving the information?" "What is *actually* said?"

Evaluation

When the student demonstrates an awareness of how advertising design and its related fields influence his life, the objective has been achieved.

Other things to consider

- Vocabulary: advertise, advertisement, propaganda, competition, point of sale, product, plus other terms utilized in the section on advertising concepts. (See list of advertising concepts.)
- People who might have need for the concept: advertising designers, commercial artists, illustrators, cartoonists, the general public.

LEVEL 5

ACTIVITY 136

Concept taught by this activity: Because their contour is unique, most forms can be identified when seen in silhouette.

Objective: The student identifies forms from their silhouettes or contour.

A sample lesson plan for achieving the objective:

Teacher preparations
- Collect appropriate prints and locate whatever photographs may be available in magazines or in the media center showing objects, people, etc. in silhouette.
- Set up conditions for creating shadows or silhouettes of students.

Teaching suggestions
- Begin with a discussion session to determine how much students already know about the concept. Ask questions such as: ''Is it possible to recognize someone from his shadow?'' ''Why?'' ''Have any of you ever had your silhouette traced and cut out of black paper?'' ''Could you tell it was you?'' (For those who haven't had the experience, it might be a good demonstration to conduct at this point.)
- See if anyone knows what the word *contour* means and then relate it to *silhouette*. (Both emphasize the outside shape of something.)
- ''How many things can you think of that have contour we can easily identify?'' Make a list or see how many each student can write down in two minutes. Then see how many things they can name that would be *hard* to identify from their outside shape. ''Does the position of an object in relation to you ever affect how easily it can be identified from its contour or silhouette?''
- ''Which would be easier to tell from its silhouette—a giraffe or a beaver?'' ''An anteater or a water buffalo?'' ''What if the anteater was curled up in a ball and sound asleep?'' ''Why does that make such a difference?'' ''How about a

dolphin and a porpoise, or a crocodile and an alligator?'' ''Why are these last comparisons more difficult?'' ''How about distinguishing between a gorilla and an orangutan?'' ''Or an elephant and a zebra?'' (This discussion should make three points: (1) unique shapes are easily distinguished, (2) shapes can be disguised, (3) we need to have a thorough understanding of what certain things really look like to distinguish them from those with a similar contour.)

Suggested art activity
Have the children do line drawings of the contours of two or three forms that they like and cut them out of construction paper. Tell them to be careful to get the details of the outside shape (contour) as accurate as possible.

Alternative art activities
- Do a bulletin board or mural of plant and animal silhouettes. (Some silhouettes could be outline contours only.)
- Do a relief sculpture of plant and/or animal silhouettes.

Evaluation

When the student demonstrates either a verbal or a nonverbal awareness of the concept, then the objective has been achieved.

Other things to consider

- Vocabulary: silhouette, contour, outline, detail, unique.
- Art materials needed: pencils, construction paper, and scissors.
- Prints:
  Harvesters by Brueghel (the trees)
  Cliff of Etretat After Storm by Courbet (boats)
  Trains du Soir by Delvaux
  Fox Island by Hartley
  Poster—Moulin Rouge by Toulouse-Lautrec

LEVEL 5

ACTIVITY 137

Concept taught by this activity: The human eye is a more complex version of the camera lens in its capacity to control light.

Objective: The student describes ways in which the human eye is a more complex version of a camera lens in its capacity to control light.

A sample lesson plan for achieving the objective:

Teacher preparations
This lesson is developed to create an awareness for the learner of how his eye operates much like a camera. Diagrams of the eye and the camera and perhaps a simple box camera to use in the classroom as part of the instruction would be helpful.

Teaching suggestions
The body of information to which the learner should be exposed could include the following ideas:
- We see objects because waves of light are reflected from them and enter the eye.
- In the eye, reflected light passes through the lens and is brought to a focus on the light-sensitive retina. The retina is like film in a camera except it changes the light waves into nerve impulses (which are like messages) and it sends them to the brain. The lens is clear in healthy eyes and when it becomes clouded, we say the person has a cataract. His vision is affected because light can't pass through the lens properly. The iris of the eye adjusts to control how much light is allowed to pass through the lens by changing the size of the pupil. The darker it is, the larger the opening is in the iris, and the brighter the light gets, the smaller the opening becomes. (Discuss experiences students have had with having their eyes dilated.)

- Discuss how we see nothing in a completely dark room but if we shine a flashlight on some object, we can then see it. Light reflects off the object and part of the reflected light enters our eyes and the light causes us to see the object.
- The lenses of our eyes and the lenses in most cameras are convex lenses. In a camera, light reflected from an object passes through the lens, is focused on a film at the back of the camera, and forms a small image. The images formed on the retina of the eye or the film in a camera are both inverted or upside down, and smaller than the objects. The shutter of the camera, like the eyelid of the eye, opens to let light in. The size of the opening through which light enters the camera is controlled by the diaphragm. If the light-sensitive film receives too much light, we say the film was over-exposed; if it received too little light, we say it's under-exposed. Discuss experiences students may have had with under- or over-exposing film.

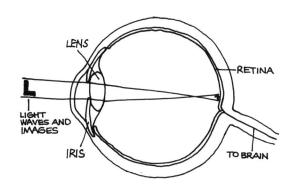

- Discuss how the brain turns the inverted image on the retina right-side up and with the camera we have the film processed and merely turn it right-side up.

   One of the marvelous things about the eye is the ability of the lens to adjust for far and near vision. It actually changes its shape by the aid of tiny muscles. (The camera lens *can't* change its shape.)
- Discuss other ways in which the eye is a more complex instrument than the camera (sees more, sees continuously, adjusts automatically or per instruction from the brain). Yet how the camera can do things the eye can't (records without emotion and provides a visual record of what was seen--the photograph).
- This activity is one often used in science and might be expanded to include concepts of near and far sightedness. The blind spot might also be discussed.

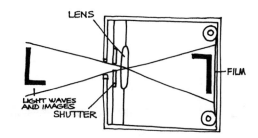

Suggested art activity
Examine the insides of cameras and discuss the various parts as they relate to the eye. See if students can identify the lens, diaphragm, and shutter, the point where film is exposed and how the camera adjusts to objects both near and far away. Discuss why the appropriate lens opening is important and what the shutter has to do with it. (The lens opening is set and the shutter speed, if set properly, allows only the right amount of light to strike the film.)

Alternative art activities
Have someone illustrate how light transmits an image when it passes through a lens.
- Look out the window. Hold a magnifying glass in between the window and a white piece of paper or a screen. Move the glass around until an image shows on the paper.
- Place a lighted candle and a paper screen about two feet apart. Darken the room. Move a magnifying glass (a convex lens) between the candle and the screen until the image of the candle appears on the screen. Will it work with a different kind of lens? Try it! Create a chart showing how this experiment was accomplished.

Evaluation

When the students' awareness is demonstrated at least on a verbal level, then the objective has been achieved.

Other things to consider

- Vocabulary: convex, concave, image, lens, iris, retina, shutter, film, light wave, transmit, inverted image, and focus.
- Resource materials: Elementary science books typically deal with this concept in sections on light.
- People who might have need for the concept: photographers, commercial artists, general public.

LEVEL 5 ACTIVITY 138

Concept taught by this activity: The student can create simple designs by laying objects or old negatives on proof paper and exposing it to light. The designs are called photograms.

Objective: The student will demonstrate an awareness of how light turns photo proof dark and then create photograms by laying objects or old negatives on proof paper that he exposes to light.

A sample lesson plan for achieving the objective:

Teacher preparations
Collect a variety of interesting objects, negatives, fern leaves, nuts and bolts, burlap, nylons, and kitchen gadgets to use in creating the photograms.

Teaching suggestions
■ Review what the student has learned about cameras and their relationships to the human eye. Discuss what the students know about film, for example, "What is film used for?" "Where does it go in the camera?" "What does light do to it?" "Why does the amount of light striking the film have to be controlled?" "What happens if we load or unload film from a cartridge in the light?" "What does it mean when we say 'the film has been developed?''

■ Explain how proof paper is paper similar to newspaper or construction paper in that it changes its appearance when exposed to light. Construction paper turns lighter and images on newspaper fade. With construction paper or newspaper, it takes quite awhile, but with proof paper, it's an almost immediate change. (Blue print paper will do the

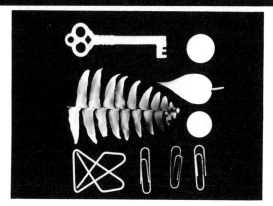

same thing as proof paper in light.) The emulsion side of proof paper has a shiny surface and sunlight or artificial light will turn it dark. (Demonstrate this for the students.) Then ask, "What would happen to the paper when I lay some object on it before I expose the paper to light?'' Let students select objects to lay on the proof paper. Place the objects on the paper in darkness and then turn on the light. As the paper turns dark, that part of the surface covered by the objects will remain light until they are removed from the paper. The light image is called a photogram. As the exposure to light continues, the shapes of the objects will gradually darken and disappear, too. Give each student or group of students an opportunity to make a photogram. Design success should be emphasized too.

■ Materials needed: a yellow safelight; 5-by-7-inch velox paper, grade 2; Dektol developer; acid fixer; stop bath (short stop); a tray (8-by-10-inch) to wash the film in; a package of blotters to dry film on; an assortment of objects to set on the film when it's exposed to light; two pairs of tongs.

Suggested art activity
The process: In a totally dark room with just the yellow safelight to see by, arrange objects on the 5-by-7-inch

velox paper. Turn on an incandescent lamp or flashlight and hold it for an 8-second count, then shut it off. The film is now exposed and needs developing just like any other film. Prepare the three developing solutions according to the instructions on each package. Arrange them in trays in front of you so that from left to right you have: (1) developer; (2) stop bath, and (3) fixer. Slide the exposed 5-by-7 velox paper, shiny side up, into the developer and, holding the edge with tongs, agitate the solution by rocking the tray gently. At the end of the development time (after the image has clearly appeared), place the print in the stop bath for 30 seconds. Using the second pair of tongs slide the print into the fixer and agitate immediately. After 30 seconds, you can turn on the room light or open the door. Wash the print for one half hour in lukewarm running water. Let it dry between blotters.

Alternative art activities

- If arrangements can be made or if funds are available for purchasing necessary materials, photograms could be made on contact paper and the film developed so that students could assist in and witness the actual photographic process.
- Take a field trip to a local photo lab or have a photographer come to the school and give a demonstration on developing pictures.
- Take a field trip to a nearby major airport and watch television-x-ray monitoring of flight bags and purses, another useful form of the photogram principle. Special training is required to perceive dangerous objects in photogram images.

Evaluation

When the student has witnessed the process described in the activity, then the objective has been achieved.

Other things to consider

- Vocabulary: photogram, proof paper, blue print paper, emulsion, negative, safelight, developer, fixer, stop bath or short stop, film blotters, contact paper.
- Art materials needed: proof paper, an assortment of objects and if desired, the items listed under additional experiences.
- Resources: Additional help may be found in books such as the *International Encyclopedia, The World Book Encyclopedia* and other available resources under the heading of photography.
- People who might have need for the concept: photographers.

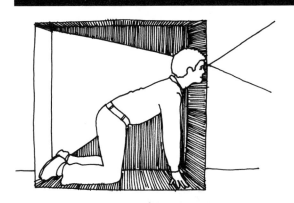

Concept taught by this activity: The student can construct a simple pin hole camera and take a picture using photo sensitized paper.

Objective: The student will construct a pin hole camera and take a picture on photo sensitized paper.

A sample lesson plan for achieving the objective:

Teacher preparations
- Have students collect materials needed for the construction of the cameras. (See descriptions of simple and complex forms of pin hole camera, below.)
- Have a sample made or ready for assembly.

Teaching suggestions
- "If you were Tom Thumb, and put into a box with the lid on, what are all the problems you would have?" (Let the "suppositional" work on them until they can *feel* "as if" they are Tom in the box.)

  "If you found a pin in the box, what would you do with it?" (One hole would be like a small window to Tom, and *light* could come in. The light hole would allow Tom to peek out.)
- "When light comes into a box and hits film, you can get an image just like Tom Thumb would see if he were in the box."

Suggested art activity
Provide students with opportunities to build and use at least one of the pin hole camera types. You might also try replacing the pin hole part with an actual lens such as a magnifying glass. This lets you see your subject as the camera would.

Note: To extend the students' understanding of how a camera functions, one or two different versions of a pin hole camera might be constructed. The simplest kind which merely demonstrates basic aspects of a camera and the more complex form which can actually be used to take a picture. Both varieties would be helpful to the student.

A simple form of the pin hole camera:
- Place waxed paper over the open end of a cylindrically shaped cereal box. Fasten the paper with a rubber band. Punch a tiny pin hole in the closed end of the box. Wrap a sheet of black construction paper around the box, so that the sheet extends beyond the end with the waxed paper. Fasten the black paper in place with another rubber band. The paper acts as a light shield.
- Place your face up to the light shield so that all outside light is blocked from your eyes. Look at some object about 100 feet away and discuss how it looks. (The image will appear upside down.)
- "What happens if the hole is slightly larger?" "Is the image sharper?" "Fuzzy?" "How big does the hole have to get before an object is seen right side up?" "How can all of this be explained?"

The more complex version of the pin hole camera:
- Obtain an oatmeal carton with a snug fitting lid. Paint the inside of the carton black. In the center of one end of the carton, cut an opening one inch square. Paste a piece of aluminum foil 2 inches or 3 inches square over the opening and punch a tiny pin hole in the center of the foil. Make a cardboard cover that can be placed over the pin hole on the outside of the carton and secured with tape so that no light gets in except when the hole is uncovered. In the opposite end of the carton, on the inside, tape four inches of black and white orthochromatic film. This must be attached in a totally darkened room or the film will be exposed. You can also do it in a room lit with a red incandescent lamp. The film should have the right side facing the pin hole, too. To take a picture you merely aim the box at a subject, uncover the hole, and replace it as quickly as possible so that the light enters the pin hole and records the image on the film. The film must then be developed and printed just as any other exposed film. The student may wish to build a small viewfinder on top of the cereal box. Be sure the picture taking is done on a bright sunlit subject and that the light source is behind you. See

that the camera is held steady or resting on something.

Alternative art activities
A student with some experience and interest in photography might want to try constructing a camera that utilizes a magnifying glass as a lens and has the potential for changing the focal length by one box sliding inside another.

Evaluation

When the student demonstrates an awareness of how the pin hole camera and its operation is related to the construction and use of any basic commercial camera, then the objective has been achieved.

Other things to consider

- Vocabulary: pin hole, camera, photo sensitized paper, light shield, inverted image, viewfinder.
- Art materials needed: wax paper, rubber bands, oatmeal or other cylindrical cartons with lids, masking tape or black friction tape, black tempera paint and brushes, black construction paper, black tempera paint and brushes, black construction paper, black and white orthochromatic film.
- Resources: Most elementary science texts which deal with light or the senses will contain a unit on the camera and the eye and describe activities relating to the pin hole camera.
- People who might have need for the concept: commercial artists, photographers, teachers.

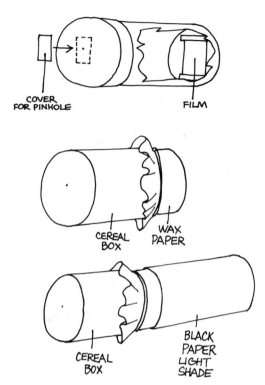

LEVEL 5

ACTIVITY 140

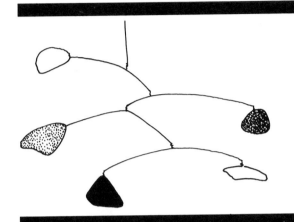

Concept taught by this activity: Space can be organized either formally or informally (symmetrical or asymmetrical). Achieve balance by adjusting weight and location, focusing attention, and with contrasts.

Objective: The student can balance parts of a design either formally or informally and achieve the balance by adjusting weights, focusing attention, or with contrasts of some kind.

A sample lesson plan for achieving the objective:

Teacher preparations
- Obtain suggested prints.
- If you are going to refer to any of the related concepts, set up the demonstrations that will be needed.
- Obtain materials for activities.

Teaching suggestions
- Ask questions such as: "What is balance?" "How can we tell when something is balanced?" "How dependent are we on balance?" (Our own balance as well as the balance of nature.) "What part does balance play in the things man makes?" "What kinds of balance can man use in the things he makes?" (formal and informal) "When you see a picture that is not hanging straight, what does it make you feel like doing?" "How would you feel if everything was not in balance?" Use a fulcrum to demonstrate balance. "How can you tell when two things are balanced?" "Why do they balance?" (same weight)

"There are two kinds of balance, formal and informal. When we balance two shapes with equal weight or size, which would that be?" "What is another name for formal balance?" (symmetrical) "Are you asymmetrical?" "When

you balance with your little brother on a teeter-totter, what kind of balance is that?" "What is another name for informal balance?" (asymmetrical)

"What is meant by balance in nature?" "What is meant by balancing the budget?" "What is meant by balancing the diet?"

"Who knows that a 'mobile' is?" "Do parts of a mobile always have to be in perfect balance?" "Why?" "Is space in a mobile an important part of its composition and balance?" Look at pictures of mobiles by Alexander Calder, father of mobiles.

"What kind of balance is used most in this room?" "In building design?" "In painting?" "Household objects?" "In advertising?" "What is the most interesting kind of balance for pictures?" "Why?" Discuss formal balance for formal subject (religious) and informal balance for informal subject (recreational). (Refer to famous architecture and paintings.) "Do artists always want balance in a picture?" "When wouldn't they?"

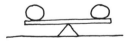

"Can you cause parts of a picture to balance by contrasts or points of emphasis?" "Give some examples." (Room, mantle, picture groups)

"Since we can't balance pictures with weights like we did the fulcrum, we have to create an illusion of balance. We call it a psychological form of balance. Does anyone have some idea about how psychological balance might be accomplished?" "Are most forms of balance in a picture psychological or real?"

- Note: Psychological balance may be achieved by any of the following:
  - By adjusting weights
  - By the location of forms
  - With contrasts in such things as color, texture, value, pattern, size, etc.
  - By focusing attention
- Note: When balance occurs around a "center," we say it is "radially" balanced.
- Look at prints of famous paintings and see if students can locate the ways in which the artists have created psychological balance and whether the balance is formal or informal.
- Discuss the following related concepts:
  - A fulcrum can be used to measure weights (science).
  - The bones of animals with a spinal column are arranged in a formal or symmetrical fashion (science).
  - Nature attempts to maintain a balance (ecology).
  - There can be formal and informal balance in music.

  - There can be formal and informal balance in poetry and literature (language arts).

Suggested art activity
Experiment with arranging a series of paper shapes (different sizes, colors, textures, and shapes) on a background and see how many different ways balance can be achieved. Have the children discuss their arrangements with others and then glue them in the arrangement that is the most unusual and yet still balanced.

Alternative art activities
- Make a mobile or stabile out of a variety of materials, for example, paper sculpture, straws, geometric figures, Christmas ornaments and cards, snow flakes, leaves, burrs. The construction may be in story form with colors.
- Make a construction of objects such as wood blocks, straws or balsa wood. Use both formal and informal balance.
- Arrange a weed, flower, or leaf arrangement in a three-dimensional form that is balanced, using all aspects of concept.
- Create a wire sculpture, stabile, abstract forms made of wire or metal banding, combined with other materials such as tin, plastic, paper or cloth. Both ends of the wire should be fastened to a base of wood, clay or plaster and twisted into an interesting shape that will balance well.
- Bind a roll of fabric with string in a spiral for almost the whole of its length, then completely immerse it into a dye bath, then let it dry. Have the students experiment to see what kind of balance they can create. These will have a tendency to have asymmetrical balance.
- Purposely create a completely unbalanced painting and then try to establish a strong emphasis in some portion of the painting by making it unusual in some way. The emphasis will help balance the painting.

Evaluation

When the student is able to create balance from imbalance in an arrangement of some kind and when he can distinguish between formal and informal balance, then the objective has been achieved.

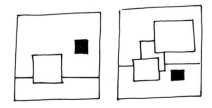

Other things to consider

- Vocabulary: fulcrum, symmetrical, asymmetrical, psychological, formal, informal, visual balance, stabile, mobile, three-dimensional form.
- Art materials needed: paints, paper, brushes, construction paper, scissors and glue. If constructions are built, such things as weeds, blocks of wood, drinking straws, balsa wood, pliers, wire, fishline, and wire cutters would be useful.
- Audiovisual materials needed: fulcrum, scales.
- Prints:
  Fur Traders Descending the Mississippi by Bingham
  Adoration of the Magi by Botticelli
  The Last Supper by Dali
  Apples and Oranges by Cezanne
  Dancing Class by Degas
  Don Manuel Osorio by Goya
  Breezing Up by Homer
  The Aficionado by Picasso
  Senecio by Klee
  The Brooklyn Bridge by Stella
  Knockout by Morreau
  Birds in Bamboo Tree by Koson
- People who might have need for the concept: painters, sculptors, architects, interior designers, illustrators, commercial artists, artists that deal with ceramics, weaving, printmaking, stage set designing, assemblages.

LEVEL 5   ACTIVITY 141

Concept taught by this activity: Symmetry gives a sense of stability and balance to a design and even when an arrangement is just "psychologically" balanced it seems symmetrical.

Objective: The student demonstrates an awareness of how symmetry can provide a sense of stability in any arrangement (two-dimensional or three-dimensional).

A sample lesson plan for achieving the objective:

Teacher preparations
Have pictures available of buildings, animals, and various objects which are both symmetrical and asymmetrical (formal and informal balance). Use the pictures as well as things inside and outside the room for your discussion period.

Teaching suggestions
Note: This lesson and the following one are extensions of #140. They could be taught separately or as a unit.
■ Review the meaning of the words *symmetry, symmetrical, asymmetrical,* and *formal* and *informal balance.* Discuss objects that have symmetrical shapes such as chairs, desks, telephones, windows, and people. Some students may observe that people are not *exactly* symmetrical because one arm is slightly longer or one eye lid droops and the other does not. Praise the students for their keen observation, but note that we are classifying objects in a "general" way only. Therefore, any object that appears to be the same on each side of its center is symmetrical and has symmetry.
■ Look at pictures or sculpture by artists along with interior

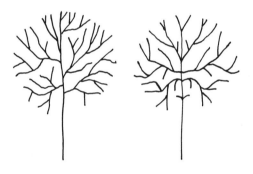

designs and have students see if they can point out those which contain symmetrical arrangements of space and those which are asymmetrical.
■ ● Discuss the terms *stable* and *stability.* (Note that with the word *stable* we are not referring to a place for animals.) "How can you tell when something is stable or has stability?" "What conditions are necessary?" "How can you make something stable which is at first not stable or rather shaky?"
  ● Refer again to the pictures and ask if the students can now select those arrangements which (psychologically) seem to be most stable or have the greatest stability.

  Note: Those arrangements which are symmetrical *also* seem the most stable. Be certain that students look at total pictures and not just at their parts. Although a comparison of objects can be made, we are more concerned with total works of art at this point.

■ Discuss the idea that if a picture has an informal kind of balance such as a large shape balanced by a small one or a large gray area by a small brightly colored one, the picture still balances like a fulcrum from its center. Thus, if you could psychologically hang the picture from its exact mathematical center, it would *still* balance because the small or brighter shapes have greater eye attraction than the larger or grayed ones.

Suggested art activity

Create either two- or three-dimensional arrangements, one of which is symmetrically designed and one which is asymmetrical. Use materials which the student can work with quickly so that a great deal of time isn't spent in this phase of the activity. For example, if the student wants to do sculptural forms, encourage him to make constructions of heavy paper or cardboard which can be quickly glued or fastened together.

Alternative art activities

- Create a mobile that has both symmetrical and asymmetrical sections.
- Look at prints and list which parts are symmetrical and which are asymmetrical. Identify characteristics which cause pictures to seem psychologically balanced.

Evaluation

Use the discussion session or oral questioning as the primary evaluation source for this concept. Look for any indications of a change in the individual's awareness of the concept. Determine whether or not the student can see the concept. In effect, see if he can tell how it influences the stability or solid look of an arrangement.

Other things to consider

- Vocabulary: stable, stability, symmetrical, symmetry, asymmetrical, formal balance, informal balance.
- Art materials needed: drawing and painting materials or media which can be quickly joined together into a three-dimensional design.
- Prints:

  Symmetrical Arrangements:
  Adoration by Botticelli
  Sacrament, Last Supper by Dali
  Blue Boy by Gainsborough
  Three Flags by Johns
  The Brooklyn Bridge by Stella
  Asymmetrical Arrangements:
  Venice by Canaletto
  Dancing Class by Degas
  Absinthe by Degas
  House at Aix by Cezanne
  Breezing Up by Homer
- People who have need for the concept: painters, illustrators, commercial artists, printmakers, sculptors, architects.

LEVEL 5   ACTIVITY 142

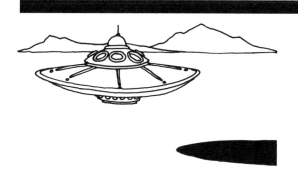

Concept taught by this activity: When a shadow is drawn or painted detached from an object, the object or figure appears in suspension.

Objective: The student demonstrates an awareness that objects or figures may appear in suspension when the shadow is drawn or painted detached from the object.

A sample lesson plan for achieving the objective:

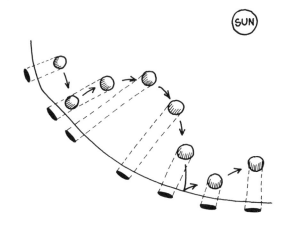

Teacher preparations
■ Assemble materials for outside activity and drawing lesson.
■ Research and collect a number of prints showing the concept.

Teaching suggestions
■ Discuss what cast shadows are and what conditions are necessary for one to see them. You might ask questions such as: "What is a shadow?" "How is a *cast* shadow different from the shadow on your face or under your chin?" "How are shadows made?" "What do shadows do in the morning?" "In the afternoon?" "At different seasons?" "How do shadows show that people or things are up in the air, for example, a bouncing ball, or clouds, and airplanes passing overhead?" "Why do we want to make shadows in some drawings?" "Do they provide information for the viewers of our pictures?" "Why don't some pictures have shadows?"
■ Take the students outside if it's a sunny day and focus in on the observation of cast shadows from objects that are in the air. These could include birds, bouncing balls, airplanes, clouds, and wires suspended between poles.

■ Display and discuss prints showing the concept. Ask the following questions: "How did the artist show that the subject of the painting or drawing is not touching the ground?" "Does the value of the shadow tell you something about the picture?" "What?" "What kinds of things can a shadow tell you about the action and composition of a picture?" "Did the artist create a mood by his own shadow?" "Identify the mood."
■ Have students take turns drawing demonstration models (on chalkboard) of the various things shadows do in suspension as established during the discussion.

Suggested art activity
Do a drawing or painting of some object in flight with its shadow on the ground.

Alternative art activities
■ Do a diagram illustrating the position of the shadow cast by an airplane as it moves across the sky or of a bouncing ball as it strikes the ground, bounds in the air and completes a full arc.

- Draw three of the five basic forms to make them look three-dimensional and with the use of the concept have them appear to float in space.

Evaluation

Use the students' pictures to evaluate how clearly the concept was taught and how well the learner is able to use the information.

Other things to consider

- Vocabulary: shadow, suspension, composition, value, balance.
- Art materials needed: jump ropes, balls, bean bags, art paper, charcoal or other drawing media, and pencils.
- Prints:
  Notre Dame by Daumier
  The Crucifixion by Dali
  Boy with a Tire by Lee-Smith
- People who might have need for the concept: painters, printmakers, commercial artists. illustrators.

Concept taught by this activity: All art is created for one or more of five basic reasons. (See Objective below.)

Objective: The student demonstrates an awareness of the five major uses of art: (1) philosophy or religion, (2) utility (use), (3) documentation (history), (4) ornamentation (decoration), and (5) self-expression. (For those financing its production, art must have an element of "collection value.")

A sample lesson plan for achieving the objective:

Teacher preparations

The following information is provided as background for the teacher to be more effective in leading the discussion.

Note: Art is created for a great variety of reasons but the way in which any art is *used* after it is finished by the artist largely determines the kinds of art produced. Considering (as much as is possible) the millions of things done by artists from the time of man's first attempts at drawing, it is not unreasonable to classify all of his efforts under five major headings.

Art is used as part of man's religious expression, for

utilitarian purposes or everyday use, to *document* events or the existence of people and places, to decorate objects, (*ornamentation*) people or other animals, and as a means for personal (*self*) *expression*. In our schools we have typically dealt only with this last use for art—self-expression. It is probably the one which influences the lives of most people the least. As you develop exercises and discussions to enlarge the student's awareness of the concept in this lesson, be certain that the student has a broader understanding of what art is and how it influences his life. At the same time, the fact that artists cannot exist without an income of some sort should also be mentioned. Some artists have been sponsored by wealthy patrons (kings, monarchs, businessmen, and foundations) and some have inherited sufficient income to maintain themselves, but most artists have had to exist by virtue of whatever their art would sell for. This reality of life has also influenced what the artist created.

Basic information about the five reasons for art.

Religion or Philosophy
This area includes the construction of all buildings which had some religious significance, for example, the Parthenon, Gothic and Roman cathedrals, churches, Mayan Temples, tabernacles, Buddhist and Shinto temples of the Far East, The Taj Mahal, and the pyramids of Egypt. It also includes the creation of religious figures (statues), the ornamentation of objects with religious symbols (altars, altar pieces, spears, masks, cups, chairs), and the designing of clothing used in religious ceremonies. Even body painting which has religious meaning would be included. The art forms of primitive peoples are heavily influenced by their religious practices and the art of the middle ages in all of the civilized world was almost entirely religion based (Christian).

■ *Utility*
Anything that was at one time influenced by an artist's design and has a practical use would come under this heading. Tables, desks, chairs, clothing, automobiles, schools, churches, factories, homes, apartments, plows, combs, staplers, telephones, light switches, computers,

dishes, furnaces, and paper clips are examples of art objects designed for use. It is true that, in the mass produced form we see it, each of these may not look too much like its original design, but each was at one time touched by the hand of the artist. This is by far the largest category and the one most influential in our lives.

- *Documentation*
Any art form which by its existence declares that an event took place or that a certain individual "looked like such and so" is a form of documentation. This would include paintings of wars or other historical events, portraits and sculptures of actual people, political cartoons, illustrations for books or stories, photographs and films of all sorts and architecture. Art is the most reliable historian.

- *Ornamentation*
Whenever the artist decorates an object to add to its beauty or aesthetic quality, the decoration pattern or design he applies comes under the heading of ornamentation. Typical examples include decoration around the frieze of a building; ornate carving on the back, arms, and legs of a chair; embroidery on a shirt or blouse; and the hanging of pictures on a wall. This area would also include the hanging or placing of objects on a form to decorate it, for example, beads, neckties, rings, sculpture, and decorative fountains.

- *The artist's own self-expression*
This last category contains all art that is created simply as an outward expression of the artist trying to communicate a feeling, attitude, or idea. Ths artist has no concern about profit or use for his product. He creates it to fulfill a personal need, and would do so regardless of conditions or lack or reward.

Note: All five areas are not distinct and exclusive; many art forms can be placed in two or more categories. Some are easy to place under a heading and some are very difficult to place. The broad awareness of the five areas is what needs developing for the student.

Teaching suggestions

- Briefly discuss what the students think art is and what artists do. Have pictures on display throughout the room showing the great variety of art objects this lesson will explore.
- Talk about the uses of art or objects designed by artists. Mention that there are five basic uses for art and see how many of the headings the students can supply. If terms like *therapy, creativity,* and *beauty* are mentioned, help them to recognize that these uses or reasons for art probably apply in all art that is created.
- Discuss whatever terms may not be familiar to the student and utilize the information provided in the "Teacher preparation" section. Use your own experience, the students, and whatever other resources you might have available.

Suggested art activity
Cut out pictures and make a display of examples of the five reasons for art, or have students do a photo study of examples of all five uses for art as found in their school community.

Alternative art activities
- Visit an art museum or invite a group of artists to talk about why *they* do art.
- Have students make a verbal or written report on the five reasons for art.
- Show films, slides, or filmstrips on art.
- Have students create examples of the five reasons for art.

Evaluation

When you are satisfied that each student has broadened

his awareness of how art is used and why it is produced, then the objective has been achieved.

Other things to consider

- Vocabulary: ornamentation, documentation, self-expression, decoration, historical, utility, utilitarian, religion, religious, frieze, architecture, decorate, design, aesthetic, ornate.
- Art materials needed: those appropriate for whatever activity the student selects.
- Prints:
Religious usage:
Adoration by Botticelli
Sacrament, Last Supper by Dali
Virgin with Saint Ines & Tecla by El Greco

Utility:
Venice by Canaletto
My Gems by Harnett
Autumn by Koryusai (umbrella and clothing)

Documentation:
Dempsey and Firpo by Bellows
Guernica by Picasso
Allies Day by Hassam

Ornamentation:
Francis I by Clouet (also documentation)
Don Manuel Osorio by Goya

Self-Expression:
Nude Descending #2 by Duchamp
Justice and Peace by Overstreet
Mural by Pollock
Les Miserables by Picasso
- People who might have need for the concept: teachers, art critics, docents, museum directors and curators, art historians.

LEVEL 5   ACTIVITY 144

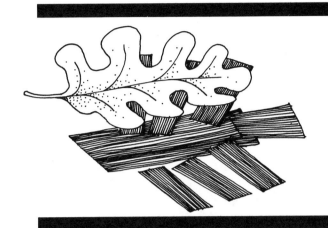

Concept taught by this activity: Art forms can be categorized, for example, large or small, realistic or abstract, and geometric or organic.

Objective: The student will demonstrate an awareness of how art forms can be large or small, realistic or abstract, and geometric or organic.

A sample lesson plan for achieving the objective:

Teacher preparations
■ Display prints of art objects where students can see them easily.
■ Be sure to have pictures of sculpture, both realistic and abstract. Also, be sure to have the measurements of some of these objects. (For example, *Mona Lisa* by da Vinci is 30¼″ by 21″) A list of these prints and objects is included in the following lesson plan.

Teaching suggestions
■ Discuss the terms *large* and *small*. Relate them to art objects which are various sizes just as people, trees, rocks, shoes, and books are different sizes.
  ● Show the class prints of painting and pictures of sculpture and have the students try to guess the size of each object. After they have guessed, tell them the actual size of the art form.
  ● Make comparisons of some art objects with objects found in the classroom. Examples:

  David by Michelangelo. 13′5″ high. This statue wouldn't be able to fit in the room because it is too large.
  Man Drawing Sword by Ernst Barlach. 31″ high. This statue isn't quite as tall as a yardstick.

Cube by Isamu Noguchi—approximately 32′ ht. (a sculpture in front of the Marine Midland Grace Trust Co.). This sculpture would probably be taller than the school building.
Art objects can be very small; ceramics would be a good illustration of this.
Calling of St. Matthew by Carravagio. 11′1″ by 11′5″ This painting is almost as tall as the statue of *David*.
Mona Lisa by da Vinci. 30¼″ by 21″. This painting is about the same height as the sculpture by Barlach, *Man Drawing Sword*.
Sistine Chapel by Michelangelo. It took Michelangelo four years to complete this work, 1508-1512.

■ *Realistic* or *Abstract:*
  ● Define *realistic* and *abstract*. *Realistic:* true to life or nature; accurate representation of real life; people and nature as seen with the naked eye; recognizable; pictorial representation. *Abstract:* little or no attempt at pictorial representation of life; imaginary idea; an artistic composition or creation characterized by designs that do not represent actual objects or designs not precisely representing concrete objects or figures, but with recognizable elements.
  ● Show the class examples of realistic art forms. Examples:

  Night Watch by Rembrandt.
  Christina's World by Wyeth.
  Girl with Braids by Modigliani. Even though Modigliani's paintings are not like Rembrandt's paintings, they are still realistic. Ask the class why "In what ways do they differ?" "In what ways are they alike?"
  Bronze Works by Rodin, Charles Russell, or Frederick Remington.
  David and *Moses* by Michelangelo. Even though these sculptures are made out of bronze and marble, they are still realistic. Referring to the statues by Michelangelo and Rodin, ask the class why these are realistic. "In what ways do they differ?" "In what ways are they alike?" Pictures of Greek sculpture would be equally appropriate.

- Show the class examples of abstract art forms.
  Examples:

  Orange and Yellow by Mark Rothko or *Composition, 1963* by Miro. Rothko deals with shapes and color relationship with no accurate representation of real life.
  Composition by Jackson Pollock. Pollock deals with the ''art'' of painting.
  Paintings by Piet Mondrian. Mondrian deals with space division and color.
  Paintings by Paul Jenkins. Jenkins deals with flowing colors and shapes.
  Sculpture by David Smith. Smith works with geometric shapes in metal.
  Sculpture by Alexander Calder. Calder works with mobiles and large metal sculptures.
  Discuss the fact that some works of art are more or less abstract than others. Use examples.

- *Geometric* or *Organic:*
  - Define *geometric* and *organic.* (a) *Geometric:* the use of geometric shapes, such as the square, triangle, circle, rectangle, cube, cone, pyramid, cylinder, and sphere; mechanical, hard edged. (b) *Organic:* not man-made; is or once was a living object. (In other words, it resembles humans, plants, vegetables, animals, leather, rope, or other organically derived product.)
  - The day before this lesson, assign the students to bring an object to class. When all the objects are assembled, ask, ''Which of these objects are organic?'' ''Why?'' ''How do they differ from the inorganic objects?'' ''Which of these objects are geometric or mechanical?'' ''Why?'' ''How do they differ from the organic objects?''
  - Have the students find objects in the room and outside which are organic and geometric. (For example, organic--trees, grass, flowers, animals; geometric--cars, stop sign, buildings, machinery.)
  - Show the class examples of geometric art forms.
    Examples:

    Sculpture by David Smith.
    Paintings by George Braque.
    Paintings by Piet Mondrian.
    Essex by Paul Chamberlain. A sculpture wall piece; an assembly of automobile parts and other metal pieces.
  - Show the class examples of organic art forms.
    Examples:

    Hay Wain by John Constable.
    Paintings by Van Gogh.
    Paintings by Rubens.
    Paintings by Monet.
    Paintings by Corot.
- The combination of two or more qualities:
  - Paintings and sculpture can have more than one quality. For instance, a painting can be realistic and organic or abstract and geometric or abstract and organic or geometric and realistic. Discuss with the class that Cezanne used geometric shapes to produce organic, realistic objects. He said that everything in nature is made up of geometric shapes. This is called Cubism. Show the class some paintings by Cezanne to illustrate this point. Paintings such as: *Card Players* or *Apples and Oranges.*

Suggested art activity
- Have the students draw a landscape using only geometric shapes. (Construction paper, crayons, and watercolors are suitable.)
- Have the students draw an organic object using only geometric shapes. (Construction paper, crayons, and watercolors are suitable.)

Alternative art activities
- Show the class prints or slides, using an overhead projector or slide projector if possible, and have the students tell you whether the art forms are (1) realistic or abstract and (2) geometric or organic. Examples are works by:

  Rembrandt--realistic and organic
  Monet--realistic and organic
  Daumier--realistic and organic
  Feininger--realistic (somewhat) and geometric
  Michelangelo--realistic and organic
  Leonardo da Vinci--realistic and organic
  Rothko--abstract and geometric
  Bonnard--abstract and organic
  Overstreet--abstract and geometric
  Duchamp--abstract and organic
  Klee--abstract and organic
  Constable--realistic and organic
- Have the students draw a geometric object using organic qualities. (Construction paper, crayons, and water colors are suitable.)

Evaluation

Were the students able to recognize the differences between the art forms and then tell you whether the forms were realistic or abstract and geometric or organic? (Solicit verbal response from the students.) Did the students use only geometric shapes as outlined in that activity? Did the students endow the geometric object with an organic quality? Any evidence of this sort would indicate a good awareness.

Other things to consider

- Vocabulary: realistic, abstract, geometric, organic.
- Art materials needed: construction paper, crayons, watercolors, and drawing paper.

- Media needed: overhead projector, slide projector.
- Prints:
  Delphic Sibyl by Michelangelo
  Moses or *David* by Michelangelo
  Ice Skating Palace by Bonnard
  Print Collector by Daumier
  Bacchus by Carravagio
  Mona Lisa by Leonardo da Vinci
  Sinbad the Sailor by Klee
  Pictures of ceramics
  The Night Watch by Rembrandt
  Christina's World by Wyeth
  Gypsy With Baby by Modigliani
  Bronze works by Rodin, Charles Russell, or Frederick Remington
  Pictures of Greek sculpture
  Orange and Yellow by Rothko
  Mural by J. Pollock
  Nude Descending #2 by Duchamp
  Bar, Folies Bergere by Manet
  Justice and Peace by Overstreet
  Le Jour by Braque
  The Hay Wain by Constable
  City Hall in Rega by Feininger
- People who might have need for the concept: teachers, art historians, museum directors, art critics.

LEVEL 5   ACTIVITY 145

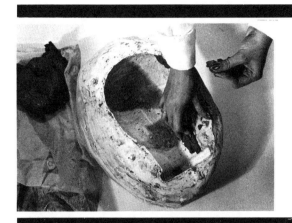

Concept taught by this activity: Forms can be made from some pliable materials by pressing them into a shape or mold.

Objective: The student will create form with a press mold.

A sample lesson plan for achieving the objective:

Teacher preparations
- Experiment with the process if it is not a familiar method of working with clay or a claylike material.
- Have all materials ready for use by the students, for example, clay, and objects such as rocks, original plaster molds, wooden bowls and balloons for forming the shapes.
- Collect any illustrations which might be available and have them displayed in the room.
- Collect any actual examples which might be available.

Teaching suggestions
- Ask questions such as: "Why do artists use clay or other similar materials to create art forms?" "What are their advantages over other materials?" "Disadvantages?" "How can clay forms be used?" "How can they be decorated?" "How can clay objects be formed?" "Who knows what a mold is?" "What do you think a press mold would be?" "Why does clay pull away from plaster when it dries?" "What are all the ways you can create texture or pattern on a form?" "How did the artists decorate these?" "What tools did he use?"
- List new terms to be used on overhead, easel chart, or blackboard. Explain the meaning of each. Use them in class daily.
- Demonstrate in front of the class the full process, using actual materials, explaining each step as you go.
- Show examples (photos or actual) of hand-made forms created by potter artists. Ask numerous questions about their construction and how they were decorated.

Suggested art activity
Wedge clay (to eliminate air bubbles). Pat or roll out flat ¼" to ½" thickness. Cut clay with the flat end of an orange stick to the shape of the mold, only slightly larger (oval, round, rectangular). Wet the mold (if plaster) slightly. Place the clay on the mold and gently press pieces into the mold. Cover lightly with plastic and allow it to dry. The clay will pull away from the mold as it dries. Gently remove with both hands. Fire in a kiln at cone 06 after the clay is thoroughly and slowly dried. Glaze if desired (or use stain or some kind of paint). Refire if glazed.

Alternative art activities
- To vary, use a piece of cloth hung like a hammock from the inside of a box. Hold with clothespins or string. Use the hammock as a mold for flattened clay. Use coarse materials for the hammock to give the clay a nice texture. Drape the clay over the outside of a rock, a dish, or a plaster mold to form it. You may attach a foot (rim, leg, or stand) onto the bottom of the form *before* it dries. The foot must be attached while the clay is still moist and the clay form must be removed from the rock or dish before it dries and breaks itself or the mold.
- Make masks over large balloons. (papier mâché, cloth strips)
- Make globe maps using round balloons as forms. (papier mâché)
- Make maracas by placing small pebbles inside balloons, inflating and tying them and inserting sticks in the end and then covering with papier mâché.
- Make pottery candy dishes by draping a clay slab over a smooth rock (or other form), which is covered with paper towel, and attaching three small legs. Fire when completely dry. The dish must be removed from the rock before it dries or it will crack.
- Construct a solar system using balloons and papier mâché. (group activity)
- Make a sand cast mold and create a new form by pressing strips of clay into the mold.

Evaluation

If the student is able to make some claylike object by pressing the material he uses into or onto some form, then the objective has been achieved. Make certain that emphasis during instruction is on the process and not on the making of some specific object.

Other things to consider

- Vocabulary: ceramic clay, mold, plaster, form (as a verb), wedge, press, kiln, fire, glaze (if needed), slab, draping, utility.
- Art materials needed: ceramic clay, original plaster molds, water and containers, orange sticks, rolling pins, (optional) pieces of plastic, balloons, papier mâché, coverings to protect clothes, tables, or desks, fabric for draping, and interestingly shaped rocks.
- Books:
  Making Pottery Without a Wheel by Carlton Ball
  Meaning in Crafts by Edward Mantil
  Sculptor with Simple Materials by Robert and Joan Dawson
- Prints or photographs or hand-made ceramics.
- Magazines:
  Ceramics Monthly
  Crafts Horizons
- People who might have need for the concept: sculptors, potters, ceramists, teachers.

Concept taught by this activity: Mosaics can be created by embedding small objects in some soft material which becomes the grout.

Objective: The student will create a mosaic by embedding objects in any groutlike material material.

A sample lesson plan for achieving the objective:

Teacher preparations
- Assemble materials and have them ready for use.
- Get mosaic examples, both actual and pictorial form.

Teaching suggestions
- Review some of the experiences the students have had with the mosaic process by asking questions such as: "How many have ever made a mosaic?' "What kinds of material did you use for the pieces (tessarae) and the background?'' "How did you attach the tessarae to their background?'' "Have any of you ever made mosaics with things like tile or rocks, or glass pieces?'' "Who knows what grout is?'' (The plasterlike substance used to fill in between the tiles used in a bathroom or in tile-mosaics.)
- Look at pictures and mosaic examples and discuss: "Why do you think an artist would use tile for his design instead of paint?'' "What materials can be used for grout?'' "For the adhesive?'' "How would you go about making a large mosaic such as a walk decoration or sun dial?'' "How might materials be used to make interesting changes of color, texture, or design?'' (combining materials, tipping tiles, different sizes) "What kinds of designs are suitable for mosaics?'' "Why could mosaics be used on buildings?'' "Why aren't more of them used?''
- Discuss the process of gluing tessarae to a stiff background and the importance of keeping the background spaces linelike in nature. The tessarae can vary in size but the spaces between them should be thin and narrow so they don't confuse or dominate the design.

- Suggest a variety of materials which might be used (see list on next page). If students need ideas offer many rather than one or two. For example, as subjects they might use still life, imaginary worlds, fish, birds and other animals, landscape, alley scenes, harbors, bridges, construction sites, farms and farm buildings.
- To help the student avoid problems and help assure success, suggest that he:
  - Cut big shapes first.
  - Use colored backgrounds to unify his composition.
  - Repeat colors for balance and unity.
  - Make the grout thick like cream and brush in between tessarae.
- List of media

Materials	Adhesive	Backgrounds
linoleum	white glue	(Should be
fabrics	airplane glue	as heavy or
seeds	school paste	heavier than
pebbles	wheat paste	materials placed
weeds and other	rubber cement	on it)
natural objects	tile cement	oak tag
found objects	Grouts include	corrugated
tile	commercial grout	board
tile scraps	plaster of paris	masonite
wood and building	spackle	box lids
scraps		plywood
broken glass*		chip board
shattered marbles	Note: copper wire,	construction
plastics	reeds, yarn, metal-	board
macaroni	lic thread and other	foil or paper
	materials may be	plates
	used as dividers	carton lids
	of shapes within	poster board
	the mosaic design	

- Mosaics are made by gluing small pieces of various materials side by side to form a design. The size, shape, color, and texture of each piece adds to the interest of the surface. By experimenting, arranging, and rearranging, children will find that they may want to put the pieces close together or farther apart or overlap them. They may want to

*Place glass under water when breaking to avoid dangers of flying particles.

cover all the parts of the design or only the main parts.

■ The design should be kept simple since the tesserae are so full of interest in and of themselves. Sketch with chalk or charcoal for a preliminary plan. Consider such principles of composition as contrast (dominant and subordinate areas), balance of color, size, form, dark and light. If the tesserae are thick or heavy, use pieces of cardboard cut from boxes as a background. (Masonite and plywood for heavier mosaics.) Vary the size and placement of the tesserae.

Suggested art activity
Select materials, an adhesive, and a background surface and create a mosaic design.

Alternative art activities
■ Decorate flower pots by covering with tile, smooth rocks, or other materials held in place with grout.
■ Make mosaic trivet using frame wood, wrought iron, and used ceramic tile, tumbled stones, plastic chips, glass, or linoleum pieces for design.

Evaluation

If the student goes through the process of making a mosaic and filling in between the pieces or tessarae with grout then the objective has been achieved.

Other things to consider

■ Vocabulary: mosaic, tessarae, grout, adhesive, unity, variety, positive and negative space.
■ Art materials needed: background materials, adhesives, grout, and tesserae as chosen by the student or teacher.
■ Books:
  The Art of Making Mosaics by Louisa Jenkins and Barbara Mills.
  Making Mosaics by John Berry.
  Mosaic Making by Helen Hutton.
■ People who might have need for the concept: craftsman, teacher, mosaic artist.

LEVEL 5   ACTIVITY 147

Concept taught by this activity: Molds can be created and duplicate forms produced by pouring slip or some other liquid into a mold.

Objective: The student will create a mold from a selected form and produce duplicates of it by pouring slip or some other liquid into it.

A sample lesson plan for achieving the objective:

Teacher preparations
- Have sufficient quantities of plaster available along with a large plastic bowl for mixing. Have sand in an appropriate container plus additional materials for making other kinds of forms which the student may wish to cast.
- Make preparations in the form of rules to protect desks and other surfaces to eliminate problems that might arise in plugging up a sink or getting plaster on clothing or furniture.
- Familiarize yourself with the process of creating forms, casting them in plaster to make a mold, and then making duplicates of the form.

Teaching suggestions
- Show examples of objects which are duplicates, for example, a set of glasses, bowls, or plaques.
- Questions: "How were these made so they were exactly alike?" "How could you produce forms that are alike?" "Is there an easier way to produce replicas of something than the methods used by cartoonists when they draw a character like Snoopy the same way all the time?"
- Discuss the use of patterns for duplicating things, for example, dress patterns, cutting several shapes at once from one pattern.
- Discuss the use of stamping out duplicate shapes with a cookie cutter.

- Questions: "What is a mold?" "Have you ever cast something from a mold?" "Is there anything in your home that was cast from a mold?" "Was your automobile made from a pattern?" "Cast in a mold?" "What kind of materials can molds be made from?" (plaster, plastic, metal, rubber) "What kind of materials can you use to pour into a mold?" (plaster, slip, plastic, resin)
- Show examples of molds and cast forms. Ask the last two questions, above, again with each example.
- Show a film or filmstrip, if available, which demonstrates the process of casting a mold. Show pictures from books or magazines.
- Questions: "Are some materials rather dangerous for use in casting?" "Which ones?"
- Discuss the notion that molds and mass production have had both social and economic impact on the world (social studies). The field of industrial arts has changed dramatically as result of molds.

Suggested art activity
From the discussion, generate enthusiasm for each student to create some kind of simple mold and to make a series of duplicate forms from that mold. Here is a rather elementary kind of solution to making a mold: Form an object in wet sand, cast the form in plaster to make a mold of the object, and then make a duplicate form by pouring slip or plaster into the mold. (sculpture, plaques, pottery) If plaster is poured into the mold, coat it first with vaseline or detergent so the plaster pieces won't stick together.

Alternative art activities
- Use a commercially formed object (like a paper cup) in combination with a shape made in sand or another commercial object for casting and then making a duplicate form.
- Make a mold by pouring plaster over a form made from a material such as wallpaper cleaner, soap, clay, nonporous styrofoam, salt and cornstarch mixture, or wax.
- Make a cast from a mold formed from aluminum foil by pouring plaster or wax into the shape formed.
- If plaster or clay duplicates are cast from your mold, paint or stain them to look like sculpture or ceramic forms.

The following information might be helpful for the teacher who is not familiar with casting objects in plaster. The process described would be used in any of the activities above.

Plaster Mixing
Partially fill a bowl or pan with water. (Plastic or rubber pan is the best.) Shake or sift plaster into the water until a small island of plaster remains above the water level. Let this stand for about two minutes. Then mix slowly with the hand until the mixture begins to set or thicken. Pour into your form or over the object you have created.

Sand Casting (Makes relief sculpture or wall plaques)
- Place moist sand in a large container.
- Make some shape or object in the wet sand, for example, an animal, a face, or an upside-down bowl.
- Fill or coat the form with plaster as described above.
- When the plaster is firm, remove it from the damp sand and brush out or brush off all particles from what has now become your plaster mold or replica of the shape you made in the wet sand.
- When the plaster mold is thoroughly dry, duplicates of it can be made by pouring slip into it or by pouring plaster over or into the mold. If slip is used, it should be left inside the mold until it starts to thicken next to the plaster (it dries from the outside in). When the wall is as thick as you want it to be, pour out the inside of the mold. When the clay form which you now have sitting inside the mold is dry, it will shrink and pull away from the plaster wall. As soon as this happens, it can be carefully removed from the mold, dried slowly, and made ready for firing in a kiln.
- If plaster is used to make the duplicate form, coat the surface of the plaster with a thin layer of liquid detergent, vaseline, or shortening so the mold and the duplicate form you are pouring won't stick together when both are hard.

Note: For the initial experience, students should only try one-piece molds and they need to be cautioned about any undercuts in the forms they cast because undercut areas will be broken off when forms are cast or pulled from a mold. (An undercut is a fragile overhang.)

Evaluation

When the student is able to make a mold and create duplicate forms from it, then the objective has been achieved.

Other things to consider

- Vocabulary: mold, cast, duplicate, slip, plaster, pattern, relief sculpture, undercut.
- Art materials needed: according to the interests of students and availability of materials, select from sand, plaster of Paris, wax, clay, slip, soap, wallpaper cleaner, styrofoam, salt, cornstarch, vaseline, detergent, or shortening, aluminum foil, boxes.
- Audiovisual materials needed: such things as cookie cutter, dress pattern, samples of sculptures, plaques, pottery, film, filmstrips, books, magazines, film loops, cast sculpture replicas, cast plastic replicas, and "Incredible Edibles." (However, the teacher must enforce the concept of molds and de-emphasize the art aspects of this material.)
- Films: "The Art of Ceramic Decorating" by Bailey-Film Associates.
- People who might have need for the concept: artists that do casting and jewelry casting, art historians, and docents.

LEVEL 5   # ACTIVITY 148

Concept taught by this activity: A design can utilize both intentional and accidental processes. Therefore, the artist must always be alert to every possibility affecting his final product.

Objective: The student demonstrates an awareness of how an artist sometimes utilizes unintentional things which affect his final art product.

A sample lesson plan for achieving the objective:

Teacher preparations

Note: We sometimes have the notion that artists always know in their "mind's eye" what their picture, sculpture, or whatever it is they're working on will look like when it's completed, that their task is simply one of making vision a reality. For some artists this may be true, but others train themselves to be very alert to everything that is happening to their product. Some painters recognize that every stroke they add to a canvas literally changes (or at least affects) all that was there before they touched it. Thus the idea an artist has to begin with can keep changing. He observes his work in progress and notes new possibilities that are even better than his original plan, and then he changes directions because of his new goals. To create an awareness of the concept, have the students experience ways in which exciting things can be created out of accidents. Display and discuss prints and other examples of art that probably changed a number of times before the artist felt he was through with the work. Have a variety of media available for students.

Even though this concept is given at this point as a lesson, it is intended that from this point on the idea of this concept be frequently brought to the students' minds so that they might develop a natural alertness to the possible improvements that could be made at every point of their art production. It would be well for each student to develop the "habit" of looking for the accidental things that might happen to improve his work.

Teaching suggestions

■ List as many accidents as you can (for example, spilled milk, crashing cars, broken dishes, burned fingers, skinned knees, unmatched socks). What are all of the *good* kinds of accidents? (Discovering diamonds, finding money, happening onto new ideas, finding a new chemical, finding a new friend, finding a shortcut)
■ Have the students participate in activities such as these:
  ● Have someone print your initials on your paper and then try to make a cartoon type figure from the letters.
  ● Have the student scribble with crayon or pencil on a piece of paper while keeping his eyes closed. Then have him create a picture or design out of the accidental markings.
  ● Wet a sheet of manila or drawing paper with clear water. While it is wet, paint three strokes of thick tempera or water color across the page, then tip the sheet and watch "accidental" blends of color occur.
  ● Play the analogies game. For example, a surprise is to the expected as an accident is to _____. (A plan, preparation, anticipation, goal) Luck is to accident as _____. (Fortune is to chance)

Suggested art activity

Create a design, collage, or picture from torn paper or fabric scraps or spill paint on the students' paper and have them create a picture or design from this planned accident.

Alternative art activities

■ Create a construction or sculpture from wood scraps. Use found objects to create a weaving, stitchery, or applique.
■ Contact local artists and interview them in relation to their experience with the concept. Report your findings to the class.
■ Discuss works of art which the artist is less likely to change much as he goes along. (Industrial designers, architects, city planners, landscape designs, and sculpture cast in

metal are good examples, but even here subtle changes might occur even though significant changes aren't likely just from the standpoint of the planning time necessary in these areas.)

Evaluation

When the student appears to recognize the importance of being alert to lots of possibilities in art and has successfully created interesting pictures or designs from accidental beginnings, then the objective has been achieved.

Other things to consider

- Art materials needed: any materials that are readily available and that students want to use are appropriate for this activity, for example, tempera, crayon, paper, fabric, found objects, watercolor, pencil, and yarn.
- Prints:
  Those which artists probably changed a great deal while they were being painted:
  Bedroom at Arles by Van Gogh
  Water Flowery Mill by Gorky
  Guernica by Picasso
  Boats at Argenteuil by Monet
  City Hall in Rega by Feininger
  Rebus by Rauschenberg
  Mural by Pollock

  Those which artists changed very little:
  The Crucifixion by Dali
  Turning the Stake by Eakins
  View of Toledo by El Greco
  Snap the Whip by Homer
  Mona Lisa by da Vinci
  Justice and Peace by Overstreet
  La Grande Jatte by Seurat
- People who might have need for the concept: Every type of artist could profit by developing the habit of watching for the accidental things that can happen to improve his work. The set designer, costume designer, commercial artist, film maker, interior designer, painter, and sculptor.

LEVEL 5

ACTIVITY 149

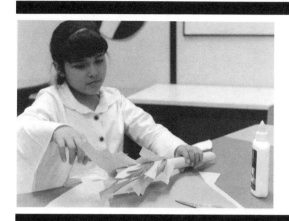

Concept taught by this activity: Sculpture can be made from paper by folding, scoring, stretching, cutting, bending, creasing, or rolling. Decorative textures can be added to any paper form.

Objective: The student will demonstrate that forms can be made from some pliable materials by folding, scoring, stretching, cutting, bending, rolling, creasing, or combinations of these.

A sample lesson plan for achieving the objective:

Teacher preparations
- Have a variety of paper and cardboard available along with scissors and paste.
- Display examples of paper sculpture (real or pictures) or have books on paper sculpture available as resources for students.

Teaching suggestions
- Talk about experiences students have had in creating art with paper, for example, paper weaving, sack puppets, and 3-D murals.
- Look at some of the examples you have been able to obtain and ask questions about how they were made. Emphasize the notion that a great variety of forms can be created simply by applying one's imagination to simple processes of cutting, folding, scoring, and stretching.
- Cutting
  - Experiment with positive and negative space using a dark color of cardboard or construction paper on a light background. Establish rules and challenge the student to see how many interesting arrangements they can create within the restrictions, for example, using straight vertical

shapes only, creating movement in one direction, creating movement in two directions, using vertical and horizontal shapes only, or adding diagonal and/or curved shapes.
  - These can be varied by starting from a rectangular shaped paper or a triangular shape or a circular shape.
  - Another variation is to create designs that are take-offs from patterns found in nature such as a wood grain or a leaf structure.
- Cutting and Folding
  - The natural take-off from cutting is cutting and folding back. The basic rule here is that nothing must be taken away or added. The part cut out (a) is left attached as part of the design but folded back to alter the outside shape of the paper. The designs may be very simple or very complicated depending on the imagination and manipulative skills of the student.
  - Combining the technique of cutting with folding back offers further possibilities and the use of tissue paper as a background or as a basic material or as a veil over the design can increase the potential for divergence in the activity.
  - For students responsible enough to use them, a single edge razor blade or an exacto knife used as a cutting instrument helps in creating much more intricate designs. Then imaginary landscapes, cities, forests, and animals can be used as design ideas.

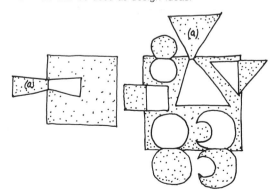

- Relief and Paper Sculpture
  (Bending, scoring, creasing and rolling, added to cutting and folding.) In addition to creating relief (a three-dimensional form with one side flat) with cutting and folding back techniques, other means may be used too. These include:
  - Tearing strips, rolling them, and pasting
  - Weaving paper and pasting the loops that are left sticking up
  - Giving short strips of paper one twist and inserting them into diagonal slits
  - Folding a narrow rectangular sheet of stiff paper length ways and cutting into the folds at right angles along the crease. Press the forms you cut in. The cuts may be few or numerous and in some sort of repeat pattern. When sections are pushed in, the feeling of relief is created. Cardboard may need to be marked with a knife before folding.
  - The above process can be used to create buildinglike designs with rectangular boxes or with hollow cylinders.
  - Short folded strips of paper can be used with paste to create buildinglike designs much like one would construct with drinking straws or toothpicks.
  - Trees, birds, fish, mammals, and so forth can be created with combinations of paper cylinders and cones, then attaching strips, curled pieces of paper, or folded shapes for details such as tails, ears, whiskers, beaks, legs, and feet. Interesting masks can be created with the same process.
- Flowers and plants
  Cut shapes of leaves and flower petals, score with point or edge of scissors, then shape. Paper may be stretched by pulling gently over scissor blade, or rolled over pencil for curling. When butcher paper is finger painted with contrasting or harmonizing colors on both sides, and dried, it may be shaped and curled to form interesting designs. (Thin finger paint with liquid starch.)
- Sticks and paper bags
  Stick puppets can be made from stiff paper attached to sticks such as pencils, rulers, tongue depressors, and popsicle sticks. Faces, animals, and other objects can be made. Paper bag puppets, like hand puppets, are decorated with the folded flap representing the opening and closing of the mouth. Crayon, paint, or paste cut paper onto the bag for decoration. Many variations should be encouraged.
- Stuffed forms
  Paper bags, socks, mittens, or stuffed fabrics make for variety in puppetry. Subjects may include imaginary animals or people, Easter bunnies, totem poles, flu bugs or insects, space vehicles, tropical fish, abstract mobiles and stabiles, performers, musical instruments, masks, birds, African animals, non-objective forms, homes of the future, and playground equipment. Collect empty boxes of all kinds, far ahead of time. Integrate with found objects. Add liquid soap to glossy surfaces which resist paint.
- Creating textures and decorating forms
  Experimenting with several kinds of paper, adhesives and decorative materials can sometimes aid the child in his need to explore many possibilities. He may wish to consider materials such as colored or white construction paper, boxes, cardboard and egg cartons, newsprint, butcher paper, craft paper, tissue, crepe, tag board, ship board, paper towels, paper bags, plates and cups, paper tubes or cores, thread, and thread cones. Also consider as adhesives staples, white glue, wheat paste, school paste, rubber cement, scotch and masking tape, pins, paper clips, string, braid and fasteners. Decoration may be done with tempera and watercolor, ribbon, yarn, braid, sequins, glitter, crepe paper and tissue paper, spray paint, found objects, fabrics, and crayons.
- Suggestions
  - Note that there are many ways of cutting, bending, twisting, curling, scoring, pleating, and folding paper.

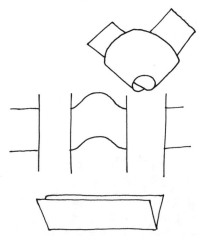

Paper may be pasted, stapled, or locked together. Paper surfaces may be textured by slitting, piercing, or crinkling. Be aware that every process and technique is usable in decorating or adding texture and detail to any form.
- Students may be further motivated by learning how paper has been used as a folk art in other countries. (Japan, Mexico, and China) Ways in which these cultures use texture as decoration and in details could be very helpful in stimulating the learner. The tie-in with social studies and language arts might prove interesting, too.

Suggested art activity
Make flowers from construction paper, tissue paper, or crepe paper, poster paper, magazines. Utilizing the flowers made by the entire group working on this lesson, create an imaginary flower garden or set up a display outside the classroom.

Alternate art activities
- Make animals or other shapes or forms from a single piece of paper.
- Create seasonal room decorations from paper. (group activity)
- Make a mobile or stabile from light cardboard. (group activity)
- Construct primitive dancers or shields or masks from cardboard. Decorate with paper.

Evaluation

When the student is able to create sculptural forms from paper, utilizing the processes included in the concept, then the objective has been achieved.

Other things to consider

- Vocabulary: pliable, scoring, creasing, stretching, folding, and rolling.
- Art materials needed: construction paper, crepe paper, tissue paper, cardboard, poster paper, scissors, rulers, pencils, magazines, paste and glue, single edge razor blade or exacto knife.
- Books:
  Creative Paper Design by Rottger (Reinhold Publication)
  Creating with Corrugated Paper by Hartung (Reinhold Publication)
- Films, film strips and other books are readily available on the subject of paper sculpture. They need to be previewed to determine their appropriateness to the level of the student.
- People who might have need for the concept: commercial artist, sculptor, window designer, stage set designer.

MATURITY LEVEL 6

Developmental stages

In this packet of lesson plans the teacher can provide the student with twenty-six art experiences that develop his awareness of how to:
- Create designs on fabric with batik and tie/dye techniques.
- Create forms that are stationary or have movement.
- Accurately render the position of an object and its parts in space.
- Recognize a variety of radial forms and their use in art.
- Create a variety of forms with macrame and knotting processes.
- Create sculptures from pliable materials by carving, cutting, or scooping away.
- Create pictures or designs by the stencil process.
- Create rhythm and motion in a design with lines and shapes.
- Visually warp a surface and create the illusion of depth with line.
- Create a balancing of complexity (detail) and simplicity in a work of art.
- Paint objects bluer, grayer, and lighter to give the illusion of distance.
- Make objects appear more distant by altering their position on a picture plane.
- Recognize that the horizon line is at the eye level of the viewer.
- Create the illusion of space by having parallel lines converge to a point on the eye level line.
- Draw or paint the value of shadows more accurately.
- Use shadow to describe forms or planes.
- Plan relief and depth with light.
- Recognize the three properties of color.
- Paint the color of a shadow more accurately.
- Use constrasts in color or value to avoid a "washed out" look.
- Create the appearance of form or volume with flat planes or shapes.
- Create form by rendering highlights, half tone, shadow edge, and reflected light.
- Create the illusion of forms with cast shadows and reflected light.
- Create the illusion of boards, water, foliage, glass, and other similar textures.
- Identify basic kinds of cameras and the use of their various parts.
- Operate an adjustable camera properly.

An explanation of level 6

This program is *not* designed for potential art students only; art skills are treated simply as a by-product of instruction.

Up through level 4, the drawings of the student are relatively accurate meters of his perceptual level. But as the learner develops the ability to portray his experience in greater detail, it becomes increasingly difficult for the teacher to evaluate the student's work by measuring his perceptions. By the time he has reached this level, the student is receiving inputs that move him into both two and three dimensional areas of art and into forms of abstraction. This complexity in his perceptual level makes analysis rather impractical.

At stages above level 4, currently beyond the experience of most students and adults in our society, all the teacher needs to do is note the number of the activity the student has completed and then pass that information on to the next teacher. Those who are sufficiently interested in art to develop skills in drawing or to specialize in some specific discipline would move beyond this "core" program and become art specialists at higher levels.

Art projects that can be used as devices for teaching a specific concept

Drawing (pencil, chalk, pen, marker, brush, etc.)
Lessons: *152, 157, *158, 159, 160, 161, 162, 163, *164, *165, *171, *172, *173

Perspective
Lessons: 158, *160, *161, *162, *163

Murals
Lessons: 159, 160, 161, 167, 171, 172

Water Color and Tempera
Lessons: 159, 160, 161, 162, 163, *167, *168, 169, 171, 172, 173

Sculpture (constructions)
Lessons: 159, 166, *170

Carving Sculpture and Other Forms
Lessons: *155, 166

Leathercraft
Lessons: 153, 166

Dry Flower Arranging
Lessons: 153, 159, 166

Stencil Designs (serigraph)
Lessons: *156, 159

Melted Crayon Painting (encaustic)
Lesson: 159

Batik
Lessons: *150, 157, 159

Knitting and Crocheting
Lessons: 157, 166

Basket Weaving
Lessons: 153, 157, 166

Weaving
Lessons: 157, 159, 166

Puppet Making
Lesson: 151

Cartooning and/or Caricature
Lessons: 159, 162, 163

Posters
Lessons: 157, 159, 167

Dioramas
Lessons: 151, *166, 170

Collage and Paper Designs
Lesson: 159

Wire Sculpture
Lesson: *157

Ceramics
Lessons: 155, 166

Terrariums
Lesson: 159

Photography
Lessons: 159, *174, *175

Printmaking (e.g., gadget and roll prints)
Lessons: 153, 156

Copper and Foil Tooling
Lesson: 157

Tie/Dye
Lessons: *150, 153, 157, 159

Mosaics
Lesson: 159

Applique (sew or glue)
Lessons: 159, 166

Rug Hooking
Lesson: 157

Holiday Decorations
Lessons: 157, 159, 166, 170

Mobiles and Stabiles
Lessons: *151, 157

Paper Sculpture

Lessons: 159, 170

Papier Mâché
Lesson: 159

Macrame
Lessons: *154, 157, 166

Snow Sculpture
Lesson: 151

---

*Key projects for the concept.

LEVEL 6

ACTIVITY 150

Concept taught by this activity: Designs can be created with batik and tie/dye techniques.

Objective: The student is able to utilize the processes of batik and tie/dye to make designs on paper or fabric.

A sample lesson plan for achieving the objective:

Teacher preparations

■ Collect and prepare materials for demonstrations and student activities. These would include cotton cloth in square shapes for such things as handkerchiefs, headscarves, and neckerchiefs, and oblong pieces for such things as towels, banners, scarves, and ribbons. T-shirts or other cotton wearing apparel could also be used. Remove any starch from the material before dyeing it.

■ Have wooden frames available for all methods of dyeing except folding or binding. The minimum size of frame is 8 ¼'' by 8¼'', the maximum 2' by 2' 8''. The wood should be 1½'' by ½''. The materials should be stretched tightly over the frames with all threads kept straight. Before dyeing, the prepared cloth must be "loosened" by dampening it. After dyeing it should be rinsed in water, smoothed out on a flat surface and dried or ironed. Thus all of the space and equipment for this process must be available.

■ Only liquid dyes penetrate lastingly into the fibers of cloth; therefore, paste dyes should not be used. To increase the adhesion of the dye, one teaspoonful of cooking salt per 3 ounce weight of cloth is added. The cloth will dry considerably lighter than it was when it was wet. Trial strips may be helpful if specific colors are needed. The dye-bath can be kept for weeks.

■ There are two distinct ways of dyeing: (1) dyeing *onto* the material; and (2) dyeing *into* the material. In the first process the dye is applied by dabbing, painting, or stippling. Blobs of color spread and their shape depends on

the method used. In the second process the material is immersed 15-30 minutes.

■ Techniques for masking areas of the material with wax were developed in Indonesia. They are known as batik. The traditional patterns of batik will not be a part of this activity. Only the basic idea of masking with wax will be used. Household candles (paraffin) and beeswax candles will both be appropriate.

Teaching suggestions

■ Dye can be applied in many different ways. Students should be encouraged to experiment with various tools and methods. The following suggestions could be made or students directed to discover them for themselves.

● Spray dye onto the fabric.

● Use a stick to blob dye, the deeper the stick is dipped, the bigger the blob. Different sizes of sticks and whether the stick is sharpened or unsharpened affect the shapes and sizes of blobs, too.

● Tilt the frame and let the dye run.

● Brush the dye onto the cloth.

● Dye from one side only, dye around the edges, dye on a diagonal, or dye just at the corners.

● Fold and dip the materials into the dye. (Inner layers of cloth absorb less dye than the outer layers.)

● Fold in a zig zag pattern.

● Fold lengthwise and diagonally.

● Fold triangularly six or seven times and dip just the corners.

● Fold lengthwise and crosswise into a square, then once more lengthwise and crosswise and once diagonally. Dip just the corners.

● Roll a long strip and dip each end (or bend and dip center portions).

● Roll and bind with string. The pressure of the binding protects the material from the action of the dye. Bind diagonally. Criss cross bindings.

● Bring all four corners of the cloth into the middle, fold the material lengthwise and crosswise, then roll it up, bind, and dye it. The tighter the binding, the clearer are the masked areas.

- Pick up the material in the middle and double it over in thick radial folds. Bind and dye.
- Fold into accordion pleats and bind with string.

■ Masking with wax or batik techniques can be done in a variety of ways. When dripping the wax onto the cloth, hold the candle close to the cloth. If it has to fall too far, the wax cools in the air and it won't have sufficient adhesion to stick to the cloth and mark it properly. After dyeing, all wax can be removed by rinsing it in hot water or by laying layers of porous paper like newsprint on both sides of the cloth and ironing the wax onto the paper. The following methods of masking with wax are suggested:
- Drop wax at random or in rows (patterns) or in rings.
- Mask for one color, mask again, and dip in or blob on a second color or a third.
- Rotate the cloth under a dripping candle to form radial designs.
- Tilt the fabric on a frame and let the wax run when it hits.
- Make a pointed wooden tool, heat it in a flame, and dip into liquid wax. The size of the blob depends on how deep the tool is dipped. Patterns can then be created by dipping and dobbing.
- Pour large quantities of wax onto cloth. Dip in cold water and crack. When the material is dyed the color penetrates the cracks and soaks into the fabric.
- Lay two pieces of cloth together and pour wax onto the top one. When they are separated, the wax is left in patches and the partial masking of the lower piece of cloth creates blurred outlines and random patterning.
- Combine wax masking ideas with the dyeing techniques suggested above.
- Pour wax onto the cloth with a heated spoon. Let it run.
- Make stamps from wood or metal, heat and dip in wax.

Suggested art activity
Have the student select one or two dyeing techniques and try them.

Alternative art activities
■ Have the student try additional techniques or make up some of his own.
■ Have the whole class contribute one or more dyed pieces to be used in a wall hanging. The teacher might sew the pieces together on a sewing machine and hang it on a long stick of bamboo or a rod.

Evaluation

When the student has successfully completed the decorative dyeing of at least one piece of cloth using a suggested technique or variation of it, the objective has been achieved.

Other things to consider

■ Vocabulary: dyeing, dobbing, batik, tie/dye, binding, masking.
■ Art materials needed: dyes, frames, cotton cloth, paraffin wax, candles, iron, newsprint paper, and dowel sticks.
■ Resource materials: Books on batik and tie/dye along with textile design are readily available in libraries and could be used for additional ideas or illustrations.
■ People who might have need for the concept: fabric designers, teachers.

LEVEL 6   # ACTIVITY 151

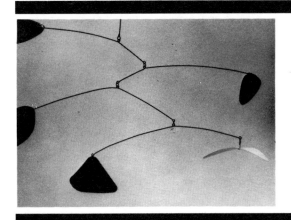

Concept taught by this activity: Created forms can be stationary or have movement.

Objective: The student creates forms that are stationary (stabiles) and forms that have movement (mobiles).

A sample lesson plan for achieving the objective:

Teacher preparations
This concept will be done in a period of two days—the first day students will make mobiles and the second day they will make stabiles.
■ Exhibit pictures of mobiles and stabiles (or just sculpture) or samples of such.
■ For the exercises suggested in this lesson have ten straws for each student (plastic), one popsicle stick for each student, scissors, glue (one bottle for four students), a spool of thread (one for four students), crayons, pins, pencils, tempera paints, brushes, cardboard, construction paper, and the numbers ten, eleven, and twelve.
■ The teacher should have stiff wire 8″ long, thin cardboard with two small shapes 3″ by 3″ and one large shape 5″ by 5″ cut out of it, and a few pins.

Teaching suggestions
■ What are all of the things requiring balance? (Scales, teeter-totters, airplanes, tight-rope walkers, skiers are a few.) What are the ways those things get balanced? (Skiers use poles; on a teeter-totter the heavier person moves closer to center, and so forth.) (Ask similar questions about space, movement and change.)
■ The discussion might go as follows: "Does anyone know what a mobile is?" (A mobile is sculpture that moves.) "What things in nature have movement?" "Is a mobile like

any of them?" "What makes a mobile move?" Since a mobile is almost always in perfect physical balance, it is also usually in visual balance and harmony.
● Help students think about such things as the swooping flight of a bird, a leaf falling, a flag fluttering and a waterfall—and that these are all movements which give them a great deal of interest or excitement.
● After they've given some of their ideas, ask such questions as: "How does a swooping flight of a bird affect its appearance?" "Is there a feeling to the movement?" "Is it different from the kind of mood or feeling of a flowing stream?" "How?"
● Wind up with the idea that mobiles are created for the sake of movement and each has particular ways in which it moves that capture an observer's attention. Ask: "Are mobiles related to sculpture, painting, drawing, or design?" "How?" (The students should get involved in stating why they think so or what makes mobiles relate to these other art forms.)
■ Ask class: "What about the space around the mobile?" "Or the space that surrounds each piece?" "Are they important?" "Why?"
■ Take the two 3″ by 3″ small shapes that you cut out as directed in the class preparation section and tie a thread to a straight pin, stick the pin into the edge of one of the cardboard shapes, then suspend it where it will move freely (you can thumbtack the end of the string to the ceiling or the arch of a doorway).
■ Let the class talk about the space around the shape.
● Doesn't it take on a life of its own?
● What about the space between the doorway—doesn't it seem different?
■ Now, take the other cardboard shape (contrasting design, 5″ by 5″ and suspend it in the same way near the first.
● Get the students involved and aware of how the two mobiles move independently, in a different manner from each other, and how they move at different rates of speed.
● Move the two pieces toward and away from each other. (a) See if students notice how the space in between

Suggested art activity

Make a large or more advanced mobile. (Hand out ten plastic straws to each student, the thin cardboard 12'' by 12'', mixed tempera, straight pins, and brushes.) Encourage students to remember everything they have talked about: mood, movement, space, color, balance. Have them cut out shapes from the cardboard and tie the thread to the pin and stick the pin in the cardboard. Then tie the other end of thread to the straw. They can stick two straws together to make them longer. The teacher can slice the straw ends to hold a shape using an exacto knife.

Alternative art activities

- Additional experiences might be enjoyed by some in either stabile or mobile projects. Altering materials and size are major change factors.
- Have students that have a strong interest in this activity build a scrapbook of pictures of mobiles and stabiles with the names of the artists that made them.

Evaluation

The student who is able to create a piece of sculpture which moves freely (mobile) with natural air currents has implemented the concept satisfactorily. Balance, design, and color are probably factors that influence the appearance of their mobiles and should be discussed.

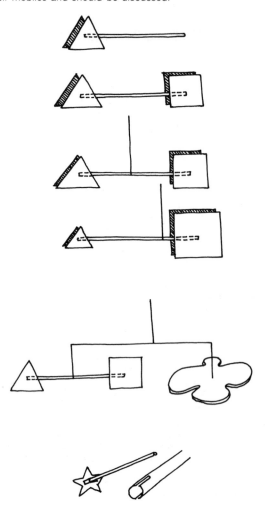

becomes involved in the movement and forms. (b) Discuss the importance of balance when two shapes are suspended from the same string. Review formal and informal balance (symmetrical and asymmetrical).

- For each student hand out two pieces of white construction paper 5'' by 7'', one bottle of glue for every four students, one popsicle stick, scissors, a pencil, and a spool of thread.
- Tell them to cut two pairs of shapes. Example: two triangles and two squares. Glue the two triangles together at one end of the stick, having the stick in between the two triangles. Have them do the same on the other side with their other shape (the two squares). See that one of the shapes is larger than the other.
- Have them tie a string (not too tight) in the middle and try to balance by moving the balancing string toward one end or the other until the stick is horizontal.
- Take one of the student's mobiles.
  - Tie it to one end of an 8 inch piece of wire (strong enough not to bend).
  - Now take the big shape you made under class preparation and balance it on the other end of the wire. Ask them: "What kind of balance is this?" (asymmetrical)
  - Have them color their shapes with their crayons and try to maintain the balance with value and color.
- Look at pictures of sculpture or of stabiles and discuss how they are different from the mobiles they have made. Discuss ways in which some forms appear to be moving when they are not, for example, a foreign race car, a rocket ship or jet fighter, and some forms of sculpture which have implied movement. Recall exercises with paper sculpture or construction which resulted in a type of stabile. Discuss Calder's mobiles and stabiles—their likenesses and differences.
- These factors they have learned will become more complex and more interesting if they construct larger and more creative mobiles. Just for a warm-up, hand out a piece of lined paper and ask them to write down everything they could use to make a mobile (sticks, twigs, fingernail files, wires, straws, fishing hooks, Christmas balls, popcorn balls, bells, sea shells, kitchen utensils, wood, cardboard, metal washers and nuts, cork, spools, and small pieces of pottery).

Other things to consider

- Vocabulary: movement, stabile, mobile, sculpture, rhythm, balance, informal balance, formal balance, symmetrical, and asymmetrical.
- Art materials needed: crayons, tempera, brushes, paper, cardboard, thread, wire, glue, straws, pins, and pencils.
- Pictures of sculpture, stabiles, and mobiles. See the works of Alexander Calder and Henry Moore (books and periodicals on these men are available in most public libraries).
- Many "baby departments" in stores have interesting commercial mobiles to hang over cribs. If you don't want to purchase such a visual aid, a store may let you borrow one for demonstrations.
- People who might have need for the concept: sculptors, artists that create mobiles, interior designers, product designers, set designers.

LEVEL 6   # ACTIVITY 152

Concept taught by this activity: Accurately rendering the position of an object and its parts in space can improve the quality of a drawing.

Objective: The quality of the student's drawings is noticeably improved as a result of his learning to accurately render the position of an object and its parts in space.

Sample lesson plan for achieving the objective:

Teacher preparations
■ Collect and display prints and colored photographs recommended or located in the school's media center.
■ Become thoroughly acquainted with the informational part of this activity.
■ Prepare a grid on acetate that students can lay over prints and photographs.

Teaching suggestions
Note: One of the keys to learning to draw accurately is developing the ability to visually and mentally judge the relative position of all parts of a subject in space. If one is drawing a dog, for example, the position and angle of the head in relation to the feet, knees, shoulders, hips, and tail must be carefully analyzed. Artists often do quick little line

drawings called action studies. In these drawings artist works only on the position of his model and earnestly attempts the placement of each part in the right relationship to every other part. Is the foot to the right or left of the head? Are the neck and shoulders perpendicular to each other? Is one wrist higher or lower than the other? These are the kinds of

questions the artist is asking himself as he compares parts of his subject to each other. The use of a grid to look through can be quite helpful in making such decisions.
■ Show the class some large colored photographs of animals. Discuss what makes some of them harder to draw than others. See if anyone has had difficulty at one time or another in drawing animals walking or running. Discuss reasons why, in relation to the concept.
■ Have students do a quick drawing of a duck walking or a bird perched on a limb. Look at some pictures of ducks walking or birds perching *after* the students finish their drawings. Discuss where the feet and legs of a bird are in relation to the body. Because the student hasn't become accustomed to checking the relative positions of parts of his subject he probably draws the legs and feet like figure A rather than figure B (see adjacent illustration). He ignored the upper part of the bird's leg and left off the knee joint.

■ Lay the grid over prints or photographs and talk about those parts of various subjects which students might need to visually analyze more carefully than others.
■ Practice a series of action drawings taking just two or three minutes on each. Use students in the class as subjects. Work only on the relative position of parts of the body. Discuss results pointing out common problems or where students as a group needed to look more carefully.

Suggested art activity
Select a human subject or some other animal and draw it doing something (show it in action).

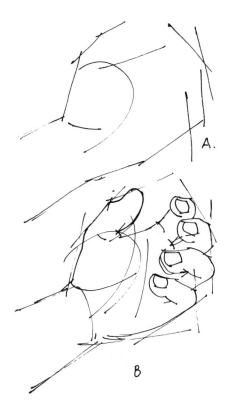

A.

B

Alternative art activities
- Do a relief sculpture of some animal running, grazing, bucking, or some other action.
- Make your own grid and compare two different drawings of the same subject (with the help of the grid as opposed to drawing without it).
- Draw your own hand. See its "total shape" in space first (no fingers, nails, or other details). Check angles, proportion, and "gesture." After the basic "layout" is completed, put in the details.

Evaluation

When the student demonstrates an ability to better analyze the relative positions of parts of a figure to its whole, then the objective has been achieved.

Other things to consider

- Vocabulary: render, space, analyze, action study.
- Art materials needed: drawing and painting media plus sculpture materials which can be easily carved.
- Prints:
  Dempsey and Firpo by Bellows
  Oath of the Horatii by David
  St. Joseph by De La Tour
  Fighting Horses by Gericault
  Young Hare by Durer
  Christina's World by Wyeth
  Knockout by Morreau
  Birds in Bamboo Tree by Koson
  Breezing Up by Homer
- Book: *The Art of Responsive Drawing* by Nathan Goldstien
- People who might have need for the concept: painter, illustrator, industrial designer, printmaker.

LEVEL 6   ACTIVITY 153

Concept taught by this activity: Radial forms may be open or closed, natural or man-made.

Objective: The student demonstrates an awareness of how radial forms may be open or closed, natural or man-made.

A sample lesson plan for achieving the objective:

Teacher preparations
- Set desks or students in semicircle for easy discussion.
- Set up a table and have objects described in the teaching activity in order with written notes for each object.
- If possible, have large photographs or pictures of objects similar to the ones described in the discussion activity placed around the room.
- Gather and get ready the materials used in the activities: paper, scissors, rubber or styrofoam stamps, ink pads, cut vegetables and fruits, thin tempera, and shallow paper plates.
  Note: Substitutions on suggested materials may be just as suitable or more so than this list.

Teaching suggestions
- To get a definition of *radial form* the following is suggested:
  - Show objects such as flowers, cut fruit (orange), a section of a log, the end of a pencil, a wheel.
  - Ask questions such as: "What do all of these have in common with the wheel?" "How are they different?" "Can you see any design or pattern that is similar in all of these things?" "Has anyone heard of the word *radial*?" "or have you heard of the word *radiate*?" "How are *radial* and *radiate* related?"
  - Show objects that are not radial forms: a square, triangle, oval (pictures or cut-out shapes). Lead a

discussion of how these are different from radial forms.
- Concept of *open, closed*
  - Show objects side by side or alternate showing open and closed radial objects: open—ripple, thumbprint; closed—pictures of octopus, starfish, daisy, orange slice, wheel, picture of cut-up pie or a snap. Have them look at each very closely and try to remember them.
  - Ask, "What do you suppose is meant by open and closed forms?" "How did these pictures show a different use of space?" "Were some open?" "some closed?"
  - Point to objects again and have students designate which are open and which are closed forms.
  - Discuss feelings received when looking at different forms: "How do you feel when you look at a closed form?" "at an open form?" "How does the eye travel?"
  - If possible, pass the objects around for closer observation.

- There was one other difference in the objects we've looked at and talked about that gives us one more way of being art critics. Some were natural and some were man-made. What is meant by these two words? Discuss objects in terms of *natural* and *man-made* until awareness is evident.

- Direct students through questioning techniques to conclude that an axis can be: (a) a point from which something rotates, for example, the earth rotating on its axis, a wheel around an axle, and the second vertebra of the neck that serves as a pivot for the head to turn on; (b) a straight line that divides something symmetrically, for example, the backbone of vertebrates, the stem of a leaf, and the trunk of a tree; (c) a line which bisects parallel cords of a curve at right angles and divides them into two symmetrical parts and a line used as the basis of measurements in an architectural drawing. Discuss the examples used throughout the room. See if students can discover most of the examples around them.

- Ask questions such as: ''Why would artists need to know about an axis?'' (''Can an artist be aware of his world without such a knowledge?'' ''How frequently is the axis used in man and in nature?'') ''Would an inventor need to know about it?'' ''How about designers of homes, cars, and machines?'' ''Are they artists?'' Discuss the following concept in science: The linea alba is the axis for the entire human body.
Note: The linea alba is an almost imaginary line but it may be seen by following down the center line of the skull, the line dividing the nostrils, through the small depression under the nose, the piece of skin between your two front teeth, and the dimple in your chin; all are part of the linea alba line.

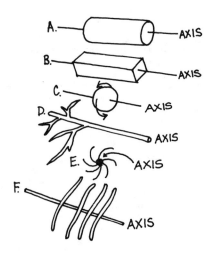

Suggested art activity
Give each student paper and scissors—preferably large sheets of butcher paper or newsprint or smaller lightweight paper from the school supplies. Have students fold as shown and then cut out their own shapes. Emphasize that the pattern cut is mirror-imaged or repeated several times in the final ''snowflake.'' This is one quality of radial forms.

Alternative art activities
- Give students rubber stamps of letters or imprint small objects and have them make radial shapes or designs by making a mark on medium weight paper and then stamping images around the point or radius. Ask each student to show his print and tell if it is open or closed, as a radial form. (This project could also be done on paper cut in circles.)

- In winter, have students use their own bodies to create radial designs in the snow. Divide the class in groups of six and lead class in several solutions.
  - Have students stand facing the center of the circle and put their arms into the circle.
  - Have one child as a radius stand in the middle of the circle, the others putting one foot next to his, making a form.

- After demonstrating these solutions, allow students to experiment on their own, using whatever number of students that works. Allot a certain amount of time and challenge students to find as many radial forms as they can in the allotted time. Allow time for several applications: sitting, standing, lying on the ground.

- Use vegetables or fruits cut crosswise, wood, or rolled corrugated cardboard cut crosswise as stamps to dip in shallow paper plates of thinned-down tempera paints. Have students stamp on fairly heavy paper.

- Use radial forms to relate fractions in math.

- Have students make some paper and divide the space into sections with just lines and without creating *any* illusions of space or depth. (Some will be created regardless of what they do.) Then have them create some new space divisions but this time using one or two that become an axis for other lines. Discuss what happens in terms of space created. (The illusion of depth should be much greater in the second design.)

- Use mirrors to show how radial forms may be made by repeating a given form or line. You may discuss symmetry in this manner as mentioned above in math to show fractions.

Evaluation

Keep track of student responses in discussion and examine radial designs until you are satisfied that the students' awareness has been changed.

Other things to consider

- Vocabulary: illusion, space, depth, axis, axle, rotate, symmetrical, axis, symmetry, linea alba, bisect, parallel, natural, man-made, mirror image, open, closed.

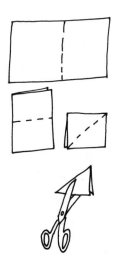

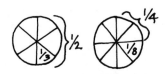

- Art materials needed: pencils, crayons, paper, scissors, rubber stamps or gadgets for imprinting, ink pads or tempera paint, and small paper plates.
- Visual aids: pictures of fruit, wheels, flowers, and other radial or nonradial forms, both natural and man-made, open or closed.
- Prints:

  Sacrament Last Supper by Dali (figure of Christ serves as an axis)

  Small Crucifixion by Grunewald (the cross is an axis)

  Nude Descending # 2 by Duchamp (the inferred diagonal line going through the hips of the figure is an axis)

  The Brooklyn Bridge by Stella (the center vertical line is an axis)

  I and the Village by Chagall   (contain radial

  Numbering at Bethlehem by Brueghel   designs and axis

  Head of a Man by Klee   examples)
- People who might have need for the concept: architect, sculptor, crafts designer, batik and tie/dye artist, industrial designer, potter.

LEVEL 6

ACTIVITY 154

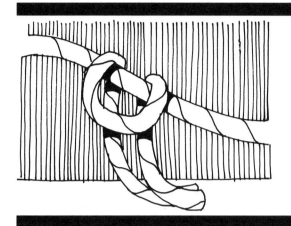

Concept taught by this activity: Wall hangings and a variety of forms can be created with macrame and knotting processes.

Objective: The student can tie from memory five of the basic knots for macrame.

A sample lesson plan for achieving the objective:

Teacher preparations
- Review the six types of knots, so that you can tie all of them.
- Obtain enough heavy cord so that each student will have enough to work with.
- Obtain tacking pins, enough for the whole class.

Teaching suggestions
- Cut a length of cord about 18 inches long as a holding cord for each of the students. Tie a knot as the first adjacent illustration shows and place two tacking pins through the knot to hold the cord.
- Next cut eight cords 24 inches long and attach them to the holding cord as illustrated in the second figure.
- Horizontal double half hitch: follow the directions as illustrated in figures 4, 5, and 6. Take the cord that is farthest to the right and pull it horizontally across the front of the rest of the cords that are hanging down (see figure 4). Take the next cord, the one that is now the farthest to the right, and loop it over the horizontal cord as is illustrated in figure 5. By repeating the same thing over and over, you then create the horizontal double half hitch (see

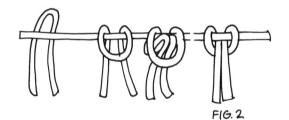

FIG. 2

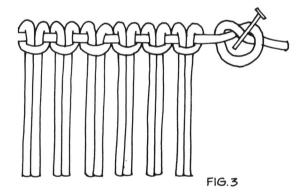

FIG. 3

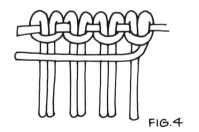

FIG. 4

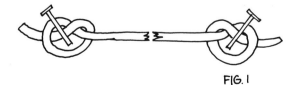

FIG. 1

figure 6). A continuation of it is illustrated in figures 7 and 8.

- Diagonal double half hitch: the only difference between the horizontal double half hitch and the diagonal double half hitch is the position in which the knot-bearing cord is held as the knotting is done (see figure 9). The designs in figures 10 and 11 can be done with the diagonal double half hitch knot.
- Vertical double half hitch: in the double half hitches that have been illustrated so far, the knot-bearing cord remains the same across a row or down a diagonal, while the knotting cords change with the completion of each knot. The process reverses in the vertical double half hitch. The knot-bearing cord changes at the completion of each knot, and the knotting cord remains the same (see figures 12, 13, 14, and 15). Starting from the left, take the first cord and run it in back of the second cord to start the knot as illustrated in figure 12. After making the knot as illustrated in figure 12, push it tightly to the top of the knot-bearing cord and then move to the next knot-bearing cord to the right as illustrated in figure 13. This process is repeated with each of the cords hanging vertically and then the process can be reversed as illustrated in figure 15. Figure 15 shows the vertical double half hitch going from right to left.
- Half knot: the half knot requires four cords. The two on the outside are tied around the two in the center as illustrated in figures 16, 17, and 18. The starting of the half knot is shown in figure 16. Figure 17 shows the half knot before it is tightened. The half knot with one tightened and another tied, now becomes the square knot, making five basic knots that can be used in an unending variety of ways is shown in figure 18.

Suggested art activity
Make a wall hanging with the macrame process.

Alternative art activities
- Make holders for hanging potted plants.
- Make a purse or bag.
- Make a belt.

Evaluation

When the student is able to tie the five knots and create something with them, the objective has been achieved.

Other things to consider

- Vocabulary: knotting, macrame, horizontal, vertical, half hitch, square knot, sampler, holding cord.
- Art materials needed: pins and heavy cord such as jewt.
- Resources: instruction sheets on macrame knots are often available at crafts and novelty stores along with examples of articles that can be made.
- People who might have need for the concept: teachers, fabric designers.

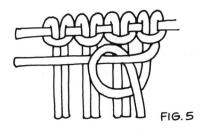

FIG. 5

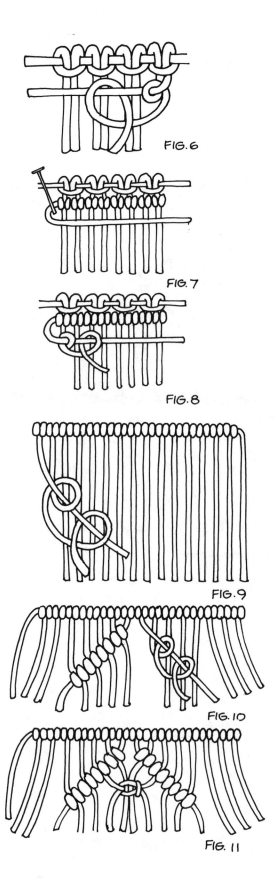

FIG. 6

FIG. 7

FIG. 8

FIG. 9

FIG. 10

FIG. 11

346

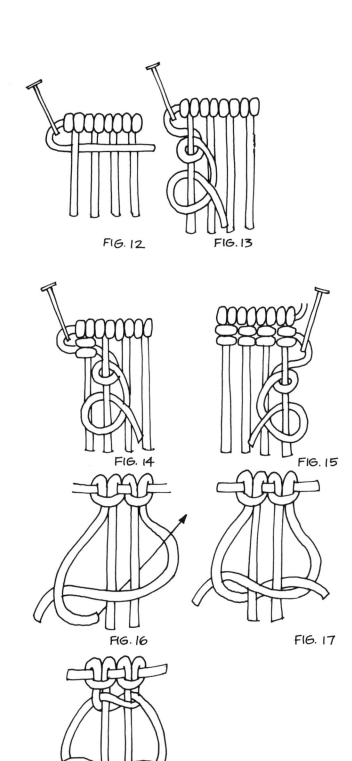

FIG. 12   FIG. 13

FIG. 14   FIG. 15

FIG. 16   FIG. 17

FIG. 18

LEVEL 6

ACTIVITY 155

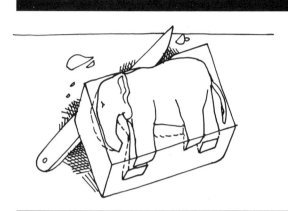

Concept taught by this activity: Sculpture can be created from pliable materials by carving, cutting, or scooping away.

Objective: The student will create a new form by carving, cutting, or scooping parts away from an original whole.

A sample lesson plan for achieving the objective:

Teacher preparations

Newspapers or other coverings should be placed on desks. Tools should be available for carving purposes. Pictures of things which appeal to the student as sculpture subjects should be displayed and pictures or, where possible, samples of student sculpture should also be available. Include examples of the in-the-round and relief types. Each student should be given paper and pencils to do small sketches of what he might like to create. Soft materials such as soap, wax, or clay blocks should be available for carving. A list of safety rules should be established and discussed thoroughly with the students, for example, not cutting towards a hand or thumb.

Teaching suggestions

- Discuss how carving parts away from the whole differs from their experience with clay or papier mâché (where they add to a form or build it up).
- Discuss the fact that with some materials one must be very careful not to carve away parts that cannot be replaced. ("If this was marble or stone and I cut too much away, what would I do?" "Can I stick more stone back on and have it look good?")
- Emphasize the need for advance planning and recommend a side view drawing which can be transferred (traced onto the material the student will eventually carve).
- If water base clay is available, have students shape it into a form that has about the same dimensions as a large bar of

hand soap. Let the clay then harden some until it holds its own shape but is easy to carve. (The advantage of clay is that it can be repaired if the student carves too much away. The student simply wraps a wet cloth around the form and leaves it a couple of hours or until it softens and then adds moist clay to it and starts over again with the mended section.) Wax can be repaired but it is more difficult to control because you have to heat it, and soap is just about impossible to mend once the mistake is made. In the latter case, the student's best alternative is to try to think of a new form which could still be carved from the soap or else just get a new bar.

- Encourage students to think of the textures associated with the animal or object they decide to carve and to pay close attention to proportion from top, side, front, and back views. This will help the student be more successful. Remember though, the focus is on the *carving process* and if he completes that he's fulfilled the objective of the activity. If clay is used, remember to save all scraps since they are re-usable. If the clay is to be kiln fired, keep the thickness of any parts limited to ½" to ¾", otherwise the objects will likely break or crack in the firing.
- Demonstrate the carving process if such an activity would seem helpful. Stress necessary safety factors.

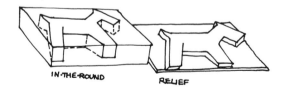

IN-THE-ROUND   RELIEF

Suggested art activity

For most students a relief type of sculpture may be preferred, especially if they want to carve an animal with long thin legs or neck. A plaque or relief kind of sculpture also lends itself to carving details such as a deer's horns or in capturing action such as a dog running. Discuss these ideas and alternatives with students but let them make the choice. In-the-round sculpture, you might note, is easier if a base is included (see illustrations).

Don't encourage students to "just do something easy." When the student wants help with his carving simply ask questions or discuss how the subject he has chosen "looks" so that his perception of it changes. Encourage students to individualize their choice of subject. Insects, flowers, reptiles, people, mammals, buildings, or anything that appeals to the student is suitable subject matter.

Alternative art activities
New experiences are possible simply by changing the kind of material carved, for example, wax and balsa wood.

Evaluation

The teacher can measure understanding of the concept by the students' work. If the student has demonstrated a good grasp of the subtractive process and what it involved, he has accomplished the objective. The *quality* of his product is *not* the issue.

Other things to consider

- Vocabulary: sculpture, subtractive process, additive process, in-the-round, relief, carving, realistic, and abstract.
- Art materials needed: wire ceramics tools (where available), knives, chisels, spoons, and objects for making texture. Any other tool for carving, scooping, or cutting. Newspapers, soft wax, large bars of Ivory soap, blocks of clay, and paper and pencils.
- Pictures of relief and in-the-round sculpture pictures of subjects which might be of interest to the class. Samples of sculpture.
- People who might have need for the concept: industrial designer, wood carver, sculptor, arts craftsman, jewelry maker.

LEVEL 6

ACTIVITY 156

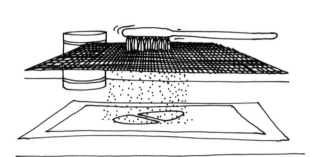

Concept taught by this activity: Pictures or repeat designs can be created by the stencil process.

Objective: The student creates pictures or repeat designs utilizing the stencil process.

A sample lesson plan for achieving the objective:

Teacher preparations
Have examples of signs, designs, and pictures created with the stencil process (silk screen and serigraph included) readily available.

Teaching suggestions
■ The stencil process may be introduced by comparing it to the concepts on shadow and photograms; for example, a shadow exists when something comes between a light source (sun) and a surface (ground). By causing something to come between paint being applied and a surface, an image is created, very much like a shadow, this time caused by paint—not light. Spray paint (using spray can of paint or a toothbrush and screen) past a ball or some shape and ask students how this idea could be used to teach about shadow. Then introduce the concept of "stencil."
■ Discuss the terms used: "Has anyone ever heard of the word *stencil*?" "What is a stencil?" "Is it anything like a silk screen or a serigraph?" "What is a silk screen?" "a serigraph?" "Have you ever seen stencil paper?" "Have you seen someone paint the address on the curb in front of their home?" "Have you seen stencils with the alphabet on them?"
Note: A stencil is made by taking a wax-coated paper or woven fabric that ink won't penetrate, cutting out letters or designs in it, and then brushing, spraying, or forcing ink or paint through the openings and onto a surface underneath it.

■ Have the students cut holes with interesting shapes in oak tag or some other kind of stiff paper. Keep sharp, crisp edges that will reproduce well. Shapes can be cut with sharp scissors or exacto knives. Print the design on another piece of paper by using a bristle brush and thick opaque tempera. Dab the paint on. Hold the brush in an upright position. Dragging the brush will pull paint under the edge of the stencil and destroy crisp edges. Be careful to lift the stencil straight up from the page rather than dragging it across the wet paint. Some prefer dipping a sponge in tempera and imprinting on top of the stencil. Soft chalks, wax crayons, and felt tip markers can also be used for stencil marking.
■ Using stencils with spatter paint techniques:
To spatter paint a stencil, you may drag a toothbrush loaded with paint across a wire screen, thus spattering paint onto the stencil. Spraying the paint can be done with a fly sprayer or small atomizer. Even the squeeze bottle which is used for deodorants and other similar products will work.

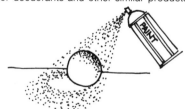

When designs are made in the stencil, doing a repeat kind of pattern increases the aesthetic quality of the finished product. The child is not likely to get very excited about reproducing one little shape. Encourage each child to create his own picture or design.
■ The commerical method of using a stencil is called silk screen and the printmaker artist's method for using stencil is called serigraph.

Silk screening uses a stencil which is supported on a screen of tightly stretched fabric. Ink is forced through this

351

fabric screen by means of a squeegee. The stencil, of course, blocks out the print so that the desired motif is printed. The whole technique need use only inexpensive materials, most of which can be made by students themselves.

To make the screen, first build a rigid rectangular frame using wood approximately 1¼'' x ¾'' and being careful to make the corners solid and square. A piece of finely woven silk, nylon, or organdy is then stretched tightly over this frame. Since this will affect all later prints, take care to make the fabric as taut as possible. It may be stapled snugly to the frame when wet so that natural shrinkage will tighten the screen. A very good method of stretching is to cut a groove all around the frame, place the fabric on top and then force a heavy cord into the groove so that it binds the fabric to the frame. This cord can be removed easily and the screen further tightened should this later be necessary.

The squeegee is ideally made of rubber although a wooden paddle tapered at one edge will suffice. The rubber squeegee used in cleaning windows is satisfactory. This squeegee should be a little shorter than the smaller inside dimension of the screen frame. In planning the print, it must be kept in mind that the inside dimensions of the frame are the critical ones.

The stencil can be cut from thin but nonabsorbent paper such as fingerpainting paper or from a commercial film. It can be as elaborate as desired and because of the screen support, might have doughnutlike objects enclosed in open spaces. Fasten the stencil to the outside of the frame with masking tape.

A spoonful of prepared screen ink or very thick tempera paint is placed in the screen and to one side. The squeegee pulls the ink across the screen. Apply considerable pressure and hold the squeegee at an angle of approximately 45° Only one application across the screen should be necessary.

Suggested art activity
Prepare a sketch or drawing and utilize the stencil process in creating a stencil design.

Alternative art activities
Additional experiences with the process implementing new or different designs.

Evaluation

When the student has created a picture or design using the stencil process, then the objective has been achieved.

Other things to consider

- Vocabulary: stencil, silk screen, imprint, serigraph, process, technique, opaque, squeegee.
- Art materials needed: tempera, oak tag, drawing paper, soft chalk, crayons, felt tip markers, sponges, scissors, cutting knives, and materials for making a silk screen for those who are interested.
- Resources: Books on printmaking, illustrations and advertisements utilizing silk screen; a visit to a professional printer who uses the silk screen process in graphics could show students how the process works at a commercial level.
- People who might have need for the concept: artists that do printmaking, serigraphs, and deal with art history.

LEVEL 6 ACTIVITY 157

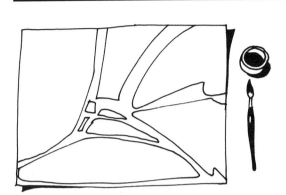

Concept taught by this activity: Lines and shapes can be used to create the illusion of rhythm and motion and lead the eye in a certain direction.

Objective: The student uses linear shapes to create rhythm and motion and to lead the eye in certain directions.

A sample lesson plan for achieving the objective:

Teacher preparations
■ Arrange desks so students face each other.
■ Materials: prepare tempera (any color) the day before (10 to 15 bottles or containers). Have 10 to 20 disposable aluminum pans available. Before class begins have one bottle and one pan for every four desks. Cutting from cardboard, have one-inch squares and two-inch squares for each student. Cut out one-inch circles, a good handful for each student, and place in bags for each, pass them out when ready to do the fourth exercise in the "teaching suggestions" section (use colored or black paper). Cut paper for each student (5" by 7" white paper). Cut paper 18" by 24", one sheet for two students (white). Have a collection of the following kinds of things with several of each: leaves of several varieties, grainy pieces of wood, pictures of wavy water or ripples, sea shells, and flowers with petals. Have these words on paper: progressive, alternative, flowing, repetitive.
■ Collect and display appropriate prints and illustrations.

Teaching suggestions
■ Begin the discussion period by asking: "Do you know what motion and rhythm are?" Lead them to recognize that motion is movement, and any kind of movement with some kind of repetition can have rhythm. Hand out a lined piece of paper and ask them to write down all the things they can think of that have rhythm and motion. (Give them one

minute.) Examples: heart beat, drum beat, violin, lightning, streets, writing, hopping, water, wood grain, grass, insect wings (their buzzing and their texture), mountains, rain, fences, train tracks, and inside a piano. "What about a girl's curly hair?" "Or objects in the classroom?" "What happens when you drop a rock in a pond?" (Are the ripples rhythmical compared to sound waves?) Ask if they've ever seen a close-up of the structured lines in an insect wing.
● "What kind of texture does an insect wing or any kind of wing have?"
● "Isn't there a linear rhythm?"
● "Can rhythm be anything other than a beat?" (Rhythm can be a sound, motion, line, or texture.)
■ Talk about four specific types of rhythm.
● Repetitive: AAAA; Hop, Hop, Hop, Hop
● Progressive: ABCD; squatting to standing up
● Alternative: ABAB; Hop, Jump, Hop, Jump

- Flowing: ABC, ABC; walking

Have a few try and clap the above rhythms with their hands. Then you can show them and have the whole class clap them out.

Read poetry that has rhythm. Pick four students and let them try (individually) to create with their bodies one of the four rhythms. Or, hand students a piece of plain paper and crayon or pencil and a lined piece of paper. Ask them to write down (on the lined paper) the different kinds of lines from nature that can make rhythm. Examples: wavy, curved, straight, horizontal, vertical, diagonal, and circles. This was to open their minds to the notion that rhythm or movement can be implied.

■ Turn to the collection of leaves, wood, words, shells, or other objects. Create a rhythm or motion from what the textures and the words suggest. For example, the rhythm in a leaf vein or a wood grain.

■ Hand out the 5" by 7" paper to each student. Hand out 1" circles to each student. Remind them of all the different rhythms they've talked about and have them create one using dots. Collect and show some to the class. Ask them if any relate to forms in nature. Do any remind them of a certain texture or rhythm? (wood, grass, feather) "Which one, if any, is repetitive, progressive, alternative, or flowing?"

Note: The students now know about motion and rhythm. By using patterns of rhythm and different kinds of lines they can create a direction or make their eye move in a certain direction.

■ Hold up one of their works (from the above exercise) that makes your eye move to the right or left, center, up or down. Ask the students, "What is it in this picture that makes your eyes move in a certain direction?" Do the same with one more picture. "Which of the four rhythms (progressive, alternative, flowing, or repetitive) shows direction most?" (progressive) Tell them that the following are ways to create progressive rhythm, to help lead the eye:
- Small to large (progressive large to small).
- Light to dark (a hole)—Pressure of brush, chalk or stamp.
- A few to a lot—(density).
- Size variation.
- Converging lines.

■ Discuss handwriting as rhythmic line and direction.

■ Hand out one 18" by 24" piece of paper to two students. Pour the bottles of tempera into the pans. (One bottle and one pan for every four students.) Students should already have the 1" by 1" and the 2" by 2" squares of cardboard on the desk. Tell them to dip the cardboard in the paint and imprint linear patterns that lead your eye in certain directions. Have them practice density, progression, light to dark, and plaid textures.

■ Develop the notion that whenever an artist places anything on his paper or canvas, even a single brush stroke, to some degree it changes everything that was already there because the environment is no longer just as it was. (It takes a great deal of experience to be that aware, but many artists are.) Then ask the students, "What's the simplest picture you could make that would give the viewer some sort of feeling for direction and distance (or measurement)?" Have the students try it. When they get through see if anyone has included just two dots in their picture. If no one thought of this simple solution, see if you can lead them to it by having them try just two different shapes, then two shapes that look alike, two lines exactly alike, and finally two dots. Help students to recognize that even when you have nothing more than two dots distance and direction are implied. Just as soon as more than one dot is applied to a surface, direction is implied and distance and measurement are also implied.

■ This concept and these exercises are not only related to art, but also to dance—where they use their bodies and improvise to something intangible, their bodies also may react in a manner never done before by them. Rhythm and motion are present in student's reaction to music—they clap to different beats and to symbols or words (see book, Threshold to Music). In physical education, rhythm and motion are part of coordination. The concept is also related to language arts—students have to use their minds and search for nouns and adjectives not only verbally but artistically.

■ It may be appropriate to introduce the students to the idea that one of the main reasons for *design* or *composition* in art is to *control the eye movement of those who look at the art.*

Suggested art activity

Discuss ways in which artists of all kinds, for example, sculptors, painters, architects, commercial artists, designers, and city planners, utilize rhythm and movement in the works they produce. Have the student select an artist whose work he enjoys and create a design, picture, or form after the style of that artist, using line and shapes to create the illusion of rhythm and motion.

Alternative art activities

■ Lay acetate or transparent paper over artists' prints and trace shapes, values, or colors which form patterns and lead the eye in a certain direction.

■ Draw or paint a picture and/or design which contains rhythmical elements.

Evaluation

The students' ability to create rhythm and movement in the exercises determines whether or not each clearly understood the concept.

Other things to consider

■ Vocabulary: rhythm, movement, alternating, progressive, repetitive, and flowing.

■ Art materials needed:
  ● Paper 18" by 24"—one for two students.
  ● Paper 5" by 7"—one for each student.
  ● Tempera, paint, bottles, aluminum pans, scissors, any tool such as magic marker, crayons, pens, chalk.
  ● Lined paper—one sheet for each student (and pencils for each)
  ● Cardboard (thick)

■ Prints:
  The Wave by Hokusai (Print not in program)
  Birds in Bamboo Tree by Koson
  Autumn by Koryusai
  Blue Boy by Gainsborough
  Snap the Whip by Homer
  Sinbad the Sailor by Klee
  Nude Descending #2 by Duchamp
  Brooklyn Bridge by Stella
  View of Toledo by El Greco
  Apples and Oranges by Cezanne
  Mural by Pollock

■ Other audiovisual materials:
  Poetry:
  "Taxi" and "Barefoot Days" by R. Field
  "Hoppity" by A. A. Milne
  "Merry Go Round" by Dorothy Baruch
  Books:
  Child Craft Poetry, Vol. I
  Threshold to Music, Teacher's Edition

■ People who might have need for the concept: painter, illustrator, commercial artist, printmaker, sculptor, interior designer, landscape architect. This concept would have a rather universal application in almost every form of art.

LEVEL 6

ACTIVITY 158

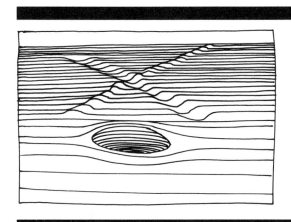

Concept taught by this activity: Lines which are actual or inferred can be used to visually warp a surface and thus create the illusion of depth.

Objective: The student uses lines to make a drawing surface appear warped and have depth or space where none really exists.

A sample lesson plan for achieving the objective:

Teacher preparations
Provide drawing paper and pencil, crayon, or ink media for making line drawings. Collect prints and other visuals needed.

Teaching suggestions
- Brainstorm on all the different ways one can take a flat surface like a piece of paper and make it three dimensional (fold it, cut and paste it, wrinkle it, and so forth). Discuss whether or not it is possible to create illusions of space, depth, or form using nothing but lines (converging lines, objects drawn in perspective, and so on).
- Ask the question: "Is it possible to make a flat surface appear dimensional without drawing realistically?" "For instance, could you make pencil lines in such a way that a flat surface appeared hilly or bumpy?" "mountainous or filled with holes and caverns?" Have students try this on the blackboard.
- Look at topographical maps and discuss how the lines create the illusion of dimension on a flat surface. The weather maps shown on television illustrating the isobars and the jet stream are another example of how lines seem to give dimension to a flat surface. Geological maps describing rock strata do the same thing.
- Have students take small (about six inches square) shapes and line them with a ruler at 1/16" or 1/8" intervals—just

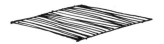

straight lines. Next have them bend and warp the lined paper and watch the lines. Next tell them to *permanently* warp the surface and do a drawing of the lines.

Suggested art activity
Have students experiment with line drawings to see if they can discover ways to create the illusion of dimension on their paper. Have them imagine the surface as being warped, mountainous, or full of holes, and then mentally trace the imaginary forms with their pencil, pen, or crayon making a striped effect as in the illustrations provided. Encourage students to try several versions that are different from each other and from every other student's, and to take patient effort to keep lines close together—detailed.

Alternative art activities
- Have students do two line drawings of a deep well: one in which the artist is looking down into it, the other in which the artist is standing on the bottom looking up.
- Draw lines which will give the impression of a specific object "under" the lines, for example, a pencil.

Evaluation

When the student can use lines to create the illusion of form or dimension on a flat surface, then the objective has been achieved.

Other things to consider

- Vocabulary: dimension, two dimensional, three dimensional, visual, visually, warp, distort.
- Art materials needed: drawing media and paper, topographical maps, and geological drawings of rock strata.
- Book: *Creative Line Design* by Rottger (Reinhold Pub.)
- Prints:
  Cheyt M by Vasarely
  Prodigal Son by Rembrandt
  Three Negro Boys by Watteau
  The Blue Cart by Van Gogh
- People who might have need for the concept: painters, illustrators, industrial designers, commercial artists, sculptors, designer craftsmen, jewelry makers. This concept would have a rather universal application in almost every form of art.

LEVEL 6

ACTIVITY 159

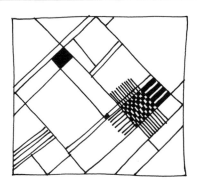

Concept taught by this activity: A balancing of complexity (detail) and simplicity is necessary in many works of art.

Objective: The student offsets details in an arrangement with areas that are comparatively simple so that a balance between the two is created.

A sample lesson plan for achieving the objective:

Teacher preparations
- Collect prints and other visuals for display and discussion.
- Create some examples of simplicity carried to the point of monotony or lack of interest and detail carried to the point of offense or chaos (see illustrations A and B for monotony).

Teaching suggestions
- Show the student a bold floral pattern used as a wall covering. Select one that would appeal to most students and yet would *not* be pleasing if one used it on all of the walls and on the drapes of a room. Discuss why the print appeals to them, where it could be used, and so forth.
- Brainstorm as to where the print or pattern would not be appropriate. Talk about how much of a room's surface could be covered with it and still have it be an enjoyable pattern. Develop the idea that the eye needs relief from detail just as the body needs an occasional rest from hard physical labor or vigorous exercise.
- Look at the artists' prints. Have the students point out the rest areas of each picture. Discuss what would happen to the arrangement if every space was as busy as those with the most detail.

Suggested art activity
Draw or paint a picture or create a design in which rest areas are carefully planned to complement areas of detail.

Alternative art activities
- Create a design or pattern with considerable detail in it. Then make one or two areas *much* more detailed so that "busy-ness" becomes a relative thing.
- Create a three-dimensional design utilizing the concept. (Use toothpicks, straws, colored poster board, construction paper, and similar items).
- Utilize the concept in a monoprint, vegetable, or gadget print.
- Do a fabric design (weaving, stitchery, or applique) utilizing the concept.

Evaluation

When the student purposefully creates a balance between detail and simplicity (rest areas), then the objective has been achieved.

Other things to consider

- Vocabulary: detail, simplicity, balancing, arrangement, rest areas, chaos, monotony.
- Art materials needed: appropriate drawing and painting equipment.
- Prints:
  Ice-Skating Palace by Bonnard
  The Smokers by Brouwer
  House at Aix by Cezanne
  Maas at Dordrecht by Cuyp
  City Hall in Rega by Feininger
  The Bullfight by Goya
  Knockout by Morreau
  Rockets and Blue Lights by Turner
  Lacemaker by Vermeer
  (Any work by Mondrian would be excellent examples of this.)

■ People who might have need for the concept: painter, industrial designer, sculptor, architect, city planner, landscape architect, interior designer, home economics teacher, art teacher. This concept would have a rather universal application in almost every form of art.

LEVEL 6

ACTIVITY 160

Concept taught by this activity: Objects usually appear bluer, grayer, and lighter as they get farther away, for example, sky, trees, buildings, mountains, and clouds.

Objective: The student will paint distant objects bluer, grayer, and lighter than those in the foreground to create illusions of depth or distance.

A sample lesson plan for achieving the objective:

Teacher preparations
Assemble appropriate prints and photographs illustrating the concept. Have painting materials ready.

Teaching suggestions
■ Have the students play with "visual metaphors" to teach the concept, for example, "A gray mountain far away . . . became the misty horizon's prey," or a simile such as: "The brightly colored airplane was as gray as its distance away," or "Distant colors so bright and gay can only be seen as light blue-gray."
■ Use a discussion period to determine how aware students already are of the concept. Has anyone looked at mountains that were far, far away? Did you notice what color they were? Do distant objects seem to appear different in color than the same things up close? How are they different? Does distance affect the appearance of things in any other way? (List the ways—color, shape, size, detail, value, grayness, and blueness.) Develop the notion that everything goes toward a middle value or neutral tint and shade.
■ Look at a variety of prints and photographs including some which *ignore* the concept. Discuss the application of the concept in each case and test students verbally to see if

they perceive the concept when it's used. Ask, "Who used the concept best?" "How can you tell?" "Do artists always intend to have great depth in their pictures?" "Why not?"

Suggested art activity
Paint a real or imaginary scene. Use color and value in such a way that the distant objects *really* look far away.

Alternative art activities
■ Tear shapes out of colored construction paper and create an imaginary landscape. Use the grayest and bluest paper for those shapes which are most distant and the brighter, darker, more intense colors for foreground objects.

Evaluation

When the student paints distant objects bluer, grayer, and lighter than objects up close, then the objective has been achieved.

Other things to consider

- Vocabulary: landscape, foreground, background, illusion.
- Art materials needed: crayons, watercolors, or tempera, construction paper, paste or glue.
- Prints:
  Blindman's Bluff by Fragonard
  Hudson River Logging by Homer
  The Return by Magritte
  Snap the Whip by Homer
  Tranquility by Gasser
  Peaceable Kingdom by Hicks
  The Scout by Remington
  The Gleaners by Millet
  Ville D'Avray by Corot
  Mona Lisa by da Vinci
  The Harvesters by Breughel
- Film: ''Discovering Perspective'' by Bailey Film Associates
- People who might have need for the concept: painter, illustrator, commercial artist, artists who draw, who do serigraphs and print making, and those who deal with art history and analysis.

LEVEL 6   ACTIVITY 161

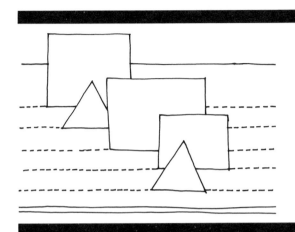

Concept taught by this activity: As the point where an object is touching ground or water gets higher on the picture plane, it appears farther away. (True only with objects on relatively flat surfaces.)

Objective: The student demonstrates an awareness that when the base of an object is raised on the picture plane it will appear farther away.

A sample lesson plan for achieving the objective:

Teacher preparations
Have appropriate materials ready, for example, drawing and painting materials, photographs and prints utilizing the concept.

Teaching suggestions
- Review some of the ways artists are able to create the illusion of depth. (Make certain *depth* and *illusion* are understood.) The students will likely mention such things as objects getting smaller, showing less detail, color and value changes, and overlapping. Refer students to prints which illustrate the concept and see if any can guess another way of creating a depth illusion.
- Have a student go to a window and lay a ruler or some other straight edge on the glass, but along the base of several objects he sees, starting with those closest to him and finishing with those farthest away. See if students notice that those objects which are farthest away start highest on the window pane. Place a sheet of tracing paper or acetate on top of a landscape, sea scene, or city scene, and rule lines indicating the base line of all major objects or shapes in the picture. Then number them in order from bottom to top. Ask the class if the numbering is also consistent with an indication of which objects are closest

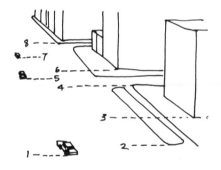

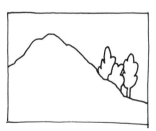

and which are farthest away. (They *should* be!)
- Look at the prints and photographs collected and see if students are now able to identify ways in which the concept has been used. Once the use of the concept is clearly recognized, ask questions such as: "Do artists *always* use this concept?" "Do they always *want* depth in their pictures?" (Note that many artists are not concerned with illusions of depth but know how to achieve it if they have a need to.)

Suggested art activity

Have students paint or draw pictures that utilize the concept. Encourage each to select a subject quite different from everyone else. Suggest that some students might want to try creating pictures which *don't* use the concept or some may even try placing larger objects higher on the paper to see if things get larger as they get farther away or to see if they can counteract the placement on the page. Discuss all results with the class, especially anything an individual student discovers in this activity which is new information for him or her.

Alternative art activities

- See if the concept works in an imprinting activity.
- Use the concept with geometric or abstract shapes or forms. See if the students can discover the exceptions to the concept. (Objects such as trees growing "over a hill" could be an exception to the concept.)

Evaluation

When the student uses the concept to create the illusion of depth in a picture, then the objective has been achieved. Verbal awareness may be an indicator of awareness along with the students' ability to *use* the concept.

Other things to consider

- Vocabulary: picture, plane, illusion, depth, base line.
- Art materials needed: drawing and/or painting media as selected by the students.
- Prints:
  Venice by Canaletto
  The Hay Wain by Constable
  Combination Concrete by Davis
  Dancing Class by Degas
  Water Flowery Mill by Gorky
  La Grande Jatte by Seurat
  Numbering at Bethlehem by Brueghel
  Tranquility by Gasser
- People who might have need for the concept: painter, illustrator, commercial artist, stage set designer, cartoonist, artists that draw, do serigraphs, printmaking, and those that deal with art history and analysis.

LEVEL 6

ACTIVITY 162

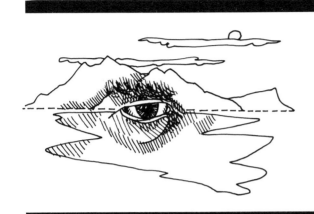

Concept taught by this activity: The horizon line is at the eye level of the viewer.

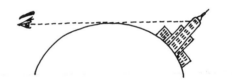

Objective: The student will accurately describe the relationship between the horizon line and the eye level of the viewer, and he will render objects as they relate to the eye level (above, below, or on the eye level).

A sample lesson plan for achieving the objective:

Teacher preparations
- Have prints displayed along with any photographs which might help to clarify the concept.
- Plan a walking tour of the building and the surrounding area to experience applications of the concept.
- Have drawing and painting materials ready for activities.
- Be prepared to take several art periods to complete this activity as it will be one of the most difficult for students to implement.

Teaching suggestions
- Review what was learned concerning the eye level line and the horizon line in activity no. 158. Then emphasize this idea: The horizon line and the eye level (the height at which we see things) are always one and the same. The horizon will *always* be at the height of our eyes whether we lie on the ground, stand on a ladder, sit on top of a 100-story building, or look out the window of an airplane at 30,000 feet above the earth. With our eyes parallel to the ground and looking straight out toward the horizon, the

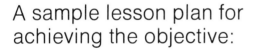

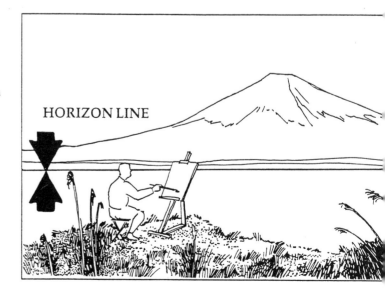

HORIZON LINE

horizon will *always* be at eye level.

■ Discuss how the concept was applied and in evidence as they did their exercises in activity no. 158. Ask the following questions: "Where did the parallel lines always meet?" (on the horizon line) "Was the horizon line always at the eye level of the viewer?" "Can you look at the pictures that were drawn and tell where the person who drew them would have had to be standing to see them in that particular position?" (They should be able to tell.)

Discuss the same ideas using prints suggested in this lesson.

■ Have students lay tracing paper over photographs of buildings and trace where all major parallel lines seem to come together. Note that all vanishing points are on the same line (horizon line and eye level line) unless you have another vanishing point up in the sky or down in the ground.

■ Have three students describe how they see objects in the room. Have one sit on the floor, one stand up, and one on a ladder. Have each in a different part of the room and then have them describe which parts they see of a desk, fellow students, and so forth. (The student sitting down will see the sides of the desk and the underside of the top and he will be looking up under the chins of classmates. The student on the ladder will see tops of desks, heads, and shoulders.)

■ If it's possible, have each of the three students take a polaroid snapshot of what he sees from his position in the room. If each took a picture of his view of the same group of students and desks, the idea that we see everything in relation to the height of our eyes might be even more dramatically demonstrated.

Suggested art activities

■ Take the students on a field trip. Decide ahead of time what area or location will be most suitable. Each student should have a sketch board of wood, cardboard, or masonite, a view finder, ruler, pencils (soft), erasers, and drawing paper. Have the class separate into two or three groups, each group to look at the horizon from a different elevation. Have the students hold their rulers at the height of their eyes. Ask them to take special notice as to what is above the edge of the ruler and what is below it.
Note: A view finder is made from two "L" shaped pieces of poster paper about 2″ by 3″ in size.

When the two pieces of paper are held in an overlapping position, then a view finder or a peep hole is made for the student to look through and select a subject to draw. (See illustration.)

■ Students will now face the problem of trying to draw objects in positions where they have more than just the one vanishing point as drawn in activity no. 158. When drawing objects with two vanishing points, stress that both points will still be on the eye level line (horizon) but the object should be drawn by starting with the line which represents the corner of the object closest to the viewer. In activity no. 158 they started with the end of the box.

Alternative art activities

■ Have each student draw a box as he sees it. Try to make certain that no two students are in the same general spot. Encourage the student to think about what he is seeing and to measure whenever he has any question as to what angle a line takes or how high the box is in relation to its width from a certain view.

■ Change positions and do another drawing.

Evaluation

When there is evidence that the learner recognizes the true relationship between the eye level and the horizon line, and

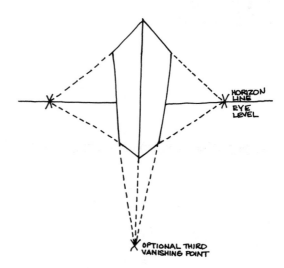

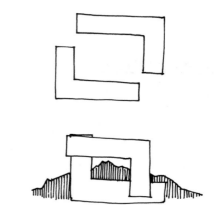

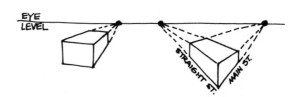

when the student is able to illustrate that relationship in a perspective drawing, then the objective has been achieved (rendering objects above, below, or on the eye level as they are seen by himself).

Other things to consider

■ Vocabulary: perspective, horizontal, vertical, elevation, vanishing point, horizon, parallel, depth, level, three dimension, perpendicular, solidity, observe.

■ Art materials needed: drawing paper, soft lead pencils, sketch board, view finders, erasers.

■ Prints:
The Blue Cart by Van Gogh
Lacemaker by Vermeer

Mlle. Violette by Redon
The Return by Magritte
6-Day Bicycle Rider by Hopper
Blindman's Bluff by Fragonard
Notre Dame by Daumier
The Smokers by Brouwer

■ People who might have need for the concept: painter, illustrator, draftsman, industrial designer, commercial artist, stage set designer, cartoonist, printmaker, artists that do drawings, prints, and deal with art history and analysis.

BIRD'S EYE VIEW

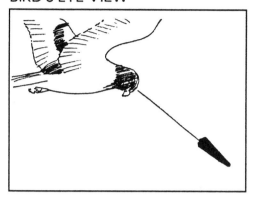

NORMAL VIEW

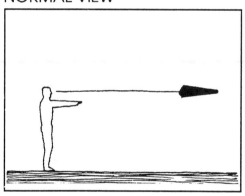

Remember, everything is drawn from the point of view of the eyes of the person doing the drawing.

WORM'S-EYE VIEW

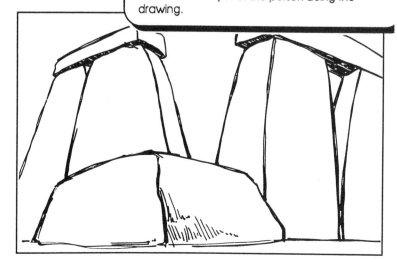

LEVEL 6   ACTIVITY 163

Concept taught by this activity: Parallel lines which appear to converge come together at a point on the eye level.

Objective: The student is able to draw parallel lines converging to a point at eye level to help create an illusion of depth.

A sample lesson plan for achieving the objective:

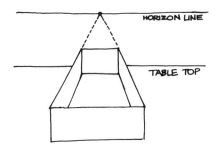

Teacher preparations
- Gather and assemble pictures with overlays marking all parallel lines. (These should be actual photographs if possible.)
- Make arrangements for overhead projector.
- Assemble and display prints which contain examples of the concept.
- Have appropriate materials for drawing or painting activities.

Teaching suggestions
- Begin by asking questions such as: "Who remembers what the horizon is?" "What determines where the horizon is?" "Does the horizon look the same to everyone no matter where they are standing or sitting (same height in relation to their eyes)?" "Why do the parallel lines seem to come together in the distance?" "Are things really getting smaller?" (Examples) "What relationship is there between the height of our eyes (eye level) and the horizon line?" "Have people sitting, standing, or in other positions describe a desk and how much they see of it. (They should conclude that everything is seen above, below, or at the height of their eyes.)

  "With your finger draw what you see out the window on the window pane. Are you drawing things in perspective?" "Why?" (If some media is available to draw on the glass

without creating a problem in getting it off, use it.)
- Have students lay transparent paper over magazine photographs and draw in the perspective lines (parallel lines) that go to a vanishing point on the horizon line. Discuss what they have done. Discuss what happened and why.
- Take a field trip and look for examples of the concept. Make thumbnail sketches of examples and discuss them in class. What problems did you have in trying to draw examples of the concept? Discuss them.
- Discuss these ideas: "Why do artists need to know about perspective?" "What would happen to a landscape scene if the artist *didn't* use perspective?" "Do some artists choose to ignore perspective?" "Why?" "Would they need to know about perspective before they could use it in a creative way?"
- Direct the attention of the students to pictures of such things as a creek, a sidewalk, a mountain road, a street, or the side of a building. Show such pictures on an overhead projector. Have students trace with their fingers where the parallel lines seem to converge. Use mounted overlays which will show how the parallel lines appear to converge to a point.

Suggested art activity

Set up some simple objects such as boxes or cubes and have the students draw them as they would appear going to one vanishing point in the distance. Have them assume that the object is sitting directly in front of them. Help the student to recognize that the parallel lines need not be long like a road before they appear to come together as they go towards the horizon line.

Alternative art activities

- Draw a group of boxlike objects as they would appear if the sides all seemed to converge to one point on a horizon line.
- Do a landscape drawing or painting in which a road, railroad tracks, or a series of objects disappears into the distance with one vanishing point. (For the student who wants to know how to draw objects seen with more than one vanishing point, a subsequent activity will be answering his need.)

Evaluation

The evaluation tool for the teacher is what the student draws after the concept has been taught. If he is able to draw objects with parallel sides that converge to some common point on the horizon line, then the objective has been achieved. The student keeps verticals and horizontals parallel.

Other things to consider

- Vocabulary: parallel, converge, eye level, horizon, landscape, illustrate, appear, identify, vanishing point.
- Art materials needed: drawing and painting media and an assortment of paper.
- Audiovisual materials needed: overhead slide projector, slides and overlays.
- Prints:
  Trains Du Soir by Delvaux
  Oath of the Horatii by David
  Tranquility by Gasser
  The Harvesters by Brueghel
  Brooklyn Bridge by Stella
  The Adoration of the Magi by Botticelli
  Sacrament of the Last Supper by Dali
  The Dancing Class by Degas
- People who might have need for the concept: painter, industrial designer, illustrator, draftsman, printmaker, stage set designers.

LEVEL 6

ACTIVITY 164

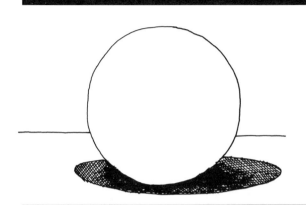

Concept taught by this activity: Shadows are darkest immediately underneath an object and gradually get lighter as they go away from the object.

Objective: In his picture the student will show that shadows are darker underneath objects and gradually get lighter as they go away from them.

A sample lesson plan for achieving the objective:

Teacher preparations
- Obtain pictures which demonstrate the concept.
- Arrange for a flashlight or spotlight.

Teaching suggestions
- Conduct a discussion asking questions which will lead into and support the concept.
- Review questions: ''What is a shadow?'' ''What causes a shadow?'' ''What makes a shadow dark in some places and light in others?'' ''Are shadows always attached to the object casting them?'' ''Do artists always show shadows in their pictures?''
- Show famous paintings in which it is very obvious that the shadows are darker closer to the object and get lighter as they go out from the object.
- Using a lamp to make shadows, have the children show value change in the object's shadow.
- Attach a large styrofoam ball or other shape to the tack board with a large pin. With a flashlight, make long shadows on a light background. Discuss the concept in relation to what the class sees. Ask questions such as: ''When shadows aren't attached, does the concept hold true?'' ''How does knowledge about the concept help the artist?'' ''What do shadows tell you about a picture?'' ''Why

don't we see shadows in the daylight on some occasions?'' ''What conditions influence how clearly we see shadows?'' ''Can you see shadows at night?'' ''Do shadows sometimes seem to be all of the same value?'' ''Does a shadow ever go from a light value next to an object to a dark value away from it?'' ''Why not?''

Suggested activity
Have the students draw an object that has a shadow which is darker closer to the object and becomes lighter as it extends out.

Alternative art activities
- Have the students select an incident or subject they have some particular interest in and paint a picture of it. See if the students still show the cast shadows darkest next to the object or form casting them as they introduce color to their picture.
- Find pictures in magazines and newspapers which illustrate the concept and prepare a display for the school.

Evaluation

The student's picture should clearly show the concept. It may not be skillfully rendered but if the shadows the student draws or paints are darkest next to the form casting them, then the objective has been achieved.

Other things to consider

- Vocabulary: The student may have need to review such terms as: lightness, darkness, highlight, shadow, cast shadow, value, more value, less value.
- Art materials needed: art media for drawing and painting plus a selection of paper.
- Audiovisual materials needed: photographs, styrofoam ball or object, spotlight.
- Prints:
  Snap the Whip by Homer
  The Gleaners by Millet
  Seven A.M. by Hopper
  The Scout by Remington

Oath of the Horatti by David
My Gems by Harnett

■ People who might have need for the concept: artists that draw, paint, or do printmaking, commercial artists of all types.

LEVEL 6

ACTIVITY 165

Concept taught by this activity: A shadow can describe the form or plane over which it falls, or it can overlap other shadows and be seen as a single dark shape.

Objective: The student draws or paints composite shadows as a single dark shape and points out how shadows can describe the form or plane over which they fall.

A sample lesson plan for achieving the objective:

Teacher preparations
- Arrange to have a strong light source, (from the window, direct sunlight, or spotlight). Shadows will be cast on wall of school in or outside.
- Obtain pictures of the moon's surface and prints which illustrate the concept. Display them for discussion.
- Display pictures showing cast shadows in a variety of situations and falling over many different kinds of forms. Use prints and photographs.
- Collect a variety of objects which change plane, for example, steps, boxes, folded cardboard, and other things that have several planes to the form.

Teaching suggestions
- Ask questions such as the following: "How do artists create the illusion of form (three dimensional)?" "What kinds of things do they need to know?" "Does the artist need to use all that he knows each time to create the illusion of three-dimensional form?" "Could the illusion of form be created with a silhouette?" "By just showing shadows?" "How much can a shadow or shadows tell us about objects or forms?"

Have the child observe and study a cast shadow when the shadow is on a ball, hole, bump, and flight of steps. Let child see pictures of moon's surface showing cast shadows. Show pictures or paintings with cast shadows to illustrate the importance of cast shadows in drawings and other art.
- Refer to some of the illustrations. Ask, "How much information would our brain lack concerning each of these objects if there were no shadows?" Discuss each picture. Do the same thing with objects in the room and just outside the building.
- Discuss ways in which artists have used the concept. Refer to prints.
- Show pictures of the moon's surface and discuss how a child can tell by the shadows in the picture what the

surface of the moon is like: ''Shadows indicate bumps and holes, craters and mountains.'' ''Light is from one direction.'' Discuss what happens as two astronauts stand together and cast one shadow: ''When do the shadows overlap?'' ''Can the shadows of flying objects overlap?'' ''Could you identify what the separate shapes were if the shadows of the several objects were cast as one?'' ''Try it.''

- A common example of simplified shadows of several objects is the game where hands are placed in certain positions and the shadow which is cast looks like wolves, birds, or other identifiable objects.
- Ask, ''How do shadows influence the appearance of shapes and forms?'' ''What does it mean to *alter* a shape?'' ''What kinds of objects or forms would you think might alter the shape of a shadow?'' (stairs, doorways, walls and floor), ''Would a shadow appear the same cast on shag carpet and a slick wooden surface?'' ''What are some other kinds of surfaces which might alter the shape of a shadow?''
- Set up an object or one of the materials you brought and then have a student come up and shine a bright light on it creating clearly defined shadows. Discuss what is seen and how each material you cast the shadow on alters the appearance of the shadow.
- Other questions that the teacher might ask could include: ''What would happen if a shadow was cast on water?'' ''How would a shadow cast on a mirror look?'' ''Would there be one?'' ''What would happen to a cloud's shadow?'' ''an airplane shadow?'' ''How would the landscape influence their shape or appearance?''

Suggested art activity
Have the students draw and paint cast shadows as they appear falling over a variety of forms and surfaces. Do *not* draw anything but the shadows and see if the uninvolved observer can tell what the forms are as described by the contour of the shadows. Do the same thing with shadows created within forms (shadows which are *not* cast shadows), then add the shapes of the forms that are creating the shadows.

Alternative art activities
- Have students cast their shadows on wall. Draw the shadows and cut them out for placement on simulated brick wall, painted wall, or other textured surface. In a mural, overlap some forms while drawing attention to how the shapes are altered.
- Draw overlapping objects casting shadows on a variety of forms or planes.
- Have the students draw an object and its shadow as it would appear on two entirely different kinds of surfaces.
- Have students select appropriate subjects in natural light indoors or outdoors.

Evaluation

When the student is able to draw or paint shadows which seem to partially describe the form over which they lie and he shows overlapping shadows as a single dark shape, then the objective has been achieved.

Other things to consider

- Vocabulary: altered, value, texture, shape, form, cast shadow, light source, influences, plane, altered composite shadows, overlapping surface, illusion of form.
- Art materials needed: pencils, crayons, charcoal, or chalk; any are appropriate with whatever paper they work well on.
- Equipment needed: photographs of groups of people or objects, a strong light, a large styrofoam ball on a stick with a stand of some sort, and other assorted objects to cast

shadows. A piece of shag carpet and other kinds of textured surfaces, convex surfaces (umbrella) and concave surfaces (cardboard strip bowed). A rumpled, wrinkled sheet, and other such forms could be used along with surfaces to demonstrate on; scissors, tape, stick, ball, surfaces of holes and bumps, steps, and boxes.
- Prints:
Christina's World by Wyeth
The Letter by Vermeer
Le Moulin de la Galette by Renoir
As Apostle Paul by Rembrandt
The Gleaners by Millet
Moneylender and Wife by Metsys
Boy With a Tire by Lee-Smith
Mona Lisa by da Vinci
Breezing up by Homer
La Grande Jatte by Seurat
Snap the Whip by Homer
- People who might have need for the concept: painter, illustrator, commercial artist, printmaker, teacher, art critic.

LEVEL 6

ACTIVITY 166

Concept taught by this activity: Some surfaces which appear flat become three dimensional with the aid of light; thus, relief and depth can be planned with light.

Objective: The student demonstrates an awareness of how surfaces which appear flat can become three dimensional when light is shown on them.

A sample lesson plan for achieving the objective:

Teacher preparations

Note: The teacher should be aware that the importance of teaching this concept is to help the student be more sensitive to and aware of form, both real and illusionary. Just as color or the lack of it can affect us, so being aware of form can help our lives to be more full and interesting.

■ Have some sort of spotlight available such as the light of a slide projector or an actual floodlight of some sort. Use a room that can easily be darkened to make full use of the spotlight. Review terms such as *opaque* (an object we can't see through) and make certain each is understood. Review or discuss with students whatever terms students may not understand.

■ Collect a number of prints and pictures showing the concept. Display them for discussion.

■ Arrange for materials used in demonstrations and for student activities.

Teaching suggestions

■ Arrange several objects on a table in a lighted room. Discuss whether the objects appear to have any depth or relief.

■ Darken the room and flood the same objects with light from one side. Discuss appearance of the objects now, as far as having depth and relief.

■ Experiment by changing the direction of the light to see how the objects are changed in form and mood.

■ Ask questions such as: "What are shadows and how are they made?" "What times during the day do shadows create the most depth out-of-doors?" "Where is the light source during these times?" "What kinds of days alter this observation?" "How do artists create the illusion of depth or relief in their paintings?"

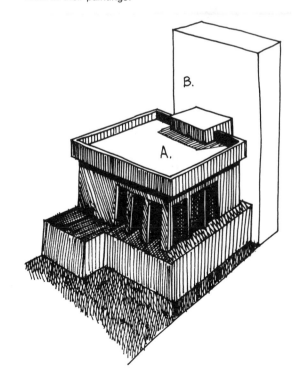

- Look at samples or pictures of sculpture. Discuss the role of shadows in enhancing the appearance of relief or depth: "What does *relief* mean?" "What does relief have to do with depth?" "If there is light, can you create depth or relief without shadows appearing on the surface?" "Why not?" "How do shadows affect the appearance of a surface, for example, your face, a piece of sculpture, the wall of a home, a section of lawn or garden, your desk?" "If an artist uses shadow on forms within a picture, does that add to the illusion of depth?" "Why?" "Find an example."
- Locate pictures in a magazine that contain strong contrasts in dark and light with sharply defined shadow areas. Cut out some of the objects, separating them from their shadows. See if this affects the feeling of depth. Note that balconies, awnings, deep-set windows, overhangs, large eaves, and other projections create ever-changing shadow patterns on a building.
- Look at pictures of contemporary architecture, especially those of tall office buildings. Compare them with some of the buildings designed at least two hundred years ago. Discuss the role of cast shadows in helping the buildings to appear more interesting. Note that even the most simple styles of architecture would seem far less interesting if the shadows of eaves, balconies, deep set windows, and other architectural variations didn't create a constantly changing pattern of light and dark contrasts. Are these patterns planned by the architect?
- Discuss how artists such as Michelangelo in his *Delphic Sibyl* used shadows to give the illusion of architecture in the background of the painting. Sculpture very often uses this concept. Discuss this art form and note how an awareness of this concept can help us appreciate forms around us and increase our perception of space.
- The teacher could then have the students create a construction, sculpture, drawing, or painting and see how well they can apply the concept.
- Discuss the need for special lighting effects both in the home and in public buildings. How does a change in lighting affect the mood or feeling of a room?

Suggested art activity
- Do a photo study of a building or set of buildings illustrating the changing effect shadows have on their appearance at different times of the day.

(OR)

- Do a sand casting of nuts and bolts or other three-dimensional objects. Discuss how the objects make shadows and create a feeling of depth or relief.

Alternative art activities
- Collect pictures of buildings which illustrate the concept and set up a display.
- Save milk and soda straws and do a straw sculpture. Discuss how lengths and thickness make a difference in the size of the shadows.
- For science make a model of the moon's surface. Ask, "What would be a good medium to use to show relief and depth (shadows)?"
- Analyze several prints of famous paintings which contain shadows and discuss how they add to the illusion of relief and depth. Discuss how the sculptor, potter, artist, and architect plan ways in which shadow areas of their forms will enhance them. Bring examples to class or have the artists themselves talk to you.
- Make clay slabs and experiment with a variety of ways in which the surface can be textured. Analyze your results and select those which cast the most interesting shadows.
- Have each student choose a partner and do a clay likeness of each other's head. "Do the eyes, nose, mouth, ears, hair, etc. show relief and depth by the shadows they make?"

Evaluation

When the student demonstrates a verbal awareness of the concept and can point out instances where it has been used, then the objective has been achieved.

Other things to consider

- Vocabulary: relief, depth, shadow, position, medium, sculpture, casting, illustration, analyze, awareness, opaque, transparent, form, two and three dimensional.
- Art materials needed: art paper, pencils, paints, butcher paper, clay, fabric, sand, plaster, nuts, bolts, straws, paper mâché or other media students may choose to use.
- Film Loops:
  "Form and Light" by Bailey Film Associates
  "Line, Surface, Volume" by ACI Films Incorporated
- Films:
  "Light" by ACI Films Incorporated
  "Discovering Dark and Light" by Bailey Film Associates
- Prints:
  Fur Traders on the Missouri by Bingham. Note how flat things look that are in shadows or dim light.
  Bacchus by Caravaggio. Why is detail seen very clearly in this print?
  Turning the Stake by Eakins
  Blue Boy by Gainsborough
  Man in the Golden Helmet by Rembrandt
  Print Collector by Daumier
  St. Joseph by De La Tour
  Seven A.M. by Hopper
  Mona Lisa by da Vinci
  Delphic Sibyl by Michelangelo
  Adoration by Botticelli
  Venice by Canaletto
- People who might have need for the concept: architect, city planner, interior designer, industrial designer, commercial artist, painter, illustrator, sculptor, crafts designer, furniture designer.

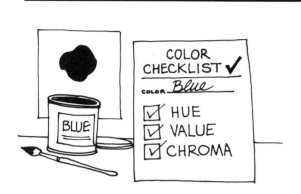

Concept taught by this activity: A color has three properties: (a) hue (all colors except black and white), (b) value (darkness or lightness), and (c) chroma (brightness or dullness; intensity).

Objective: The student demonstrates an awareness of the three properties of color to the extent that he can look at two given colors, name the hue and correctly identify which is darker in value and which is most intense.

A sample lesson plan for achieving the objective:

Teacher preparations
Collect appropriate prints, painting materials, and other visual aids used in the discussions.

Teaching suggestions
■ "What are all of the things with an orange (pick any color) hue?" (List on board.) "List all of the *dark, medium,* and *light* orange things." "Which are brightest?" "Which are most dull?" Discuss the three terms used in the concept, determining first whether or not students are familiar with them and finally seeing that each word is clearly defined.
■ The teacher could start by having two students stand up that have on shirts or sweaters that are the same hue but are of different value and chroma. Have the class determine which is the darkest value and which is the brightest chroma. Select other students and do the same thing until there is some certainty that the students have the idea of the concept.

■ Provide each student with a number of swatches of paper about two inches square and have them all take half of them and arrange them in order of their value from dark to light. Then have the students arrange the rest in order of their intensity—from dull to bright. Then select at random about five students to display their selections. Discuss whether or not the arrangements were accurate and make adjustments, as needed. Try the same sort of things with paint chips, colored tile, or other materials that have multiple colors.
■ Discuss relative differences in hue, value, and chroma with other things in the room, for example, books, clothing, and crayons. Look at prints and other illustrations and discuss the relationship between value and chroma. Help students develop the capacity to make even subtle distinctions.

Suggested art activity
Show each of the art prints and from each picture have the student list five color areas in order of their value, no. 1 being the lightest and no. 5 the darkest. Then have him order them in terms of intensity.

Alternative art activities
Do a bulletin board or display case explaining and illustrating the concept.

Evaluation

When the student identifies the three properties of color to the extent that he can meet the requirements of the objective, then the activity may be concluded.

Other things to consider

■ Vocabulary: hue, value, chroma, intensity.
■ Prints:
Apples and Oranges by Cezanne
Combination Concrete by Davis
Bedroom at Arles by Van Gogh
Water Flowery Mill by Gorky

Head of a Man by Klee
Sinbad the Sailor by Klee
Justice and Peace by Overstreet
Before the Start by Lapicque
■ People who might have need for the concept: interior designer, painter, illustrator, commercial artist, house painter, color consultant.

LEVEL 6

ACTIVITY 168

Concept taught by this activity: Shadows appear as darker, grayer, and less intense versions of whatever color they rest upon.

Objective: The student paints shadows as darker, grayer, and less intense versions of whatever color they rest upon.

A sample lesson plan for achieving the objective:

Teacher preparations
■ Collect appropriate prints and whatever colored photographs are available in the school's media center. There are numerous pictures containing shadows that are intended for science and social studies but which make excellent resources for this concept. The shadows can be either cast shadows or the shadows that are on the surface of something.
■ Have a color wheel available as a resource.

Teaching suggestions
■ The following body of information may be helpful as a means of knowing what lies behind the concept itself. Discussion should be pointed towards the student *discovering* these kinds of things.
  ● Using the color wheel as a visual resource, the color of a shadow tends to swing in hue toward the next lower adjacent color and then in to the center of the color wheel toward gray. Thus if the color of grass is green, the shadow will be blue green and in toward gray.
  ● Shadows take on the color of whatever they rest on, therefore, shadows appear to be transparent rather than opaque.
  ● Cast shadows almost always show tinges of a hue that is complementary to the color of the light source. If the light source is yellow light, the cast shadows will contain

tinges of violet. If the light source is blue light, the cast shadow will contain tinges of orange.
  ● Shadows seldom have hard edges. When they are drawn or painted with hard edges they seem to be below or above the surface they're supposed to be resting on.
  ● Shadows are less intense than the color they rest upon.
■ Don't present the preceding information as a formal lecture. The student will be able to use the information best when *he* discovers it. Begin with a discussion on shadows. (Start with what the student already knows.) Ask, "What color is a shadow?" "What color is the shadow on (Joe's) shirt?" "or (Mary's) dress?"
■ Look at the color of shadows on clothing, carpeting, grass, brick, hair, and whatever other environments they can be seen on. Discuss each in terms of whether or not the concept is really true. Shadows which rest on surfaces that are grayed hues or on the warm side of the color wheel will be more difficult for students to visualize.

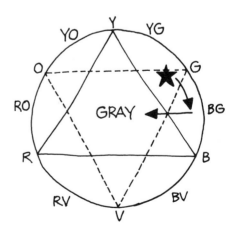

■ Discuss the use of the concept in art prints and in photographs. Discuss why old masters' paintings contain so many brown or blackish shadows. Colors changed with age and repeated varnishings (artist didn't know the concept).

Suggested art activity
Paint a picture of a favorite object or animal with its shadow.

Alternative art activities
■ Illustrate a portion of a story about shadows.
■ Do a group project on the color of a shadow by making a mural, frieze or bulletin board display.

Evaluation

When the student paints shadows as darker, grayer, and less intense versions of whatever color they rest upon, the objective has been achieved.

Other things to consider

■ Vocabulary: intensity, chroma, hue.
■ Art materials needed: standard painting materials as available in the classroom.
■ Prints:
 Still Life with Pipe by Chardin
 Blue Boy by Gainsborough
 Tranquility by Gasser
 Snap the Whip by Homer
 6-Day Bicycle Rider by Hopper
 My Gems by Harnett
 Le Moulin de La Galette by Renoir
 Women In a Garden by Monet
 Lacemaker by Vermeer
 The Scout by Remington
■ People who might have need for the concept: painters, illustrators, architectural renderers, commercial artists, art critics, docents.

LEVEL 6   ACTIVITY 169

Concept taught by this activity: Designs and pictures may appear "washed out" when the creator is fearful of using contrasting colors or values.

Objective: The student strengthens contrasts between values (or colors) when it appears that his picture or design has a "washed out" look.

A sample lesson plan for achieving the objective:

Teacher preparations

- Even though there may be times when an artist wants his picture or design to have very little contrast in it (as he portrays a certain mood or feeling), some students will work with such a limited range of values their designs will look "washed out" and lacking in spirit, vitality, and energy.
- Collect samples of "washed-out"-looking designs. If none are available, create one or two examples. Note that student work is a good resource. Look for those which contain just three basic value changes—the white of the paper, a few dark areas in between and a middle value.

Teaching suggestions

- "Who are the most energetic ones in this class?" "What do they do that makes us think they are energetic?" (They exercise a lot, run, jump, laugh, talk fast.) "How many sources of energy can you name?" (Things that produce heat, for example, food, wood, paper, coal, gasoline, gas, atoms, electricity, the sun.) "What happens to a pair of blue jeans that are washed with too much bleach in the water?" "Why do some of your clothes generally get a little lighter in color every time they're washed?" "How could a painting or drawing become anemic or washed out looking?" "In art,

when we say it looks anemic we mean it lacks contrast, spirit, vitality, and energy."
- Look at the art print *Print Collector* by Daumier. Have two students look at it very carefully and count the number of value changes they can find. Have them count to themselves and then tell the class how many they discovered. Make the point that students typically use only three or four value changes in a picture and frequently use only two—the white of the paper and the dark of their pencil. Look at other art prints and discuss what each might look like had they not used the concept.
- Discuss that some pencils (6-H) are too "hard" (hard lead or graphite) to get nice *darks*, and some pencils may be too "soft" to get nice sharp light lines and tones. (2-H is a "medium" pencil, and HB is a good softness.)

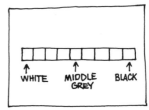

Suggested art activity

Do two designs or pictures exactly alike as far as the outline in the drawing part is concerned. Then render one with just three value changes and render the other as technically as possible.

Alternative art activities

- Analyze illustrations out of magazines or books. Note how close relationships between values are used to create mood, for example, pictures of fog, illustrations of nighttime, desert scenes in the bright sun, a heavy snowstorm.
- Make a collection of pictures with different ranges of values to place on the bulletin board.

■ Ditto a 1″ by 8″ "bar" on paper to be shaded in by the
students. Have them go from white to black in nine steps, in
other words, create a design in which the nine steps can be
identified. Discuss ways in which this activity causes
everyone to avoid anemic looking drawings.

Evaluation

When he expands his range of values used in a design or
picture to at least five or six changes, then the objective has
been achieved.

Other things to consider

■ Vocabulary: "washed out," anemic, contrast, contrasting.
■ Art materials needed: drawing and painting materials.
■ Prints:
Print Collector by Daumier
Quay Le Pouliguen by Vuillard
Iliad Study by Ingres
Fur Traders on the Missouri by Bingham
Ville d'Avray by Corot
Mlle. Violette by Redon
■ People who might have need for the concept: painter,
illustrator, commercial artist, interior designer.

LEVEL 6 ACTIVITY 170

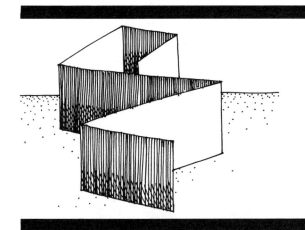

Concept taught by this activity: Flat planes may be organized into shapes which have the appearance of volumes or forms.

Objective: The student demonstrates an awareness that one can create height, width, and depth with flat planes that are combined to make specific shapes.

A sample lesson plan for achieving the objective:

Teacher preparations
Collect prints and other helpful illustrations available within the school. Be prepared to discuss the concept both from actual or real situations and illusionary ones.

Teaching suggestions
■ Review some of the terminology in the concept. For example, a flat plane is any flat surface such as a piece of paper, and volume refers to an object with the capacity to hold air, liquid, or mass within its outside structure.
■ In the discussion have a brainstorming session on the variety of flat planes students might see inside and outside the room. Move from this discussion to a listing of the kinds of things that can be made from simple flat planes. "How many three-dimensional forms could you make from a flat piece of paper?" "Would all of them have volume?" "Which ones wouldn't?" Relate this discussion to student's experience with paper sculpture.
■ Use illustrations such as those included with this activity to help the student recognize ways in which flat planes can be used to create forms and volumes.
■ Review ways in which artists create illusions of depth, then ask questions such as: "In pictures where artists have painted in an abstract way, is there still some feeling that

some shapes are closer to the eye than others?" (Look at some of the recommended prints.) "How does the artist create that feeling?" (Some colors seem closer than others, overlapping creates depth, some textures influence the appearance of space, and detail might be a factor.)
■ Discuss what happens to the illusion of depth when two shapes which first overlap only touch each other now. "What happens to the feeling of space when you separate the shapes?" "Does the feeling of space seem different in each case?" "When is the feeling of space least noticeable?" (When they touch each other.) Encourage free expressions and divergent opinions.

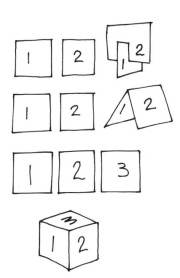

Suggested art activity

By folding, slotting, and gluing processes, have the students create a variety of three-dimensional forms or volumes. Then have them try drawing some of the shapes, noting that flat planes can be altered to become three-dimensional forms or volumes.

Alternative art activities

- Have the students create two or three designs or pictures using the same shapes in each but purposely creating depth in one and minimizing it in the other by having all shapes touch without any overlapping. Encourage students to originate shapes of their own and let them use as many as they like. Let the students select their own media in creating the designs.
- Using nothing but flat materials such as paper, or railroad board, create a three-dimensional form or construction.

Evaluation

When the student demonstrates either a verbal or nonverbal awareness of the concept, then the objective has been achieved.

Other things to consider

- Vocabulary: volume, plane, form, linear perspective.
- Art materials needed: construction paper, glue, or paste, scissors, drawing paper, pencils, crayons, or felt-tip pens.
- Prints:
  Adoration by Botticelli
  House at Aix by Cezanne
  Tranquility by Gasser
  6-Day Bicycle Rider by Hopper
  Justice and Peace by Overstreet
  Cheyt M by Vasarely
  The Letter by Vermeer
  Print Collector by Daumier
- People who might have need for the concept: sculptor, painter, industrial designer, commercial artist, architect, engineer, interior decorator.

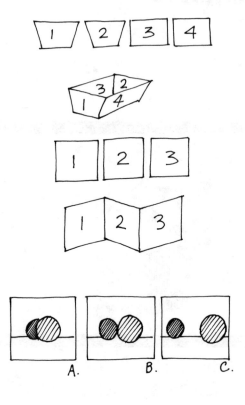

LEVEL 6

ACTIVITY 171

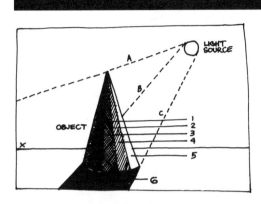

Concept taught by this activity: Forms can have areas of highlight, light or half tone, and a shadow edge (or core line).

Objective: The student will be able to render the basic forms with highlight and half tone, and a shadow side with its shadow edge.

A sample lesson plan for achieving the objective: (This lesson and lesson no. 172 go together. They are written as two lessons so that the student would not have too much information given to him at one time.)

Teacher preparations
■ Make preparations for the room to be darkened. Have some of the basic forms available—a sphere, cube, cone, cylinder, and pyramid.
■ Place the forms on a table or desk that has been covered with white paper.
■ Have a spotlight or strong light to shine on the forms after the room lights have been turned off.
■ Several art prints of masters' works should be displayed that illustrate this concept. (Suggested prints are at the conclusion of this activity.)

Teaching suggestions
■ "What are all of the things which can give off light?" (Sun,

moon, candle, flashlight, match, fire, reflections.) "How many ways can light rays hit objects?" (Directly, near miss, not at all, glancing.)

This learning experience could begin by listing the terms *highlight, half tone,* and *shadow edge* or *cone line* on the blackboard. The students could then be led to identify these factors in the masters' prints that are displayed in the room. The students should be able to identify the light source that the artist has used and be able to explain how that light has caused each of the items mentioned in this concept to appear.
■ When the students give indication that they can see the items mentioned in this concept in the masters' prints they should then practice seeing them on real forms. The lights could be turned out and a spotlight used to illuminate some basic forms. The students should be able to identify the highlight, half tone, and shadow side with its shadow edge on all of the basic forms of sphere, cube, cone, cylinder, and pyramid. Motivate students to the point that they detect the subtle differences between areas.

Suggested art activity

Select an object or some living thing and draw or paint it, indicating areas of highlight, light or half tone, and a shadow edge or core line. The position of the light source could also be indicated.

Alternative art activities

Additional opportunities and choices of subject will provide alternative activities.

Evaluation

When the students are able to draw the basic forms with a highlight, half tone, and shadow side, you have met the objective of this activity.

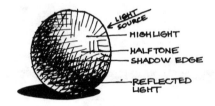

Other things to consider

The teacher must keep in mind that the importance of this concept is for creating the optical illusion of form (making an object look like it has depth).

- Vocabulary: highlight, half tone, shadow edge, core line, shadow side.
- Art materials needed: drawing materials, a spotlight, and objects to draw.
- Prints:
  The Man With the Golden Helmet by Rembrandt
  The Crucifixion by Dali
  Bacchus by Caravaggio
  Blue Boy by Gainsborough
  My Gems by Harnett
  Lacemaker by Vermeer
  Mona Lisa by da Vinci
  Moneylender and Wife by Metsys
  Knockout by Morreau
- People who might have need for the concept: painter, illustrator, commercial artist, industrial designer, cartoonist, printmaker, art historian.

LEVEL 6

ACTIVITY 172

Concept taught by this activity: Forms will usually cast a shadow and contain areas of reflected light.

Objective: The student can render forms with a cast shadow and areas of reflected light.

A sample lesson plan for achieving the objective: (This lesson is a continuation of activity no. 171.)

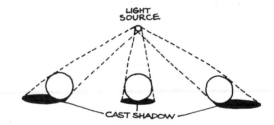

Teacher preparations
■ Drawings done by the students in activity no. 171 could be displayed in the room so that they could be referred to as visual aids.
■ Several of the prints of masters could also be on display, particularly some showing the use of cast shadow such as *My Gems* by Harnett or *6-Day Bicycle Rider* by Hopper.
■ A spotlight and a variety of basic forms (sphere, cube, cone, cylinder, and pyramid) should be obtained.

Teaching suggestions
■ Go outdoors and look for unusual shadows and objects casting them. Look for examples of shadows being cast by reflected light (like from the white cement of the sidewalk upward). Have students come back in and make a list of the unusual shadows found outdoors.
■ Review what a cast shadow is, how it is caused, and where one would look for one. Review what reflected light is, how it is caused, and where one would look for it.
■ A review of the concept in activity no. 171 could precede a discussion on cast shadow and reflected light. As in the preceding activity, the student should be able to identify cast shadows and reflected light in the works of artists and with actual forms.

■ A discussion of the masters' prints could be used to identify the places where the concept has been used and how it helped the artist to show dimension and form.
■ When the students are able to see the concept being used in the masters' prints, have them look for the same things with the spotlight and the basic forms. Have them analyze how the shape of the cast shadow changes as the position of the light changes and how the reflected light changes as the light changes. Discuss ways in which surfaces and/or objects can influence the reflected light seen.
■ Lead the students to discover how the light source determines the location and shape of the cast shadow. Note that the shadow is *like* the shape of the object and that the shadow extends out from the spot where the sphere touches the ground (see illustration). The idea that light travels in a straight line is important in this discussion and in the illustrations.
■ Hold a piece of white paper next to the neck of a student with a light reflecting off the paper and onto the skin of the individual. Do the same thing with colored paper. When the skin appears lighter or colored, then reflected light makes the change seen.
■ Note that the reflected light may appear lighter in value than it really is. This is because it usually is seen in between the two darkest areas—the shadow edge and the cast shadow.

Suggested art activity
Do a drawing of at least two geometric forms as they would appear with light coming from the upper right hand side of them.

Alternative art activities
Have the student do a drawing or painting of some subject he has interest in. Incorporate all of the value changes or areas studied in this and the preceding lesson, specifically, highlights, light, light or half tone in the light side and shadow, shadow edge, reflected light, and a cast shadow on the shadow side.

Evaluation

When the student draws or paints a picture showing reflected light and a cast shadow along with areas of highlight, half tone, and shadow and shadow edge, then the objective has been achieved.

Other things to consider

- Vocabulary: highlight, light, half tone, shadow, shadow edge, core line, reflected light, cast shadow.
- Art materials needed: pencil, eraser, charcoal, paint such as watercolor or tempera, brushes, and paper.
- Prints: utilize those suggested in the preceding activity, plus
  The Gleaners by Millet
  The Crucifixion by Dali
  The Scout by Remington
- Film: "Discovering Light and Dark," Bailey Film Associates
- People who might have need for the concept: painter, illustrator, commercial artist, industrial designer, stage set designer, cartoonist, printmaker, art historian.

LEVEL 6   ACTIVITY 173

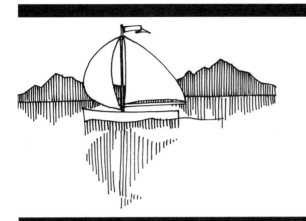

Concept taught by this activity: When shadows and other value contrasts are perceived accurately, the illusion of boards, water, foliage, glass, and other similar textures can be created.

Objective: The student creates the illusion of some common textures by accurately rendering contrasts in value.

A sample lesson plan for achieving the objective:

Teacher preparations
Note: It is not expected that most students will be able to implement this concept very skillfully. Any individual who tries to carefully recreate the contrasts in value he sees on a textured form will likely be successful. The teacher should do all that is possible to help students recognize how important seeing values accurately is to artists. The teacher then simply provides opportunity for the student to "try out" this new information. This lesson is an extension of activity no. 126, level 5.

Collect appropriate prints and have drawing materials available to the student.

Teaching suggestions
■ Review what was accomplished in lesson no. 126.
■ Have students do rubbings of several rough textures in the room. Discuss: What role does value contrast play in helping us to see texture? What would an artist need to know about value to create the illusion of textures in this room?
■ Have the students draw a three-inch square on another piece of paper and *copy* one of the textures that they made from their rubbings, the object being to copy the rubbing texture almost exactly. To do this, they must concentrate on shapes, values, lines, and dark and light patterns.

■ Have each student select two objects to draw—one that has rough texture and one that has a smooth shiny texture. Here again, the student should concentrate on the shadows and values that he sees, trying to copy them as accurately as possible. Keep the drawings no larger than 2″ by 3″

Suggested art activity
Have the students compose and sketch a still life, landscape, or anything of a realistic nature, again concentrating on creating the illusion of the textures by accurately rendering contrasts in value. Students should be told that the most *unusual* use of shadow-values will be rewarded.

Alternative art activities
■ For advanced or highly motivated students: The teacher could even pose a problem for the students to solve such as: drawing a sphere, cylinder, and cube sitting on a black shiny surface. Each of the three objects might have a different texture.

■ Discuss how artists create the illusion of textures. Try to copy in every detail some part of an artist's painting that creates the illusion of texture and write down whatever was learned from the experience.

Evaluation

When the student has made a conscientious attempt to utilize changes in value to create the illusion of texture, then the objective has been achieved. Reward unusual perceptions and renderings of shadow-values.

Other things to consider

■ Art materials needed: pencils, paper, and crayons.
■ Prints:
The Blue Cart (drawing) by Van Gogh
Young Hare (drawing) by Durer
Christina's World by Wyeth
Virgin Forest by Rousseau
Man In the Golden Helmet by Rembrandt
Bar, Folies Bergere by Manet
Blue Boy by Gainsborough
Bandaged Ear by Van Gogh
Iliad Study (drawing) by Ingres
■ People who might have need for the concept: painter, illustrator, printmaker, commercial artist.

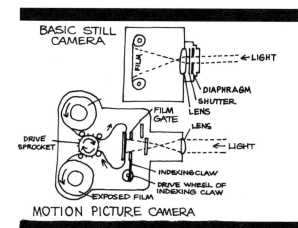

BASIC STILL CAMERA

FILM

←LIGHT

DIAPHRAGM
SHUTTER
LENS
LENS

FILM GATE

DRIVE SPROCKET

←LIGHT

INDEXING CLAW
DRIVE WHEEL OF INDEXING CLAW
EXPOSED FILM

MOTION PICTURE CAMERA

Concept taught by this activity: Basic kinds of cameras (including still and movie) can be identified as can their various parts: aperture, shutter, view finder, film advance, built-in light meter.

Objective: The student identifies basic camera types and correctly names parts of the camera and their function.

A sample lesson plan for achieving the objective:

Teacher preparations
Note: Activity no. 174 may well be taught as part of a photography unit that includes no. 175. Activity 174 helps the student identify the basic parts of the camera and what they do; in no. 175 he learns to set or operate each part properly.

Have at least one example of the two kinds of cameras available for demonstrations—a still camera and a movie camera. Study this lesson thoroughly and the cameras that are being used so that everything is clearly understood and instruction can be given. The temptation will be for the teacher to do all the talking but even in this sort of activity where all instruction becomes convergent (there is one correct answer to most questions), it is still important for students to *discover* what the parts are.

Teaching suggestions
■ Ask questions such as: "What kinds of cameras are these?" "Which one is a still camera?" "Where does the film go?" "Do both use the same kind of film?" "Why not?" "How do you open the camera to put the film in?" "Does it matter how it goes in?"
■ Below is a list of the parts of these cameras. See how many of them can be correctly located (on *both* cameras).

Film advance knob
Lens
View finder
Shutter release button
Aperture
Flash attachment & flash bulb
*Zoom lens control on a movie camera and built-in light meters

Tune exposure control
Distance setting
Film speed setting
Shutter speed setting
Lens opening (aperture) setting

■ Enlarge the students' concept of a camera by asking: "How is a still camera different from a movie camera?" (See illustration.) "Which control would you move to adjust the camera from taking a picture that had no action and then taking one with *fast* action?" (the shutter speed setting) "What might happen if you set the camera for a distance of thirty feet and tried to take a picture of someone two feet away?" (Photo would probably be out of focus or blurred.) Continue asking these kinds of questions until every part of each camera and the purpose they serve has been thoroughly taught.

Suggested art activity
Have students work in teams to see if everyone can learn the correct name for all major parts of two basic kinds of cameras.

Alternative art activities
■ Develop a game based on naming parts of the two kinds of cameras. It could be organized like a "spelling bee."
■ Bring in a guest photographer to show and explain some of the more technical aspects of camera use.

Evaluation

When the student can identify most of the parts on the two basic cameras and describe what each thing does or how it operates, then the objective has been achieved.

Other things to consider

■ Vocabulary: film advance knob, shutter release button,

*May or may not be on the cameras used in your classroom.

diaphragm, aperature, time exposure, film speed, shutter
speed, zoom lens, still camera, light meter.
- Resources: The sections on cameras and photography in
  most school encyclopedias deal with the ideas utilized in
  this lesson and provide additional information or illustrations
  for both student and teacher.
- People who might have need for the concept: photographer,
  photo engraver, newspaper and magazine photographer,
  costume designer, aerial photographer, commercial artist.

LEVEL 6

ACTIVITY 175

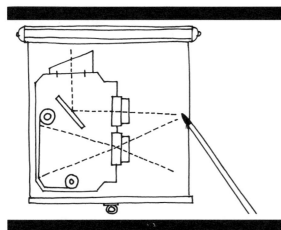

Concept taught by this activity:
To operate an adjustable camera, load film, compose with a view- finder, focus, choose the lens opening, manipulate shutter and aperture controls, set film speed, and hold the camera steady.

Objective: The student demonstrates competency in the operation of an adjustable camera.

A sample lesson plan for achieving the objective:

Teacher preparations
Have an adjustable still camera available for demonstration purposes and encourage students who have had some experience with this kind of camera to bring one from home. Be certain they get their parents' approval and that cameras can be stored in a safe place during the time they are at school.

Teaching suggestions
■ Review aspects of activity no. 174 and encourage students who are familiar with the operation of an adjustable still camera to instruct the class through some sort of demonstration. Clarify points that are missed or taught hurriedly. Ask lots of questions about the operation of the camera.

Demonstrate loading and unloading film, looking through the viewfinder, and choosing the correct distance, lens opening, shutter speed, and film speed for any given situation.
■ Discuss the importance of holding a camera steady. The slower the shutter speed the more important this becomes.
■ Discuss some of the common mistakes people make taking pictures. This might include such things as:
Common mistakes and how to avoid them.
● Cutting off heads. Make sure *all* of the subject appears in the viewfinder at the *exact* moment that the picture is snapped.

● Poor background. Check the viewfinder to see that trees or other objects do not "grow" from the subject's head.
● Poor focus. Stand at least six feet from the subject.
● Tilted camera. Keep the camera level when you snap the picture.
● Camera movement. Hold the camera steady and press the shutter release button gently.
● Obstructed lens. Make sure that the camera strap or your finger does not cover part of the lens.
Lighting concerns
● Front lighting is seldom useful for portraits. The sun shines directly into the subject's face, causing him to squint. The sun also casts harsh shadows under his eyebrows, nose, chin, and cheekbones.
● Side lighting produces dark shadows on one side of the person's face. Fill in the shadows by using a flashbulb or take the picture near an object that reflects light, such as a light-colored building.
● Back lighting forms bright highlights on the subject's hair and shoulders, but a dark shadow may cover his face. Light from a flashbulb will fill in the shadow area and improve the photograph.
● Flash fill-in, used with back lighting. Produces good detail and even lighting. For close-ups, cover the flash reflector with a white handerchief to prevent overexposing the front of the subject.
Composition ideas
● Composition is the arrangement of objects in a photograph. Good composition produces a pleasing photograph. For good composition, have only one center of interest in a picture and use a plain background so that all interest will be focused on the subject. When photographing distant landscapes, include a large object in the foreground to give the picture depth. Balance light and dark tones to create dramatic contrast in the picture. Study the lines and shapes of your subject material. Certain lines and shapes suggest feelings of peace, dignity, or action. Use these lines and shapes to make your photography create a mood.
● Light and dark tones used together create striking photographs. Add emphasis by contrasting dark against

light or light against dark.

- Horizontal lines suggest peace and rest. A picture is more interesting if the horizontal line is off-center and does not cut the picture in half.
- Vertical lines emphasize height and create feelings of dignity and grandeur.
- Diagonal lines suggest action and movement. They may also suggest conflict.
- Balanced objects at the front, back, and sides create order in a photograph and give a feeling of depth.
- Radiating lines can be used by a creative photographer to form interesting patterns and abstract shapes.
- Triangular lines and shapes direct attention to the center of interest. Triangles can suggest rest or movement.

Suggested art activity

Give each student opportunity to set the camera, compose a picture through the viewfinder, and take a picture. After the film has been developed and prints made, display each student's picture or pictures.

Alternative art activities

Show the students' pictures of the same subject that were taken with different settings of the camera to demonstrate what different effects take place.

Evaluation

When each student has had at least a minimal opportunity to put the concept into practice, then the objective has been achieved.

Other things to consider

- Vocabulary: focus, focusing, composing with the viewfinder, composition, lighting effects.
- Resources: The sections on cameras and photography in most school encyclopedias deal with the ideas utilized in this lesson and provide additional information or illustrations for both student and teacher.
- People who might have need for the concept: photographers, commercial artists, teachers.

MATURITY LEVEL 7

Developmental stages

In this packet of lesson plans the teacher can provide the student with thirty-one art experiences that develop his awareness of how to:
- Recognize ways in which light is reflected.
- Recognize that sunlight and some artificial light contain the spectrum of colors, that color is reflected light, and that transparent and opaque materials reflect color in different ways.
- Recognize that perception requires the development of mental imagery.
- Resolve some drawing problems by dealing with large or simple shapes and forms first and details last.
- Group shapes and forms in aesthetic arrangements.
- Group objects in a variety of ways.
- Recognize when complements neutralize or accent each other.
- Recognize ways in which the value of one shape influences another.
- Recognize the influence a given environment has on a color.
- Recognize the balancing characteristics of complements.
- Recognize ways in which colors may seem to be passive, receding, aggressive, and advancing.
- Recognize the varied role of the artist in society.
- Identify contemporary uses of photography and careers associated with the art.
- Create mosaics by imbedding hard objects in a material which will solidify.
- Laminate thin sheets of various materials to create a variety of forms.
- Use strong contrasts to attract attention and graduated contrasts to lead the eye from one shape in an arrangement to another.
- Create formal and informal arrangements of shapes.
- Create unity without monotony through the repetition of shapes or forms.
- Recognize the role of practice in skill development.
- Define the attitude and position of a model with line.
- Utilize several concepts in perspective and value to create a drawing or painting.
- Create a design in fabric with the process of hooking.
- Recognize procedures in the development of film and its use in photography.
- Overcome common problems in picture taking.
- Create a film strip or slide presentation.
- Overcome at least four common errors in drawing.
- Create a better balance between positive and negative spaces.
- Improve scale and proportion.
- Deal with basic problems in foreshortening.
- Recognize the role media plays in determining the eventual outcome of the artist's product.
- Analyze and discuss works of art by naming and recognizing materials and techniques.

---

*Key projects for the concept.

An explanation of level 7

This program is *not* designed for potential art students only; art skills are treated simply as a by-product of instruction.

Up through level 4, the drawings of the student are relatively accurate meters of his perceptual level. But as the learner develops the ability to portray his experience in greater detail, it becomes increasingly difficult for the teacher to evaluate the student's work by measuring his perceptions. The student is receiving inputs that move him into both two and three dimensional areas of art and into forms of abstraction. This complexity in his perceptual level makes analysis rather impractical.

At stages above level 4, currently beyond the experience of most students and adults in our society, all the teacher needs to do is note the number of the activity the student has completed and then pass that information on to the next teacher. Those who are sufficiently interested in art to develop skills in drawing or to specialize in some specific discipline would move beyond this "core" program and become art specialists at higher levels.

Art projects that can be used as devices for teaching a specific concept

Drawing (pencil, chalk, pen, marker, brushes, etc.)
Lessons: *179, 180, 181, 191, 192, 193, *194, *195, 196, *201, *202, *203, *204, 205, 206

Perspective
Lessons: 194, *196, 204

Murals
Lessons: 179, 180, 181, 182, 191, 192, 193, 194, 201, 202, 203, 204, 205, 206

Water Color and Tempera
Lessons: *182, 183, 184, 185, 186, 191, 194, 195, 196, 202, 203, 204, 205

Sculpture (constructions)
Lessons: 179, 180, 181, 190, 191, 194, 205

Carving Sculpture and Other Forms
Lessons: 180, 181, 194, 205

Leathercraft
Lessons: 190, 191, 192, 193, 194, 205

Dry Flower Arranging
Lessons: 180, 181, 191, 192, 193, 194, 205

Stencil Designs (serigraph)
Lessons: 180, 181, 191, 192, 193, 194, 205

Melted Crayon Painting (encaustic)
Lessons: 179, 180, 181, 182, 191, 194, 205

Posters
Lessons: 179, 180, *182, 188, 191, 192, 193, 194

Dioramas
Lessons: 180, 182, 191, 192, 193, 194, 201, 202, 203, 204, 205, 206

Collage and Paper Designs
Lessons: 180, 182, 183, 184, 185, 186, 191, 192, 193, 194, 205

Batik
Lessons: 180, 182, 183, 191, 192, 193, 194, 205

Knitting and Crocheting
Lessons: 191, 192, 193, 194, 205

Cartooning and/or Caricature
Lessons: 179, 180, 181, 191, 194, 202, 204

Wire Sculpture
Lessons: 180, 191, 192, 193, 194, 205

Ceramics
Lessons: 180, 191, 192, 193, 194, 205

Terrariums
Lessons: 180, 191, 192, 193, 194, 205

Photography
Lessons: 180, *188, 191, 194, *198, *199, *200, 205

Printmaking (e.g., gadget and roll prints)
Lessons: 180, 183, 184, 191, 192, 193, 194, 205

Copper and Foil Tooling
Lessons: 180, 191, 192, 193, 194, 205

Tie/Dye
Lessons: 180, 191, 192, 193, 194, 205

Mosaics
Lessons: 180, 181, *189, 191, 192, 193, 194, 205

Basket Weaving
Lessons: 191, 192, 193, 194, 205

Weaving
Lessons: 180, 182, 191, 192, 193, 194, 205

Puppet Making
Lessons: 190, 191, 194, 205

Paper Sculpture
Lessons: 180, 191, 192, 193, 194, 205

Papier Mâché
Lessons: 180, 191, 192, 193, 194, 205

Macrame
Lessons: 180, 181, 191, 192, 193, 194, 205

Applique (sew or glue)
Lessons: 180, 182, 191, 192, 193, 194, 205

Rug Hooking
Lessons: 180, 181, 182, 191, 192, 193, 194, *197, 205

Holiday Decorations
Lessons: 180, 181, *182, 183, 184, 186, 191, 192, 193, 205

Mobiles and Stabiles
Lessons: 180, 181, 190, 191, 192, 193, 194, 205

Snow Sculpture
Lessons: 191, 192, 193, 205

*Key projects for the concept.

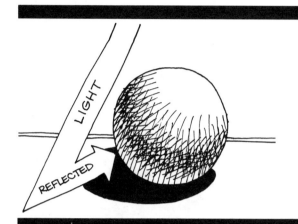

Concept taught by this activity: Light is reflected when it travels from one surface to another. Light may be reflected in many directions.

Objective: The student demonstrates an awareness that many things reflect light and the light may be reflected in many directions.

A sample lesson plan for achieving the objective:

Teacher preparations

Assemble appropriate illustrations and materials for implementing the concept.

Note: We have no vision without light, and the joy and satisfaction of sight is greatly enhanced when we become more aware of light and of those things that reflect light. Even though light is the means by which we see the world around us, we do not know exactly what it is. It can be described only in terms of what it does. Some of the things that light does are important for some types of artists to perceive. This concept may not seem like an art concept to the teacher or his students, but remember that what the student or the artist does in his craft will not change until his awareness or perception changes. Therefore, once the concept of this lesson is thoroughly discussed and a variety of applications for it experienced, the student will never see all of the things that relate to this experience in the same way again. As a result, his vision of art will never be the same again. Light is a form of energy--heat, radio waves, and x-rays. The speed, frequency, and length of its waves can be measured. Its behavior in other ways makes it similar to these other forms of energy, too. But light is the only type of energy that is directly visible, and

therefore, it is the most useful. Glowing objects--the sun and stars, a fire, an electric lamp--can be seen because they give off light themselves. But it is important for the artist to realize that other objects can be seen because they reflect light. This is to say that even colors are reflected light. One ancient experimenter, Hero of Alexandria, did discover one of the first laws of light. He noticed that the angle of a light ray coming to a mirror was the same as the angle of the reflected ray leaving the mirror. From this he decided that light rays always take the shortest possible distance--a straight line--between an object and the eye. Later it was shown that this is not always true, for light rays do bend under certain conditions. It soon became known that rough surfaces reflect in the same way as mirrors. However, because they are rough, the reflection is diffused. Thus, light falling on this page-- which is rough compared with the surface of a mirror--is reflected in all directions. The page can be seen from any point in the room by the light reflected from it. A mirror reflects light much more accurately, in the exact shapes of the objects that send light rays to the surface of the mirror. One interesting effect of reflection is the position of the "apparent image," which seems to be behind the mirror. If a pencil is held six inches in front of a mirror, for example, it can be shown that its reflection (or apparent image) on which the eye focuses, is at an imaginary point that is six inches *behind* the surface of the mirror.

Teaching suggestions

■ Think of as many things as you can which are shiny (windows, table tops, glass, shoes, car bumpers, hub caps, water, ice, marble). Ask questions such as: "Where does light come from?" "How do we know when light is present?" "A long time ago a man developed the theory that light always travels in a straight line. Is that true?" "How can you bend light?" "What is a reflection?" "Can you see a reflection without light?" "*Where* do you see reflections?" (water, mirrors, hard shiny surfaces, oily surfaces) "When you look at the reflection of trees in a lake, is the image bent any?" "Why does a stick look like it is bent when it is poked into water?'' ''Why are the ocean, lakes, and rivers the color of the sky that day?''

- Develop a game that would challenge the students to determine: (a) where light was coming from on any given object, (b) where it was receiving reflected light, (c) from what source, and (d) where its color was being reflected on any other object or surface. The student should be brought to realize that matt surfaces reflect light differently than slick shiny surfaces.

- Using the prints, discuss how this concept has been used by different artists. (Use the same kinds of questions listed above.)

- Single objects, such as a white vase, could be set up with different colors of construction paper under them to show the effect of color being reflected. Perhaps an orange piece of paper could be set under a white shiny vase and an orange paper under a matt white vase or white paper under a black shiny vase and white paper under a black matt vase. The students could then try painting one of the objects showing the reflected lights involved.

- Brainstorm on the kinds of things that are capable of reflecting light. Begin with the obvious (white paper and hard shiny surfaces) and end with the subtle ones (skin and objects with dark hues and matt surfaces). Discuss how light can reflect in many directions and that one object can receive light from several directions and thus cast multiple shadows and reflect light in a variety of ways. Discuss the fact that *anything* we can *see* is reflecting light to our eyes!

- Analogy practice: A tree is to its reflection as _____. (For example, a boy is to his shadow, a mother is to her daughter, a voice is to its echo.)

Suggested art activity

Try bending a reflecting light from a variety of surfaces to another but differing type. Ask, ''If I held a pencil like this at an angle to a mirror or a pool of water, what angle would its reflection have?'' Have students find out and then make a picture illustrating what they have learned.

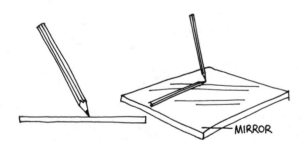

Alternative art activities

- Make a chart or bulletin board illustrating these related concepts in science.
  - Because light travels in a straight line, it cannot go around an object, it either goes through the object or the object stops it.
  - Materials differ in the amount of light they reflect, absorb, and allow to pass through them.
- Have students bring mirrors to class and draw selfportraits.

Evaluation

When the student demonstrates an awareness of the concept, then the objective has been achieved.

Other things to consider

- Vocabulary: reflection, path of light, reflected, light waves, frequency, energy.
- Art materials needed: drawing materials, pencil or crayons, paper and still life objects.
- Prints:
  Man In the Golden Helmet by Rembrandt
  My Gems by Harnett
  Turning the Stake by Eakins
  A Bar at the Folies Bergere by Monet
  The Moneylender and His Wife by Metsys
  Seven A.M. by Hopper
  St. Joseph by De La Tour
  Les Miserables by Picasso
- People who might have need for the concept: color consultant, lighting technician, painter, illustrator, interior designer.

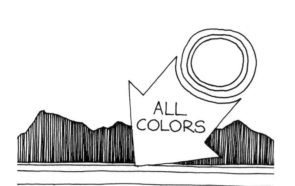

ALL COLORS

Concept taught by this activity: Sunlight and some artificial light contain the spectrum of colors. Color is reflected light; colored opaque materials reflect colors differently than transparent ones.

Objective: The student demonstrates an awareness of color as reflected light and how surfaces influence reflection. He can describe how light can appear as a spectrum of colors.

A sample lesson plan for achieving the objective:

Teacher preparations
Obtain a prism, the appropriate prints listed, and arrange for the room to be darkened as needed.

Background information

Artists recognize that a keen awareness of the opaque and transparent qualities of objects can add dimension to the ability they have to express themselves. Artists also recognize that subtle differences they see are influenced by the relative opaqueness or transparency of things. If your favorite color is red, you'll react rather differently to each variation of that color. If it's a luminous red, you react differently than when it's lustrous or iridescent, filmy or transparent. An artist may not think of color as a thing by itself, but he is concerned about how he might represent the extra beauty and feelings which the opaque and transparent dimensions of texture can lend to his creative act. The artist who cannot perceive and perhaps portray opaqueness and transparency is missing a part of his "vocabulary of expression." Such effects as luster,

iridescence, and luminosity add further dimension to transparency. Naturalistic painters have tried to achieve the qualities which are seen in life, but abstract art is a field where these qualities could be exploited in unusual ways. They could complement unusual forms and areas of color (instead of appearing as mere flat impressions of pigment). They could, also, resemble other textures altogether and thus offer new visual enjoyment. In brief, the most conventional of color schemes may turn readily to intriguing color effects if resourcefulness and skill are used.

Teaching suggestions
- Discuss what the student already knows about color. Ask questions such as: "What happens to the color in a room when there's no light at all?" "Does something have to give off light before we can see color?" "What does the word *reflect* mean?" "Can a color be reflected?" "What is a prism?" "What is it used for?"
- Hold a bright colored sheet of paper next to some other object that is white or nearly white. "Where does the color come from that is seen on the white surface?" Point out where reflected light is occurring elsewhere in the room.
- Demonstrate that a beam of light can be broken down into the spectrum of colors by passing through a glass prism. (Put a dark lens covering with a small hole in the center of a slide projector to obtain a small beam of light that can be directed through the prism onto a screen or a white piece of paper.) Ask questions such as: "What makes a rainbow?" (droplets of water acting as prisms) "Can we create a rainbow in the room?" (a fine spraying water sprinkler can be used for this, outside) "Why is color and light studied in science?" "Why does the artist need to know about color?"
- Discuss the terms *opaque* and *transparent*. See if students can readily distinguish between the two. Have examples of each previously identified and brought to the room. Select appropriate art prints containing illustrations of opaqueness and transparency.
- Relate the concepts of color reflection and the spectrum of colors. Then discuss how transparency affects color reflection. Ask questions such as: "Will *all* glass objects reflect some color?" ("If they didn't, would you see the

color?'') "Which colors of glass reflect a color best?" "If you had two green objects, both of which were exactly the same color but one was glass and the other painted wood, what differences would you find in their appearance?" "Would the color appear the same?" "Would light passing through the glass one influence the appearance of it?" "Why?" "What does the transparency of something do to its ability to reflect light?" "Are there other kinds of things that are transparent besides glass?" (porcelain dishes, plastic, paper are *somewhat* transparent.)

■ Discuss these related concepts: (Science)
  ● White light is made up of all the colors of the rainbow.
  ● If some light rays are absorbed and some reflected by an object, the object will have the color of the rays it reflects.
  ● Black is a lack of color or the absence of reflected light. White is a mixture of all colors in sunlight. (The opposite is true when the artist works with paint or pigments.)

■ Additional things to study:
"If light comes from the sun, the compounds of the earth either reflect or absorb the colors in the light. How can this be demonstrated?"
Note: This earth is colorless. The color we see is coming to us from the sun in the form of white light. When the light from the sun reaches the earth the compounds (materials) of the earth either absorb (take in) or reflect (shine back) the light (color) that it receives. Where there is no light, there is no color. Not only is color not seen in a dark room, but also the color is not there. The color of an object depends on the material or compounds of the object and the light in which the object is seen. A red-orange sweater looks red-orange because the material from which it is made--wool--and the pigments of the dyes that are in it have the capacity to absorb all the colors coming in the form of light and to reflect only the red-orange to the eye of anyone seeing it. The artist must be aware that an object of any given color reflects that color to other near objects so when painting a picture he recognizes that those reflected bits of colors are influencing what he sees.

Suggested art activity
Bring transparent and opaque objects to class or have students bring some. Have students draw or paint several objects, trying to create the illusion of opaqueness and transparency. Discuss the differences they found between transparent and opaque objects and how that enabled them to create the illusion of both. (The student need not do this skillfully since this is rather a complex problem even for older students or adults.)

Evaluation

When the student demonstrates a verbal awareness of how transparent objects reflect light in ways different from opaque ones and is able to use a prism to show that light contains a spectrum of color, then the objective has been achieved.

Other things to consider

■ Vocabulary: opaque, transparent, spectrum, luminous, iridescent, pigment, prism, reflected light.
■ Art materials needed: drawing and painting materials.
■ Prints:
Boats at Argenteuil by Monet
Fur Traders on the Missouri by Bingham
The Cradle by Morisot
Bacchus by Caravaggio
Seven A.M. by Hopper
Sacrament, Last Supper by Dali
Bar, Folies Bergere by Monet
Money Lender and Wife by Metsys
■ Films:
"Discovering Color," Bailey Film Associates
"Color and Pigment In Art," Coronet Film
■ People who might have need for the concept: painter, illustrator, color consultant, interior designer, stage designer, stage technician, lighting technician, photographer.

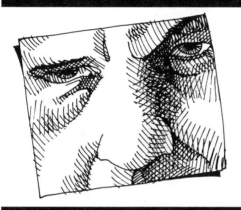

Concept taught by this activity: Perception of an object may be hindered by one's inability to visualize the "whole" of something.

Objective: The student demonstrates an increase in his ability to perceive something in his mind and draw it. When shown only a small portion of a familiar form, he can mentally add the missing parts.

A sample lesson plan for achieving the objective:

Teacher preparations

Note: Perception is a mentally conscious activity. To perceive an object takes mental work. The more we deal with the process of *really* looking at an object, the better we can remember its characteristics. "Really looking" should include firsthand or in-life experiences with the object. "Really looking" demands intense study. The viewer must analyze lines, angles, proportions, colors, values, textures, spaces, shapes, and arrangements at a highly refined level. Visual perception comes from this kind of "looking" and remembering the relationships perceived. (This concept activity is related to level 3, activity no. 106.)

■ Collect suggested prints and display them for discussion.
■ Have drawing and painting materials ready for use.

Teaching suggestions

■ Suggest drawing an object or living thing that the student has only a superficial acquaintance with, for example, a farm tractor or rooster for the urban student or a skyscraper or tenement for the rural student. Have the student describe his subject in detail, then draw upon the class and whatever resources are available within the school to clarify and enlarge upon the student's first effort. Question students regarding one's ability to draw something without ever having seen it or after a minimal experience with it.

■ Discuss experiences of people who have gone to great lengths to study something even at the peril of their lives. The example of Leonardo da Vinci and Michelangelo dissecting human bodies at a time when it was a criminal offense to do so is a classic example. Their drawings of the human body changed dramatically when their awareness changed.

■ Discuss the old principle of bleeding the sick to cure all afflictions. The practice was a result of not really perceiving that each illness had an individual cause, few of which had anything to do with the blood. Use the example of amateur portrait painters who spend such a disproportionate time getting a likeness that they end up with two pictures--one is a face and the other is what's left.

■ Point out how most artists make a conscious effort to work on their "total" product at the same time and not just start at one side and work across. Their concern is with the "whole" rather than its parts.

■ Discuss how they are able to fill in what's missing in the print *St. Joseph* (what's hidden in the shadows?), but how many have sufficient awareness to duplicate the picture from memory?

■ Remind the students that if we look carefully we will see many interesting details, but if we get too interested in some specific detail, we will miss the "essence" of the *whole* thing. Sometimes a shadow of a person can "look like" the person without showing any detail. A silhouette can give the "essence" of the person--no eyes, nostrils, or colors need be shown, but the "wholeness" is still there. The person can be recognized from the silhouette, even though details are not visible.

■ Using a soft pencil and a sheet of paper, draw a five-inch square. Use a ruler if it is helpful. Inside the square draw a simple organic shape. Make it large enough to allow parts of it to touch the borders of the square. Leave the organic shape white, but shade in the spaces around it, for example, it should look like a puzzle piece. Don't make the shape too complex. Next, take a second sheet of thin paper (for tracing) and draw another five-inch square on it. Inside this second square, draw the first organic shape again, as accurately as possible. Have the student analyze where it is off. Look at the ''whole'' of each shape, whether white or gray. Put the thin paper over the first one and check the accuracy that way. Have students cut out the various shapes and draw each.

Suggested art activity
Select a subject or some part of art that has normally been difficult to draw. Study it intently. Caution the students to not just ''look'' but to *analyze*, causing their minds to deal with great detail, as have the other artists discussed above. Look at ways others have drawn or painted it. Try to know it so well you can see it in your mind in great detail. Then draw it.

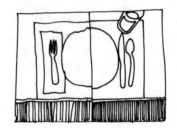

Alternative art activities
- Do the same thing as suggested above except make a sculpture, modeled or carved.
- Collect pictures of common things and cut out all but one section or part. Have the students draw the missing portions matched up to the remaining portion. This could be a group or class activity. Discuss which were recognizable when just the ''part'' was seen. Display the work showing drawings completing the objects which are shown.

Evaluation

When the student has completed one of the activities and demonstrates a heightened awareness of the concept, then the objective has been achieved.

Other things to consider

- Vocabulary: perception, visualize, mentally rendering.
- Art materials needed: drawing or painting materials.
- Prints:
  Cliff of Etretat After the Storm by Courbet (boats)
  St. Joseph by De La Tour
  Fox Island by Hartley
  Les Miserables by Picasso
  Man with Helmet by Rembrandt
  Poster—Moulin Rouge by Toulouse-Lautrec
- Book: *The Art of Responsive Drawing* by Nathan Goldstein
- People who might have need for the concept: painter, sculptor, printmaker, illustrator, commercial artist, docent.

LEVEL 7   ACTIVITY 179

Concept taught by this activity: Many problems in drawing and painting can be resolved more easily when the student deals with large or simple shapes and forms first and details last.

Objective: The student is able to solve drawing and painting problems by beginning with the large or simple shapes first and tackling details later.

A sample lesson plan for achieving the objective:

Teacher preparations
Assemble appropriate art prints and materials for drawing activities.

Teaching suggestions
- Ask: ''What are the opposites of simplification?'' (complexity, detail, chaos, hubbub, confusion) ''Complete this analogy: Details are to shape as _____
_____'' (For example, blades of grass are to lawn, or pattern is to dye).
- Discuss various ways objects can be simplified in the beginning. Stress the notion that drawing the largest and most obvious aspects of a form can make the rendering of the details easier.
- Consider treating complex forms as geometric shapes. As students progress through this experience, stress over and over that they should never use this idea as a crutch. That even though students can learn more easily by starting the subject of their drawing as an oval, triangle, or whatever shape is appropriate, they *still* need to continually sharpen their observation and must avoid stereotyped ways of drawing things.
- Have the class practice identifying the *basic* shapes in objects and have them study the relative locations and sizes of the several basic shapes that might be found in specified

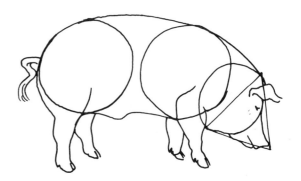

objects. Next, have them practice drawing some simple forms by first starting with the basic shapes they see. Lay tracing paper or acetate on top of some of the art prints, tracing only the basic shapes to illustrate how artists used this principle.

Suggested art activity

Have students select something which is normally a difficult subject for them to draw. Have them follow this procedure:
- Identify the basic or simple shapes they see in it first in the same relative positions they see them in.
- Vary the simple shapes and combine them until they better resemble the subject.
- Finally, add all details to the drawing.
Have the students practice working with their large muscles with large movements in their drawings and reserve their small muscle use for detail work at the end.

Alternative art activities

Follow the same procedures outlined in the suggested art activity above and apply them to the creation of a piece of sculpture.

Evaluation

When the student can describe ways in which complex forms can be treated simply in drawing and thus increase his chances for success, then the objective has been achieved.

Other things to consider

- Art materials needed: drawing and painting media.
- Prints:
  Adoration by Botticelli
  Harvesters by Breughel
  Bedroom at Arles by Van Gogh
  My Gems by Harnett
  Birds in Bamboo Tree by Koson
  The Scout by Remington
  The Brooklyn Bridge by Stella
  Moneylender and Wife by Metsys
- People who might have need for the concept: painters, sculptors, illustrators, commercial artists, printmakers, industrial designers.

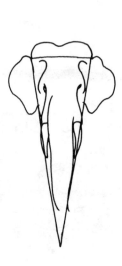

LEVEL 7 ACTIVITY 180

Concept taught by this activity: Grouping, as opposed to the lining up of shapes, usually creates a more interesting and aesthetically pleasing arrangement.

Objective: The student is able to group shapes as one way of creating more interesting and aesthetically pleasing arrangements.

A sample lesson plan for achieving the objective:

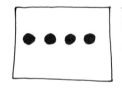

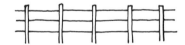

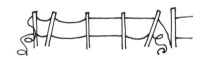

Teacher preparations
Assemble appropriate prints and art materials.

Teaching suggestions
- Discuss aspects of the concept to determine how much the students already know about it. Use questions such as: "What do the words *unity, monotony,* and *conflict* mean to you?" "Can shapes conflict with each other?" "How?" "Can shapes have unity?" "How are those with unity different from those which conflict?" "Can conflicting shapes be unified?" "When would we want unity in a picture?" "What if everything is so unified it's boring?" "Then what do you do?" "What if we just lined everything up in a row in our picture?" "Would it be all right if we made each shape a little different from all the others and *then* placed them all in a row?" "Why not?" "How does grouping of dissimilar forms give unity to a design but eliminate monotony or boredom?" "Has grouping been done in this room?" "Where?" "Why?" "In your home?" "Can you tell about it?" "Would artists use this idea of grouping?" "Why?"
- Divide the group into two teams. Suggest a variety of objects which might be arranged in a design. Team A must always arrange their objects in rows. Team B can try *other* methods in utilizing the space in their arrangements. (Suggest such things as furniture, letters and words,

automobiles, trees, houses, and toys.) Discuss the results. Which are the most interesting? Why?
- Look at art prints and discuss how the artists have used the concept. Look at interior designs, commercial advertisements, and illustrations. Has the concept been used there, too?

Suggested art activity
Find a picture in a magazine in which "grouping" needs to be used, or a picture in which it *is* used. Do a tracing of the picture on thin paper showing the proper grouping which is used successfully. Display the actual pictures and the tracings, side by side, so all students may benefit from the various examples.

Alternative art activities
- Do abstract designs utilizing the concept.
- Arrange bulletin boards utilizing the concept.

- Collect pictures from magazines that illustrate the concept. Include examples of "lining up" with pictures of condominiums or apartment houses that appear in monotonous rows.

Evaluation

When the student tries to use grouping in his arrangements to create greater interest and develop some sort of aesthetic quality in his design, then the objective has been achieved.

Other things to consider

- Vocabulary: grouping, unity, conflict, aesthetic, clustering, disorganized.
- Prints:
  Le Jour by Braque
  I and the Village by Chagall
  Dancing Class by Degas
  Apples and Oranges by Cezanne
  The Numbering at Bethlehem by Breughel
  The Night Watch by Rembrandt
  The Bullfight by Goya
  Le Moulin de la Galette by Renoir
  La Grande Jatte by Seurat
- People who might have need for the concept: landscape architect, architect, interior designer, sculptor, painter, commercial artist, printmaker.

LEVEL 7

ACTIVITY 181

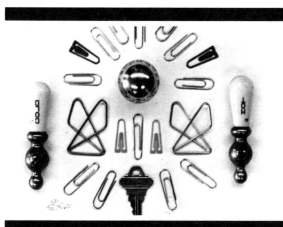

Concept taught by this activity: Objects may be grouped or arranged in many ways: horizontal, vertical, and diagonal directions; by size, shape, or function; and according to color or texture.

Objective: The student groups objects in a variety of ways and in harmony with their size, shape, function, color, and texture.

A sample lesson plan for achieving the objective:

Teacher preparations
Note: When the student becomes aware that grouping is a desirable thing to do in the arrangement of a design or picture, then the objective is to lead him to an awareness of the many ways this can be done. He needs to become *so* aware of this design factor that it becomes an automatic consideration to him anytime he observes or attempts to do any art work.

Collect appropriate prints and a variety of art media. This concept can be implemented with any materials the students might choose but imprinting and pasting activities lend themselves best to it. Bring a sack filled with many assorted objects to categorize.

Teaching suggestions
■ Fill several sacks with various objects (spools, spoons, rocks, all kinds of objects). At random ask students to empty the contents of their sack (on the floor or a table) and put them into categories, for example, red items, plastic items, metal items. This exercise gives the students practice in *flexible* thinking--the ability to recognize categories and sets. Since the student has already had a recent experience with grouping, review what was done and introduce this lesson by brainstorming on all the different ways one might group objects. Use the students' own clothing, objects in

the room and outside the class as examples or resources in addition to art prints and pictures from magazines.
■ Ask questions such as: "Should the "kind" of thing you're grouping influence how you go about it?" (grouping elephants vs. fence posts or automobiles vs. houses or lamps) Bring in the effects that size, shape, and function have.
■ "Would the colors of objects in a grouping influence how you arranged them?" "What if you were arranging lamps and three were red, two were black, and one was light green? Would it matter which ones were next to each other?" "Why?"
■ The same sort of discussion on texture would be as valid as the above one on color.
■ Look at prints and identify ways in which size, shape, function, texture, and color may have influenced the arrangement or groupings of objects and people by each artist. Help students to be aware that it takes a great deal of practice and continuous analysis for one to use this concept well and with any consistency.

Suggested art activity
Do vegetable prints, gadget prints, or pasted collage designs using colored paper to implement the concept.

Alternative art activities
■ Have the students paint a design or picture of some favorite subject utilizing the concept and describing how they went about the task.
■ Have a committee prepare a display for the room or hall built around the concept.

Evaluation

When the student demonstrates an awareness--either verbally or nonverbally--of the concept, then the objective has been achieved.

Other things to consider

- Art materials needed: any art materials would be appropriate but those which cause the student to work abstractly and allow him to analyze and alter his decisions will bring greater success.
- Prints:
  Christina's World by Wyeth
  Marilyn Monroe by Warhol
  Rebus by Rauschenberg
  The Bullfight by Goya
  House at Aix by Cezanne
  Still Music by Shahn
  La Grande Jatte by Seurat
  Breezing Up by Homer
  Seven A.M. by Hopper
  Women In a Garden by Monet
- People who might have need for the concept: architect, landscape architect, interior designer, city planner, painter, sculptor, printmaker.

LEVEL 7

ACTIVITY 182

Concept taught by this activity: When a color and its complement are mixed together, each tends to gray or neutralize; but when placed side by side, each emphasizes or intensifies the other.

Objective: The student points out ways in which complements can either dull or neutralize or emphasize and accent each other.

A sample lesson plan for achieving the objective:

Teacher preparations
Collect appropriate prints and photographs. Assemble painting materials such as crayons, chalk, tempera, or watercolors. Display a color wheel.

Teaching suggestions
- Review the complementary colors. Have students pick them out on a color wheel or refer to examples in the room.
- Use students to demonstrate ways in which colors influence each other when mixed. Have a container of pale orange (white added to orange) and let a student mix some of it with a small amount of violet, brown, black, and blue (each in turn with a clean brush). The orange will make a gray out of the blue and thus neutralize it most. See if students are able to pick this out.
- Discuss why artists gray their colors. (To control intensity; gray harmonizes well with other colors.) Compare the brightness of pure colors with similar hues in prints by famous artists.
- Go outside and as you walk around the building ask questions such as: "Are all of nature's colors bright and hot looking?" "What if the sky was red all the time?" "Why does mother nature reserve her bright colors for accents?" "Do artists do the same thing?" "In what way do colors change as they appear farther away?" (bluer and grayer)

- Take colors and place their complements in cellophane over the top (blue over orange, yellow over violet, and red over green). "What happens to the two colors mixed this way?" "Do a picture in which all but your accent colors have been grayed by adding their complement and white."
- Discuss what might happen if the eye mixed the colors, for example, tiny dots of red scattered among tiny dots of green. "Would you still get a grayed or neutral tone?" (yes) (Have someone try it after several have had an opportunity to commit themselves.) The comics offer a good source—study them with a magnifier.
- Experiment with small geometric shapes in blue, violet, and green by placing them on backgrounds of red, yellow, and orange to see which combinations seem to clash the most. (Complements will contrast stronger than any other combinations.) See if it makes any difference in the way complements accent or emphasize each other if one is lighter in value or grayer in hue. Discuss the results. "Are there only three sets of complementary colors?" "Why do artists want colors to be neutral one time and contrasting another?"
- Look at prints or color photographs which contain colors that are seen next to or against their complement. Discuss the effect this has on them. Students should conclude that complements placed next to each other or overlapped in any way will emphasize or accent each other.
- Discuss the validity of each of the following statements. Are they true? when? always? When a color wheel is made by mixing the three primary colors, each wheel will be different as done by the individual student. No matter how many colors there are on a wheel, the color across from any given color is its complement. When complementary colors are seen together in nature, they are usually harmonious or dulled. When complementary colors of high intensity are placed next to each other, a visual conflict occurs.
- See if students can point out places where the concept has been used in the room, on themselves, and outside the room.

Suggested art activity
Use one or more of the sets of complementary colors and make an abstract picture. Many kinds of paper could be

used with different and interesting results, for example, construction paper, tissue paper, or cellophane paper which can be overlapped to show other colors through. Discuss the results of the overlapping. When using construction paper, discuss the effect on intensity when placing one complementary color directly on the other or side by side as compared with having white or a neutral paper showing in between.

Alternative art activities
■ Make a realistic picture with realistic forms using only one set of complementary colors. Repeat the same picture using the colors as they would be used realistically. Compare and discuss results.
■ Make a mobile using only one set of the complementary colors, either in their high intensity or dulled or neutralized.
■ Have students find pictures in magazines where complementary colors are used directly on top of each other or as the predominant colors but in a dulled tone.
■ Have students think of complements in nature such as red berries on green bushes. Or, go on a walk to find these things.
■ Find an appropriate picture or pictures that contrast in the use of complements and have the student write his own reactions.

Evaluation

When the student demonstrates an awareness of the effects complements have on each other, then the objective has been achieved.

Other things to consider

■ Vocabulary: complement, accent, emphasize, contrast, clash, intensity, hue.
■ Art materials needed: any painting media is appropriate for this activity along with such things as colored paper, cellophane, scissors, paste, magazines, and materials for making a mobile.
■ Film: "Color and Pigment in Art," a Coronet Film
■ Prints:
The Small Crucifixion by Grunewald
Head of a Man by Klee
The Letter by Vermeer
I and the Village by Chagall
Bedroom at Arles by Van Gogh
Before the Start by Lapicque
La Grande Jatte by Seurat
Zebegen by Vasarely
■ People who might have need for the concept: painters, illustrators, docent, art historian, art critic, commercial artist, printmaker, architect, interior decorator, color consultant, window designer, house painter, cartoonist, landscape architect, display designer, fabric designer, set designer.

LEVEL 7

ACTIVITY 183

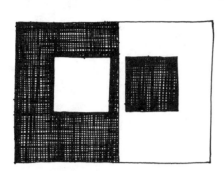

Concept taught by this activity: Each value is directly affected by the value of shapes that surround it: dark values may appear to come forward or light ones recede or even vice versa.

Objective: The student identifies some of the reasons (why or how) a given value is influenced by the shape or shapes surrounding it.

A sample lesson plan for achieving the objective:

Teacher preparations
Note: This is an extension of activity no. 182 and a preliminary to numbers 184, 185, and 186. It could be taught concurrently or separately from each.
■ Collect and display suggested prints. Add photographs or other pictures housed in the library (or media center) that further illustrate the concept.
■ Have materials ready for demonstrations and suggested art activity.

Teaching suggestions
■ Have three "weights" of some sort in front of the class. One is something quite light, such as an egg; another heavier than the egg; and a *very* heavy object. Have several students lift the light object, then the very heavy one. Last, have them lift the middle weight. Ask if it is lighter than the first weight. Many will say that it is. What has made the heavier middle weight *seem* lighter than the first was? It contrasts with the very heavy weight. This is true with shades, tones, and colors as well.
■ Review to whatever degree is necessary what the students remember about the influence complementary colors have on each other.

■ Ask questions such as: "Do you suppose shades without color could have the same sort of influence?" "For example, would a black circle look any different on a white background than it would on a middle gray or dark background?" "Why?" "How can you find out for sure?" "Is it possible for someone to make a shape appear lighter or darker by just changing its background?" "Who can prove their answer?"
■ Have the students experiment with pieces of construction paper and other kinds of paper that range in value from white to black. Test four or five shapes with values against a variety of backgrounds ranging from white to black. Discuss ways in which each seems to change in relation to its background. Ask, "Which shape (value) seems closest to you?" "Does the shape look lighter or darker now?" "Does it make any difference if the shape is smooth or textured?" "Can one shape appear to come forward in one setting and backwards in another?" Remind the students that colors have values of dark, gray, and light.
■ Discuss ways in which this concept might influence how we see things in life, for example, a room in our home or at school. Discuss how value relates to color. Talk about value relationships in photography.
■ Look at the art prints and other pictures. Ask, "Where has the artist used the concept?" "Why does the figure of Christ (*Crucifixion* by Dali) seem to come forward?" "Why do the white floor tiles (*The Letter* by Vermeer) seem to float above the floor?"

Suggested art activity
Do a series of swatches illustrating what happens when a

specific value is placed in front of a series of colored backgrounds ranging in value from white to black. Have each student work with a different color. Have them experiment with textures on the colors, too.

Alternative art activities
- Create a design or picture that seems to have depth but only because the concept has been applied. (no linear perspective)
- Do a display for the room or the hall illustrating the concept to teach the idea to other students.

Evaluation

When the student can describe the influence of one value on another in any given circumstance, then the objective has been achieved.

Other things to consider

- Vocabulary: recede, affected, influence, linear perspective.
- Art materials needed: tempera paint or crayons, paper, pencils, scissors, paste, and colored paper.
- Prints:
  Fur Traders on the Missouri by Bingham
  Guernica by Picasso
  The Crucifixion by Dali
  Water Flowery Mill by Gorky
  Man in the Golden Helmet by Rembrandt
  The Letter by Vermeer
  St. Joseph by De La Tour
  Don Manuel Osorio by Goya
  Composition 1963 by Miro
  Cheyt M by Vasarely
  Any of Josef Albers color studies are excellent examples.
- People who might have need for the concept: painters, illustrators, commercial artists, sculptors, craftsmen, printmakers, architects, interior designers, display designers, fabric designers, set designers.

LEVEL 7

ACTIVITY 184

Concept taught by this activity: It is difficult to have a colorless gray because the neutral takes on the appearance of any adjacent colors. A color is affected by its environment.

Objective: The student points out examples of how neutral colors take on the appearance of whatever is adjacent to them.

A sample lesson plan for achieving the objective:

Teacher preparations
Review activity no. 122 in which the students discussed the symbolic nature of art. Collect appropriate illustrations and whatever kinds of examples are available. Be aware of examples that exist in and around the student, too, especially those which are part of the natural (nature) environment.

Teaching suggestions
■ Begin the discussion by asking questions such as: "What does the word *neutral* mean?" "If we were to note that some colors are neutral, which ones would we be talking about?" (black, white, and gray) "If all shades of gray are truly neutral, will they go with any other color without clashing?" "Can something be gray and yet be a mixture of gray and another color?" (blue gray, reddish gray, greenish gray, for example) "If the gray is *totally* neutral, will it have another color evident in it?"
■ To fully answer the last question students must clearly understand that a neutral will *not* be a hue or tone of some other color. (What makes it *appear* that way is the color adjacent to it or behind it. Have students with grays and colored chips or sheets of paper and see if they can come to this conclusion themselves.)
■ Discuss the following story: Mr. X painted one wall of his basement a pale lavender. When he got through his wife

asked, "Why did you paint the wall white?" "It isn't white, it's lavender," said the husband. Four days later the wife looked at the wall again and said, "It looks like lavender to me now, but will it go with the carpet we're buying?" (The carpet was blue with some lavender tones in it.) After the carpet was installed the wife looked at the wall again and declared, "Now the wall looks blue; why is that?" "That's just what I hoped would happen," answered the husband mysteriously.

What did happen? Did the wall really change colors like the wife thought? How does this story apply to the concept?
■ Establish in the opening discussion that this lesson deals with the influence *environment* has on color. What we know about a color and the impressions we have concerning it are altered by any change in environment—whether it's symbolic, cultural, or natural. You may want to discuss the terms used in the concept itself first, for example, "What does *environment* mean?" "Can our environment change?" "Are there different kinds of environments?" "Can we experience several at the same time?" "How could the environment be symbolic?" "How do the terms *symbolic* and *cultural* relate to each other?" "Would cultures such as the Polynesian, Chinese, Indian, and American attach *different* meaning to the same color?" "Would people in one part of the world be more familiar with shades or tints of some colors than people in another area?" (Eskimos in the Arctic as opposed to natives in a tropical area as opposed to people in a large American city.) "Wouldn't the color blue, for example, have a somewhat different meaning to each culture then?"
■ Review some of the lessons in which students have discussed ways in which colors influence each other. Move from those ideas into a discussion of how the natural environment has an influence, too. (A red tulip seen against green foliage, dark rich soil, a dark blue sky, or an orangish gray fence.)
■ Set up committees to further investigate the ideas discussed. This could be an excellent way to find answers to unanswered questions or to extend class awareness of the concept. Be sure that at least the natural and cultural

influences are investigated. Physiological effects of color might also be a part of the natural environment discussion. Design art projects using some of the symbols or motifs of different cultures, for example, Indian paintings, totems, and religious symbols.

■ Look at prints and whatever other resources are readily available and discuss whether or not the artist was aware of this concept.

Suggested art activity
Look at a series of colors placed next to and/or in back of neutral gray shapes. Each time ask what color the gray is. "Does the gray take on the color it is next to or in front of?" It should if the amount of gray is similar in size to the color. Have students locate examples of the concept in magazines, prints, or paintings by artists. Look especially for the use of this concept in home and yard magazines.

Alternative art activities
■ Do a collage or paint a design that demonstrates the concept.
■ Create a personal symbol to show what kind of a person you feel you are.
■ Design a coat of arms, a shield, a symbol for your school or an industry.
■ Make a collection of artifacts that have symbolic design and color. Display and discuss. (Indian jewelry and art, Japanese prints, totem poles, tiki heads)

Evaluation

When the student demonstrates an awareness of the concept, the objective has been achieved.

Other things to consider

■ Vocabulary: neutral, colorless, adjacent, hue, tone, shade, mood, influence, environment.
■ Art materials needed: colored paper, magazines, paints, paper, scissors, glue or paste, and brushes.
■ Prints:
I and the Village by Chagall
Harvest Scene by Gauguin
Before the Start by Lapicque
Boats at Argenteuil by Monet
Rebus by Rauschenberg
Virgin Forest by Rousseau
The Rhine Maidens by Ryder
The Letter by Vermeer
Look at two or three prints at once and imagine how a color in one would look if it were seen in the environment of another.
■ People who might have need for the concept: painter, house painter, interior designer, illustrator, commercial artist, artists that do serigraphs, prints, stage design, advertising and cartoons.

LEVEL 7

ACTIVITY 185

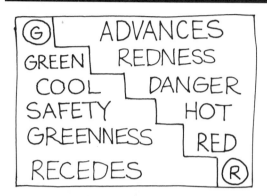

ADVANCES
REDNESS
DANGER
HOT
RED

GREEN
COOL
SAFETY
GREENNESS
RECEDES

Concept taught by this activity: Every pair of complementary colors shows a balancing of opposites such as cool and warm, red and green, or light and dark. The complement of a color neutralizes the given characteristic.

Objective: The student demonstrates an awareness of how complementary colors may balance opposing characteristics.

Note: In art the word *complement* means opposite. It is opposite in warmness and coolness, darkness and lightness, and opposite as far as ingredients are concerned. Complements cancel or neutralize the effect of each other and visual balance is made easier.

A sample lesson plan for achieving the objective:

Teacher preparations
■ Collect suggested prints and whatever other pictures might be helpful.
■ Assemble art materials for the suggested activity.

Teaching suggestions
■ Review aspects of previous lessons on complements.
■ Brainstorm briefly on a variety of opposites. First ask for all of the opposites students can think of, next ask for all of the hot and cold things, salty and peppery things, love and hate examples. (See if any of the opposites apply to color.) "How are complementary colors opposite?" Discuss ways other than placement on the color wheel.
■ The process of after-image could be experienced again with this concept with the explanation that our sight mechanism puts in the complement even when there is not one in existence. This can give the artist clues as to compatible intensities of complementary colors.
■ Discuss whether or not cool-opposite-warm colors have a neutralizing effect or if dark-opposite-light or gray-opposite-pure colors have a neutralizing effect. "Are there any characteristics of complements that *aren't* opposites?" (Texture may or may not be since it's a separate element. Darks and lights are complements in some cases but not others.) After this discussion ask, "Do the complements *still* seem to balance or neutralize each other?"
■ Discuss the art prints in terms of the warmth and coolness of colors--their redness or greenness, darkness or lightness. Multiple ways of describing the characteristics of colors and how one characteristic is the opposite of the other and has a balancing or neutralizing effect like complements do.
■ The "opposition" principle and "balancing-off" principle are well taught in the use of similes and metaphors. Discuss how a successful simile takes two apparently opposite, unlike things and surprisingly creates a harmony and relatedness. For example, "The fluff floated in the air like a newborn colt chasing his shadow." (Fluff is very light and inanimate. A colt is relatively heavy and animate.)

Suggested art activity
Paint a picture using nothing but complements. List ways in which the colors used had a neutralizing or balancing effect on each other.

Alternative art activities
■ Create a design from complements using colored tissue paper.

■ Do a stitchery, weaving, or applique using complementary colors.

Evaluation

When the student points out a variety of ways complements balance or neutralize each other, the objective has been achieved.

Other things to consider

■ Vocabulary: exemplifies, balancing of color, opposites.
■ Art materials needed: drawing and painting materials, and for alternative activities, colored tissue paper and materials for fabric designs.
■ Prints:
Harvest Scene by Gauguin
Tranquility by Gasser
Sinbad the Sailor by Klee
Flowers and Parrots by Matisse
Mlle. Violette by Redon
Zebegen by Vasarely
Boats at Argenteuil by Monet
The Old King by Rouault
■ People who might have need for the concept: interior designer, floral arranger, architect, landscape architect, painter, illustrator, commercial artist, color consultant, art critic, art historian, docent.

LEVEL 7

ACTIVITY 186

Concept taught by this activity: Colors may seem to be passive and receding, aggressive and advancing.

Objective: The student identifies ways in which colors may seem to be passive and receding, or aggressive and advancing.

A sample lesson plan for achieving the objective:

Teacher preparations
- Have materials and magazines ready.
- Review lesson and background information.
- Have pictures displayed as examples to refer to. (Colored chips or colored paper could also prove helpful.)

Teaching suggestions
- Have a question and answer session to get students thinking about characteristics of color learned from previous discussions and how they relate to this lesson. Ask the following questions: "Is seeing color something we learn or something we just do automatically?" (It is a learned process. Blind people who gain their sight have to learn to see color.) "How does the eye see each color separately when light is made up of all the colors?" (All of the colors in light are absorbed by the object except the color it is, and that one reflects back. Discuss spectrum, rainbows, and prism.) "When we see colors, each color has special characteristics and we need to talk about some of them so you can learn to use color better."
- Discuss characteristics of color and refer to chips (samples) of pure color: (1) warm—cool; (2) aggressive—passive; (3) advancing—receding; (4) dominating—submissive; (5) opaque—transparent (kinds of paint rather than colors); (6) bright—dull. "Which colors fit which characteristics?" Name or list them.

- Discuss some of the prints suggested. "Which characteristics can you find that they've used?" "Do you think artists understood the characteristics we've discussed?" (Have children squint their eyes while looking at prints. The aggressive colors will come out and the passive ones fade.) Ask: "Who needs to know about these things?" "What professions?" "Why?" (designers, decorators, manufacturers, businessmen, landscape artists) "What helps or tools do you imagine those people would use?" (Lead students to discover training is needed and also color chart displaying the characteristics of color . needed.)
- A review of passiveness, recessiveness, advancing, and so on can be conducted musically. Some music is loud, dominant, and aggressive. Some is quiet, peaceful, recessive. Play examples and let the students call out descriptions. Hold up colors which are more like the music being played. (Accept all student responses except those which are obviously out of character and interpretation.)

Suggested art activity
Considering the psychological effects of color, design two color schemes for a room—one that would calm down a nervous, aggressive person and one that would be very exciting and stimulating to a shy, quiet person.

Alternative art activities
- Do a landscape picture (painted or collage) and try to destroy perspective by using color opposite to the way it is seen in nature. (Have shapes get brighter and warmer in the distance.) Use pictures or outdoor scenes to look at and reverse.
- Design and draw a paper model of yourself and two additional outfits for the model. Color one outfit with an aggressive color, the second a passive color, and the third both a passive and an aggressive color.

Evaluation

When the student demonstrates an awareness of the concept either verbal or nonverbal, then the objective has been achieved.

Other things to consider

- Vocabulary: aggressive, passive, warm, cool, dominant, submissive, advancing, receding, opaque, transparent, bright, dull, shade, tint, collage, spectrum, prism, absorb, reflect.
- Art materials needed: pencils, paper, paint, color chips, colored paper, magazines, scissors, paste or glue, and brushes.
- Film: "Discovering Color" by Bailey-Film Associates
- Prints:
  Before the Start by Lapicque
  Composition 1963 by Miro
  Combination Concrete by Davis
  Zebegen by Vasarely
  Water Flowery Mill by Gorky
  Orange and Yellow by Rothko
  The Old King by Rouault
  The Brooklyn Bridge by Stella
  Virgin Forest by Rousseau
- People who might have need for the concept: color consultant, interior designer, painter, commercial artist, docent, stage set designer, serigraph artists, printmakers, display technicians, cartoonists, interior designers.

LEVEL 7

ACTIVITY 187

Concept taught by this activity: Artists fulfill numerous functions in society and explore a great variety of interests.

Objective: The student demonstrates an increased awareness of what artists do and how their work contributes to their society.

A sample lesson plan for achieving the objective:

Teacher preparations
- Collect and display examples of the kinds of work artists do. This could include examples of architecture, industrial designs such as lamps, TVs, and cars, landscape architecture, commercial art such as TV advertising, package design, and illustrations for books and magazines, fashion design, interior decoration, sculpture, painting, and ceramics.
- Arrange a walking tour to follow the discussion and have students list everything they see that was probably at one time designed by an artist. This tour could include other parts of the building and a short distance from the school. (The building itself plus fixtures, furnishings, landscaping, signs, and other accoutrements ought to be items that students would list.)

Teaching suggestions
- Ask, "If you were given enough money to hire an artist for all day today, what would *you* have him do for you?" "If we gave each of you all the knowledge and skills required to be an artist, what would you do for *yourself* today?" "Complete this simile: The statue was as calm and beautiful as _____." Ask the students to make a list of the things they think artists do. Ask questions such as: "What is an artist?" "What are all of the things artists do?" "When is a person considered an artist?"

- Extend the list by mentioning that "*everyone* who creates an original design for *anything* used by man is an artist." "What else could be added to our list?" The eventual and total list should ultimately include the following: architects, city planners, landscape architects, interior decorators, mural painters, landscape and figure painters, draftsmen, portrait painters, abstract painters, sculptors, commercial illustrators, fashion designers, sign painters, advertising designers, package designers, printmakers, graphics designers, art directors, art teachers, potter artists, ceramists, jewelry designers, industrial designers, glass blowers, furniture designers, lapidary artists, weavers, textile designers, rug makers, tapestry designers, lithographics artists, metal sculptors, artist welders, art historians, art critics, color consultants, automotive designers, photographers, layout men, cartoonists, stage designers, costume designers, musicians, actors, actresses.
- Discuss how different our lives would be if none of the people listed above existed.
- Have students investigate and then report on how the role of the artist began and how it has changed as society has changed. This could be a committee assignment.

Suggested art activity
- Make a collage or montage of the great variety of things artists produce.
- Report on the kinds of skills and tools various artists utilize.

Alternative art activities
Make a mural depicting the functions of art and artists. Schedule a series of visits by artists representing some of the more unusual areas of art.

Evaluation

When the student can identify from two to three times as many vocational opportunities available in art as compared with those he knew prior to this experience, then the objective has been achieved.

Other things to consider

■ Art materials needed: magazines, art paper, drawing and painting media.
■ Books:
  Art as Image and Idea by Feldman
  Art Search and Self-discovery by Schinneller
  Art in Everyday Life by Goldstein
■ Films:
  "Art in Our World"
  "Changing Art in a Changing World," Bailey Film Associates
  "Art, What Is It, Why Is It," Encyclopedia Britannica Films
■ People who might have need for the concept: teachers, art critics, art historians, docents.

LEVEL 7

ACTIVITY 188

Concept taught by this activity: Contemporary uses of photography and careers associated with the art can be identified.

Objective: The student identifies contemporary uses of photography and careers associated with those uses.

A sample lesson plan for achieving the objective:

Teacher preparations
Assemble materials, listings, or charts required for discussions and activities. Include, if possible, one of the films available from Kodak on teenage film makers.

Teaching suggestions
- Set the scene for a discussion of photography—its uses and potential as an art form and some of the careers associated with it. Ask questions such as: "Is photography really an art?" "If a camera will reproduce anything you aim it at far better than anyone could draw or paint, where is there any art to photography?" (The imagination and creativity is dependent on the person using the camera.)
- Discuss the body of knowledge required of a photographer: "What does he need to know about cameras (the great variety of kinds and quality requires constant study and updating), lenses, filters, light meters, film, film developing, picture enlarging, tripods, and other equipment which he uses?"
- "What kind of education and experience must one have to be a photographer?" "How would an art background assist the individual?" "How important is a sense of color and design to a photographer?" "What techniques does he need to explore?" "How are chemistry and physics important to a photographer?"
- If many of these questions cannot be answered appropriately in class, have students do research on them

or invite a photographer to come to class with his equipment and provide the assistance needed. (Over 65,000 people make a living from photography and it is also one of the major hobbies.)
- Discuss the various kinds of jobs photographers do. (TV cameramen, movie cameramen, studio photographers, equipment and supply salesmen, aerial photographers, police photographers, photoengravers, newspaper and magazine photographers.) You might also talk about professions or careers that could use photography (commercial artists, advertising agencies, illustrators of all kinds, art teachers, painters, sculptors, product and package designers, art supervisors, potter artists, stage designers, sign painters, and parents).
- Look at some of the movies available from Kodak that represent prize winners in their film making contests.

Alternative art activities
Develop a display or bulletin board on photography showing the different phases or careers, have examples of the pictures people in those careers take, and show what kinds of art experiences and knowledge assist the photographer in doing a better job.

Evaluation

When the student demonstrates an increased awareness (verbal or nonverbal) of the role photography plays as an art form and careers associated with it, then the objective has been achieved.

Other things to consider

- Vocabulary: tripod, filter, light meter.
- Art materials needed: An assortment of cameras and photographic equipment. Examples from a variety of careers in photography. Several high quality magazines on photography as resources.
- People who might have need for the concept: (See list in "teaching suggestions" section.)

LEVEL 7 ACTIVITY 189

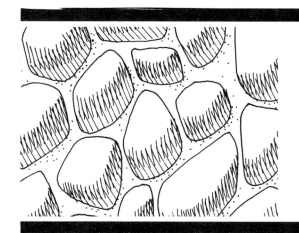

Concept taught by this activity: Mosaics can be created by embedding hard objects in a material which will solidify.

Objective: The student will demonstrate that forms can be created or altered by embedding hard objects in a material which will solidify.

A sample lesson plan for achieving the objective:

Teacher preparations
- Assemble materials needed for this activity. If a mosaic is done, a stiff board such as ½″ plywood with ¼″ square wire nailed to the surface is needed for the cement to stick to the surface.
- Be familiar with the processes and be prepared to demonstrate any of the various steps.
- Display examples for discussion.
- If plaster is used, set up materials for plaster mixing so that desks and other surfaces are protected. Allow for quick setting of plaster. Have means for cleaning and disposing of excess plaster without clogging the sink.

Teaching suggestions
- In one minute, have the students make as long a list as possible of places they have seen tiles used. (bathroom, shelves, walls, floors, murals at church) Review this experience by making mosaics set in grout. Announce that there are still other processes, similar to the experiences they have had, by which mosaics and other forms may be created. (See activity no. 146 for review.)
- "Who can describe how a stone fireplace is laid?" "Is the process different from laying brick?" "Or the laying of a hearth?"
- "Are some mosaics done by embedding pieces?"
- "Have fossils come about as a result of embedding?"

"How?"
- "Why would an artist want a wall hanging to be partially three-dimensional?" "Who are some artists that create assemblages?"
- "How many different materials can objects be embedded in?"
- "What kinds of soft materials are available that we could set tessara into and create a mosaic?" "What other kinds of things could be made by the embedding process?" (The embedding process is analogous to sticking a hand or foot in mud or snow.)

Suggested art activity
Form a mosaiclike design by embedding tessera or objects in sand and pouring plaster onto the design so that the objects become embedded in the plaster once it has set.

Alternative art activities
- Make a wall plaque by embedding colored glass or tile in thick plaster of Paris.
- Make floral or weed arrangement for table or mantle decoration by embedding the objects in plaster of Paris. (Or Christmas wreaths or other decorations in linoleum paste)
- Embed mosaic pieces for a design in clear or colored melted plastic. (Jewelry can be made by this method also.)
- Cover can with chicken wire that will hold plaster to its surface and embed rocks, glass, and other objects for decoration. (May be used as planter.)
- Make a mosaic by embedding the tessera in white cement or some other material which hardens slowly.
- Describe a ceramic form (sculpture or pot) with tesseralike shapes embedded in the clay (the pieces would be glued into the places made for them after firing).

Evaluation

The object the student makes by the process of embedding serves as evidence that the objective has been achieved.

Other things to consider

■ Vocabulary: embedding, solidify, fossil, mosaic, tessera.
■ Art materials needed: Depending on the activity selected, the following materials might be used: plaster of Paris, found objects, linoleum paste, wallpaper cleaner, plastic, cans, chicken wire, white cement or other similar material, plywood, a heavy screen wire, nails or carpet tacks, and some kind of found or commercial tessera, clay and glass or tessera of some kind which are colorful.
■ Books:
Mosaics for Everyone by Sister Mary Magdalene, Immaculate Heart College Press
Creative Clay Design by Rottger, Reinhold Co.
Ceramics Art in the School Program by Supensky, Davis Pub.

LEVEL 7   ACTIVITY 190

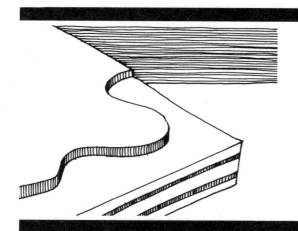

Concept taught by this activity: As a prelude to various art crafts, the student can create a variety of forms by laminating thin sheets of various materials.

Objective: The student laminates thin sheets of some material as part of learning to create objects in some of the various art crafts.

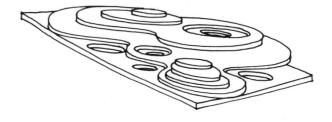

A sample lesson plan for achieving the objective:

Teacher preparations
- Assemble materials for demonstrations and student use.
- Have samples of laminating available, for example, wood and cardboard.

Teaching suggestions
- Discuss the meaning and purpose of laminating: "Does anyone know what the word *laminate* means?'' "Why do craftsmen laminate wood?'' "Why is plywood (a form of laminated wood) able to fulfill certain roles in building that regular boards cannot?'' "Is corrugated cardboard a form of laminated paper?'' "What advantage does corrugated paper have over regular paper?'' "How is that like corrugated potato chips?'' Develop from your discussion the notion that both strength and appearance are of major importance in laminating.
- Discuss what kinds of materials can be laminated. (plastic, paper, wood, cloth, and others) Brainstorm on the kinds of forms or objects one might possibly create with the laminating process. Look at examples of laminating and discuss their possibilities for use.

Suggested art activity
Laminate pieces of white card stock or poster board to create a relief kind of design somewhat after the order of a contour map.

Alternative art activities
- Create three dimensional or relief designs by laminating sheets of balsa wood, plastic, or cardboard in layers at various heights.
- Laminate materials together and carve them into a new form or combine laminated pieces together as new shapes or forms.

Evaluation

When the student has created a design or form utilizing the laminating process, the objective has been achieved.

Other things to consider

- Vocabulary: laminate, laminated.
- Art materials needed: glue, paper, pencils, a choice of materials such as balsa wood, smooth cardboard, plastic, or corrugated cardboard.
- Books:
  Creating with Corrugated Paper, a Reinhold Publication
  Creative Wood Design, a Reinhold Publication
- People who might have need for the concept: designer craftsmen, woodworkers, carpenters, cabinet makers, furniture designers, sculptors, architects, cartographers.

Concept taught by this activity: Strong contrasts of hue or of value tend to attract our attention immediately, while gradual changes lead us progressively from one shape to the next.

Objective: The student demonstrates a recognition of how differently strong contrasts affect the viewer, as opposed to how gradations in contrast affect the viewer.

A sample lesson plan for achieving the objective:

Teacher preparations
- Because much of what artists deal with is visual it becomes very important for the artist to intimately understand how to attract visual attention when the need calls for it. This concept, if understood and practiced, can give great strength to observing and creating art.
- Collect and display recommended art prints and appropriate illustrations found in the media center or library.
- Have art materials available for the suggested activity.

Teaching suggestions
- Brainstorm for examples of the concept located in the room, on an individual's dress, and outside the classroom or the school building.
- Have the students evaluate an advertisement out of a magazine and have some of them explain to the rest of the class how this concept had been used to sell a product. Evaluate an interior design or a television commercial.

Suggested art activity
Create a calendar for the room and by using this concept draw attention to special days and holidays.

Alternative art activities
- Make a display built around another area of the curriculum, keeping this concept in mind as it is done.
- As a team activity, arrange and decorate the room for a parent back-to-school night.
- Have a team of students put up an art exhibit in the hall built around this concept, making it understandable to the rest of the students in the school.
- Do the scenery for a class puppet show or production. Depict the special scenes using this concept.

Evaluation

When the student can describe the differences in how gradations in contrast affect the viewer as compared with strong or abrupt contrasts, the objective has been achieved.

Other things to consider

- Art materials needed: pencils, paper, and paint or those materials required for any alternative activity.
- Prints:
  St. Joseph by De La Tour
  Fox Island by Hartley
  The Return by Magritte
  The Scout by Remington
  Zebegen by Vasarely

Rockets and Blue Lights by Turner
Quadrille by Toulouse-Lautrec
Fighting Horses by Gericault

■ People who might have need for the concept: painter, illustrator, commercial artist, industrial designer, architect, landscape architect, city planner, interior designer, fashion designer, stage set designer, printmakers of all types.

Concept taught by this activity: When the interval between like shapes is repeated in a uniform order, the design becomes more formal. Unequal spaces create a more informal arrangement.

Objective: The student describes ways in which the space or interval between like shapes affects the formal or informal quality of an arrangement.

A sample lesson plan for achieving the objective:

Teacher preparations
- Assemble and display suggested art prints and whatever illustrations may be available in the school media center or library.
- Have materials ready for suggested art activity.

Teaching suggestions
Note: This is another design or arrangement tool. It is similar to learning a word that enlarges one's vocabulary. You do not need to use the word every time you speak, but only when that word will say what you want to say. This concept is used by artists in a similar way. When it is part of them, they can use the idea to create formal or informal order. The student should first be able to detect the use of this concept in works of art ranging from architecture to drawing. The student should also be able to tell when it has been used properly.
- Review the student's understanding of the terms *formal* and *informal.* Talk about pattern and the need for repetition.
- Discuss the principle that informal designs or patterns are usually more dynamic or active than formal ones.
- An "interval" can be a space vertically or horizontally or *any* way, and it can be *heard* in music as well as *seen* in

art. A realistic artist will often vary an interval for interest just as musicians often use similar variations. Listen for some.

Suggested art activity
Create either a formal or informal design and demonstrate an understanding of the concept. A construction with wood blocks or paper could be done in addition to drawing or painting.

Alternative art activities
- Create flower or weed arrangements in applying the concept.
- Create a fabric or wall pattern with imprinting. Have one formal design and one informal.

Evaluation

When the student can describe or illustrate ways in which the space or interval between like shapes affects their formal or informal quality, the objective has been achieved.

Other things to consider

- Vocabulary: interval, regulated, uniform, formal, informal.
- Art materials needed: wood scraps, glue, heavy paper, scissors, paint, and paper.

- Prints:
  Three Flags by Johns
  Rebus by Rauschenberg
  Justice and Peace by Overstreet
  Still Music by Shahn
  Zebegen by Vasarely
  Cheyt M by Vasarely
- People who might have need for the concept: sculptor, painter, printmaker, commercial artist, architect, interior designer, landscape architect, city planner, designer craftsmen, potter, art historian, docent.

LEVEL 7

ACTIVITY 193

Concept taught by this activity: The repetition of parts of a design tends to create unity but may create monotony.

Objective: The student creates unity without monotony by using repetition in a design.

A sample lesson plan for achieving the objective:

Teacher preparations

Note: This is another design or arrangement tool, and please note that the concept says "TENDS TO." If the other elements of a composition (such as color and value) are not unified the composition will not appear to be unified even though there is a repetition of the parts of the design. "Parts of a design" refers to elements that make up the design or arrangement, such as line, color, form, value, texture, space, and shape.

■ Collect suggested prints and whatever other illustrations might be helpful.

■ Have materials for the suggested art activity ready for use.

Teaching suggestions

■ Repeatedly tap a ruler on a desk or beat a drum in a monotonous rhythm. Ask the students all of the words they can think of to describe what they hear. Reward responses like "boredom" and "monotony." Give the beat a little variety and do the same thing.

■ Review the students' understanding of unity, repetition, and monotony. Relate the terms to music, dancing, and marching. Relate them to the ways in which plants grow in nature as compared with planted areas in parks. "What creates unity?" "Why is repetition needed?"

■ Review the art prints and other illustrations. See if students can point out ways in which the artist unified his picture with the repetition of shapes.

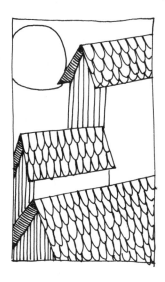

Suggested art activity

Create two designs that use the same motif. Have repetition in one carried to the point of creating monotony. Use repetition in the second design to create unity *without* monotony.

Alternative art activities

Apply the concept in creating: (a) a fabric design, (b) a construction, (c) paper sculpture, (d) a painting, and (e) a print.

Evaluation

When the student uses repetition to create unity without monotony, then the objective has been achieved.

Other things to consider

- Vocabulary: unity, variety, monotony, repetition.
- Art materials needed: pencils, paint, paper, and whatever materials are needed for the alternative activities.
- Prints:
  Figure Five in Gold by Demuth
  City Hall in Rega by Feininger
  Virgin with Saints Ines and Tecla by El Greco
  Three Flags by Johns
  Composition 1963 by Miro
  Guernica by Picasso
  Orange and Yellow by Rothko
  Cheyt M by Vasarely
- People who might have need for the concept: architects, interior designers, commercial artists, painters, sculptors, printmakers, potters, teachers, docents, art historians, art critics.

LEVEL 7

ACTIVITY 194

Concept taught by this activity: Skill development in art is the result of practice, either mental or physical, or a combination of the two.

Objective: As a result of practice, the student demonstrates skill development in drawing.

A sample lesson plan for achieving the objective:

Teacher preparations
■ Collect and display art prints and appropriate illustrations selected from those in the school media center.
■ Have material for the selected art activity ready for use.

Teaching suggestions
■ Name everyone who gets better (or skilled) by doing the skill over and over again. (Basketball players, golfers, musicians, mathematicians, actors and actresses, artists, weightlifters, runners, almost everyone.) Ask questions such as: "How many of you take some sort of music lessons?" "Do any of you have to practice any during the week?" "Why does the music teacher *insist* on practice?" "Concert pianists, even after performing for twenty or thirty years, still practice eight hours a day. Why in the world would they do such a thing?" "How many of you think you can't draw?" "How many think you can?" (Compare the amount of time the "yes" group has practiced drawing with those who say they can't.) Make the point that *anyone* who wants to can learn to draw well. The secrets are (1) *wanting to* and (2) *practice.*
■ Discuss the notion that practice can be either physical, mental, or a combination of the two. Research has shown that practicing a skill in the mind can be as helpful as physical practice; for example, shooting free throws with a basketball for an hour may be no more effective than practicing it mentally for the same period of time. Have the class try this idea as an experiment. Any skill the class

chooses could be used for the experiment.
■ Discuss art prints in terms of what things took the most practice and which artists seemed to have the greatest skill in (1) drawing, (2) color usage, and (3) arrangement of space.

Suggested art activity
Select some object or a part of a living thing and practice the drawing of it. Draw it over and over—ten times or more for a complicated subject and one hundred times for something simple. Observe that the thing has not become more simple, but the *ability* to do has increased.

Alternative art activities
■ Have the students set a goal of doing at least ten drawings a week, keeping them, and building a portfolio with them. The drawings should be reviewed by the teacher so that the student doesn't spend his time just practicing the things he does wrong over and over.
■ Have each student do a number of drawings for a back-to-school exhibit.

Evaluation

When the student has improved his drawing skills so that he and other students can point out areas of improvement (comparing his first drawing with the last), then the objective has been achieved.

Other things to consider

■ Art materials needed: drawing and painting media.
■ Prints:
Iliad Study by Ingres
The Old King by Rouault
Lacemaker by Vermeer
Rebus by Rauschenberg
Mona Lisa by da Vinci
Marilyn Monroe by Warhol (photo—silk screen)
Still Music by Shahn

Mural by Pollock
Leisure by Leger
Venice by Canaletto

■ People who might have need for the concept: all artists, engineers, doctors, skilled laborers, craftsmen.

LEVEL 7   ACTIVITY 195

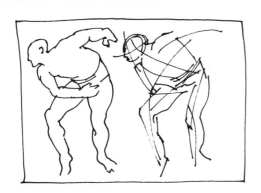

Concept taught by this activity: The attitude and position of a model can be defined with lines, for example, contour drawings and gesture studies.

Objective: The student enlarges his feeling for form, proportion, and detail through experiences with contour drawing.

A sample lesson plan for achieving the objective:

Teacher preparations
■ Have drawing materials available. Display prints and any appropriate pictures available from the school library or media center.
■ Note that gesture studies and contour drawings are merely exercises. Gesture studies are used to help the student define the action or position of a figure and contour drawings help the learner to develop a feeling for the figure in space and the relationships of its parts.

Teaching suggestions
■ Hold up any interesting object and ask the students what they would be able to see if the lights were *almost* off (very dim). Have them draw the object as if it were quite far away in very dim light. Discuss that when only the outside edge, or outline, can be seen--we call that its contour. We can trace a contour with a pencil or ink line.
■ Discuss what the word *contour* means. Note that the word refers to the outline or silhouette of something *plus* its interior forms. In any case, contour drawings are strictly *line* drawings, and the exercises suggested contribute to the awareness of the student *only* when they are carefully and thoughtfully done. A contour drawing of the United States would be an outline of its silhouette, mapping every detail of its precise shape. A contour drawing of the interior would include outlines of each state, etc., plus contour lines

describing the changes in elevation. This last aspect gives a feeling of "form" to the map (see activity no. 157).

Note: The major goal in this activity should be that of motivating the student to *practice* enough contour drawings for the time to affect his drawing ability. As the concept states, contour drawing *does* seem to enlarge the students' "feeling" for form and proportion, but it does not happen through one or two quick applications. Motivate the student so that he is willing to devote a good amount of time observing the outside contour as well as the interior of an object as he draws the lines that describe it. As indicated in the note in the "teacher preparations" section, contour drawings are also valuable in helping the student to develop a feeling for the space a figure occupies and how its parts relate to each other in space.
■ Discuss the word *gesture*. Have two students come to the front. Ask one to stand stiffly, arms down, as if at "attention." Have the other student act like a baseball pitcher, freezing the action. Ask the class which position is most interesting? Which shows the most action? Discuss that the "baseball player" has more "gesture." Students are inclined to draw people so that they look rather stiff. They underestimate the action. Gesture studies or small, quick line drawings help the student to establish the action or position of the figure. It's also helpful in getting at the altering of proportions. If the student has described the position of the figure in two or three minutes, then he won't be disturbed if he has to change his drawing when he discovers some of the proportions aren't accurate.

Suggested art activity
■ Do a contour drawing of just the outside shape of an object. This drawing, done on white paper, might be taped to a sheet of black paper and the shape cut out of the black paper so that it could be displayed and a discussion of how much the contour or, in this instance, the outside shape contributes to our perception of it. Then have the students practice doing contour drawings without looking at their paper, looking only at the object as they draw it. Encourage them in either instance to work slowly and carefully. With the first part they should look carefully, too.

In the drawings without looking, have them *think* carefully. It should be discovered that in some instances drawing without looking reveals a great deal, but in other instances not so much.

■ Do a series of gesture studies. With lines, locate the position of the head, hands, feet, and other parts in relation to each other and the angle of the head compared to the shoulders, trunk, and hips. Measure or check proportions and make corrections as needed.

Alternative art activities

■ Do a contour drawing putting in the interior characteristics that define the object (such as the shirt collar, the belt or waist above trousers, eye glasses, etc.).

■ Discuss ways in which form, proportion, and detail have improved as a result of this experience. Discuss art prints in terms of how well the artist seemed to sense the gesture and contour of a figure.

Evaluation

When the student does a variety of contour drawings that are carefully and thoughtfully done and that have a clear outline of the objects or figures, then the objective has been achieved.

Other things to consider

■ Vocabulary: outline, contour, silhouette, form, proportion.
■ Art materials needed: drawing media and paper.
■ Prints:
  Dempsey and Firpo by Bellows
  The Smokers by Brouwer
  Dancing Class by Degas
  The Small Crucifixion by Grunewald
  Knockout by Morreau
  Poster—Jan. 18 to Feb. 12 by Shahn
  Quadrille by Toulouse-Lautrec
  Leisure by Leger
■ People who might have need for the concept: painters, printmakers, illustrators.

LEVEL 7   ACTIVITY 196

Concept taught by this activity: The student should combine perspective and value concepts previously taught for use in drawing or painting.

Objective: The student will create the illusion of three-dimensional objects seen in two point perspective with light coming from one direction. (See activities no. 161, 162, 163, 171, and 172.)

A sample lesson plan for achieving the objective:

Teacher preparations
■ Assemble appropriate prints and whatever other illustrations are available in the school's media center that will help with the teaching of the concept.
■ Acquire an assortment of drawing materials and different kinds of paper for students to select from.

Teaching suggestions
■ Ask, "How many objects, or things, can you list which can be drawn in perspective, in two minutes?" "Complete this analogy: Trick is to a magician as _____ is to an artist." (illusion, perspective)
■ Review the activities listed in the concept above. The student should have a clear awareness of each idea before he tries putting them to use in one picture. Skillful application of each is not necessary but understanding and awareness are. Students should respond correctly to questions such as: "How does the appearance of an object change when you raise the base of it in a picture?" (It tends to look farther away.) "What does the horizon line have to do with the eye level?" (It is the eye level of the

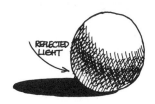

viewer.) "How can parallel lines converge in the illusion of distance?" (By using vanishing points.) "What is an example of reflected light?" (Golden windows at sunset, water reflecting on a ceiling or tree above it.) "Where is there a highlight in this room?"
■ Have the student illustrate each of the previous questions with small pencil sketches.

Suggested art activity
Have the student mentally take a cardboard box apart and draw what it would look like with the light coming from himself or some other source. If this is too complicated for the student, have him draw an actual box with a spotlight on it or in direct sunlight. Caution the student to think carefully about where the darkest shadows would be in relation to highlights and to compare all other values with either of the two extremes. For the perspective part, he needs to establish an eye level line (horizon line) with vanishing points and have all converging lines going to one point or the other. He needs to be alert to ways in which textures become very apparent when values are rendered accurately. You may review this task by using an actual box and a spotlight for experimentation and example.

Alternative art activities
■ Do the same sort of exercise with an imaginary building as the subject or object. If the student wishes, any other subject that contains cubelike and spherical shapes would be equally appropriate. The forms could even be imaginary ones.
■ Create an imaginary scene or a design utilizing the five concepts.

437

Evaluation

When the student has completed at least one exercise in which he has combined concepts 161, 162, 163, 171, and 172 into one drawing, the objective has been achieved.

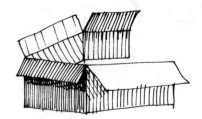

Other things to consider

- Vocabulary: perspective, value, linear perspective, eye level, horizon line, render, vanishing points.
- Art materials needed: spotlight, pencils, crayons, an assortment of paper for drawing, and cardboard boxes opened up.
- Prints:
  Numbering at Bethlehem by Brueghel
  Venice by Canaletto
  The Crucifixion by Dali (the cross)
  Snap the Whip by Homer (the school)
  Still Life with Pipe by Chardin (the box)
  Tranquility by Gasser
  Trains du Soir by Delvaux
  Seven A.M. by Hopper
  Christina's World by Wyeth
- People who might have need for the concept: painter, illustrator, industrial designer, draftsman, artists that do stage designing, cartoons, serigraphs, and printmaking.

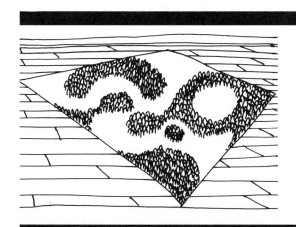

Concept taught by this activity: Floor coverings, wall hangings, and other fabric designs may be created with the process of hooking.

Objective: The student will demonstrate an understanding of the hooking process.

A sample lesson plan for achieving the objective:

Teacher preparations

Acquire the basic materials. This would include such things as: burlap, two-ply monk's cloth or scrim for the backing (scrim is sometimes called rug canvas), a rug hook or Columbia Minerva punch (a loop latch hooker if you use scrim), needle, yarn, a frame, stapler, staples, wrapping paper, and a crayon or felt tip marker.

Teaching suggestions

Note: The technique of rug hooking employs the use of a tool with a hooked end to pull and push yarn back and forth through a background material. It is effective when combined with weaving or stitchery; like weaving, it can stimulate the student to experience the excitement of working with smooth, rough, hard, and soft yarns. Designing varied arrangements of color, texture, and pattern will challenge the learner. Ranging from shag effects to low relief rugs, this art may take the form of inviting coverings for floor or wall hangings.

■ Two basic rug hooking procedures may be used as a beginning for making any rug or wall hanging. The first method involves the use of a backing fabric of burlap or monk's cloth and any one of three tools: the punch needle, shuttle hooker, or hand hook (with a crochet needle as a possible substitute for the last). The second method makes use of a tool called the loop latch hook and a backing material of scrim.

■ To use the punch needle and burlap in the first method, decide on the rug size; then cut burlap for a backing, allowing several extra inches on each edge for a margin.

Use a handmade frame of soft wood, a ready-made picture frame, or one of the specially designed stretcher or rug frames. Stretch the backing tightly over the frame and fasten with staples or carpet tacks. Cut a piece of wrapping paper the size of the proposed rug. With crayon, felt tip pen, or chalk, draw a bold design that will fill the space inside the margin. Avoid tiny detail and line drawings. To transfer the design, sketch directly on the burlap with a felt pen, cut out the shape, and use it as a pattern.

To use the punch needle, thread the yarn through ring at top of the handle and then through the inside point. Pull about a foot of yarn through the needle; then drag the yarn back, with tension, so it will gradually slip into the tube and handle. Set the loop gauge for the length of loop wanted. Point the open side of the punch needle in the direction the hooking will take. Push the needle through the backing until it hits the handle, keeping the hand firmly on the burlap. Pull the needle back to the surface. Do not jerk, but glide it from one loop to another. Continue the process of punching the needle back and forth through the burlap. When a small amount of hooking has been completed, the loops will begin to hold one another tightly.

■ Ideas for design are everywhere: a painting or print, cut paper shapes, an experience, unusual views of common objects, objects viewed through a microscope, shapes of buildings, nature--all the endless visual patterns in our daily lives offer constant and changing sources.

■ A variety of textures result from snipping the end of each loop to give a velvety appearance; shearing the tops off the loops; sculpturing the loops, giving a low-relief effect; varying the length of loops, making some high and others low; combining clipped and unclipped loops; or combining yarn, strips of fabric, or leather. When all parts of the design are finished, remove the rug from the frame, then fold back the edges and stitch. Paint latex sizing over the back of the finished piece to give body to the rug, hold the yarn securely in place, and prevent slipping on the floor. If the rug is to be a wall hanging, sizing will not be necessary.

■ *Scrim background.* The loop latch hook, used when working with a scrim backing, knots the yarn into the backing. For this type of rug hooking, cut a piece of scrim, leaving enough material on all four sides to turn back for a finished edge. With a felt tip marker, draw a design on paper to match the size of the rug. Place the paper under the scrim, and with the felt pen trace the lines of the design on the material. Because of its stiffness, the fabric does not need to be placed on a frame. Cut pieces of yarn the length desired, usually about two inches. To avoid interrupting the hooking process for constant cutting and measuring, prepare enough pieces at one time to complete a small section. Bring the two ends of yarn together and hold between the fingers to form a loose loop. Put the hooker through the loop and under one strand of the scrim. Pull the two ends of the yarn up to the point of the hook and place them between the hook and latch. Close the latch and pull the hooker back through the scrim and also through the previous loop, holding the ends of yarn with fingers to form a knot in the yarn. Continue this process, keeping the loops close together.

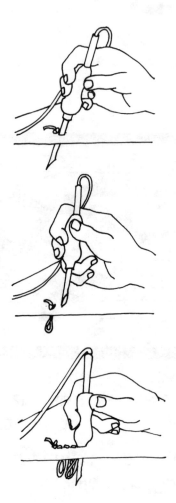

- An unusual variation to the hooking technique is rug hooking at the easel. A large piece of scrim is attached to a wood frame, then placed on an easel, which serves only to a wood frame, then placed on an easel, which serves only to hold the frame. Several students can work simultaneously as each makes his design for a particular area of the piece. This group approach to rug hooking enables each person to see his design emerge as each shape becomes a part of the finished piece.

Suggested art activity
Create some sort of hanging or floor covering by hooking.

Alternative art activities
Create a wall hanging by hooking.

Evaluation

When the student demonstrates an ability to utilize the process of rug hooking, then the objective has been achieved.

Other things to consider

- Vocabulary: hooking, scrim, punch, loop latch hooker, sizing.
- Art materials needed: See list in "teacher preparations" section.
- Resources: books, filmstrips or single loop films on hooking. Some may come under the heading of weaving.

LEVEL 7

ACTIVITY 198

Concept taught by this activity: The student should witness film development and learn about the equipment and procedures used in the developing process.

Objective: The student demonstrates an awareness of the following:

- How film is developed, the equipment and materials used in the process, and
- The basic kinds of printing paper (contact or enlarging) available and identifiable in terms of weight, finish, tone, and contrast, and their appropriate use in making various kinds of photographs.

A sample lesson plan for achieving the objective:

Teacher preparations

- Contact a photographer friend and arrange to have a demonstration of the film developing process. Some school district media centers have such people available or a local junior or senior high school teacher may be competent in this area.
- If there are funds available, the teacher may wish to collect or purchase the materials outlined in this activity and have them available for demonstrations in the future.
- *Where to work.* Since photographic films and papers are sensitive to light, they must be handled in a darkroom. For processing film in a film developing tank, you need a darkroom only while you are loading your film into the tank. But during this time, it must be *really* dark. Here's a good way of determining if a room is dark enough. If after staying for five minutes in the room or closet that you're checking, you still can't see a sheet of white paper placed against a dark background, the room passes inspection. You can make doors light-tight by putting heavy cloth over the cracks. For printing or enlarging you don't need total darkness. You can use a ''safe'' light in the darkroom so

that you can see what you're doing. Just make sure that the only light in the room is supplied by a suitable safelight lamp, and keep the lamp at least four feet from the photographic paper. Closets like a custodian's room are good places for temporary printing darkrooms, since they provide the three major essentials: running water, electrical outlets, and a good working surface. Use a sheet of plastic, such as a plastic tablecloth, under the trays to keep spills off the counter top.

- *Equipment and materials.*
  - To develop your film, you need a film developing tank. Make sure that the developing tank you use will accept the size of your film. You can develop your film in trays, as a temporary substitute, by seesawing the length of film through the solutions. However, it's better and easier to use a film tank. There is less chance of scratching the film, and after you load your film into the tank in the dark, you can carry out all the remaining steps in the light.
  - To make prints the same size as your negatives, you need a printing frame or a contact printer to hold the light-sensitive photographic paper in contact with your negative during exposure.
  - In addition, you need four photographic trays a little larger than the largest prints you expect to make. Instead of trays you can use shallow pans or dishes such as pie plates made of glass, plastic, or china. Don't use metal unless it's enamelware or stainless steel. You also need a kitchen measuring cup, a photo thermometer, and a safelight such as a BROWNIE Darkroom Lamp, Model B, or a KODAK Darkroom Lamp with a Safelight Filter OC (light amber). Some minor items that will be useful are spring clothespins and several quart jars for storing solutions. A photo blotter roll is helpful for drying prints. Your photo dealer will be glad to help you select the equipment you'll need. He may sell photo darkroom kits which include the basic items.
  - For developing your films, you can use Developer D-76 or a MICRODOL-X Developer. For prints and enlargements, use a VERSATOL Developer or DEKTOL Developer. After development, you'll need a stop bath

and a fixing bath. (The KODAK Tri-Chem Pack includes convenient individual packets of developer, stop bath, and fixer, and other companies may have similar packets.) Before drying the film, you may want to use a photo flow solution, which minimizes water marks and drying streaks on the film and speeds drying.

- Photographic papers are supplied in a variety of speeds, contrasts, surface textures, image tones, stock tints, and weights. To get started, we suggest you use VELOX Paper for your contact prints and MEDALIST Paper F for your enlargements. The no. 2 printing grade is suitable for average negatives that have been properly exposed and developed. Later, you may want to get some no. 3 and no. 4 paper if you have some low-contrast negatives (in which there is little difference in density between the lightest and darkest portions), or no. 1 paper if you have some high-contrast negatives (in which there is a very large range of densities).

Teaching suggestions

Introduction: Photography is a fine art. Artistic photographers use many of the same concepts in design and awareness that painters use. This activity teaches you about how photographers develop and enlarge their exposed film. It is part of their "technique."

Developing your film.

- Label three jars "Film Developer," "Stop Bath," and "Fixer." Mix the three solutions according to instructions with the chemicals. Make sure each solution always goes back into its correct jar—even a few drops of stop bath or fixer could ruin the developer.
- Pour the proper quantity of developer into the tank. Check the temperature with your thermometer. If the solution is warmer or cooler than recommended, adjust the temperature.
- To cool the developer, put the tank into a larger pan of cold water, and stir the solution until it reaches the temperature recommended in the instructions. If the solution is too cool, use warm water.
- Take your tank and your roll of exposed film into your "darkroom." Be careful not to spill any developer.
- In TOTAL DARKNESS, rip the "Exposed" sticker on rolls of film. Use a bottle-cap remover to open 35mm magazines. Break open 126 cartridges by bending the two cylindrical chambers toward the label. Roll the film into the apron or reel according to the instructions included with the tank.
- Lower the loaded film apron or reel into the developer solution in the tank and begin timing. Raise and lower the film several times. Put the cover on the tank and turn on the lights.
- Agitate the tank by rotating it back and forth for about five seconds at thirty-second intervals. At the end of the developing time (see the film or developer instructions) pour the solution back into the "Developer" jar. When pouring, tip the tank only slightly at the start.
- With the tank tilted a bit, pour the stop-bath solution into it through the opening in the top. Agitate gently for about 15 seconds and then pour the liquid back into its original jar.
- Pour in the fixer solution and agitate as before. At the end of the fixing time pour the solution into its jar.
- Remove the tank cover and wait. Place the tank under a moderate stream of 65 to 75°F water and let the film wash for about a half hour. Take it from the apron (or reel) and rinse both apron (or reel) and tank.
- Run the film through a tray of PHOTO-FLO Solution, diluted according to the instructions on the bottle.
- Hang up the film with a film clip or clothespin at each end. Let the film dry in a dust-free place.

Developing your prints.

- Arrange four trays in front of you so that, from left to right, you have developer, stop bath, fixer, and wash water. Mix the three solutions to the recommended temperature by placing a small, deep bowl of warm or cool water in the tray

of solution. Don't spill any of the water into the solutions.

- Take the exposed paper from the printer easel and slide it, shiny side up, completely into the developer with your left hand. Rock the tray gently for 60 seconds by tipping up first one end, then the other.
- Take the paper out of the developer with your left hand and, after letting it drain for a second or two, slide it into the stop-bath solution (center tray). Agitate the tray for about 15 seconds in the same way as before.
- With your right hand, withdraw the paper from the stop bath and slip it into the fixer. You can turn the lights on after thirty seconds. Leave the print in the fixer for 5 to 10 minutes and keep it separated from any other prints in the tray. Again, agitate the tray frequently. Avoid overfixing.
- After fixing, transfer your prints to the wash tray. Wash them for about an hour in gently running water at a temperature between 65 and 75°F (or for five minutes each in twelve changes of water). Don't let a strong stream of water strike the face of the prints.
- Dry the prints between white photo blotters with the picture side toward the linen surface. Or, you can lay the prints on a clean towel, and cover them with a second towel.

Suggested art activity

Make certain each interested student has an opportunity to see the developing and printing process and to learn about printing papers. Wherever possible, allow the student opportunities to perform parts of the process.

Alternative art activities

- Provide opportunities for demonstrations and/or lectures by a local photographer for students with a high interest in photography.
- Go to an exhibit on photography.

Evaluation

When the student is able to briefly describe the developing and printing process in photography and demonstrates an awareness of the different kinds of printing paper, the objective has been achieved.

Other things to consider

- Vocabulary: safelamp, darkroom, developing tank, light-sensitive photographic paper, negative, exposure, photographic tray, photo blotter roll, developer, stop bath, fixer, photo flow solution, printing paper, film cartridge, film magazine, agitate film.
- Materials needed: compose a list of materials from the section on teacher preparations.
- People who might have need for the concept: photographers of all sorts, commercial artists, and science teachers.

LEVEL 7

ACTIVITY 199

Concept taught by this activity: Good photographs require an understanding of depth of field, proper lighting, backgrounds, correcting for parallax, and the most effective view of the subject.

Objective: The student takes photographs which do not contain any of the common defects associated with the novice photographer.

A sample lesson plan for achieving the objective:

Teacher preparations
Have examples representing each of the more common mistakes children or adults first make in picture taking. Become familiar with each of the errors and the conditions which cause them.

Teaching suggestions
■ Before initiating any discussion, review the following body of information.

● Common mistakes and how to avoid them
Poor background: Check the viewfinder to see that trees or other subjects do not grow out of the head or compete with the main subject.
Chopping off parts of the subject: Make sure all of the subject appears in the viewfinder at the exact moment that you snap the picture. When parts are cut off, they should not cut off at points like the top of the head, the neck, waist, or knees. This can also be a parallax problem (see below).
Out of focus: Focus problems cause blurred, fuzzy pictures and stem from being too close to the subject for the kind of lens the camera has. A good general rule is to stand at least five feet from the subject.
Tilted camera: The subject looks like its going up or down hill when it should be level. Keep the camera level

when you snap the picture.

Camera movement: Here again the subject may be blurred or fuzzy. Hold the camera steady and press the shutter release button gently. The slower the shutter speed the more steady the camera must be held. When taking movies, it's best to hold the camera steady and let the subject move past it, towards it or away from it.

Obstructed lens: Black shapes cutting across the picture are generally caused by a camera strap or finger that got in front of the lens when the photo was taken.

Jerky movement: When movies are taken and only a few seconds of film is exposed before the subject is changed, the film looks jerky. Allow five to ten seconds for each shot.

- Lighting

  Hazy or cloudy sunlight is best for taking pictures of people. There are no dark shadows across the face in this kind of light.

  Bright sunlight is best for landscapes. Details stand out more sharply and strong contrasts strengthen the picture.

  Side lighting produces dark shadows on one side. These can be reduced by a flash bulb or by taking the subject's picture next to something that will reflect some light onto the shadow area.

  Top lighting is when the light is directly overhead. Unattractive shadows will appear under a person's eyebrows and nose. These can be corrected the same way side lighting problems are corrected.

  Front lighting causes the person to squint because the light shines directly into the person's face and casts harsh shadows. Change the subject's position.

  Back lighting is light coming from behind the subject and places the person's whole face in shadow. A lens shade is needed for the camera and flash fill-in or reflected light can get rid of the overall shadow effect.

- Composing pictures

  Light and dark contrasts create striking photographs— either light subjects against dark backgrounds or dark subjects against light backgrounds.

  Horizontal lines can suggest peace and rest but the picture is more interesting if the major horizontal line is off center and doesn't divide the picture in equal parts. The same is true of vertical lines which give a feeling of height, dignity, and grandeur.

    Diagonal lines suggest action and movement or perhaps conflict.

    Radiating lines such as tree branches or spokes in a wheel can form interesting patterns and be used in an abstract way.

    Inferred triangles can direct attention to a center of interest and give solidity to an arrangement.

    Informal balance can be used to give depth to a picture and to create a more interesting or dynamic arrangement.

- Filters

  Filters hold back the light of certain other colors. Thus a *yellow filter* deepens the sky tone and provides contrast between sky and clouds. A *red filter* makes the sky almost black but washes out skin tones. A *green filter* provides the same sky tones as yellow, produces normal skin tones, and makes flowers stand out from a green background. A *polarizing filter* reduces the glare from shiny surfaces such as water or glass.

- Parallax problems

  There is a difference between what the viewfinder shows and what the lens records on the film with most cameras. The photographer needs to make certain that important aspects of the picture are not on the edges of the viewfinder when framing is done. The closer you get to a subject the more this can be a problem.

- Depth·of field

  Inexpensive cameras have a somewhat narrow range in which all parts of the subject will stay in focus, particularly if the lighting is not adequate. Cameras with adjustable lenses and a greater range in the f stop can take pictures in which even the most distant figures will photograph as sharply as those up close.

■ With cameras and a discussion session, assist students in drawing upon their experience as you dispense the information related to this lesson. If the sum total of their experience is not sufficient, make individual or group assignments to investigate the answers to specific questions. Don't just tell them everything. Have students bring examples of some of the mistakes commonly made.

Suggested art activity
As a class activity, illustrate the whole lesson and the findings of the class on a bulletin board.

Alternative art activities
■ Have the class determine if there are any situations where the above mentioned items would not be considered errors in photography; for example, some pictures might be taken for "effect" that might call for the photographer to violate the rules. It could be like purposely misspelling a word for effect. If it is not obvious it loses its effect.

■ Go on a field trip to a photography exhibit or have a photographer put up an exhibit in the class or school.

Evaluation

When the students describe common errors in picture taking along with their solutions and can point out ways in which his own picture taking ability has improved, then the objective has been achieved.

Other things to consider

■ Vocabulary: depth of field, parallax, filter, lighting, reflected light, flash fill in, polarizing filter.
■ Resources: professional photographers, encyclopedias, and books or magazines on photography.
■ People who might have need for the concept: photographers of all kinds, teachers, and all fields of commercial art.

LEVEL 7

ACTIVITY 200

Concept taught by this activity: The student can create a filmstrip, slide presentation, or movie by writing script, sketching a storyboard, and recording music and dialogue.

Objective: The student demonstrates an awareness of various educational media and their processes of production, and creates a media presentation of his own design.

A sample lesson plan for achieving the objective:

Teacher preparations
- Have available (either in the classroom, the school office or library, or from student homes) a 35mm slide camera and projector, a movie camera and projector (super-8, 8, or 16 will do), screen, material for making overhead transparencies (acetates, india ink for cellulose, thermo-fax machine) overhead projector, paper for storyboards and poster visuals, cassette or tape recorder. Be familiar with the machines or have someone available who is.
- If possible, discuss with other adults who have experience in drama, television, or advertising media, good methods of helping students produce their programs. (Actual examples of storyboards, recordings, and dramatic acting would be helpful.)

Teaching suggestions
- "How to get an idea"—(finding the problem).
  - What are all of the things you could make a short movie or slide show of? (Make a list of script ideas such as "our family," "our town," horses, mountains, the ocean, art, stories, "our school," "How to" lessons, "my dog," and similar subjects.

- Decide on a category, then make a list of all the possible things you could show in a program about that category, for example, "What are all of the things I could show about my dog?" (Running, sitting, begging, sleeping, heeling, doing tricks.) Then, "What are all of the settings I could show him in?" (Up a tree, on a roof, under a bush, in school.) Now ask, "What are the most unusual ways to show him sleeping?" "Running?" "Can I 'modify' these ideas?" "Can I do just the 'opposite?'" "How can I change it to be unusual?"
- Selecting the media.
  Have students analyze availability of cameras, costs (film and other materials), and goals of the presentation (if little motion to be shown, why use a movie?). Also consider time involved and personal interest in a specific media. Then have students decide whether to use slides, movies, posters, or some other media.
- The plan.
  - Write a script. Begin with rough notes, ideas in any order, and thumbnail sketches. Then put them into a sequence and write a formal script.
  - Draw a "storyboard."

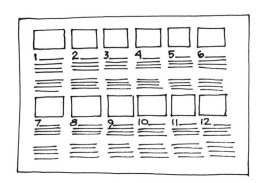

445

(1) Have the students use rulers to draw many rectangles of 1″ by 1½″ proportions such as 2″ by 3″ on as large a sheet as possible. Begin, for example, with a 30″ by 40″ sheet. Under each rectangle put the scene description and sound, for example, "Cue 'My bedroom with only the bed visible, at 5 p.m.' Show picture on wall. No music yet." Under the scene description, put the script which fits that exact scene, for example, "This is the room where the great inventor grew up as a girl."

(2) Do sketches in the rectangles, showing as accurately as possible what the scene should look like. Rectangle #1 would be the opening title and credits, and so on in sequence. (Commercially made storyboards are available in some art stores.)

- Review completed storyboards and make any necessary changes or improvements.

■ The production.

- The students now simply follow the storyboard and script, using cameras or equipment as necessary. (Students may draw on clear acetate sheets with India ink or markers if they are doing their presentation for the overhead projector.)

- When students present their program to the class, it is important for the teacher to set a climate for fun and positive acceptance. No negative reactions, boos, and so forth, are acceptable--only applause, "wow," "neat," and so on are acceptable. Any violators do not get to watch the presentations that day.

- Alternate media activities

(1) Students create an imaginary story, without formal script or storyboard, by going one by one up to the overhead projector, drawing something on the projector, and having the student just preceding them tell a story that goes with their drawing. (An ordinary grease pencil may be used. Students could pre-draw an acetate before going up if desired.)

(2) Have a television station send a representative to talk about storyboards and television.

Evaluation

Observe whether students are aware of storyboards, scripts, and general media processes by looking at their programs, listening to discussion, and asking questions.

Other things to consider

■ Vocabulary: script, dialogue, drama, cassette recording, scene, media.
■ Art materials needed: see "teacher preparations" section.
■ People who might have need for the concept: television workers, actors and actresses, commercial artists, advertisers, illustrators, educators, and cartoonists.

LEVEL 7

ACTIVITY 201

Concept taught by this activity: The student's efforts in drawing are enhanced when he develops an awareness of errors that commonly occur at this level.

Objective: The student will point out ways in which he has worked to personally overcome one or more of the errors commonly made at this level. Four important ones are: (a) having forms that seem to occupy the same space; (b) using so much detail that form is lost; (c) making the parts stronger than the whole; and (d) using hard, monotonous outlines.

A sample lesson plan for achieving the objective:

Teacher preparations
- Help students to recognize that being able to draw well takes a great deal of practice and a constant awareness of the error that creeps into his drawing. Skill is seldom the result of one or two attempts. (Review activity no. 194)
- Try to locate work from other students which contain*:
  - Figures or objects which occupy the same space in perspective. (Not simply overlapping but one sitting in or on top of the other.)

*See illustrations

- Subjects so detailed it's hard to tell what the form was supposed to be.
- Examples of a student getting so concerned with certain parts of his picture that the "overall" appearance suffers.
- Figures or objects with dark, monotonous outlines that separate one from the other.

Teaching suggestions

- Brainstorm concerning the most frequent errors students have noted in their own work or in the work of others their age. If errors are mentioned that are of concern equal to or greater than those in this lesson, they may be treated as well. Trace a student's footprint with chalk. Ask the class how many of them could stand on that one footprint without touching any other part of them to the floor. (One, or perhaps two if they stood on top of the other.) Emphasize that each object in a drawing needs *its* own space on which to stand too.
- Set up a series of still-life type drawing problems. Have the student select one and then as he works, have him pay particular attention to the common errors mentioned in this concept.
- Encourage the student to automatically check his work for the errors mentioned in the concept and any others he may be making.

Suggested art activity

Go on a sketching field trip so that the students might be able to do at least three sketches. This field trip could be to a location like the city dump where they could draw items that are piled on top of each other and stacked at unusual angles. After returning from the field trip, have the students display their sketches and note the drawing errors.

Alternative art activities

- Fill a sketchbook with drawings done outside of school.
- Conduct timed drawing sessions of up to five minutes each. Hold evaluation sessions following several of them so that students are aware of the mistakes they still need to correct.
- Practice with different types of drawing media should be encouraged during this process, but do not make the changes too dramatic or too often or the student will give all of his attention to the drawing media rather than to the concept mentioned in this activity.

Evaluation

When the student has demonstrated an awareness of at least two errors he is making in his drawing and has corrected them to a noticeable degree, then the objective has been achieved.

Other things to consider

- Vocabulary: form, space, perspective, outlining.
- Art materials needed: drawing and painting materials.
- People who might have need for the concept: painter, draftsman, illustrator, commercial artists of all types, stage set designer, cartoonists, printmakers of all types.

LEVEL 7   ACTIVITY 202

Concept taught by this activity: To create more aesthetic arrangements artists sometimes need to adjust the relationships between positive and negative spaces.

Objective: The student will examine the relationships of positive and negative shapes in his subject and alter them when it strengthens the aesthetic quality of the arrangement.

A sample lesson plan for achieving the objective:

Teacher preparations
Collect appropriate prints and assemble a variety of drawing and painting materials for students to select from.

Teaching suggestions
■ Go to activity no. 178 and have the class do the last activity under ''teaching suggestions'' and discuss which shapes are positive or negative. Review the terms *positive* and *negative shapes*. Note that negative space (areas that are basically background shapes) needs to receive equal consideration with the major objects (positive space) in any design.
■ • Talk about several prints and have the students categorize all the objects in the pictures into one of two planes—the foreground or subject and the background. Have several students that seem to get the idea trace with their finger around the overall general shape that they would consider the positive shape. The negative shapes are what is left.
 • When all of the students seem to understand the idea of the positive and negative general shapes, have the class talk about those that seem to have the most interesting and aesthetic arrangements of space and shapes.

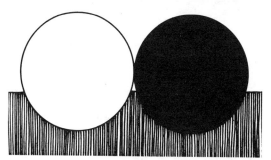

• By putting some butcher paper over several art prints, some of the students could make tracings of some of the prints discussed. Put the prints up to the window so that they can see the outlines through the butcher paper. Lead the students to see why an artist seldom copies nature just as it is, but he rearranges what he is looking at. See that they are looking at shapes which are rather ordinary looking and need alterations to be made more interesting. (See pictures.)
• Positive space (trees and stump) seem lost in all the negative space (sky and ground). The shapes aren't very interesting and there's little accent or emphasis anywhere.

 By enlarging two of the trees and the stump and moving them over to the left, space divisions are much more interesting and unequal in size. We now have a point of emphasis with the trees and stump.
• Landscape scenes, as seen from the school or perhaps from the windows of the classroom, could be discussed as to what might go into an artist's painting—or what might be left out.
■ Look at art prints and discuss the question: ''If the artist had placed _____ in some other position or in _____ position, how would that have affected the positive and negative space relationships?'' ''Would the picture have been as interesting?'' ''Why not?''

Suggested art activity
Select an interesting subject that doesn't seem to be very well arranged. Make a series of sketches rearranging the elements of the subject until at least one has been changed for the better. Do a painting, sculpture or whatever of the final sketch.

Alternative art activities
Do other versions of the concept in media such as cloth, clay, yarn, paper, or found materials.

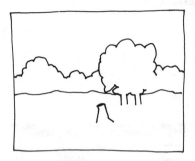

Evaluation

When the student can identify ways in which he might alter the subject, when he's looking to develop a more aesthetic relationship between positive and negative shapes, then the objective has been achieved.

Other things to consider

- Vocabulary: aesthetic, positive, negative, space relationships, arrangement.
- Art materials needed: Any drawing or painting materials are appropriate for this activity plus tracing paper or acetate and felt tip markers.
- Prints:
  Fur Traders on the Missouri by Bingham
  Venice by Canaletto (What if the buildings were seen all in a row?)
  Snap the Whip by Homer (What if the boys were all in a line--none falling and all the same size?)
  The Gleaners by Millet
  Christina's World by Wyeth ("How would the space divisions look if Christina was almost home?")
  The Scout by Remington ("Trace the figure of the Indian and horse. Change their position or size in the picture, then discuss how well they work when they're changed.")
  Notre Dame by Daumier ("What if the bridge was seen only in the distance?")
  Allies Day, May 1917 by Hassam ("What makes this arrangement unique?")
  Women in a Garden by Monet ("What makes this arrangement somewhat unusual?")
- People who might have need for the concept: painters, illustrators, sculptors, printmakers, photographers, interior designers, commercial artists, architects, landscape architects, crafts designers, potters.

LEVEL 7   ACTIVITY 203

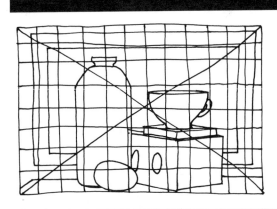

Concept taught by this activity: When the student can visually align aspects of a subject vertically, horizontally, or some other way, then proportions and scale relationships can be improved.

Objective: The student visually aligns his subjects vertically and horizontally (or some other way) in an effort to improve proportions and scale relationships.

A sample lesson plan for achieving the objective:

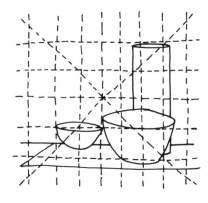

Teacher preparations
■ Have yarn and whatever drawing and painting materials are available ready for use.
■ Make a large grid with wooden frame and string or rope strung through it for the lines.

Teaching suggestions
■ This activity is an extension of activity no. 152. A review of the previous lesson might be a good starting point for discussion.
■ The student is easily deceived as to the space he sees between forms or parts of forms. Because his experience in visually and mentally analyzing proportions and space relationships is limited, it is helpful to give the student some physical guidelines to think with. A large grid as suggested in "teacher preparations" above is an excellent device that can be used to help students align parts of a subject to the whole or to each other. As he looks through the grid, the student immediately knows what things are at the same height and which parts align vertically. As he works through this sort of exercise over a period of time, he'll be able to

maintain the grid in his mind even when he doesn't actually have it, and he can find ways of using other things in the environment as a grid substitute.
■ Discuss methods that individual students may have used to help them "see with greater understanding." This might include such things as starting with the large or simple shapes first and drawing details last; seeing everything as a variation of the cone, cube, cylinder, or other standard form; and measuring ratios or proportions with a pencil or brush and the thumb.
■ Have the student use background shapes such as bookcases and desks to serve as a substitute grid.
■ When doing figure drawings, take masking tape and attach yarn at strategic points on the figure, for example, extending from shoulder to wrist or shoulder to knee. Seeing a line extending from one part of the figure to another helps the student "see" those distances and space relationships more accurately.

- Show two simple "house drawings." (One should have the verticals drawn inaccurately.) Discuss with the students.

Suggested art activity
Look through a grid and draw some subject that is normally difficult to do. Draw it without the grid and show what a difference it makes when one has something tangible with which to mentally analyze space relationships. (A smaller grid using heavy cardboard as a frame rather than wood is an alternative to the wooden frame.)

Alternative art activities
- Make a grid with tape on a window and have the students draw a landscape by looking through the grid.
- The idea of using a grid as an aid in drawing could be used in taking a small drawing done by one of the students, gridding it, and then enlarging it for a bulletin board by use of a larger grid; for example, if one-inch squares are used on the small drawing, one-foot squares might be used on the bulletin board. Then show both drawings together.

Evaluation

When the student demonstrates the ability to utilize objects in the environment of his subject to visually and mentally align aspects of it vertically, horizontally, or some other way and thus improve proportions and space relationships, then the objective has been achieved.

Other things to consider

- Vocabulary: alignment, visually align, scale relationships.
- Art materials needed: grid, yarn, tape, and drawing and painting materials.
- People who might have need for the concept: painter, illustrator, printmaker, industrial designer, stage designer, sign painter, mural painter.

LEVEL 7 ACTIVITY 204

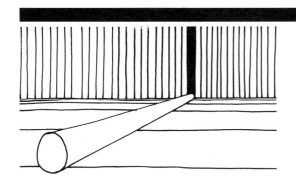

Concept taught by this activity: In dealing with foreshortening, the student's past experiences may confuse what he sees; therefore, careful proportions can be essential to the student's success.

Objective: The student carefully measures all size relationships when dealing with problems in foreshortening.

A sample lesson plan for achieving the objective:

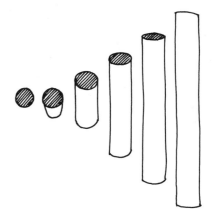

Teacher preparations
- Have the room prepared for exercises in foreshortening: controlled lighting, a tall stool or short ladder, and a variety of objects to draw.
- Collect and display art prints suggested along with any other appropriate illustrations.

Teaching suggestions
- Face the class and have the students take out a pencil to measure with. Still facing the class, hold out your arms so they are perpendicular to your body. Have the students measure the length of your arms by the method taught in activity no. 129. Then start turning your body very slowly, full circle with arms outstretched. As you turn, have the students move their thumb on their pencil up or down if the length of your arms seems to change. Discuss what happened and why. Cause the students to discover the explanation for the problem.
- Note that the students experienced foreshortening when they went through the measuring experience. (Did the length of your arms change as you turned towards them? No, they just became foreshortened!)
- Discuss ways in which the eye can be deceived by what it sees (optical illusions) or by the limitations of one's experience.

- If it's appropriate to do so, have the class go outside and gather around a tree. Walk slowly around it. Call attention to one special branch and ask how it appears to change as the student walks around it. Students should conclude that some branches may appear to be foreshortened (seem to be shorter than they are). Ask questions such as: "How does the length of the branch seem to change?" "How does it make you feel?" "As the branch comes toward you, how does its appearance change?" "How could you show this in a drawing?" "What would your drawing look like if all branches came from only two sides (two dimensional) like veins in a leaf?" "Is foreshortening necessary to make the third dimension?" "Could you build a tree house if a tree had branches coming from two sides opposite each other?" "How you can show this concept in your sketch?" "Look at drawings typical of primary grade children. Why do trees seem so two dimensional?"

Suggested art activity
Set out a variety of objects ranging in complexity. Have each student draw any of them. It is important for the student to realize that practice and strong concentration will be needed in order to draw complex objects foreshortened accurately. Many students avoid drawing objects in a foreshortened position and never develop the skill which in turn stands in the way of future drawing.

Alternative art activities
- Draw the arm in four positions: straight up, leaning back, stretched forward, and foreshortened.
- Draw the human body posed in a lying and sitting position upon mats, using foreshortening. (A student can model.)
- Place someone on a high stool or ladder and have the class draw him from their own positions, seated on the floor.

Evaluation

When the student can draw a foreshortened object more accurately than before, then the objective has been achieved.

Other things to consider

- Vocabulary: foreshorten, distortion, second dimension, third dimension.
- Art materials needed: drawing materials and paper.
- Prints:
  Dempsey and Firpo by Bellows
  Mona Lisa by da Vinci
  Delphic Sibyl by Michelangelo
  Flowers and Parrots by Michelangelo
  Knockout by Morreau
  Bacchus by Caravaggio
  Virgin with Saints Ines and Tecla by El Greco
  Lacemaker by Vermeer
- People who might have need for the concept: painter, sculptor, illustrator, commercial artist, industrial designer, printmaker, docents, and stage set designers.

LEVEL 7

ACTIVITY 205

Concept taught by this activity: The media used limits or enlarges the eventual outcome of creative activity.

Objective: The student demonstrates an awareness of how the artist's choice of media can limit or enlarge the eventual outcome of his creative activity. The decision to draw in ink rather than chalk or to carve in wood rather than marble pre-determines the eventual form and the impact it will have.

A sample lesson plan for achieving the objective:

Teacher preparations
■ Review the activity for a clear understanding of the concept.
■ Collect prints and other appropriate materials that might be available in the media center or library.
■ Be aware of the divergent thinking required in thinking of various materials. Also be aware of the problem of an artist being a "jack of all trades--master of *none*."

Teaching suggestions
■ Set up an imaginary situation to stimulate discussion and introduce the concept. For example, "What media would you choose if you were an artist and you had been commissioned to create an outdoor piece of sculpture for a large midwestern city and the scale was such that your final work had to be at least thirty feet high?" Hold a brainstorming session on what media would or would not be appropriate for the size involved and the problems of exposure to all of the elements. "How would the choice of media affect the design?" Compare the kinds of things that can be done with clay, stone, wood, steel, or plastics. "How much detail would you use or even need on something so big?" "What sort of design would be appropriate with very modern skyscrapers all around it?" "How would these needs affect your choice of materials?"

■ It might be interesting to discuss a problem that is almost the reverse of the one above and discuss the implications of media in the new situation. For example, "What if you were employed to engrave embossed decorative lettering on brass or to do highly detailed illustrations for a medical textbook. Which tools and media would be appropriate now?" "Why not use school watercolor brushes and watercolors?" "Or tempera paints?" "How about engraving in clay?" "Wouldn't that be easier?"

■ Discuss the implications of employment for the artist with a wide range of media skills versus one who only works with a single media. "What effect would the breadth vs. depth have on *skills?*" "Which well-known artists worked in more than one media?" "Look at the issue from the view of an employer."

"What kinds of artists would you look for and what kinds of media would you want them to work in if you were an architect or builder, a grocery store owner, a newspaper publisher, the owner of an advertising agency, an owner of an exclusive department store, an art gallery director, or other?"

■ See if the class can discover local situations where the media used in some art form was not appropriate for its environment or its design.

■ Look at art prints and discuss what each might have looked like had it been done with some other media (specify a media).

Suggested art activity
Make a chart tracing a similar problem to those discussed above through a realistic conclusion, showing what kind of artist would serve what needs and the media he would have to use in serving the employer best. Display the charts throughout the school.

Alternative art activities
- Have a committee do a bulletin board built around this concept and make displays with different media to show its effectiveness for the location.
- Have a group do a mural using different media and give a report as to which media worked the best.
- Make sets for a puppet show and brainstorm about the material that could be used and would work the best.

Evaluation

When the student demonstrates an increased awareness of the concept (by responses to discussion and participation in activities), then the objective has been achieved.

Other things to consider

- Prints:
  The Smokers by Brouwer
  City Hall in Rega by Feininger
  Blindman's Buff by Fragonard
  The Bullfight by Goya
  Moneylender and Wife by Metsys
  The Aficionado by Picasso
  The Rhine Maidens by Ryder
  Thatched Cottages by Vlaminck
- People who might have need for the concept: advertisers, architects, decorators, fashion designers, film makers, industrial designers, museum and art gallery directors, T.V. set and costume designers.